ABSOLUTELY NULL AND UTTERLY VOID

Pope Leo XIII, 1903

from a photograph in the possession of the Earl of Halifax, of a portrait painting

Absolutely Null and Utterly Void

THE PAPAL CONDEMNATION OF ANGLICAN ORDERS, 1896

BY
JOHN JAY HUGHES

CORPUS BOOKS *Washington—Cleveland*

Corpus Instrumentorum, Inc.
1330 Massachusetts Ave., N.W.
Washington, D.C. 20005

LIBRARY OF CONGRESS CATALOG CARD NUMBER: 68–30988
First Printing 1968
PRINTED IN THE UNITED STATES OF AMERICA

PATRI AVOQUE MEO SACERDOTIBUS
QUI IN DIEBUS SUIS PLACUERUNT DEO
ET INVENTI SUNT IUSTI NECNON
GULIELMO THOMAE MANNING
SUCCESSORI APOSTOLORUM

We pronounce and declare that Ordinations carried out according to the Anglican rite have been and are absolutely null and utterly void.

LEO XIII

13TH SEPTEMBER 1896 PAPAL BULL *APOSTOLICAE CURAE*

ACKNOWLEDGEMENTS

Thanks are due to Geoffrey Bles Ltd for permission to reproduce extracts from *Charles Lindley, Viscount Halifax*, by J. G. Lockhart, and to the Cambridge University Press for permission to reproduce material from *The Historian and Character and other Essays*, by David Knowles. The author would like also to thank the Revd Christopher Lash for his help with proof-reading.

CONTENTS

ABBREVIATIONS xvii

INTRODUCTION 1

PART ONE: THE CONDEMNATION

1 THE ANGLICAN SUCCESSION 9
The succession secured 12; The succession disputed 17; Barlow 21; Further links with the Latin hierarchy 24; A true succession? 25

2 THE PROTAGONISTS 28
Viscount Halifax 28; The Abbé Portal 32; The plan 34; Cardinal Vaughan 37

3 THE CAMPAIGN FOR REUNION IS LAUNCHED 46
'Dalbus' on Anglican Orders 46; Portal's first visit to England, August 1894 49; Portal's visit to Rome, September 1894 54; Cardinal Rampolla's letter to Portal 58; Portal's second visit to England, September 1894 60; Further efforts for reunion 63

4 THE BATTLE IS JOINED 65
Cardinal Vaughan in Rome, Winter 1895 69; Dom Francis Aidan Gasquet 72; A fatal delusion 74; 'We desire peace with all our hearts' 76; Halifax visits the pope 79; Drafting the pope's letter 81; Gasquet's 'Leaves from my diary' 82; Final work on the pope's letter 85; Lord Halifax persists 86; The papal letter Ad Anglos *90*

5 DOVES VERSUS HAWKS 92
Platform oratory 92; Opposition moves behind the scenes 97; The Revue Anglo-Romaine *101*

6 The papal commission to investigate Anglican Orders 105

Cardinal Vaughan's representatives on the commission 106; The continental members of the commission 110; Two members are added to the commission 113; Lacey and Puller 116

7 The English case against the Orders 121

Critique of these arguments 126; The history of the English reformation 128; Theological arguments 134; The Appendices 137; Evaluation 145

8 The commission at work 149

The available sources of information 150; The commission's meetings 153; The commission is terminated 159; The final vote on validity 162; The appeal to precedent 165

9 Pressing for a condemnation 168

Gasquet and Moyes' Risposta *169; A danger to the church? 178; The promised fruits of a condemnation 180*

10 The condemnation 185

Cardinal Rampolla's absence from the Feria V meeting 188; The decision 191; Apostolicae curae *192*

11 Post-mortem 199

Lord Halifax 199; The Abbé Portal 210; Canon Moyes 214; Dom Gasquet 217; Merry del Val 223; Cardinal Vaughan 227

PART TWO: THE HISTORICAL ARGUMENTS OF THE BULL

12 The Marian restoration 245
The difficulties of the enquiry 248; The treatment of Edwardine Orders by Queen Mary and her bishops 250; Bishop Bonner's treatment of Edwardine Orders 255; Papal treatment of Edwardine Orders in the Marian period 258; The Holy See the best interpreter of its own acts? 269; The 'form of the church' and the 'accustomed form' 271

13 A clerical bridegroom and an episcopal spy 276
'A certain French Calvinist' 278; The Gordon case 280

14 A reappraisal of Anglican Orders 284

Appendix 1 295

Bibliography 309

Index 343

ILLUSTRATIONS

1 Pope Leo xiii, 1903 *frontispiece*
2 Charles Lindley, second Viscount Halifax, 1897 *facing* page 28
3 Fernand Portal, 1895 *facing* page 29
4 Gasquet's diary: the original manuscript and the published version *following* page 83
5 Merry del Val's letter to Canon Moyes, *c.* 1 May 1896 *facing* page 158
6 Merry del Val's letter to Canon Moyes, 30 June 1896 *facing* page 159
7 Cardinal Vaughan's letter to Lord Halifax *following* page 203

SOURCES OF THE ILLUSTRATIONS

Nos 1–3 are from photographs in the possession of the Earl of Halifax, and are reproduced by his permission, as is No 7, a reproduction of a letter from the Hickleton Papers. The manuscript of Gasquet's diary in No 4, and No 5, are from the Gasquet Papers, and are reproduced by permission of the Abbot of Downside. No 6 is from the Westminster Archives, and is reproduced by permission of Cardinal Heenan.

ABBREVIATIONS

AER	*American Ecclesiastical Review,* Washington 1889——
AODI	Francis Clark, *Anglican Orders and Defect of Intention,* London 1956
AO(E)	*Anglican Orders (English)*, London 1957
ASS	*Acta Sanctae Sedis,* Rome 1870–1908
BP	Edmund Bishop Papers
Burnet-Pocock	Gilbert Burnet, *The History of the Reformation of the Church of England* (ed. Nicholas Pocock), Oxford 1865
ClRev	*Clergy Review,* London 1931——
CTS	Catholic Truth Society
DAFC	*Dictionnaire apologétique de la foi catholique*
DNB	*Dictionary of National Biography*
DS	Denzinger-Schönmetzer, *Enchiridion symbolorum, definitionum et declarationum,* Freiburg 1965[33]. (References to previous editions are placed in parentheses.)
DTC	*Dictionnaire de théologie catholique*
ESR	Francis Clark, *Eucharistic Sacrifice and the Reformation,* London and Westminster (Md) 1960
Gibson	E. S. Gibson (ed.), *The First and Second Prayer Books of Edward VI,* London and New York 1910
GP	Gasquet Papers
GR	*Gregorianum,* Rome 1920——
HP	Hickleton Papers
IER	*Irish Ecclesiatical Record,* Dublin 1880——
IThQ	*Irish Theological Quarterly,* Dublin 1906–1922
JES	*Journal of Ecumenical Studies,* Philadelphia, 1964——
JEH	*Journal of Ecclesiastical History,* London 1950——

JThS	*Journal of Theological Studies,* London
LACT	*Library of Anglo-Catholic Theology*
Leo XIII	Viscount Halifax, *Leo XIII and Anglican Orders,* London 1912
LThK	*Lexikon für Theologie und Kirche,* Freiberg 1957–65[2]
n.d.	no date
n.p.	no place
NRTh	*Nouvelle Revue Théologique,* Louvain 1925——
OA	J. Moyes, F. A. Gasquet, *Ordines Anglicani,* London 1896 (privately printed)
PP	Portal Papers
PS	Parker Society
RAR	*Revue Anglo-Romaine,* Paris 1895–96
RBén	*Revue Bénedictine,* Maredesous 1890——
RMP	E. C. Messenger, *The Reformation, the Mass and the Priesthood,* London 1936–37
SPCK	Society for Promoting Christian Knowledge
t.	tract
ThSt	*Theological Studies,* Baltimore 1940——
WAr	Westminster Diocesan Archives

ABSOLUTELY NULL AND UTTERLY VOID

INTRODUCTION

The subject of Anglican Orders is one on which not much can be said that has not been said before.

—Canon Estcourt (1873)[1]

Almost a century has passed since Canon Estcourt began his study of Anglican Orders with the above sentence. A glance at the bibliography at the back of this volume will show what a flood of literature has poured from the pens and typewriters of partisans on both sides of this controversy in the last hundred years alone. Most of this literature is indeed, as Estcourt indicated, repetition of what has already been said before. Is another book on Anglican Orders justified? To this question most people would return the answer encountered with such monotonous regularity in the *Summa theologica* of St Thomas Aquinas: *Videtur quod non*—it would seem not. The horse has been flogged dead. And even if there were still enough life in the weary and long-suffering frame for another lope round the track, surely the last thing we need in the present climate of improved relations between separated christians is another book on so controversial a topic, with all the memories of past polemic and strife which such a study must inevitably arouse. In the present ecumenical situation a book about Anglican Orders must be as *déplacé* as the Communist Manifesto at a disarmament conference.

If this account of the papal condemnation of Anglican Orders in 1896 merely awakens old passions, moving Roman Catholic readers to fresh attempts at justification of what was done by their forefathers seventy and more years ago, and confirming Anglicans in the conviction that Rome is invariably devious and cunning, then clearly this book had much better never have been written. I venture to hope, however, for a response at once more positive and more

[1] E. E. Estcourt, *The Question of Anglican Ordinations Discussed*, London 1873, 1.

christian. A generation of Roman Catholics which has seen the pope publicly ask forgiveness for sins perpetrated in the past against the separated brethren in the name of 'the preservation of catholic truth' need hardly feel defensive or apologetic at concrete evidence of such failings. Sober penitence for the shortsightedness and rigidity of many highly placed catholics in a previous generation can be tempered, however, by legitimate thankfulness for others in equally high places who displayed greater breadth and deeper charity. Nor is there any real reason to fear that the net result of these pages will be an increase of Anglican complacency and triumphalism. No portion of the church militant is quite free from these unlovely faults. But Anglicans have a particularly vigorous tradition of self-criticism, and it seems hardly likely that a church which is capable of producing such bishops as Trevor Huddleston and John A. T. Robinson will relapse into a comfortable sense of its own superiority. Both Roman Catholic and Anglican readers will, it is hoped, ponder seriously the truth succinctly stated in 1895 by one of Anglicanism's greatest sons: that when the Roman Catholic Church acknowledges its own errors, which its (at least numerical) superiority easily permits it to do, it is adopting the best means of leading other christians to acknowledge theirs.[2]

Quite apart from such considerations there are objective reasons to justify the investigation undertaken here. The condemnation of Anglican Orders in the Bull *Apostolicae curae*, and even more the use which numerous catholic apologists have made of this condemnation during the ensuing decades in a flood of polemical literature inevitably offensive to Anglicans' most deeply held convictions and most precious religious experiences, have created a feeling of injustice and resentment which hamper the development of that frank and charitable discussion of dogmatic differences for which Lord Halifax and the Abbé Portal worked

[2] Cf. p. 88 below.

(with but small thanks) for more than three decades, and which is now so widely desired by responsible members of both churches. If Anglican resentment at the rejection of their orders is not shouted from the housetops this is due to exemplary reserve and politeness of Anglicans in ecumenical relationships, which moved no less an authority than Cardinal Heenan to remark in 1963 that 'there is in the whole world no group of men more courteous than the clergy of the Church of England'.[3] But the feeling of injustice is there none the less, and it would be foolish to ignore it. In 1897 the Archbishops of Canterbury and York, in their scholarly and dignified Reply to *Apostolicae curae*, said that the Bull 'aimed at overthrowing our whole position as a church'.[4] More recently the widely respected late Bishop G. K. A. Bell of Chichester has called the 1896 condemnation 'one of the sharpest and most public rebuffs that the Church of Rome can ever have administered to a peaceable Christian communion'.[5] In March 1966 Dr W. J. Bolt, representing the staunchly protestant *Church of England Newspaper*, opened an interview with Cardinal Heenan by telling him that the papal condemnation of Anglican Orders was 'accepted as a stigma, as much among the Low Church as among the High Church elements of Anglicanism'. Dr Bolt's first question was whether *Apostolicae curae* would 'remain a permanent barrier to closer association and unity', and whether the Cardinal did not think that 'all dialogue [would] be uneasy until your church officially offers a redefinition or elaboration of that decree'.[6] A few weeks later the Anglican Archbishop of Wales,

[3] J. C. Heenan, 'Catholiques anglais et anglicanisme', *Lumière et Vie* 64 (August–September 1963), 86.

[4] *Anglican Orders (English)*, London (SPCK) 1957, 23. Cited hereafter as AO(E). This modern reprinting of the Bull *Apostolicae curae* and the Reply of the Anglican Archbishops is cited for reasons of convenience. The authentic text of the latter document is that of the original Latin edition: *Responsio Archiepiscoporum Angliae ad Litteras Apostolicas Leonis Papae XIII de Ordinationibus Anglicanis*, London 1897.

[5] G. K. A. Bell, *Christian Unity: the Anglican Position*, London 1948, 68.

[6] *Church of England Newspaper*, 25th March 1966, 16. The interview was reprinted the week following on the front page of the London *Catholic Herald*.

Dr Edwin Morris, stated publicly that as long as the condemnation of the Orders 'remains unchanged and authoritative . . . it constitutes an insuperable barrier between Anglicans and Rome'.[7]

A conviction so widespread cannot be banished merely by insisting that it is unjustified and that the wholly negative verdict of *Apostolicae curae* was the only one permitted by the facts. The number of such demonstrations produced in the seven decades since the Bull's appearance is legion, and he must be blind or worse who would maintain that this mass of apologetic literature has had any very large measure of success save amongst those already convinced. The feeling of injustice on the Anglican side will be diminished only to the extent that Roman Catholics are able to show that they are just as interested as Anglicans in getting at the truth in this matter, and that they are willing to consider with an open mind all that can be said in favour of the Anglican case. This must include an active desire to lift the veil of secrecy which still surrounds the 1896 condemnation, and which cannot but nourish the widespread suspicion that the closed Roman investigation of Anglican Orders in that year was neither free nor fair.

The present volume makes no attempt to settle the central question of validity. Its interest is confined almost exclusively to historical questions. Although we shall be concerned chiefly with the events surrounding the papal condemnation of Anglican Orders in 1896, the narrative is prefaced with an account of the origin of the Anglican hierarchy in the sixteenth century. Without the information presented in this initial chapter most readers would be unable to understand many aspects of the subsequent controversy. Two additional chapters deal briefly with the treatment of Anglican Orders during the Marian restoration of 1553–58, and with two cases cited as precedents in the Bull *Apostolicae curae*. These chapters differ from those which precede

[7] London *Church Times*, 22nd April 1966, 13.

them in that they contain no original historical research. They are an attempt merely to summarise and assess the results of existing studies, and are intended to serve as a stimulus to further research by other scholars.

Amongst the very large number of people who have helped me, and to whom I have expressed my indebtedness where I could in the footnotes, I should like to single out for special thanks Abbot Dr Laurentius Klein OSB of St Matthias' Abbey, Trier, who suggested in January 1965 that I undertake the research which led to this book, and Professor Dr Erwin Iserloh of the faculty of catholic theology at the Westphalian Wilhelms-University, Münster in Westfalen, whose own painstaking scholarship in the fields of ecumenical and historical theology afforded me a model for emulation, and who kindly accepted this study as the first part of a dissertation for the doctorate in theology. I am indebted to correspondents too numerous to list here and to all those who offered me hospitality and assistance during my researches, especially to the director of the St Paul's Guild of New York City, who generously relieved me of all financial cares for a period of almost three years. I should like to record my special gratitude to the Abbot and monks of Downside Abbey, who opened to me the doors of their house and of their magnificent library for weeks on end. I am indebted in a special way to Dom Daniel Rees, my companion in numerous dusty searches amongst the Gasquet Papers. The Holy Ghost Fathers at Upton, Notts, edified me with their piety and simple goodness during two extended visits; and my sojourns with the Ampleforth Benedictines in Yorkshire and at St Benet's Hall, Oxford, were a continual source of merriment and delight. My good friend and former classmate Fr Simon Mein SSM, Prior of the House of the Sacred Mission, Kelham, graciously offered me hospitality and the use of the excellent Kelham library for extended periods. I recall with special pleasure numerous profitable discussions of some of the lesser trod byways of theology and church history with that outstanding contemporary representative of the great tradition of British eccentricism Bro. George Every SSM. I am indebted to the second Earl of Halifax for permission to use his grandfather's correspondence in the Hickleton Papers, and to his archivist, Major T. L. Ingram, for much practical help. Amongst my pleasantest experiences during the writing of this book I must reckon a fascinating conversation with the Revd H. Francome Painter, who regaled me for two hours with his recollections of the second Lord Halifax. And when I received from the eldest daughter of Canon Lacey, now Mrs R. H. Hawkins of Windsor Castle, a letter telling me she could remember going as a very little girl to London to see her father off to Rome in April 1896, 'and Father Puller was there and Lord Halifax', I felt I could almost sense the dead rising up to greet me. Through the kindness of Père M. Join-Lambert I was given access to the papers of the Abbé Portal in the Oratorian house at Montsoult, where during two visits I was privileged to partake of conversation and food of a kind which only the eldest daughter of the church is able to supply. Finally, I am deeply grateful to the Apostolic Delegate in Great Britain, the Most Revd H. E. Cardinale, for his encouragement and assistance, and to his Eminence Cardinal Heenan for permission to use the archives of the Archdiocese of Westminster. I am indebted in a special way to the archivist Miss Elizabeth Poyser. For reading the manuscript in whole or in part and offering valuable criticisms, I am especially grateful to Professor Dr J. G. Remmers, Münster, and to the Revd Frs H. R. Bronk, L. B. Guillot, and A. J. Stacpoole OSB.

In sending this book upon its way I am reminded of a principle which, like so much that is good and fine and true, I learned as an Anglican:

Magna est veritas, et praevalebit.

John Jay Hughes
Münster in Westfalen, November 1967

PART ONE
THE CONDEMNATION

I

THE ANGLICAN SUCCESSION

The Church has nothing to gain from the propagation of vain legends, and nothing to lose from the manifestation of the truth of history.

—Pope Pius XII[1]

At the early hour of five in the morning of Sunday 17th December 1559 passers-by on the south bank of the Thames at Lambeth, across the river from Westminster, and boatmen dropping downstream on the tide, could have seen the flickering of candlelight through the windows of the chapel of Lambeth Palace, the official London residence of the Archbishops of Canterbury. Servants passed to and fro within the chapel, throwing their shadows upon walls and windows. Last-minute questions were asked, and instructions given. Singly, and in pairs, a small but distinguished group of leading churchmen and citizens of London entered the palace and took their places within the chapel, for despite the early hour there was nothing secret about what was being done. An event was about to take place which was to give rise not only to a form of christianity and a manner of worship of singular beauty but also to an acrimonious and confused controversy which has lasted from that day to this: the consecration of Matthew Parker as Queen Elizabeth's first Archbishop of Canterbury.

The last-minute preparations betokened by the quickly moving shadows visible through the chapel windows were the culmination of an entire year of slow but careful manoeuvring by the Queen and her ministers to make this consecration possible. The previous queen, Mary, and her cousin, Reginald Pole, the last Roman cardinal to hold the

[1] Angelo Belardetti (ed.), *Discorsi e Radiomessaggi di Sua Santità Pio XII*, ix, Rome n.d., 471.

see of Canterbury,[2] died within twelve hours of one another on 17th November 1558. Mary's half-sister, Elizabeth, acceded to the throne and inaugurated a period of slow and cautious religious change in a protestant direction. A new Act of Supremacy was passed by parliament in April, giving the Queen the title of 'Supreme Governor', replacing the title of 'Supreme Head' of the church which her father, Henry VIII, had assumed in 1534. This act repealed the heresy laws of Mary's reign, and provided that no matter was to be judged heretical except upon the authority of the canonical scriptures, of the first four General Councils of the church, or of the parliament with the assent of the clergy in convocation. This Act of Supremacy also imposed upon all clergy and upon most political officials an oath embodying the terms of the act. Refusal of the oath resulted in loss of benefice or office. This act gave Elizabeth a position different from that held by her father.

> No longer was the throne occupied by a crowned theologian, confounding Parliaments and bishops with God's learning; its occupant was an adroit and devious politician, operating through the interstices of Statute Law.[3]

Anglicanism is unique amongst the churches of christendom in that it is established not upon a confession of faith (apart from the ancient credal statements of the undivided church) nor upon the teachings of a particular reformer, but upon the use of a common liturgy. The new liturgy was imposed in the spring of 1559 by the Act of Uniformity. This restored the second and more protestant Prayer Book of Edward VI (the '1552 Book'), but with several changes of considerable significance. The aim was to achieve as wide an adherence as possible to the liturgy which was to constitute the basis of uniformity in the national church. Offensive references to the pope were eliminated, in the hope of

[2] Pole was also the last Roman cardinal to cross the threshold of Lambeth Palace until the first visit of the Jesuit Cardinal Bea to Archbishop Ramsey on 5th August 1962. (Information kindly supplied by the Revd Canon J. R. Satterthwaite of the Church of England Council on Foreign Relations.)

[3] A. C. Dickens, *The English Reformation*, London 1964, 303.

gaining the assent of his adherents to the establishment of religion. No longer were Englishmen to pray:

> From the tyranny of the bishop of Rome and all his detestable enormities . . . Good Lord deliver us.[4]

The words of administration at Holy Communion had been in 1552:

> Take and eat this, in remembrance that Christ died for thee, and feed on him in thy heart by faith, with thanksgiving.

And for the cup:

> Drink this in remembrance that Christ's blood was shed for thee, and be thankful.

To these words were now prefaced the following:

> The Body of our Lord Jesus Christ, which was given for thee, preserve thy body and soul unto everlasting life.
> The Blood of our Lord Jesus Christ, which was shed for thee, preserve thy body and soul unto everlasting life.

From henceforth it would be impossible to maintain that the Church of England was officially committed to the denial of the real presence of Christ's body and blood in the sacrament. Moreover, the so-called 'Black Rubric', inserted illegally into the 1552 Book while it was being printed, was eliminated entirely. This had stated that although the communicants were commanded to kneel to receive the sacrament,

> it is not meant thereby that any adoration is done, or ought to be done, either unto the Sacramental bread or wine there bodily received, or unto any real and essential presence there being of Christ's natural flesh and blood.[5]

Finally, the new book imposed by this Act of Uniformity enjoined the use of the ornaments of the church and

[4] Petition from the Litany of the First and Second Prayer Books of 1549 and 1552.

[5] E. C. S. Gibson (ed.), *The First and Second Prayer Books of Edward VI*, London and New York (Everyman edition) 1910, reprinted 1952, 393. (This work will be cited henceforth as 'Gibson'.) When this rubric was reinserted in the English Prayer Book of 1662 it was carefully reworded to say that the kneeling did not signify any adoration 'unto any *corporal* presence of Christ's natural flesh and blood' (emphasis supplied).

ministers which had been in use 'in the second year of the reign of King Edward VI'. This provision was to cause trouble with the Puritans, who hated the old ornaments and vestments, which they considered the dregs of popery. The Marian bishops spoke and voted against the act in the House of Lords, but could not prevent its passage.

The succession secured

Of the twenty-six English and Welsh sees no less than ten were either vacant through death upon Elizabeth's accession or became vacant within a few months through the death of the incumbent. Fifteen of the sixteen remaining diocesan bishops were deprived in the summer or autumn of 1559 for refusing to take the oath of supremacy. Anthony Kitchin, Bishop of Llandaff since 1545, acquiesced in the new arrangements and retained his see until his death in 1563. The Queen's former tutor, Matthew Parker, was appointed Archbishop of Canterbury in the summer of 1559. He was a Cambridge scholar, and had remained in seclusion in England during Mary's reign when many of the reforming clergy fled abroad. His presence in England during these crucial years was significant. For it meant that, although wholeheartedly committed to the reforming cause, Parker had never lived amongst the protestant churches of Germany and Switzerland, and took no part in the fights and wrangles of the refugees during their continental exile. These troubles were the historical birth pangs of the subsequent Puritan agitation against the Anglican *via media*.

Parker tried by every means he knew to avoid the burden of episcopacy, writing long letters of self-depreciation and even refusing to appear when summoned. But in the end he was forced to yield to the Queen's will.[6] Parker's most recent

[6] Cf. the original correspondence printed by Gilbert Burnet, *History of the Reformation of the Church of England* (ed. N. Pocock) v, Oxford 1865, 538–52. (This work will be cited henceforth as 'Burnet–Pocock'.)

biographer gives the following account of the new archbishop:

> There can be little doubt that Bacon, Cecil and the Queen were supremely right in their insistence that he should be Archbishop. The model they had in view was a church catholic but reformed, its historic roots unsevered, avoiding the errors of Rome . . . and the excesses of protestantism. Parker was exactly right for the task. . . . He really believed quite passionately in the sort of Christianity which was envisaged—dignified, preserving continuity with the past, maintaining all that seemed essential to catholicity while shedding medieval accretions. He was gentle and conciliatory in dealing with critics either on the right hand or on the left. He laboured all he could to correct abuses and to raise the standard of the clergy. And he was eminently one whose character commanded respect—without guile or duplicity, humble and without self-seeking or love of money; mild and conciliatory yet unyielding where he thought principles were concerned, even to standing up against Bacon or the Queen herself; honest and dominated by a real love of justice; the trouble he often took to secure fair dealing for quite lowly folk is striking.[7]

The Queen's difficulties were by no means at an end, however, when Parker had finally been compelled to accept the primacy. For it was then necessary to arrange for his consecration, and this raised legal difficulties. Acting under the provisions of the restored Henrician legislation for the consecration of an archbishop, the Queen's writ of consecration was issued on 9th September to Tunstall, the aged Bishop of Durham, and to the Bishops of Llandaff, Peterborough, and Bath and Wells. These four were the only diocesan bishops still in possession of their sees at that time. When they all declined to act the position was difficult. For although there were other bishops who could be had, the lawyers appear to have felt that the existing legislation specified *diocesan* bishops. A further difficulty was the doubt as to whether the Edwardine Ordinal, the rite which it was proposed to use for the consecration, was legally authorised by parliament. The Act of Uniformity establishing the Prayer Book was assumed to have authorised the Ordinal as well. But in fact it legalised only the Prayer Book, and the

[7] V. J. K. Brook, *A Life of Archbishop Parker*, Oxford 1962, 344f.

Ordinal had not originally been part of the Prayer Book. The Ordinal had been separately authorised and compiled in 1550, a year after the appearance of the first Prayer Book in 1549. Minor changes were made in 1552 when the second Prayer Book was authorised by parliament. The Ordinal was generally considered to be part of the Prayer Book, but Cecil, Elizabeth's principal Secretary of State, maintained that it was not. Since nothing had been said about the Ordinal in the Act of Uniformity, it was, according to this view, illegal.

Both difficulties, the lack of bishops qualified to act, and the lack of an authorised rite, were got over by use of the royal authority. Every step in the process was most carefully recorded, and the documents are still extant, including a paper outlining the procedure proposed, with comments by Cecil and a reply by Parker to one of his points.[8] On 6th December the Queen issued letters patent for Parker's consecration. They were addressed to Kitchin, Bishop of Llandaff, Barlow, Bishop-elect of Chichester, Scory, Bishop-elect of Hereford, Coverdale, formerly Bishop of Exeter, Bale, Bishop of Ossory, and two suffragan bishops, Hodgkin of Bedford and Salisbury of Thetford. Any four of these bishops were to confirm Parker's election by the chapter of Canterbury and to consecrate him. These letters patent contained a special provision, the famous 'Supplentes' clause, in which the Queen stated that she supplied by her royal authority anything lacking in the persons of the bishops to whom the letters were issued or in what was required by the law for the confirmation and consecration of the archbishop-elect. The signatures of six leading ecclesiastics and lawyers were obtained to a statement certifying that this was all perfectly legal and within the Queen's competence. From the strict legal point of view, however, it probably was not. Parker's election was duly confirmed on 9th December 1559

[8] There is a facsimile of this document in Estcourt, *The Question of Anglican Ordinations*, 86. The account given here is based upon that in Brook, op. cit. 81–5.

in the Church of St Mary-le-Bow, London, by Barlow, Scory, Coverdale, and Hodgkin. They adjourned afterwards to a convivial luncheon at the Nag's Head Tavern in Cheapside, an apparently harmless repast which was to have consequences long after the death of all the participants which none of them could possibly have foreseen at the time.

It was these same four bishops who, shortly before six o'clock on this Third Sunday in Advent 1559, were gathering in Lambeth Palace chapel to consecrate Matthew Parker as the seventieth Archbishop of Canterbury in succession to St Augustine. A detailed description of the ceremony may still be read in the register which is preserved at Lambeth. The rite used was that of the Ordinal as revised in 1552. Parker's biographer gives the following account of the ceremony, based upon the contemporary description in the register.

> Preceded by four candle bearers, Parker, robed in scarlet gown and hood, entered the chapel accompanied by the four bishops. After matins and a sermon by Scory, Parker and the bishops withdrew, to re-enter—Parker in a linen surplice, Barlow in silk cope (as celebrant; his two assistants were similarly robed), Scory and Hodgkin in surplices, but Coverdale, typically, in a long woollen gown. After the Gospel the three other bishops presented Parker to Barlow, the official documents were produced, the oath to the Supremacy was taken. Then after interrogatories, prayers and suffrages 'according to the form of the book set forth by the authority of Parliament', the four bishops all laid their hands on the new Archbishop, and all four recited the words of consecration. Except that all four said the words instead of the presiding bishop alone, the service was clearly that of Edward's Second Book. It is specially noted that no pastoral staff was given to the new Archbishop.[9]

At the close of the eucharistic celebration the bishops left the chapel by the north door and returned re-robed. Parker wore rochet, black chimere, and a collar of sables. Proceeding to the west door Parker gave white wands of office to his new steward, treasurer, and controller, and the procession marched out.

[9] Brook, op. cit. 85.

There is independent evidence confirming the contemporary record of the Lambeth register. The new archbishop wrote in his personal memoranda:

> On the seventeenth of December, in the year 1559, I was consecrated Archbishop of Canterbury. Alas! alas! O Lord God, for what times hast thou kept me . . . [10]

And the contemporary diarist Henry Machyn wrote of the consecration as of something generally known in London:

> The XVIJ day of Desember was the nuw byshope of [Canterbury,] doctur Parker, was mad ther at Lambeth.

Four days after his own consecration Parker and three of his consecrators consecrated four other bishops for vacant sees. Parker carried out a number of further consecrations in the new year. The new hierarchy was thus firmly established, in unbroken succession to the old.

The fact of Parker's consecration is as well attested as any historical fact can be. The evidence for it is actually stronger than the evidence for many other events of history which have never been disputed. The defects mentioned above, for the remedying of which such elaborate legal measures were devised, have nothing to do with the sacramental validity of the consecration. They concern only the legal regularity of the act. From a strict legal point of view the consecration was probably irregular. Edmund Bonner, the deprived Bishop of London, was able to embarrass the government by raising this point in 1564. The case against him was dropped in order to avoid a ruling on the question. And in 1566 parliament passed an act specifically legalising

[10] John Bruce and T. T. Perowne (eds.), *The Correspondence of Matthew Parker* (PS), Cambridge 1853, x. The original roll of parchment containing these words (in Latin) is preserved in Corpus Christi College, Cambridge.

[11] H. Machyn, *The Diary of Henry Machyn, Citizen and Merchant-Taylor of London, from A.D. 1550 to A.D. 1563*, ed. J. G. Nichols (Camden Society), London 1848, 220. Cf. also the contemporary reference to Parker's consecration in the letter of Thomas Sampson to Peter Martyr, 6th January 1560: Hastings Robinson (ed.), *The Zurich Letters* (PS), Cambridge 1842, 63. The attempt of J. C. Whitebrook, *The Consecration of the Most Rev'd Matthew Parker*, London and New York 1945, to prove that Parker was consecrated on or before 29th October 1559 by Anthony Kitchen, Bishop of Llandaff, has been refuted by F. J. Shirley, *Elizabeth's First Archbishop*, London 1948.

the Ordinal and declaring that all episcopal consecrations since Elizabeth's accession were in accordance with the laws of the realm.

The four bishops who consecrated Parker represented in their own persons the Latin and the reformed hierarchies. Barlow and Hodgkin had been consecrated in Henry's reign with the old Pontifical rite; and Scory and Coverdale had been consecrated in 1551 by Pontifical bishops using the rite of the first Ordinal of 1550. The extraordinary pains taken to obtain bishops for this crucial consecration is in marked contrast to the continental reformers' complete lack of interest in the maintenance of episcopal succession.[12] Whatever may have been the motives which dictated the care taken to preserve the succession in England, the fact itself is indisputable—and significant.

The succession disputed

One would think that an event so well documented and attested would have been recognised by all as historical. Such was not to be the case, however. There may have been some uneasiness amongst the Elizabethan reformers regarding the irregularity of Parker's consecration according to the existing statute law. The archbishop himself recorded his consecration in his work *De Antiquitate Britannicae Ecclesiae*, which was printed in 1572 and in which he set out to trace the course of religion from Augustine 'until the days of King Henry VIIIth, when religion began to grow better, and more agreeable to the Gospel'.[13] But not very many copies of this work were distributed. Although known and referred to by contemporaries, the circumstances of Parker's consecration were not widely publicised.

In the great running controversy between Harding and Jewel, which fills four huge volumes of the Parker Society's

[12] Cf. Norman Sykes, *Old Priest and New Presbyter*, Cambridge 1957, 108ff.
[13] Cited from Brook, op. cit. 323.

invaluable publications, the first Elizabethan Bishop of Salisbury was challenged on the question of episcopal succession by his Roman Catholic opponent:

> Show us the register of your bishops continually succeeding one another from the beginning, so as that first bishop have some one of the apostles or of the apostolic men for his author and predecessor. . . . You bear yourself as though you were bishop of Salisbury. But how can you prove your vocation? . . . Who hath laid hands on you? . . . How and by whom are you consecrated?[14]

Jewel's answer was not particularly clear or helpful. Indeed it requires considerable perseverance even to find it. For only after more than a dozen pages of rhetoric on the subject of succession in general, including the pope's, do we find what we are looking for:

> Ye demand of me, whether I be a bishop or no? I answer you, I am a bishop, and that by the free and accustomed canonical election of the whole chapter of Salisbury, assembled solemnly together for that purpose: of which company you, M. Harding, were then one; . . . Our bishops are made in form and order, as they have been ever, by free election of the chapter; by consecration of the archbishop and other three bishops, and by the admission of the prince. And in this sort not long sithence the pope himself was admitted . . . without the emperor's letters patent, the pope was no pope . . .[15]

During Elizabeth's reign Roman Catholic apologists habitually referred to the Anglican prelates as 'parliament bishops', and wrote as if they had not been consecrated at all.[16]

In 1604, forty-five years after Parker's consecration, the world was for the first time given a fanciful and scurrilous account of Parker's consecration which was to plague the controversy over Anglican Orders for almost three cen-

[14] John Ayre (ed.), *The Works of John Jewel* iii (PS), Cambridge 1848, 321.
[15] Op. cit. 334.
[16] Cf. Thomas Stapleton, *A Counterblast to M. Hornes vayne blaste against M. Fekenham*, Louvain 1567, fol. 7ff, 301, 458; *idem*, *A Fortresse of the Faith . . . etc.*, Antwerp 1565, fol. 141–4; *idem*, *A returne of vntruthes vpon M. Iewels Replie*, Antwerp 1566, 'The Fourth Article', fol. 130; *idem*, *Tripliciter inchoata adversus . . . WHITAKERI Duplicationem*, Antwerp 1596, 240f; Richard Bristow, *A Brief Treatise . . .*, Antwerp 1574, 93ff; *idem*, *A Reply to Fulke . . .*, Louvain 1580, 319; Nicholas Sanders, *Rise and Progress of the Anglican Schism* (trans. David Lewis), London 1877, 275ff.

turies. This was the famous 'Nag's Head Fable', and it was first published by an Irish Jesuit named Christopher Holywood in 1604 in his work *De Investiganda vera ac visibili Christi ecclesia.*[17] The tale came as a godsend to opponents of Anglican Orders, who took it up at once and repeated it with variations and elaborations in numberless works of controversy. Although there are various versions of this legend, in essence it asserted that the deprived Bishop of London, Bonner, had warned Kitchin of Llandaff not to consecrate Parker, and that he was consecrated by Scory and others (some versions say Scory alone) after a dinner held at the Nag's Head Tavern, Cheapside. The rite was said to have consisted of the imposition of a bible upon Parker's head accompanied by the utterance of the words: 'Take thou authority to preach the word of God sincerely', or some such formula. The grain of truth in this fable was the luncheon at the Nag's Head Tavern following the canonical confirmation of Parker's election on 9th December, eight days before his consecration on the 17th. It is not impossible that some discussion of the arrangements for the consecration, and perhaps even a rehearsal of the ceremony, took place on this occasion. This could have given rise to the legend, in early versions of which a reported eyewitness account by a servant at the Nag's Head plays a prominent part.

The importance which Anglicans have always attached to the possession of a valid episcopal succession is illustrated by the remark reportedly made by King James I to the Archbishop of Canterbury upon hearing this tale for the first time.

> My Lord, I hope you can prove and make good your ordination, for by my soul, man, if this story be true, we are no Church.[18]

The fable was easily refuted by producing the original register of Parker's consecration with its detailed description of the ceremony. On 12th May 1614 Archbishop Abbot of

[17] Antwerp 1604; Holywood sometimes used the name 'à Sacrobosco'.
[18] Burnet–Pocock v, 553 n. 13.

Canterbury had four Roman Catholic priests who were then in prison brought to Lambeth so that they might personally inspect the register and convince themselves of the truth.[19] This somewhat naïve proceeding proved to be self-defeating, for it gave rise to the charge that the register was a forgery, fabricated to meet the exigencies of controversy. And so the Nag's Head Fable continued to be repeated despite numerous refutations. Falsehoods have long lives, and this one continued to find its way into polemical works long after it had been disproved even by Roman Catholic scholars.[20] It was discussed in 1841 by Archbishop Kenrick of St Louis, who, although not prepared to vouch for the complete accuracy of the tale, commended it to his readers as probable.[21] Even the canonist Gasparri was led into including the fable in his work on ordination in 1894.[22] The repetition of this absurd legend by men of the calibre of Kenrick and Gasparri is especially regrettable in view of the fact that the truth about Parker's consecration had long since been available in standard Roman Catholic works. The English catholic historian John Lingard had printed a true account of the consecration in his ten-volume *History of England*, which appeared in the 1820s.[23] And a full century before, Fleury's vast *Histoire Ecclésiastique* in thirty-six volumes had given a remarkably detailed description of the ceremony, obviously taken from the account in the Lambeth register.[24] A final

[19] Estcourt, *The Question of Anglican Ordinations*, 153.

[20] Rather like the libels about a female 'Pope Joan' that one can still find in older protestant works. The present writer was once assured in all seriousness by an Anglican priest in the United States that Pope Joan had actually existed.

[21] Peter Kenrick, *The Validity of Anglican Ordinations Examined*, Philadelphia 1841.

[22] Pietro Gasparri, *Tractatus Canonicus de Sacra Ordinatione* ii, Paris 1894, 279, no. 1111, n. 1. The error was eliminated in subsequent editions, and it will be seen that, once apprised of the true facts, Gasparri was a moderate advocate of the Anglican claims at the time of the 1896 investigation.

[23] John Lingard, *The History of England* v, London 1823, 155f and 630f. Cf. also Lingard's detailed refutation of the fable in his 'Three Letters on Protestant Ordinations', *The Catholic Magazine and Review* 5 (Birmingham 1834), 499–503, 704–15, 774–82.

[24] Claude Fleury, *Histoire Ecclésiastique pour servir de continuation à celle de Monsieur l'Abbé Fleury* tôme 31, Paris 1733, 335–8. The actual author of this volume is J. C. Fabre.

instance of the hardihood of this oft-refuted fable is supplied by a letter written in 1895 by the then Bishop of Rochester, Randall T. Davidson, to Lord Halifax.

> I have lately had an opportunity of inquiring in detail as to the teaching given by theological professors at Rome to a candidate for Holy Orders. After going through many years of training, both in Scotland and at Rome, he has decided that he cannot accept the Roman position, and has sought Anglican Orders instead. His account of the teaching he has received, and the evidence given by his note-books, is certainly remarkable. It seems perfectly clear that the 'Nag's Head' fable is at this very hour being taught by recognised theological professors as a fact of history, and there is much other teaching of a similar sort.[25]

Barlow

Another objection of a similar kind made its appearance only a dozen years after the Nag's Head Fable. In 1616 Anthony Champney, a Roman Catholic priest resident at Paris and Douay, published a polemical work with a top-heavy title characteristic of the age: *A Treatise of the Vocation of Bishops, and other Ecclesiasticall Ministers. Proving the Ministers of the pretended Reformed Chvrches in generall, to have no calling: against Monsieur du Plessis, and Mr Doctour Field: And in particuler* [sic] *the pretended Bishops in England to be no true Bishops. Against Mr Mason.*[26] Champney pointed out that there was no record in Cranmer's register of the consecration of William Barlow, who was Parker's chief consecrator. Arguing that Barlow had never been consecrated at all, Champney maintained that Parker's consecration was null because his chief consecrator was not himself a bishop. It was an objection in its way as frivolous as the Nag's Head Fable. Archbishop Bramhall had no difficulty in answering the objection in 1658 in his work *The Consecration and Succession of Protestant Bishops Justified.*[27] But the

[25] Viscount Halifax, *Leo XIII and Anglican Orders*, London 1912, 191. Henceforth cited as *Leo XIII.*

[26] Douay 1616; Latin translation, Paris 1618.

[27] The Hague 1658, printed in Bramhall's 'Works' (LACT), Oxford 1844; the passage about Barlow is on pp. 136–47.

claim that Barlow was never consecrated flourished well into the present century, owing to the mare's nest of difficulties which it raised.

Barlow had an unusually chequered career, even considering the stormy times in which he lived. He was elected Bishop of St Asaph on 18th January 1536, but was translated to the see of St David's on 10th or 11th April of the same year. The confirmation of his election to the latter diocese is recorded as having taken place in Bow Church, London, on 21st April 1536, when Barlow himself was present. On 29th May the *congé d'élire* for Barlow's successor at St Asaph describes the see as vacant 'per liberam transmutacionem Willelmi Barlowe episcopi ultimi electi'. There is no extant record of when or by whom Barlow was consecrated. He remained Bishop of St David's from 1536 to 1548. In the latter year he was translated to the bishopric of Bath and Wells. He resigned his see upon Mary's accession, and after being caught trying to flee the realm he was imprisoned in the Tower. He made shift to escape by recantation and by republishing an anti-Lutheran tract which he had first issued in 1531. His second attempt at flight was successful, and he is reported to have been a minister of the church of the English exiles at Emden in East Friesland during Mary's reign. He returned to England after Elizabeth's accession, and was Bishop-elect of Chichester at the time of Parker's consecration.[28]

That no record of Barlow's consecration has survived does not disprove the fact. It is certain that he was taken for a bishop throughout his lifetime, and he is so recorded in documents from the three sees that he held. He had great difficulties with his chapter at St David's, who accused him of heresy, but never of occupying the see without consecration. In fact the charge that he was never consecrated was

[28] These facts are taken from Barlow's biography in the DNB and from Claude Jenkins, *Bishop Barlow's Consecration and Archbishop Parker's Register: with some new documents*, London 1935, reprinted from JThS, October 1922.

not raised until eighty years after he was made Bishop of St Asaph and St David's. His consecration is no more doubtful than that of innumerable other bishops of whose consecration there is also no surviving record. Professor Norman Sykes has written:

> Indeed an unusual degree of credulity is needed to reject the fact; and in a sphere of study where more than in most branches of learning probability is the very guide of life, the historical student may rest content that Barlow was duly consecrated to the office and work of a bishop.[29]

The objection has been a favourite one with opponents of Anglican Orders none the less. The frequency with which it has been raised may be seen from the amount of space devoted to its refutation by those who have written in defence of the Orders. Denny and Lacey, writing in 1895, devoted no less than thirty-one pages to demonstrating that Barlow had really been consecrated. The hypothesis that Barlow was not a bishop found an advocate as late as 1922, however, when Mgr A. S. Barnes published his book *Bishop Barlow and Anglican Orders: A Study of the Original Documents*.[30] The arguments presented in this work were so fairly dealt with by Dr Claude Jenkins in a review of the book in the *Journal of Theological Studies* in October 1922[31] as to leave not one stone upon another of the imposing but flimsy edifice erected by Mgr Barnes with such great care and ingenuity. Dr Jenkins' review is a classic example of scholarly detective work in the interpretation of ancient records and documents. But Bishop Barlow being dead, yet lives: the bogus objection that he was never consecrated continues to find its way into otherwise reputable works written in dependence upon older authorities.[32]

This objection is more than usually frivolous, since even if there were reason to doubt Barlow's consecration, the defect would still not invalidate Parker's consecration. For

[29] Norman Sykes, *William Wake* i, Cambridge 1957, 350.
[30] London 1922. [31] Reprinted 1935; cf. n. 28 above.
[32] Cf. e.g. Michael Schmaus, *Katholische Dogmatik* iv/1, Munich[5] 1957, 658 nr. 3.

we have already seen that all four consecrators joined equally in laying on hands and in reciting the words of consecration. Any defect in one would have been remedied by the others.

Further links with the Latin hierarchy

The controversy about Anglican Orders has centred around Parker's consecration because he is the most prominent link between the old papal hierarchy and the new English one. He was himself consecrated, as we have seen, by representatives of both hierarchies, and all Anglican bishops in the world today (and hence all clergy whom they have ordained) can trace their orders back to Parker.

Parker is not the only link with the Latin hierarchy, however. Another bishop who appears in the table of consecration of all present Anglican bishops is William Laud, who was consecrated for the see of St David's in 1621, and translated to Bath and Wells in 1626, to London in 1628, and to Canterbury in 1633. Although Laud derived his orders from Parker, two other bishops consecrated with the Latin Pontifical also appear in his table of consecration, thus providing independent links with the pre-reformation church and hierarchy. One of these is Hugh Curwen, who was appointed by the catholic Queen Mary to the see of Dublin and consecrated on 8th September 1555 by Bonner in St Paul's Cathedral, London, according to the form of the Pontifical. Curwen retained his see under Elizabeth, resigning it in 1567, when he was translated to the see of Oxford. He died Bishop of Oxford in 1568. Curwen participated in various episcopal consecrations after Elizabeth's accession,[33] and his name appears in Laud's table of consecration printed by Denny and Lacey.[34]

[33] Cf. Edward A. Stopford, *The Unity of the Anglican Church and the Succession of Irish Bishops*, Dublin 1867.

[34] Edward Denny and T. A. Lacey, *De Hierarchia Anglicana Dissertatio Apologetica*, London 1895, Appendix I, 184ff; cf. Tables i and vii. It is noteworthy that in the new *History of Irish Catholicism* Curwen is passed over in complete silence. Cf. F. M. Jones, 'The Counter-Reformation' in P. J. Corish (ed.), *A History of Irish Catholicism* iii/3, Dublin 1967, 8 and 16 n. 7.

The other bishop in Laud's table of consecration who provides an independent link with the old hierarchy is Marco Antonio de Dominis, who was consecrated Bishop of Segni in the state of Venice in 1600 and made Archbishop of Spalato[35] in 1602. He came to England in 1616 after a fight with the Archbishop of Traù, and was admitted into communion with the Church of England. In 1617 he joined in the consecration of George Monteigne as Bishop of London. Monteigne was one of Laud's consecrators four years later.[36]

A true succession?

If 'apostolic succession' means nothing but an unbroken chain of episcopal consecrations stretching back across the ages to the apostles and so to Christ himself, then Anglican bishops have as good a claim to stand in this succession today as any bishops anywhere. One by one all attempts to prove that the historical succession is not intact in the Anglican Church have broken down. The condemnation of Anglican Orders in 1896 preserved a discreet silence about the historical arguments which opponents of the Orders had advanced for more than three centuries. In the circumstances this was tantamount to an admission that the Anglican version of the historical facts was correct. It is true that a quarter of a century later Mgr Barnes argued that despite

[35] The modern Split in Yugoslavia.

[36] Cf. Denny and Lacey, op. cit. 184, Table i. De Dominis returned to Italy and the Roman Catholic Church in 1622, having obtained from the newly elected pope, Gregory XV, a relative and countryman of his, a promise of pardon and a large pension if he would return and recant. Despite warnings of his friends upon no account to put himself within reach of the Inquisition, De Dominis retained his confidence in his luck and wit, both of which were considerable, and which had served him well in many past scrapes. He fell into a trap after his return, however, and was arrested by the Inquisition. He died in prison in 1624. The *Dictionary of National Biography* describes him on the authority of numerous contemporary writers as 'corpulent, irascible, pretentious, and exceedingly avaricious', and adds: 'His intellectual and literary powers were very considerable. . . . As to his honesty, all his contemporaries, both Anglican and Roman, seem to be agreed that he had none.' Cf. also Vittorio Gabrieli, 'Bacone, La Riforma e Roma nella versione Hobbesiana d'un cartegio di Fulgenzio Micanzo' in Mario Praz, *English Miscellany* No. 7, Rome 1956, 195–242, esp. 225–33, where references to further literature on De Dominis may be found.

the silence of the Bull in 1896 about the historical argument, it

> remained . . . exactly as cogent and decisive as before. To omit to use an argument, when others are available which are sufficient without its use, is not to throw any doubt upon its efficacy and power.[37]

Barnes' attempts to revive the doubts about Bishop Barlow's consecration involved, as a contemporary reviewer in *The Times* wrote, 'an intricate series of suppositions and deductions which it may well perplex the brain and exhaust the patience of experts to unravel and appraise.'[38] And the devastating refutation which the book received a few months later merely showed how injudicious it had been to try to revive arguments abandoned in 1896 for the best reason there is: because they had been disproved.

But apostolic succession means more than the mere maintenance of an intact series of episcopal consecrations. There may be an essential change at some point in this historically uninterrupted chain of consecrations which means that after this point the consecrations do not have the same theological significance they had before. When Anglican Orders were condemned in 1896 it was theological objections of this kind which formed the only arguments of substance advanced in favour of the condemnation. The historical arguments in *Apostolicae curae* are of a purely formal kind, being confined to an appeal to precedent: the allegedly unbroken practice of the Holy See in rejecting the Orders. The consideration of the Bull's theological arguments lies beyond the scope of this book. We are concerned here with the story behind the condemnation of 1896. It is the record of a pioneer attempt to bring about a theological and practical *rapprochment* between the churches of Canterbury and Rome, an attempt at what we today call ecumenism in an age dominated by a very different spirit. The attempt aroused on both sides a response which shows that even in the pole-

[37] A. S. Barnes, *Bishop Barlow and Anglican Orders* vi.
[38] *The Times*, 30th May 1922.

mical atmosphere of seventy and more years ago there were not a few who were hoping and praying for a more positive approach. The attempt failed, as the world judges failure. But precisely because of this failure the attempt is an unusually good example of the seed having to fall into the ground and *die* if it is to bring forth fruit.[39]

[39] Cf. John 12:24 and 1 Cor 15:36.

2
THE PROTAGONISTS

It is necessary to desire unity and to be convinced that God wills it more than anything else.

—Lord Halifax[1]

Tarry not for corporate reunion, it is a dream and a snare of the evil one.

—Cardinal Vaughan[2]

Viscount Halifax

The investigation of Anglican Orders undertaken in Rome in 1896, which led to their condemnation in the Apostolic Constitution *Apostolicae curae*, owes its origin to a chance meeting on the island of Madeira in the winter of 1890 between the Abbé Portal and Lord Halifax. Charles Lindley Wood, second Viscount Halifax, was an altogether extraordinary man. A professional journalist who had known him well during the last decade of his very long life wrote of Halifax soon after his death in 1934 at the age of 94: 'I never met another man quite like Lord Halifax.'[3] A son of the old Whig aristocracy, born to wealth and privilege, a close friend of the Prince of Wales and later King Edward VII, Halifax was an aristocrat to his fingertips. He was brought up as a Low Church Anglican, but contact with Dr Pusey and with the successors of the Tractarians at Oxford converted him to the Anglo-Catholic view of the Church of England and its heritage. This led Halifax to join the English Church Union, a society of Anglican clergy and laypeople for the defence and maintenance of catholic principles in the Church of England. He was elected president of the union in 1868 at the age of only twenty-nine. For

[1] Letter to Portal, 8th January 1894, *Leo XIII*, 72.
[2] Speech at Hanley, 28th September 1896; cited from J. G. Snead-Cox, *Life of Cardinal Vaughan* ii, London 1910, 228.
[3] Sidney Dark, *Lord Halifax, A Tribute*, London 1934, 13.

Charles Lindley, second Viscount Halifax, 1897

from a photograph in the possession of the Earl of Halifax

Fernand Portal, 1895

from a photograph in the possession of the Earl of Halifax

fifty years he was to hold this post, which provided him with the one all-absorbing interest of his life.

Halifax was a masterly and imperious man, conscious that he was born to lead and command, but also to serve. He was also a deeply religious man, possessed, as his son's biographer has written, of 'a deep and pathetic humility'.[4] In his later years especially he became more and more a man of prayer. He had as a matter of course a private chaplain, who lived in his house and said mass daily in his chapel. Long after such an arrangement had become an anachronism Lord Halifax could not bear to terminate it.[5] His chaplain was a part of his life like butlers and servants and tenants. He loved them all, cared for them in season and out with generosity and, when necessary, with sternness, always motivated by the spirit of *noblesse oblige* which was as native to him as the air of his well-loved Yorkshire dales. He never missed daily mass unless circumstances rendered attendance impossible. When on the continent he attended mass every day in the local Roman Catholic church, though without communicating.

> Not that . . . he would have had any personal hesitation in so doing [his son has written], but he would have judged it embarrassing for the Romans if they had known and disingenuous to do it without their knowing.[6]

So great was Halifax's reverence for the gift of Holy Communion, and so profound his own sense of unworthiness,

[4] The Earl of Birkenhead, *The Life of Lord Halifax*, London 1965, 14. The early chapters of this admirable work supplement the successful but somewhat uncritical biography of the second Viscount by J. G. Lockhart, *Charles Lindley, Viscount Halifax* 2 vols, London 1935–36.

[5] The following incident, related to the author by the priest concerned, illustrates the devotion Halifax inspired in those who served him. As he was nearing the close of his ninth decade, Halifax often said to his chaplain: 'Oh you will stay with me till I die, won't you: then I'll know I'll be properly buried.' About this time the chaplain was offered the bishopric of the Windward Islands. He was torn between his loyalty to Lord Halifax and his desire to accept the offer. He sought advice from trusted counsellors, who told him: 'Halifax is the greatest layman the Church of England has produced for at least a century: you should stay with him to the end.' The chaplain took this advice, and refused the mitre. It was never offered to him again.

[6] The Earl of Halifax, *Fullness of Days*, London 1957, 25.

that until almost the end of his life he never communicated more than three times a week. When he was about ninety Halifax asked his chaplain if he might receive more often. He was told there was not the slightest objection, and thereafter Lord Halifax made his communion daily.[7] Another of his chaplains has written:

> I always found that, however early I went to the chapel to say my preparation before Mass, there was always kneeling in the front row of seats on the right and wrapped in the French cloak which he always wore, quite still, and almost invisible, the venerable figure of Lord Halifax. Under his chair was Gyp, his old, much-loved dog, who never left him night or day and always went to Mass with him, at any rate at Hickleton. . . . There was an intensity about him and the sense of entire recollection when he was praying; . . . During Mass he made all the responses quietly but audibly; he received Holy Communion with deep devotion, and, returning to his prayer-desk, knelt and again remained quite still. And so did he remain for a long long time. I have known him not to leave the chapel for his frugal breakfast for two hours after he had received our Divine Lord.[8]

The secret of the man is in those words, and the answer too to the riddle which puzzled the numerous Roman Catholics, from Pope Leo XIII on down, who hoped and expected that Halifax would join their fold and could never understand why he did not. For at least the last thirty years of his life Halifax was the continual target of Roman Catholic 'convert makers'. Various methods were used to obtain the 'submission' of this prominent and devout Anglican. None of them was successful. When Halifax was well over eighty, an Anglican priest accompanying him on a visit to Rome was offered immediate ordination to the priesthood of the Roman Catholic Church by a Roman cardinal in return for his own 'submission'. The Anglican priest assured the cardinal that his own conversion would not affect Halifax for a minute. When the priest added that in any case there was the

[7] Information kindly supplied by the Revd H. Francome Painter.
[8] Cited from Lockhart, *Halifax* ii, 358. Halifax's habits of devotion were continued by his son. Cf. Birkenhead, *Halifax* 472.

matter of his own conscience to be considered, the cardinal told him he must simply make an act of faith in the Church of Rome. The offer was rejected.[9]

Cardinal Mercier, whose acquaintance with Halifax began when the English peer was well into his ninth decade and ripened into deep friendship, was more tactful in his approach—and more christian. Pointing out to Halifax one day in conversation that his faith differed in nothing from that of a Roman Catholic, Cardinal Mercier asked his friend if he did not think his conversion would lead many others to take the same step. 'Oh, your Eminence,' Halifax replied, 'if I thought my conversion were a duty I'd take the step at once. But I think the result would be exactly the opposite of what you suppose. People would say: "He's so old. He's let himself go." '[10]

The fact of the matter is that Lord Halifax never thought for a moment of 'becoming a catholic', despite frequent suggestions of Roman Catholic friends that he should do so, any more than he thought of 'becoming an Englishman'. He knew that he was a catholic already. He considered the assertion that he did not receive the body and blood of Christ at Anglican altars as absurd as the statement that God did not exist. Much has been made of the fact that Halifax represented in his day a small minority in the Church of England. But in his unshakeable belief in the reality of Anglican sacraments he was at one with the overwhelming majority of faithful Anglicans, then and now.

In the winter of 1889–90 Halifax took his family to the island of Madeira. It was there that Halifax met the Abbé Portal.

[9] This story, with additional details and the name of the cardinal who made this offer, was related to the author by the Anglican priest concerned. For a somewhat similar incident, involving a celebrated 'convert-maker' in the United States who has since been rewarded with a diocese, cf. W. D. F. Hughes, *Prudently with Power: William Thomas Manning, 16th Bishop of New York*, West Park, N.Y., n.d. [1964], 236.

[10] Cited from Jean Guitton, *Dialogue avec les Précurseurs*, Paris 1962, 132.

The Abbé Portal

Etienne Fernand Portal was then a man of thirty-four, sixteen years younger than Halifax. A member of the Society of St Vincent de Paul, a Lazarist, he was a disciple of the great French reforming bishop Dupanloup. He was already in touch with other younger clergy in the French church who were working for intellectual and spiritual renewal. Portal was associated with men like the church historian Duchesne, the Abbé Klein, and Loisy, who was later to come to grief in the modernist crisis of the first decade of the new century—a fate which Portal himself happily avoided. The French priest and the English peer took to each other at once. Portal was a man of deep spirituality, with a ready wit, gaiety, charm, and boundless enthusiasm. From Halifax, Portal gained his first knowledge of the Church of England, which he had previously regarded as just another protestant sect.[11] Both in their talks that winter

[11] It was not the first time that an Anglican had taken pains to dispel the ignorance of Frenchmen about English religion. Matthew Parker, Queen Elizabeth's first Archbishop of Canterbury, reports a conversation he had with the French ambassador in 1564 which must have been very like the first conversations between Halifax and Portal more than three hundred years later.

'The substance of his inquisition was much for the order and using of our religion; the particularities whereof I discoursed unto him. He noted much and delighted in our mediocrity [i.e. moderation], charging the Genevians and the Scottish of going too far in extremities.

'I perceive that they thought, before their coming, we had neither *statas preces*, nor choice of days of abstinence, as Lent, etc., nor orders ecclesiastical. Nor persons of our profession in any regard or estimation, or of any ability, amongst us. And thereupon, part by word and partly by some little superfluity of fare and provision, I did beat that plainly out of their heads. And so they seemed to be glad, that in ministration of our Common Prayer and Sacraments we use such reverent mediocrity, and that we did not expel musick out of our quires, telling them that our musick drowned not the principal regard of our prayer. They were inquisitive of the abbeys suppressed: and after they knew that they were converted to the maintenance of canons and preachers, both keeping hospitality and preaching God's word, and employed to the maintenance of grammarians and of beadmen, with other distributions to the poor villages yearly, with a portion also appointed to the repairing of the ways, etc. they wished the like to be universally concluded. . . .

'For the days of our abstinence, I informed them that we were more religious in that point than they be; and though I made them a fish supper on Friday night, I caused them to understand that it was rather in respect of their usage at home than for that we used so the Friday or other such fasting days, which we observe partly in respect of temperance and part for policy, not for any scrupulosity in choice of days. I signified unto them that we had both bishops and priests, married and not married, every man at his liberty, with some prudent caution provided for their

in Madeira, and in the numerous letters which the two men exchanged in the years following,[12] there was one recurrent theme: christian reunion. More than two decades later Halifax was to write of these first conversations in Madeira:

> I remember . . . adding how impossible it seemed to me to read the seventeenth chapter of St John's Gospel without being on fire to do what little we could to promote the fulfilment of the prayer offered by our Lord for his Church before his passion. 'Did not,' I said, 'the whole state of the world and of the Church cry out for such an endeavour? And was it not a cause almost of despair, and certainly of the deepest grief, to realise how much indifference, ignorance, and prejudice had to do with keeping Christians apart?'[13]

It was the message of John XXIII being preached by an English peer when Angelo Roncalli was a little peasant boy in an obscure village in the hills of northern Italy. Portal responded warmly. Halifax's biographer writes of the abbé:

> Like Halifax, he had a mind which minimised practical difficulties by comparison with ultimate ends, a characteristic which was the strength, as well as the weakness, of both men.[14]

The two friends decided to do all in their power in their respective circles to promote the desire for reunion. They felt it was important to find some concrete question which would provoke discussion, and help to bring responsible representatives of their two churches into contact with one another. They were convinced that if only the two sides could stop talking *at* each other, and begin to talk *with* each other, and even listen to one another, the whole climate might be changed. It was for those days a daring idea—too daring, as the sequel was to show. And yet even in that

---

sober contracting and conversation afterward; they did not disallow thereof. In fine, they professed that we were in religion very nigh to them. I answered that I would wish them to come nigher to us, grounding ourselves (as we do) upon the apostolical doctrine and pure time of the primitive Church' (T. T. Perowne, *Correspondence of Matthew Parker* [PS], Cambridge 1853, 215f).

[12] A large number of these letters are printed by Halifax in *Leo XIII and Anglican Orders*; further unpublished correspondence is in the Hickleton Papers (HP) and the Portal Papers (PP). The letters of both men are in French, of which Halifax had an excellent idiomatic knowledge, though it is said that he spoke it exactly like English (cf. Dark, *Lord Halifax* 21).

[13] *Leo XIII* 9f.

[14] Lockhart, *Halifax* ii, 42.

pre-ecumenical age the idea was to find a surprising measure of response, as the correspondence published by Halifax in 1912 shows.[15] But this response was not sufficient to overcome the opposition of those in both churches who regarded reunion as an impossible dream, and rejoiced to keep it so.

The plan

In January 1892 Portal wrote to Halifax:

> Your Church should publish a thesis proving decisively that your Orders are valid, which, if not an official publication, should be written by one of your most learned theologians. And why not take advantage of the present pontificate? Leo XIII is a broad-minded and conciliatory man, and would, I am sure, examine most carefully both the opportuneness of raising the question and the question itself. . . . Believe me, my dear friend, this will always remain the first question to be resolved; and it is an easier one to bring forward in that the answer depends on questions of fact, not of faith. To bring forward the question would be, I think, a great step, as it would mark the opening of negotiations, and in this, as in so much else, it is the first step that counts.[16]

Halifax doubted the wisdom of Portal's suggestion and replied on 29th January 1892:

> The state of mind of both sides makes me fear that, at the moment, no good would come of such a request. A more hopeful approach would be for the Archbishop of Canterbury to ask the Pope to allow English representatives free access to the Vatican Library and all archives of the Roman Court.[17]

He went on to say that he had recently been talking to the Bishop of Rochester,[18] who thought that if some assurance could be received that such a request would not be refused it might be made. But Portal was not to be brought from his idea and renewed his suggestion in subsequent letters.[19]

[15] In *Leo XIII and Anglican Orders*.
[16] Arthur T. Macmillan, *Fernand Portal (1855–1926), Apostle of Unity*, London 1961, 22f.
[17] Macmillan, *Portal* 23.
[18] Randall T. Davidson, later Archbishop of Canterbury.
[19] That the initiative in the reunion movement, which opponents managed to divert into the blind alley of a purely Roman investigation of Anglican Orders and so to their condemnation by the pope, came from Portal and not from Halifax is

Crucial to Portal's proposal was his contention that the validity of Anglican Orders depended, as he said, 'on questions of fact, not of faith'. At the time Portal was writing it is true that the historical facts were still disputed. Opponents of the Orders were still repeating the old objections about Archbishop Parker's consecration and that of his chief consecrator, Barlow. *Apostolicae curae* was to signal a definite gain by abandoning these objections. But the theological significance of the historical facts remained in dispute even after the facts themselves were established and conceded. Halifax realised this, and his initial reserve is understandable.

For neither Portal nor Halifax was the question of the Orders ever more than a means to an end, a device to initiate discussion, and if possible a round table conference, between Anglican and Roman Catholic theologians. What they were striving for was not primarily the recognition of Anglican Orders by the Holy See, but a *rapprochement* between their two churches, with the ultimate goal of corporate reunion. The question of orders interested them only

---

confirmed by Portal himself in a statement he supplied in 1910 to Paul Thureau-Daugin, who was then writing a book on Cardinal Vaughan.

'It is very clear from our correspondence [Portal wrote] that the initiative for our campaign did not come from [Lord Halifax]. I pressed Lord Halifax incessantly for two years to make his church known in France through articles in newspapers or reviews, articles written either by himself or by me on the basis of documents which he would send me. He did not do this because of his numerous duties, and perhaps also because he did not realize as I did the opportunity which was presented by the general policy of Leo XIII. Therefore I decided to begin myself. This movement for union with the Anglican Church differs from previous movements in its initial point: it did not come from England but from France; it was promoted by a French priest acting under the influence of Leo XIII. I need not remind you of the magnificent *élan* there was at that time amongst French Catholics of all ranks. Our movement shared in this new spirit. It was connected with the ideas of reunion that were being talked about with regard to the Oriental Churches. Our correspondence shows further that it is correct to say that Lord Halifax aroused and directed the whole movement in England, but it would not be correct to say the same with regard to France. I was not an instrument in his hands' (contained in letter of Portal to Halifax, 3rd December 1910, HP A4.213).

With this may be compared Halifax's own statement: 'Beyond an earnest desire for reunion, and a determination never to say a word which might embitter controversy, I had hitherto done little to further the cause I had at heart—the moving impulse came from the Abbé, he was the mainspring of all our action' (*Leo XIII* 38).

as a means of opening a dialogue between the theologians on both sides. The motives and actions of the two men were misunderstood and misrepresented by those in both churches who were opposed to what the two friends were attempting. Halifax dealt with the most common misrepresentation in a speech to the English Church Union in April 1896, at the time the investigation of the Orders was going forward in Rome. It had been charged, he said, that this investigation was due

> to the passionate insistence with which Lord Halifax and a section of the English Church have been seeking to obtain a recognition of the validity of those Orders from the Holy See, and the motive which is assigned for such alleged action on my part is the desire to obtain from Rome an assertion that the English clergy are in possession of the power enjoyed by a validly ordained priesthood, to consecrate the Holy Eucharist, and to offer the eucharistic sacrifice. We desire the reunion of Christendom, and we desire it with passionate earnestness. And because we desire it, and, because we have seen that if ever Rome and England are to be brought together it can only be accomplished by finding some common ground on which both sides may be brought into contact, and because such a ground seemed best supplied by the question of Orders, we have been glad that the question has been raised. Who can doubt that if in consequence of having all the facts brought before it, the Roman Church were to recognise the validity of our Orders, one great obstacle in the way of reunion would be removed. It is, then, as a means to this end, the reunion of Christendom, not because we have any doubt as to the Orders of the English Church, or require a recognition from Rome to add to our complete assurance of their perfect validity, that the question has been brought forward in France, and is now being discussed at Rome.[20]

These assurances Halifax repeated many times over. Roman Catholics hostile to the reunion movement refused to take him at his word. They consistently interpreted the campaign for reunion as an astute attempt by High Church

[20] *Leo XIII* 293. Cf. also the letter written on 24th January 1921 by Portal to Cardinal Mercier:

'The question of Holy Orders was chosen as providing a suitable meeting ground for Anglicans and Catholics, where they could discuss, not only the validity of Anglican Orders, but also other problems which separate them. . . . I thought there were sufficient points of contact to enable the question to be discussed profitably. It was not really necessary to come to any final decision on the validity of Anglican Orders: that could have been left to the end, after all other problems had been discussed' (Macmillan, *Portal* 34).

Anglicans to obtain from Rome an endorsement of their claims to catholicity in order that they might be in a better position to attack the Roman Catholic Church in England.

It is easy to dismiss Halifax as a totally unrealistic dreamer. A dreamer and an enthusiast he was. He was quite aware of this, and aware too that he could speak for only a small minority in the Church of England. He wrote afterwards:

> No one, certainly neither the Abbé Portal nor myself, supposed that such reunion was an immediate possibility. No one, least of all the Abbé and I, who for so long had discussed the matter in all its bearings, ignored the fact that those who shared my opinions on the subject of reunion with Rome were but a small minority in comparison with the much larger number who were in general accord with my objects and the principles of the Oxford Movement. What the Abbé and I maintained . . . was that great movements were generally the result of determined action on the part of resolute minorities . . . [21]

Cardinal Vaughan

Despite his soaring idealism, Lord Halifax was in many ways a practical man of affairs. The very fact that he was able, in an age so largely dominated by fierce religious controversy and polemic, to arouse so much positive interest in reunion is evidence of his shrewdness and practical sense. It was clever tactics, but also an instance of Halifax's transparent honesty, when he called on the Archbishop of Westminster, Cardinal Vaughan, in July 1892 to enlist his help in the movement for reunion between the two churches.

> I insisted how much might be done by a friendly and sympathetic attitude on the part of the authorities of the Roman Catholic Church to bring back the Church of England into communion with the Holy See, how much the Cardinal could himself do on that behalf, that nothing was so great a cause of irritation as the attitude adopted by those authorities in regard to the Orders and sacraments conferred by the Church of

[21] *Leo XIII* 385. A letter written by Halifax to Portal on 6th May 1894 contains a prophetic remark which testifies to Halifax's realism about the length of time necessary to achieve reunion: 'The reunion of Christianity is to be *the work of the next century*, and I pray God night and day that we may contribute to it' (*Leo XIII* 84, emphasis supplied).

England. . . . I urged . . . that in regard to Holy Orders there was no doctrinal difference between England and Rome, as might be supposed to exist in other cases, as, for example, in the relation of the Holy See to the whole Church, but merely a question of fact: had the Church of England, or had it not, preserved the succession, and what was admitted on both sides to be necessary for the transmission of a valid priesthood. . . .

To this the Cardinal replied that the question of Rome was the crucial question, that it was the question which would have to be settled in the end, and that it was therefore better to begin with it—exactly the opposite course to that which I had advocated.[22]

A modern Roman Catholic writer in England has commented on this difference of view:

Psychologically, Halifax was right, and Vaughan was wrong; for the wider the measure of agreement which could be reached on other matters, the more favourable would be the atmosphere in which discussion about the Roman Primacy would be initiated.[22a]

Not only at the outset of the reunion campaign, but throughout its entire course, Halifax kept in close touch with Cardinal Vaughan, even sending him copies of important letters, and of the lengthy memoranda which he liked so much to draw up. At the beginning of January 1895, just as Vaughan was about to leave for Rome to do all he could to thwart Halifax's efforts, Halifax, who was ill, sent his friend Athelstan Riley to give the cardinal a full report of all that Halifax had done and was doing, and to plead once again for Vaughan's support.[23] Vaughan did not hesitate to use the information thus supplied to him to frustrate what Halifax was trying to accomplish. Both in private and in public he consistently misrepresented the motives of Halifax and Portal. Thus in February 1894, while the movement was still in its infancy, Vaughan wrote to a correspondent.

Halifax and his party are anxious to get some kind of recognition—anything that can be twisted into a hope of recognition will serve their purpose.[24] They wish to keep people from becoming Catholics individu-

[22] *Leo XIII* 12f; cf. also 64.

[22a] Humphrey J. T. Johnson, *Anglicanism in Transition*, London, 1938, 48

[23] Cf. *Leo XIII* 173–7.

[24] Thus the text of the original letter preserved at St Joseph's College, Mill Hill. In his biography of Vaughan, Snead-Cox softened his cousin's phrase to 'anything that can suggest a hope of recognition . . .'. I am grateful to the archivist at Mill Hill, Fr Thoonen, for drawing my attention to this change.

> ally and tell them to wait for a corporate reunion. This will never be till after the Last Judgement—and all the poor souls that will be born and die in heresy before the reunion must suffer in their own souls for this chimera of corporate reunion. They are also most anxious to get some kind of assurance about their Orders, at least the statement that they are possibly valid! But this again is to keep souls back from submission to the Church.[24a]

It is important to emphasise Halifax's long-continued efforts to obtain support for the reunion movement from Cardinal Vaughan. For it was a charge at the time, and the charge has been frequently repeated since, that the movement was underhand; that it was conducted jointly by dishonest Anglicans, anxious to strike a blow at Rome, and by continental catholics whom they had duped; and that it was all done behind the backs of the Roman Catholic hierarchy in England, who claimed to be the only people in the Roman Catholic Church capable of really understanding Anglicanism.

Cardinal Vaughan was honestly convinced from the outset that Halifax's movement was a threat to the Roman Catholic Church and faith. He made use of every means at his disposal to thwart what Halifax and Portal were attempting. Given his convictions, it is difficult to see how Vaughan could have acted otherwise. To appreciate his motives, it is necessary to understand something of the man.

Herbert Vaughan was in many ways a worthy antagonist to Lord Halifax, although the two men were so far apart in temperament that there was never the slightest basis for mutual understanding. Vaughan was a descendant of the old catholic aristocracy of England, small in numbers but great in supernatural faith and courage, which had kept the faith when Roman Catholic priests were outlawed and the celebration of mass was treason. Vaughan was the eldest of thirteen children. His mother was a convert to catholicism of deep piety, who prayed for an hour each day that all her

[24a] J. G. Snead-Cox, *The Life of Cardinal Vaughan*, ii, London 1910, 182.

children would receive religious vocations. Her prayers were granted. All five of her daughters entered convents, and all eight of her sons seminaries. Six of the eight became priests, and three of them bishops. Herbert Vaughan grew up on his father's country estate, surrounded by his rabbits and ponies and dogs, a hero to all his younger brothers and sisters. He loved sport and hunting, but when he became a priest he gave these things up for ever: the hardest thing he ever did, as he confessed later.[25] As a priest his interests were simply and solely religious. Cardinal Manning, who would not generally be considered the broadest of men, rebuked Herbert Vaughan once for being too narrow, too exclusively interested in religion and religious things. 'This makes you sharp,' Manning told him, 'and inhuman to your fellow creatures.'[26] Vaughan's biography reveals him as a man of intense prayer, with a deep humility which was little appreciated because of an aloof manner and a want of tact based upon a complete unawareness of the effect of his words and actions on others—a trait which was a special handicap in his journalistic work as editor of *The Tablet*, a post he held for a number of years prior to his appointment to the see of Salford in 1872 at the age of forty. His cousin and biographer wrote of him:

> All his life he had an impatience, which was half contempt, for the graces of style, and he had very little feeling for the values of words. His busy, eager, adventurous life, though it had directed his studies into one channel, had left him little time for the acquirement of such learning as would entitle him to be considered, and still less to consider himself, a specialist in any branch of either theology or philosophy. All these deficiencies might have been compensated for by a saving common sense, which he certainly had, but that it was yoked with a certain strange simplicity of heart which sometimes led him into the oddest blunders. His had been a very solitary life—in crowds he had been alone. . . . His was an innocence which in a journalist became disconcerting. His baffling unworldliness created difficult situations. Quite unconscious of offence, he would take some theological proposition and apply it to a human instance with very little regard for the special circumstances and

[25] Snead-Cox, *Vaughan* i, 17. [26] Ibid., 458.

> without a thought for such an irrelevancy as the feelings of the person concerned.[27]

This ruthlessly logical approach caused Vaughan to criticise Anglicans for 'refusing absolutely to push the speculative truths of the faith to their ultimate consequences and to draw legitimate conclusions from premisses'.[28]

Vaughan was a tall man with clear-cut features, 'one of the handsomest men of his time', his biographer writes, whose 'splendid presence would have served to distinguish him in any assembly.'[29] The extremely brisk manner in which he was accustomed to dash through Pontifical ceremonies earned him the nickname of 'the scarlet runner'. When Vaughan learned of this he broke down and wept at the thought of the scandal and disedification he had given, resolving in the presence of his very young chaplain to make amends in the future.[30] Some years after Vaughan's death his lay friend Wilfrid Ward wrote that the cardinal's career had displayed

> a curious combination of romantic ideals with intensely unromantic details. The romance of self-devotion for the cause of God and the Church was intense. He fostered it by habits which would seem to ordinary Englishmen superstitious—as when he placed the Papal brief appointing him Bishop of Salford in the hands of the statue of Our Lady that he might receive from her his new commission. He would fill his imagination with the ideals for which he worked. He had the romance attaching to devoted action. But, once the great aim was determined on, he was wholly unromantic and most practical in carrying it out. He often overrode, almost brutally, the romance of ordinary home life and human love if they stood in his path. Nothing could be more practical than the means he took. He followed the well-known General's advice to his soldiers—he kept his powder dry while he said his prayers.[31]

The narrative contained in the following chapters offers abundant confirmation of this characterisation.

It will readily be understood that the subtleties of theology

[27] Snead-Cox, *Vaughan* i, 192f.
[28] Preface to P. Ragey, *L'anglo-catholicisme*, Paris 1897, xv. Vaughan's preface is dated 12th April 1897.
[29] Snead-Cox, *Vaughan* ii, 406. [30] Ibid., 380f.
[31] *Morning Post*, 16th August 1910, 4.

were not for Herbert Vaughan. His was a simple view of the faith and of the church: those who were not for her were against her. He liked to be able to identify friends and foes easily, and was supremely confident of his ability to do so. A recent description of two of his successors in the see of Westminster could be applied to Vaughan without alteration: 'deeply religious, wonderfully humble, unbelievably narrow culturally and theologically'.[32]

It was characteristic both of Vaughan's theological outlook and of the methods which he considered appropriate for the propagation of truth that as editor of *The Tablet* during the years prior to the First Vatican Council he steadfastly refused to publish any views critical of papal infallibility or questioning the opportuneness of a definition. English catholics were deeply divided on the issue, and the paper received numerous letters from anti-infallibilists and inopportunists. Vaughan ignored all such communications. He was certain that the doctrine would be defined in the end, and did not wish to create difficulties in the minds of the faithful by publishing opinions criticising a doctrine to which all Roman Catholics would soon have to give the interior assent of faith.[33] Vaughan's biographer, who was himself editor of *The Tablet* when he came to write his cousin's life, has admitted that in the infallibility question the paper was guilty of dogmatism, that it was intolerant of all opposition, impatient of the attitude of those who dreaded the consequences of a definition, and always ready to cry down and discredit opponents by suggestions of disloyalty or by open accusations of Gallicanism.[34] Vaughan's attitude towards the proponents of Anglo-Roman reunion in the mid-1890's was strikingly similar to the policy he had adopted as the young editor of *The Tablet* three decades previously. There was the same dogmatism, the same intolerance of opposition, and the

[32] *Herder Correspondence* 2 (1965), 329. The reference is to Cardinals Griffin and Godfrey.

[33] Cf. Snead-Cox, *Vaughan* i, 202.

[34] Cf. ibid., 231.

same readiness to cry down and discredit opponents by suggestions of disloyalty (in the case of Roman Catholics like Portal and Duchesne) and open accusations of cynical and interested motives (in the case of the Anglicans). Vaughan's solution to the problem of reunion was characteristically simple and straightforward. It was summed up in the single word 'submission', which he repeated in season and out with a sublime disregard of its negative psychological effect. Individual submission to the see of Peter, he said in a speech at Bristol on 9th September 1895, was the only hope there was for reunion, and the greatest obstacle to this submission was pride.[35]

It is clear that Vaughan could not hope to comprehend the position of a man like Lord Halifax. The Church of England as a thoroughly protestant and Erastian institution he could understand. It was something he could come to grips with. This was the familiar enemy, the age-old foe which had oppressed his forefathers. He knew how to deal with it. But a church which claimed to be, and never to have ceased to be, 'the ancient Catholic Church of this land', which denounced him and his with scorn as 'the Italian mission',[36] which claimed to feed its children in the eucharist with the true body and blood of Christ, and to forgive their sins in the sacrament of penance as truly as the pope himself —this was too much for Herbert Vaughan. He quite naturally felt that a church which so acted and spoke was trespassing on his own preserve. To speak, as Lord Halifax and his friends did, about a gradual *rapprochement* between the two churches, to advocate friendly theological discussions between the representatives of truth and of error in the hope that such discussion might lead one distant day to a corporate reunion of the churches, this was to him a snare and a delusion, a trick of Satan to keep people back from the truth.

[35] Cf *The Tablet* 54 (1895), 415.

[36] This was a favourite phrase with a man like Archbishop Benson of Canterbury. Such language was severely condemned by Halifax, who always spoke of the Roman Catholic Church with the greatest respect.

Vaughan's attitude can only be understood against the background of English catholic history. His considerably more broad-minded friend Wilfrid Ward, who tried, with small success, to play the honest broker between Vaughan and Halifax, wrote:

> Can we be surprised that the descendants in England of those whose lives were ruined by fines and disabilities, or who were martyred for adherence to Catholic doctrines, should be slow to understand that those who persecuted or killed them belonged to a Church which for the most part potentially agreed with them?[37]

But even Ward admitted that Vaughan

> had deep down in him a strong contempt for the Church of England when it assumed any pretensions to deal on an equality with Rome. This is a sentiment not in itself incompatible with sympathy for its members. Something of the same sentiment is visible in the appendix to Cardinal Newman's 'Apologia'. It is a natural consequence of a belief that the great idea of a Catholic Church is actually realised in an existing polity and communion. External bodies necessarily become insignificant by comparison. But while Newman's past and his love for his old friends enabled him to write what he wrote without offence, Vaughan's blunt and apparently haughty demeanour had a very different effect. Again, individual Anglican clergymen were not as a rule congenial to him. To this there were marked exceptions, however. Bishop Temple and Cardinal Vaughan, both blunt and direct, understood and liked one another. But even with Dr Temple he had the habitual feeling that their co-operation as being that of a prelate of 'the Church' with a clergyman outside it must be social rather than religious. When Temple was made Archbishop of Canterbury Cardinal Vaughan wrote him a warm letter expressing a hope that they might have many opportunities of working together 'for the happiness of the people of London and the good of their common country'. Temple in his reply echoed the wish, but added, 'May I not also say in the service of our common Divine Master?' The Cardinal showed me the letter and appreciated its humour, but did not, I think, repent of his own omission.[38]

Years later the Birminghan Oratorian Dr Humphrey Johnson wrote of Vaughan:

> The Cardinal saw clearly the inherent Protestantism of the Anglican system, but lacked understanding of the Anglican mentality. . . . Catho-

[37] Cited from Maisie Ward, *The Wilfrid Wards and the Transition*, London 1934, 280.

[38] Ward, art. cit. in n. 31 above.

lics were wont to reassure their Anglican friends that what they took for tactlessness in the Cardinal's character was nothing but the essentially British quality of bluntness, to which the incredulous Anglicans replied that the Cardinal-Archbishop seemed to them most un-English in outlook. In reality, Vaughan was both English and un-English. He belonged to an archaic and nearly vanished phase of English life, the England of the old Catholic squires, excluded so long for their loyalty to the faith of their ancestors from their normal share in public life enjoyed by members of their class. But he had no mental kinship with the England of his age.[39]

Such was the man on whose stubborn and unyielding opposition the soaring hopes of Halifax and Portal were to suffer shipwreck.

[39] Op. cit. in n. 22a above, 148f.

3
THE CAMPAIGN FOR REUNION IS LAUNCHED

What a moment is this to be fingering the trinkets of Rome.

—Archbishop Benson[1]

'Dalbus' on Anglican Orders

The correspondence between Halifax and Portal contains a number of references to a defence of Anglican Orders which Halifax had promised his friend that he would write. What with one thing and another, however, Halifax seems never to have got down to it, and in the end the task was undertaken by Portal. The resulting work was first published in *La Science Catholique* in December 1893 and January 1894 under the pseudonymn of 'F. Dalbus', and was subsequently issued in the form of a brochure.[2] This publication attracted a great deal of attention on both sides of the Channel, and was widely reviewed.

Portal argued that the historical facts of Parker's consecration as well as that of his chief consecrator, Barlow, were firmly established, so that the material succession of the Anglican hierarchy was intact. The sacramental form of the Ordinal, taken in itself, he considered adequate. But he contended that Barlow's intention in consecrating Parker must be considered doubtful; and that therefore the consecration of the bishop upon whom all subsequent Anglican ordinations depend was doubtful because of a probable

[1] Edward White Benson, *Fishers of Men*, London 1893, 122.

[2] F. Dalbus, *Les ordinations anglicanes*, Paris and Lyon [2]1894. All quotations are from this second edition, which was expanded by the inclusion of several letters to the author, including one from John Wordsworth, Bishop of Salisbury, and replies by Portal. Before publication Portal sent the portion of his pamphlet dealing with the historical facts of Parker's and Barlow's consecrations to the Anglican Cowley Father Fr F. W. Puller for his criticisms. See letter of Puller to Halifax, 12th January 1894, in HP A4.243.

defect of intention.[3] Portal concluded that Anglican Orders were certainly invalid because the suppression of the 'tradition of the instruments' in the 1552 Ordinal amounted to an omission of essential matter.[4]

The final pages of the work are devoted to the subject of reunion. Portal argues that in any future negotiations for reunion the question of orders is bound to arise, and that this question will have to be resolved either prior to doctrinal agreement or immediately thereafter.

> And if it must be treated in any case, it would be better to treat it first in accordance with the elementary principle of diplomacy that when two opposing parties wish to negotiate they ought to look not for the things that divide them, but for those which unite them, not for opposition, but for points of contact. In order to enter into discussions it is necessary to seek some common ground on which each of the parties can venture without giving up any of the rights to which it lays claim. But the question of Orders appears to us to constitute an extremely favourable terrain upon which negotiations might be started without touching upon any irritating questions.
>
> The Anglican Church believes that it has genuine Orders, the Roman Church acts as if it does not. This policy is dictated by prudence, and not by passion. Since the Anglicans have such great confidence in the validity of their ordinations, why do they not offer to furnish the proof of this validity? They have no right to remain in their insular dignity and to content themselves with mere assertions of the reality of their hieracrchy.[5]

The Anglican bishops, Portal argued, should submit the proofs of their orders. They would find that the Holy See was prepared to study such proofs in the most sympathetic spirit.

Despite its negative conclusion on the subject of the

[3] Portal made use of the erroneous 'principle of positive exclusion' which says that when the minister of a sacrament has simultaneously two mutually conflicting intentions they automatically cancel each other out and invalidate the sacrament, without any consideration of the question, which intention was in reality stronger and predominant. For a preliminary discussion of some of the fallacies underlying this principle see the present author's 'Ministerial Intention in the Administration of the Sacraments', ClRev 51 (1966), 763–6. Cf. also J.–M, Tillard, 'Sacramental Questions: the Intentions of Minister and Recipient', *Concilium* 4 (1968) 61–7.

[4] In the middle ages and for centuries thereafter it was the all but universal view of Latin theologians that the essential matter of ordination was not the laying on of hands but the *porrectio intrumentorum*: in the case of the priesthood the delivery of the chalice and paten to the ordinand.

[5] Portal, op. cit. 36f.

Orders, Portal's pamphlet was extraordinarily well received by Anglicans, who were pleasantly surprised by the calm and sympathetic tone of the work, so strikingly different from the polemical tone of most previous Roman Catholic works on Anglican Orders. Closer to home, Portal's negative conclusion was praised by Roman Catholics eager to maintain the traditional negative attitude in this question. But more discerning critics pointed out that the grounds upon which Dalbus' negative conclusion was based were defective. They pointed out that the tradition of the instruments was a comparatively late innovation in the rite of ordination; and that to condemn orders conferred without this ceremony as invalid due to a defect of essential matter was to condemn all orders conferred in the west for at least a thousand years, as well as the Orders of the Orthodox, who had never used this ceremony. One of those who expressed this opinion was the well-known church historian the Abbé Duchesne, then a professor at the Institut Catholique in Paris, in a review of Dalbus' work in the *Bulletin Critique* for July 1894.[6] Duchesne also rejected Dalbus' arguments about intention.

> There have been unbelieving bishops elsewhere than in England. We should not forget that a part of the French clergy derives its ordination from M. de Talleyrand.[7]

Duchesne concluded that Anglican Orders could be considered valid. This expression of opinion from a theologian with a European reputation attracted wide notice.

Portal's condemnation of Anglican Orders for a reason which he knew would be rejected by Roman Catholic theologians was tactical. Within a few weeks of the pamphlet's appearance Portal was writing to Halifax:

> I have already received some reactions to my articles. The chief one is surprise at the whole thing, and, as I had foreseen, a great reluctance to

[6] Paris 5 (1894), 262; the complete French text is most readily available to English readers in A. C. Headlam, *The Doctrine of the Church and Christian Reunion*, London [2]1920, 283f. Duchesne repeated his view in a private letter to Portal, later printed by Halifax, *Leo XIII* 78ff.

[7] *Bulletin Critique*, loc. cit. in foregoing note.

admit the third part.[8] One of my friends wrote to me yesterday: 'You will certainly have great difficulty establishing the nullity of Anglican ordinations because of the suppression of the tradition of the instruments; also in your claim that the Church can in the course of time change or change to some extent the matter of certain sacraments.' This was foreseen.[9]

Halifax passed on this information to friends in England who objected to Portal's negative conclusion. On 4th August 1894 Halifax wrote to the scholarly Bishop of Peterborough, Dr Mandell Creighton, that it was necessary 'to read between the lines' of Portal's work. 'The Abbé Duchesne's letter upon it was foreseen—and intended.'[10] And later the same month Halifax told his good friend William Charles Lake, Dean of Durham, that Portal knew his arguments about intention and the necessity of the tradition of the instruments

would be rejected by his own people, and the consequent result of the whole would be one favourable to us. And so it has turned out, for the Abbé Duchesne, who is the greatest historical authority in France, has already written in our favour—while the *Moniteur de Rome*, the *Univers* and the *Monde*, and even the organ of the French Jesuits have followed suit more or less in the same direction.[11]

Portal's brochure had been widely noticed and had inspired a rash of articles on Anglican Orders and the Church of England. To Halifax and Portal it seemed that their campaign had got off to a good start.

Portal's first visit to England, August 1894

The next step was Portal's first visit to England in August 1894. How this came about is best told in the abbé's own words:

Lord Halifax . . . thought that my trip should be delayed until the following year. . . . My purpose in making this trip was to collect information about the revival of the religious orders and congregations in the

[8] The third part contained the argument that Anglican Orders were invalid because the tradition of the instruments had been eliminated from the Ordinal.
[9] Portal to Halifax, 29th January 1894, PP.
[10] HP A4.254.
[11] Halifax to Lake, 20th August 1894, HP A4.232.

> Anglican Church. If I visited mostly in the more Catholic circles this was because I intended to describe chiefly this side of the Anglican Church in the book which I was preparing. I did not ignore other aspects of Anglicanism, but since I had only a month at my disposal I went where it was most important to go. This is the sole reason why I had only a limited interest in the English [Roman] Catholics.[12]

Although Halifax had originally thought that the time was not yet ripe for such a visit, he threw himself into the project with enthusiasm when it was once settled that Portal was coming. Halifax was the most generous of hosts at all times, and on this occasion he outdid himself. Anyone entertaining a foreign visitor will wish to show him the things in his own country of which he is most proud. This fact, combined with Portal's own special interest, was responsible for the fact that visits to Anglican religious houses and the Anglo-Catholic institutions and parishes which they served should bulk large in the programme. Halifax did not conceal from Portal (as was alleged)[13] the existence of a large protestant element in the Church of England, and a few visits were made to churches and institutions representing this side of Anglicanism.[14] Halifax took Portal to see the Bishop of Peterborough, Dr Mandell Creighton, as well as the Archbishop of York, Dr W. D. Maclagen. Both visits took place in an atmosphere of great cordiality, the welcome at York being especially warm. The archbishop told Portal that he tried to follow the methods of St Charles Borromeo and Bishop Dupanloup in the administration of his diocese. And as he bade farewell to his two visitors he said:

> Let us hope that we are at the beginning of something really great in the interests of the Church.[15]

Halifax and Portal were moved to tears. As they took their

[12] Contained in letter of Portal to Halifax, 3rd December 1910, HP A4.213. In this letter Portal communicates to Halifax the statement which he (Portal) has given to Thureau-Daugin. Cf. n. 19 in previous chapter.

[13] This charge has been made times without number. Cf. for instance the (anonymous) review of Lacey's 'Roman Diary' in *The Tablet* 84 (1910), 1014–16, 1015 col. 1.

[14] Cf. the account of Portal's itinerary, *Leo XIII* 96

[15] *Leo XIII* 98f.

places in the carriage for the homeward journey Portal grasped his friend's hand and said with deep emotion:

> C'est la note d'une grand piété qui distingue cette maison.[16]

The distinguishing note of two subsequent incidents was less auspicious. Cardinal Vaughan, who had been apprised of the abbé's visit by Lord Halifax, invited the French visitor to lunch with him. Through some mischance the letter went astray, and Halifax arrived without his friend, who was unaware of the invitation and still in the country. This gave considerable offence. Cardinal Vaughan was both mystified and suspicious when he learned of the round of visits to high Anglican dignitaries being made by this French priest, and feared that things were being done and said behind his back of which he could not possibly approve. When the visitor did not even come to pay his respects to the head of the hierarchy of his own church during his visit to England, the existing suspicion was turned into deep-rooted distrust. Halifax himself learned of the invitation to Portal only upon reaching Archbishop's House, where he found that Canon Moyes, a member of the cardinal's staff, and the liturgist Mr Edmund Bishop had also been invited to lunch to meet the abbé. Halifax at once explained the misunderstanding and offered apologies.[17] A letter written twelve years later by Bishop indicates that Halifax's explanation was never accepted.

> Lord Halifax and Portal were asked to lunch by Cardinal Vaughan; I was there, delighted with the prospect of talking to the Abbé, and perfectly ignorant of the intrigue that was afoot. Lord Halifax came; we had lunch, conversation—most friendly and interesting, but from the Abbé Portal

[16] *Leo XIII* 98f; cf. Lockhart, *Halifax* ii, 49.

[17] *Leo XIII* 100. A diary note by Portal fixes the date of his visit to the Archbishop of Canterbury as Wednesday 15th August (PP). Halifax reports that he lunched with Cardinal Vaughan the day previously, which would be Tuesday 14th. On 12th August Halifax had written from his London house in Eaton Square to Portal, who had remained at Hickleton: 'Nothing from Cardinal Vaughan, so I think there is no point your bothering about him' (PP, bound volume of copies of letters from Halifax to Portal, 80). This letter indicates that an invitation from that cardinal was hoped for and expected, and shows that two days previous to Halifax's luncheon with Vaughan no word had been received from him.

nothing but excuses for his absence. That's how the thing is done—with all such clerics, including Mgr Duchesne.[18]

In view of Halifax's transparent honesty, shown amongst other things by the fact that he kept Cardinal Vaughan informed of everything he was doing, despite Vaughan's known and increasingly bitter opposition, such an interpretation of this incident is hardly a credit to those who adopted it. Unfortunate though this misunderstanding was, however, its importance should not be exaggerated. It is inconceivable that Cardinal Vaughan would have taken a different attitude towards the reunion movement, even if Portal had called on him. We have already seen that Halifax's attempt two years previously to win the cardinal's support had met with a sharp rebuff.[19]

The day after this unhappy misunderstanding Halifax and Portal were received by the Archbishop of Canterbury, Dr Edward White Benson, at his country residence at Addington. Benson's official biography by his son shows him to have been a man of very moderate High Church views. Like many Church of England prelates before and since, Benson had been a headmaster before becoming a bishop. He was also something of an amateur scholar: his work on Cyprian,[20] on which he worked at odd hours for several decades, is characterised by a deep reverence for the life and faith of the 'undivided church' of Cyprian's day, which Benson sees as having been corrupted by Roman autocracy.[21] His diary entries during his trips abroad show that he had a strong archaeological and aesthetic interest in Roman Catholic churches and liturgy, and a keen appreciation of the services

[18] Nigel Abercrombie, *The Life and Work of Edmund Bishop*, London 1959, 227.

[19] Cf. pp. 37ff above.

[20] E. W. Benson, *Cyprian: His Life, His Times, His Work* (ed. A. C. Benson), London 1897.

[21] The English Oratorian Fr H. I. D. Ryder praised 'the loving minuteness, the careful scholarship with which every phrase of [Cyprian] is dwelt upon'. While deploring the book's strong anti-Roman bias, he found 'sound criticism' in its uncontroversial parts, and wrote that the style reminded him in places of Cardinal Manning—a tribute which Benson fortunately never had to read, for the book was published posthumously. (Cf. H. I. D. Ryder, 'An Anglican Presentation of St Cyprian', AER 18 [1898], 13–36, 35f.)

for Holy Week in the Roman rite, which Benson admired because they were so scriptural and said so much about Christ's sacrifice on Calvary. But devotions like the rosary he considered trivial and 'un-English'. Despite his appreciation of the positive aspects of Roman Catholic teaching, Benson was deeply distrustful of the Roman Catholic Church as an institution. He considered that it invariably put policy above principle, and stipulated before he would permit Halifax to bring Portal to see him that he could not consent to receiving 'emissaries'.

> It should be clear to him that *I* have no doubts as to our Orders which make me more grateful to him for seeing the facts, than I should be grateful to him for acknowledging the Copernican or Newtonian systems, but that I honour him for saying so in the teeth of the ignorance which surrounds him.[21a]

Holding such views, Benson was understandably vexed to be linked in any way with the Roman Catholic Church. At a later stage in the reunion movement he confided to his diary:

> Cannot stand the English Church Union thanking the Pope and the Archbishop in one resolution—a new form of things which the Reformation was supposed to have ended.[22]

Benson's interview with Halifax and Portal can best be described in Halifax's own words.

> The tone was more intellectual and less spiritual than that at Bishopthorpe,[23] but it did very well. The Archbishop was much interested and very kind, and I think the Abbé produced a very good impression. Mrs Benson and the female part of the establishment very much to the front, but not in a disagreeable way[24]—although it was very interesting and amusing too—only with a considerable element of tenterhooks, as you can easily understand.[25]

[21a] Arthur C. Benson, *The Life of Edward White Benson*, ii, London 1900, 592.
[22] Diary, Trinity College Cambridge, entry for 5th July 1895, 187.
[23] The residence of the Archbishop of York.
[24] Halifax told Mrs Mandell Creighton, wife of the Bishop of Peterborough, that he would like to burn all bishop's wives (Macmillan, *Portal* 37).
[25] Lockhart, *Halifax* ii, 50f.

The archbishop's biographer explains that 'the female part of the establishment' had been deliberately brought to the fore to emphasise the unofficial character of the interview. And he quotes one of those present as saying that Benson had 'talked "with his paws in the air", ready to dart away at the least sign of any proximity to dangerous subjects'.[26] The archbishop warmed up a bit towards the end of the interview, however, promising to supply Portal with any information he needed for the book he was planning, and twice expressing the hope that their contact would not end with this visit.[27] But after the tremendous warmth of previous visits there was, understandably, a certain feeling of disappointment. 'We are far from York,' was Portal's regretful comment as they came away.[28]

Portal's visit had been undertaken on his own initiative. Its primary purpose was to gather material for a book. 'It was only circumstances,' he wrote later, 'which gave my trip an entirely different character'. And it was doubtless the circumstances which we are about to relate that prevented the abbé from ever writing the proposed book about the revival of the religious life in the Church of England.

> I returned [to France] more convinced than ever—'ardent' is too strong an expression in my opinion—and resolved simply to pursue my plan of making the Anglican Church better known amongst us. A few days after my return I was summoned to Rome in the course of a retreat which I was conducting. I had not requested such a summons nor had any such request been made on my behalf, nor did I expect anything of the kind.[29]

Portal's visit to Rome, September 1894

The summons here referred to came in the form of an intimation that the Cardinal Secretary of State, Rampolla,

[26] A. C. Benson, *E. W. Benson* ii, 593.
[27] Macmillan, *Portal* 40; confirmed by Portal's diary note (PP).
[28] Lockhart, *Halifax* ii, 50.
[29] Letter of Portal to Halifax, 3rd December 1910, HP A4.213; cf. Chapter 2, n. 19 above.

would like to see Portal in Rome.[30] Informed of this surprising turn of events, Halifax dashed over to Paris to confer with his friend before his departure for Rome. They spent the day together in excited discussion, and in the evening Halifax returned to England and the abbé left for Italy. There he gave Cardinal Rampolla, at the latter's request, a full account of all he had so recently seen and heard in England. Rampolla considered the matter so important that he took Portal the next day to see the aged Leo XIII. This audience, which lasted almost an hour, was recorded by Portal in a memorandum which he wrote immediately afterwards.

> [Portal] detailed to the Pope the various things he had seen in England, what he had been able to observe of the spirit that animated the houses of Sisters and religious communities, and what he had learnt of the general practices and principles of those who represented the Oxford Movement. He said he evidently had not seen the whole of the Church of England, and that he knew how much of a very different character existed within it; that there were many who sympathised much more with Protestants than with Catholics, but that the English episcopate contained men of first-class ability, undoubted piety and great learning. . . . He alluded to the fact that though the Archbishop of Canterbury was afraid of compromising himself, he recognised the duty of working for the cause of reunion.[31]

Writing about this audience sixteen years later, Portal explained:

> My effectiveness came not from my enthusiasm, but entirely from the fact that I was able to say: 'A few days ago I heard and saw this, that, and the other.'[32]

The pope asked Portal what he thought about Anglican

[30] The background of this summons is as follows: on 11th July 1894 Halifax had, at Portal's request, sent his friend a long letter explaining his ecumenical ideas. (This letter is summarised below pp. 204–8.) Portal noted later at the bottom of this letter: 'In the last days of July '94 a copy of this letter was sent to M. Levé [editor of the *Monde*], who communicated it to M. Lorin. M. Lorin sent on a copy to Rome. I had joined to the copy a brief report telling, if I remember correctly, the origin of my relations with Lord Halifax. This communication of M. Levé determined my summons to Rome' (PP, bound volume of letters from Halifax to Portal, 75).

[31] *Leo XIII* 119.

[32] Letter cited in notes 12 and 29 above.

Orders, and the abbé replied that he considered them doubtful.

> In speaking of my pamphlet I explained that our purpose in raising the question of Orders was to create a point of contact which would give an opportunity to the representatives of the two churches to discuss, in the spirit of charity, the differences which separated them.[33]

The pope said no one had ever talked to him about England as the abbé had done, and he wondered whether anything could be done, and what. Portal ventured to suggest that the pope should write a private letter to the two English archbishops, suggesting conferences on the subject of orders as a point of contact which would give an opportunity for representatives of both sides to discuss the differences which separated them. Asked if he believed the archbishops would reply to such a letter, Portal replied that he did. After some further discussion the pope said he would write the letter.

A few days later, however, he had thought better of it, and it was decided that to avoid the possible risk of a rebuff from the Anglican side, it would be more politic for the letter to be written by Cardinal Rampolla, as Secretary of State, to Portal. This could then be shown to Halifax and the archbishops, and if it produced a corresponding response on their part, the way would have been prepared for the direct approach which Portal had suggested. The abbé objected that this course, although apparently more prudent, was in fact less so, since it did not oblige the archbishops to make any response at all. But he was unable to alter the decision which had been taken. This change of plan, which was in the circumstances fully understandable, was to have an unfortunate result. For it enabled the Archbishop of Canterbury to say that in fact no serious approach had ever been contemplated, and that the whole thing was an attempt to use the sincere enthusiasm of Halifax and Portal to compromise the official chief of the Anglican Church.[34]

[33] Macmillan, *Portal* 43.

[34] Cf. A. C. Benson, *E. W. Benson* ii, 593.

Whether a direct approach would have had the desired effect it is impossible to say. It is easy to make out a case for the negative answer. Successful negotiations of any kind can be conducted only on the basis of mutual trust. We have already remarked Archbishop Benson's deep-seated distrust of the Roman Catholic Church. To this must be added the corresponding hostility of Cardinal Vaughan to any such approach. And yet distrust can be overcome by generosity, humility, and goodwill on the other side. This was abundantly demonstrated by the pontificate of Pope John XXIII. Could Leo XIII in the wholly different climate of the 1890s have made the kind of approach which would have overcome Benson's distrust (as well as Vaughan's) and allowed a response to be made in the spirit manifested throughout by the Archbishop of York?[35] We cannot say. However, a letter written by Benson to Halifax some months later indicates that the archbishop would not have rejected out of hand a really sincere and generous offer of joint conversations:

> I believe you really know how I sympathise with the far-off desire and hope of the unity of Christendom; but it would be impossible for me to frame and approve any answer to a question which has not yet been asked [i.e. a proposal of joint theological conferences] . . . You, however, know something at least of my views, and the strength of them, as to the gain which would accrue to Christendom if the Church of Rome would take pains to understand the history and principles of the Church of England, and you are able to judge of what would be our attitude towards any genuine and gracious attempt to understand the facts of our position. To extend their study and knowledge of these points would be productive only of good; and as it must precede any action of any sort, it must be welcomed by any one and every one who 'loves the truth in peace'.[36]

This letter displays no awareness that the Church of England might also have things to learn about the 'history and principles' of the Church of Rome. Had conversations been entered into in this spirit, they could hardly have led to any

[35] In a letter to Portal dated 27th March 1896 the Archbishop of York accepted the idea of joint conversations. Cf. *Leo XIII* 280ff.
[36] *Leo XIII* 193.

positive result. Men on both sides were guilty of thinking that reunion was a one-way street.

However, a letter to Halifax from the scholarly Bishop Creighton of Peterborough shows that even in that pre-ecumenical age there were some who realised what was needed.

> At present Nonconformists do not discover their poverty; the Romans do not discover their want of contact with actual life. That is their real defect. They are upholding a system, not making it operative on life: greater knowledge of our Church would help them greatly in this, *and we need to know something of the greater versatility and adaptability of their methods.*[37]

Cardinal Rampolla's letter to Portal

The letter which Cardinal Rampolla gave to the Abbé Portal is a remarkable document. The original French text may be read in *Leo XIII and Anglican Orders.*[38] The letter is dated 19th September 1894, and begins by thanking Portal for the pamphlet on Anglican Orders by 'Dalbus' as well as for his 'interesting account of the theological work and outlook of some of the most distinguished members of the Church of England', and of their desire for reunion. Rampolla says that despite his numerous duties, he has been able to read Dalbus' pamphlet.

> I was delighted to find so intricate a subject examined with such complete impartiality and in the spirit solely directed to the search for truth in the spirit of charity. Although I cannot go into the question itself, I cannot but approve of the authors' conclusion, since it is entirely in accord with the sentiments expressed a short time ago by the Holy Father in his apostolic letter to the princes and people of the world.[39]

The conclusion here referred to was Portal's argument that the Anglican bishops should present the proofs of their

[37] *Leo XIII* 190f, emphasis supplied.
[38] *Leo XIII* 153ff. The translation in the English edition of Portal's biography is incomplete: Macmillan, *Portal* 45f.
[39] The second sentence in this passage is lacking in Macmillan's English translation.

orders, and that the Holy See would consider such proofs in the most generous spirit.[40] It is important to note what Rampolla wrote in this letter about Portal's treatment of the Orders question. For exactly two years later it had been decided at Rome to take an entirely different line about the matter. *Apostolicae curae* said:

> Hence it must be clear to everyone that the controversy lately revived had been already definitely settled by the Apostolic See, and that it is to the insufficient knowledge of these documents that we must perhaps attribute the fact that any Catholic writer should have considered it still an open question.[41]

It is remarkable that the Cardinal Secretary of State was one of those so ill-informed as to consider a question to be still open which had in fact 'been already definitely settled by the Apostolic See'. The pope himself appears to have shared this ignorance. For when he received Portal for a brief farewell visit in September 1894 Leo XIII told the abbé, who had noticed a copy of the brochure by 'Dalbus' on the pope's table 'I have read your work; it is very well done.'[42]

Rampolla's letter continues by stating Dalbus' view that the increasing influence of the Oxford Movement in the Church of England was dispelling old prejudices and would finally

> bring back into unity with the visible Church of Christ the daughter of Rome, and that noble English race which received its Christianity from Gregory the Great. Thus the English will become fully deserving of the great destiny to which they have been called by providence. No doubt whatever can be raised as to the affectionate reception that this nation

[40] Cf. p. 47 above.

[41] *Anglican Orders (English)*, London (SPCK) 1957, 9. Cited hereafter as AO(E). This modern edition of the Bull in the official English translation prepared at the time by Merry del Val and Gasquet (cf. p. 198 below) is cited throughout for reasons of convenience. The authentic text of *Apostolicae curae* will be found in the *Acta Sanctae Sedis* xxix (1896–97), 198–201.

[42] *Leo XIII* 122. As late as March 1896 Cardinal Rampolla was still unaware that the question had already been definitely settled by the Holy See. Replying to a letter from Halifax of 20th March 1896, Rampolla said that no decision on the validity of the Orders was imminent, but that the question was being carefully studied by the Holy See, which was given full considerations to all arguments pro and contra (cf. *Leo XIII* 278).

would receive from its ancient mother and mistress if this happy return were accomplished . . .

The pope ardently desired reunion, Rampolla wrote, and would spare no pains to smooth the road to it.

A friendly exchange of ideas and a more careful and profound study of former beliefs and practices of worship would be the most useful means possible to prepare the way for this desired union. All this ought to be accomplished without any touch of bitterness and recrimination, or pre-occupation with worldly interest, in an atmosphere wherein one would breathe the spirit of humility and Christian charity alone, with a sincere desire for peace, and ardent devotion to the immortal work of love accomplished by a God who prayed that all his own should be one in him, and did not hesitate to cement this union with his blood.

May the members of the Anglican Communion have the conviction, living and profound as it should be, that the unity of the Church is the express will of Jesus Christ, that the divisions and various forms of religious beliefs are the cause of a state of things repugnant to reason and displeasing to God; that those who help to maintain such a state of things render themselves guilty before God and before society for depriving it of the greatest boon: *then* the hope of the return of England to the one centre of unity will not be in vain.

Bossuet says: 'A nation so intelligent will not long remain in such bewilderment. Her respect for the teaching of the Fathers, and her careful historical studies will bring her back to the teaching of the early centuries. I cannot believe that the hatred of the See of Peter from whom she received her Christianity will continue.'[43]

The letter concluded with an expression of hope that these prophetic words might be fulfilled, and repeating the assurance that reunion was the most ardent wish of Pope Leo XIII.

Portal's second visit to England, September 1894

With this letter in his pocket the abbé travelled non-stop clear across Europe, from Rome to Hickleton and Lord Halifax,[44] who had received from Portal fragmentary reports of the exciting events at Rome and who was by this time treading air. The Archbishop of York was for the

[43] *Leo XIII* 154f. [44] Ibid., 15.

moment unavailable, but Halifax succeeded in running the Archbishop of Canterbury to earth at a country house in Somerset which had been lent to him by the Headmaster of Eton, Dr Edmund Warre, so that Benson might have a quiet holiday rest, undisturbed by visitors and official business. Preceded by a barrage of letters and telegrams (it was before the days of the telephone) in which he neglected to mention that he would be bringing the abbé with him, and disregarding a hint that such a visit was not propitious at the moment, Halifax descended upon the archbishop at 9 a.m. in the morning of 28th September. The abbé poured forth his astonishing tale, and showed the archbishop the letter which he had brought from Rome.

If the interview six weeks previously had had 'a considerable element of tenterhooks', as even the ebullient Lord Halifax had recognised, this one was like an encounter with an aroused and distrustful porcupine. The archbishop was totally unprepared for the revelations which were made to him, and suspected that the whole thing was a plot to compromise him. The change of plan after Portal's first audience with the pope seemed to him ominous. It left the pope completely uncommitted. The letter had been written, he pointed out, by an agent who could be repudiated at any time. Though friendly in tone, it was completely vague, and contained expressions which Anglicans could not allow, such as the reference to Rome as England's 'ancient mother and mistress'. The difficulties in the way of reunion were manifold; there was not only the infallibility but the pope's claim of supremacy over all earthly rulers.[45] And the

[45] During an interval in the conversation Portal said to a member of the archbishop's entourage that such an understanding of the papal claims as Benson had criticised would be laughed out of court in any dogma class at his seminary. Told of this demurrer afterwards, the archbishop wrote that he still considered his understanding of the pope's claim of temporal sovereignty to be correct. Portal commented, quite correctly, that the conversation had shown that if the Anglican Church was misunderstood by Roman Catholics, the Roman Catholic position was equally misunderstood by Anglicans. It was precisely the existence of such misunderstandings on both sides which showed how much need there was for the kind of friendly conferences which Halifax and Portal desired. Cf. the account of the interview in A. C. Benson, *E. W. Benson* ii, 597ff.

friendly expressions of Rampolla's letter were nullified by the very different utterances of the pope's principal representative in England.

This was a reference to the militant speech which Cardinal Vaughan had delivered little more than a week previously to a meeting of the Catholic Truth Society at Preston, in which he had heaped scorn and abuse upon the Anglican Church.[46] The cardinal emphasised that the only possible basis for reunion was the individual submission of Anglicans to the infallible authority of the Holy See. After describing the results of the catholic revival in the Church of England, Vaughan suggested that these might possibly be the work of Satan, trying to lead simple souls astray, though he preferred to believe that they were due to the influence of the Holy Spirit.

Archbishop Benson said that until Cardinal Vaughan's utterances were repudiated he must take them, and not a purely private letter from one Roman Catholic to another, as representative of the official Roman Catholic attitude towards Anglicans. This was to remain Benson's position throughout, and he found it confirmed by the absence of any contradiction from Rome of Vaughan's increasingly militant and hostile utterances. The archbishop also expressed the opinion that Portal had seen only one side of the Church of England, so that the pope could not have gained from the abbé a fair picture of the religious situation in England.

Halifax and Portal laboured with might and main to get the archbishop to seize the opportunity which had been presented to him. They pleaded with him to write a letter in response to Rampolla's *démarche* which could be used to obtain the direct approach from the pope which had originally been planned. The most they could obtain from Benson was a promise to consider the matter. Halifax and Portal

[46] Text in Cardinal Vaughan, *The Re-Union of Christendom*, London 1894; excerpts in *Leo XIII* 107ff.

came away bitterly disappointed by the reception they had received.

Further efforts for reunion

During the autumn Halifax tried repeatedly to get from the archbishop the letter he desired, even submitting a number of drafts for Benson's consideration, which caused the primate to write in his diary:

> Halifax is like a solitary player of chess, and wants to make all the moves on the board himself on both sides.[47]

Halifax had a certain amount of help from the Archbishop of York, who was much more sympathetic. But in the end he had to be content with a letter from Benson which, although not entirely negative, was far from what he had hoped for.

The new year saw the publication of a cogent defence of Anglican Orders by the Anglican scholars, E. Denny and T. A. Lacey, *De Hierarchia Anglicana*.[48] Written in Latin, the book was soon read by Roman Catholic theologians on the Continent, and its solid and exact arguments made a considerable impression. Duchesne wrote to Lacey that he had had opportunity since publishing his favourable review of Portal's earlier work to study the question more closely, and had read Estcourt's book, at that time the most recent presentation of the case against the Orders. He concluded:

> The position you defend seems to me to be indisputable. I have already expressed this opinion in the *Bulletin Critique*. . . . The arguments of your opponents seem strangely like those used by the Donatists to defend themselves against the Catholics.
>
> I can tell you that my colleague, Mgr Gasparri, has completely abandoned the opinion he expressed in his treatise on Holy Orders.[49] . . . Since then he has made himself acquainted with the documents as well as with your proofs. In consequence, he has made it known in a useful

[47] A. C. Benson, *E. W. Benson* ii, 608. [48] London 1895.
[49] i.e. the opinion that Anglican Orders were invalid.

quarter that he shared your opinion, and has given the reasons for his change of mind.

May it please God, amid all these studies and controversies, to point out a path which will lead us to unity, or at least bring us as close to it as possible. Rest assured that on my side I will do all in my power to secure the due appreciation of your merits, a result which will be attained when you are better known.[50]

The concluding paragraph of this letter, especially when taken in conjunction with the letter of Cardinal Rampolla to Portal, shows that even before the turn of the century it was possible for Roman Catholic theologians to envisage a way to reunion which promised greater hope of success than that proposed by Cardinal Vaughan: complete submission of non-catholics to the Roman Catholic Church as it then was.

[50] *Leo XIII* 195f. Halifax reprinted the text of this letter in his *Further Considerations on Behalf of Reunion*, London 1923, 55f.

4

THE BATTLE IS JOINED

We must be entirely resolved on both sides to look at things from the other's point of view. We must give full weight to anything that the other side puts forward, and be determined to sin (if we sin at all) on the side of charity and peace rather than on that of a severity which prevents appreciation of all those considerations which permit a favourable judgement.

—Lord Halifax[1]

Surely Lord Halifax must be under some strange hallucination if he imagines there could be the slightest use in approaching the Protestant Bishops on the subject of reunion—the conditions for them must be absolutely impossible.

—Cardinal Vaughan[2]

Through Lord Halifax and Wilfrid Ward, Cardinal Vaughan had learned of all that was passing in England and Rome. Ward had spent two days with Portal during his first and longer visit to England in August. He had subsequently received from Halifax a long memorandum in Portal's handwriting describing his audience with the pope and his second interview with the Archbishop of Canterbury in September, when Cardinal Rampolla's letter was read and discussed.[3] Vaughan became thoroughly alarmed at the prospect that the pope might write a friendly letter to two protestant archbishops whom he considered to be mere laymen and state officials presiding over a sham church. The cardinal was convinced that any kind of recognition of this church by Rome would be a disaster for the Roman Catholic cause in England. Moreover, in Vaughan's view any letter the pope might write 'must necessarily be in substance an invitation to the archbishops to come and make their submission'.[4] Since he knew that such an invitation would be indignantly rejected, the cardinal felt bound to do everything in his

[1] Letter of Halifax to Portal, 8th January 1894, *Leo XIII* 72.

[2] Snead-Cox, *Cardinal Vaughan* ii, 172. (Undated letter of Vaughan to Wilfrid Ward, 1894.)

[3] Cf. *Leo XIII* 125, 142f, 158.

[4] Snead-Cox, *Cardinal Vaughan* ii, 176.

power to prevent it. He resolved to proceed to Rome for this purpose in January 1895.[5]

Vaughan's assumption that any letter from the pope to the English archbishops 'must necessarily be in substance an invitation to come and make their submission' was unjustified. On 22nd November 1894 Lord Halifax had given Wilfrid Ward Portal's detailed account of his audience with Pope Leo in September, in which the abbé had suggested that

> His Holiness could write a private and secret letter to the Archbishops of York and Canterbury, inviting them to work with him for the union of the churches. . . . This letter could be presented as a mark of deference towards the representatives of the Anglican Church.[6]

Ward had read the abbé's memorandum and felt that it showed 'great tact and perception',[7] a judgement that should be borne in mind in assessing the torrent of abuse and misrepresentation which has been poured upon Portal by Roman Catholic controversialists in England for more than half a century. Along with this memorandum Halifax also gave Ward his own sketch of the sort of letter Halifax thought the pope might write to the archbishops. This suggested draft said nothing at all about 'submission', but was simply the plea of an old man, who knew that he had not long to live, to the English archbishops to work with him for 'the restoration of visible communion amongst all those who call on the Name of Christ our God', and for 'that peace which can only come through the truth and by a recognition of that Catholic faith of which the bishops of the whole Church in union with the Primate of Christendom are the guardians'.[8] Ward had found the sketch of this proposed letter 'touching', but thought there were several phrases which Rome could

[5] Vaughan was no stranger at the Vatican. As Bishop of Salford he had absented himself from his diocese for two whole years (1879–81) to fight a jurisdictional battle at Rome against the claims of the religious orders in England to exemption from episcopal control. Vaughan won the fight and with it the gratitude of the entire English hierarchy.

[6] *Leo XIII* 115; cf. 134. [7] Ibid., 158. [8] Ibid., 135.

not adopt.[9] Both of these papers, Portal's memorandum and Halifax's suggested draft of a papal letter to the English archbishops, soon found their way into the hands of Cardinal Vaughan.[10] The cardinal was thus able to see for himself that what was proposed contained no suggestion of the invitation to the archbishops 'to come and make their submission' which he assumed must be the substance of any papal letter to these prelates.

Halifax himself gave Cardinal Vaughan an independent account of what he and Portal were proposing. Learning of the cardinal's imminent departure for Rome, Halifax, who was laid up in bed and unable to go out himself, sent his friend, Mr Athelstan Riley, to see Vaughan at the beginning of January 1895. Riley told the cardinal about the letter it was hoped that the pope might write. Nothing was said about the archbishops being invited to make their 'submission'. What was suggested and hoped for was a plea from an aged pope who was much respected in England

> to promote peace as far as possible before his death. . . . It should carefully avoid all controversial matters. . . . At the same time the letter should gently hint that there are grave questions between us quite apart from the matter of the validity of Anglican Orders. This would prevent any suspicion that Rome was abandoning her principles . . . [11]

Mr Riley told the cardinal, in the name of Lord Halifax,

> that Rome had nothing to lose and everything to gain by taking such a step as that now under discussion. Even in the case of her receiving a rebuff from the Anglican bishops she would be the gainer, for such action would have won the respect of all right-minded people, who had the interests of Christendom at heart.[12]

There was nothing visionary or unrealistic about the proposed letter itself, though opinions will inevitably differ

[9] *Leo XIII* 158.
[10] *Leo XIII* 162 n. 2. An undated memorandum in Gasquet's hand in the Gasquet Papers (GP) at Downside states that the documents referred to in the text above were shown to Gasquet by Wilfrid Ward. Gasquet quotes parts of Portal's memorandum in the original French.
[11] *Leo XIII* 174f.
[12] Athelstan Riley's memorandum of his conversation with Cardinal Vaughan in early January 1895 is printed in *Leo XIII* 174ff.

about the results which such a letter might have produced in 1895. The proposals of Halifax and Portal took account of Anglican sensitivity by avoiding any suggestion of submission, while at the same time carefully guarding the dogmatic claims of Rome by referring to grave questions apart from orders which separated the two churches, and to the fact that reunion could never come about through doctrinal compromise. The charge that the letter was to be, and could only be, an invitation to the archbishops 'to come and make their submission' originated with Cardinal Vaughan and his supporters. This charge has been repeated countless times since in an effort to discredit the reunion movement and to justify the action of Vaughan and his friends in wrecking it. Thus *The Tablet* wrote in 1911:

> What more foolish or hopeless plan could have been imagined than the Abbé Portal's suggestion to Leo XIII to write a letter to the Archbishops of Canterbury and York, inviting their and the English nation's submission to the Holy See?[13]

Like many polemical attacks, this was a complete waste of powder and shot, for no such suggestion had ever been made. But the misrepresentation goes on apace. As recently as 1959 Mr Nigel Abercrombie wrote that Portal had told the pope he had only to ask for the archbishops' submission to receive it.

> An enthusiastic French priest, the Abbé Portal, had persuaded himself, and was apparently persuading the Roman authorities, that the Pope had only to make the first move with the Archbishop of Canterbury, and the Church of England would quickly be brought into Catholic obedience.[14]

There is nothing in Portal's statements to justify this charge. Documentary proof of its falsity has been in print since Halifax published his book in 1912.

A lone exception in the chorus of abuse and misrepresentation was the English Jesuit and controversialist Fr Sydney

[13] *Tablet* 117 (1911), 287 col. 1: anonymous review of A. Gasquet, *Leaves from My Diary*. It is interesting to note that by 1911 it was not only the archbishops but the whole English nation which was to have been invited to make this 'submission'.

[14] Nigel Abercrombie, *The Life and Work of Edmund Bishop*, 209.

Smith, who gave a fair and accurate summary of what Halifax and Portal had done in the course of an article in the *Month* for April 1912. Fr Smith drew attention to the fact that Halifax had sent Athelstan Riley to explain to Cardinal Vaughan in January 1895 'the whole programme of what was proposed', and added:

> It is just to Lord Halifax to mention this interview, as it shows that he was not wishing to keep the Cardinal in ignorance of the steps he was taking.[15]

Cardinal Vaughan in Rome, Winter 1895

Cardinal Vaughan reached Rome on the evening of 19th January 1895.[16] Despite the fact that he had been fully informed in writing as well as orally by Wilfrid Ward and Athelstan Riley of all that had been done and proposed, the cardinal proceeded to give Leo XIII a seriously misleading account of Portal's activities.[17] He conflated the two visits that Portal had made to England, and told the pope that on the first and longer visit in August Portal had 'allowed it to be understood that he came with the knowledge and, in an unofficial way, on behalf of Rome'.[18] This was quite untrue, for Portal's first visit had been entirely private, for the purpose of collecting material for his book. He could not have made the alleged intimations even if he had wanted to. For it was only after his return to France that he was summoned to Rome and learned to his surprise and astonishment that the pope was interested in England. Vaughan added that

> the said French priest studiously avoided paying even the visit of courtesy due to English ecclesiastical authority, and indeed, kept out of the way of Catholics altogether.[19]

[15] S. F. Smith, 'Leo XIII and Anglican Orders', *Month* 119 (1912), 341, and 345.
[16] Snead-Cox, *Cardinal Vaughan* ii, 176.
[17] Cf. Snead-Cox, *Cardinal Vaughan* ii, 176f; Gasquet later published an account of this audience, as related to him by Vaughan himself, in his *Leaves from My Diary, 1894–96*, London 1911, 9ff.
[18] Gasquet, *Leaves* 10.
[19] Ibid.

This was equally untrue. Halifax had explained to Vaughan that Portal's failure to appear for the cardinal's luncheon was due solely to the miscarriage of the invitation. Far from having 'kept out of the way of Catholics altogether', Portal had spent two whole days of his visit with Vaughan's friend, Wilfrid Ward. While Ward was at Hickleton with Portal and Halifax it was

> generally admitted [Halifax wrote later] that an opportunity had presented itself for working for reunion, but that such reunion could not be the work of today or tomorrow, inasmuch as I and those who sympathised with me only represented a comparatively small party in the Church of England, a remark which led to my observing that great movements were generally the work of minorities, and that this was a matter which had to be looked at in the light of faith, rather than in that of human calculation.[20]

During this visit Wilfrid Ward told Portal that his opinion about Anglo-Roman reunion had become more optimistic:

> Ten years ago I would have said the thing was absolutely impossible, but today I am no longer of the same opinion.[21]

In bidding the abbé farewell on 18th August, Ward promised his help in the campaign for reunion, and said he would see Cardinal Vaughan as soon as possible and try to influence him in favour of the reunion movement.[22] And a few days later Ward wrote to Halifax:

> what 'a real satisfaction' it had been to him to see members of the French Church enter into English affairs in such a sympathetic spirit. . . . 'Once a thoroughly fair and sympathetic spirit comes to exist among us all, the truth will gradually be got at on all sides. Our people have very much to learn. It is curious how fifty years ago Cardinal Wiseman alone took the sympathetic view of the situation which I rejoice to see is spreading.'[23]

We have already seen that Wilfrid Ward was in close touch with Cardinal Vaughan, whom he kept fully informed of everything that had been said and done.

[20] *Leo XIII* 101. [21] Portal's Diary note, Friday 17th August 1894, PP.
[22] *Leo XIII* 101.
[23] Ibid. For Wiseman's view cf. p. 177 n. 26 below.

The effect of Cardinal Vaughan's statements to the pope was to distress Leo greatly and convince him that Portal was acting in a thoroughly disloyal and irresponsible manner. It is difficult to understand how Vaughan, with the full facts at his disposal, could have given such a misleading account of them. He was thus able to deal a serious blow to the efforts of Halifax and Portal for a *rapprochement*.

Both in this audience, and on numerous other occasions, Cardinal Vaughan emphasised that England was a thoroughly protestant country, and that there was not the slightest chance of reunion. Since to him reunion could only mean submission to the Roman Catholic Church as it then was, this statement was perfectly true. What Halifax envisaged was a gradual drawing together through an improvement in the climate of public opinion in the two churches, as well as through friendly conversations between their theologians involving on both sides explanations of doctrinal points in terms calculated to be as sympathetic as possible to the other side. There was never any meeting of minds on this point. Cardinal Vaughan habitually stated Roman Catholic doctrines in an integralist manner sure to be as unacceptable as possible to his countrymen. If Vaughan's frequent statements of the hopelessness of the Roman Catholic cause in England are understandable, given the state of public opinion in the country at that time and his own integralist view of the Roman Catholic position, it is a little difficult to understand the apparent delight he took at each fresh piece of evidence that England was incurably protestant and anti-catholic. Despite his burning missionary and proselytising zeal, Vaughan seems never completely to have overcome the view of those members of the old catholic aristocracy in England who regarded their church as a sort of exclusive club, which would be spoiled by the influx of too many outsiders.

Dom Francis Aidan Gasquet

While Cardinal Vaughan was thus doing everything he could to prevent any *rapprochement* between Rome and Canterbury, the Downside monk Dom Francis Aidan Gasquet was working away in the archives of the Holy Office at Cardinal Vaughan's request, trying to dig up fresh evidence against the validity of Anglican Orders. Gasquet had attained swift renown only seven years previously with the publication of the first volume of *Henry VIII and the English Monasteries*,[24] a work which at once became an historical best-seller. And in 1890 he had brought out in collaboration with his lay friend Edmund Bishop a work which formed a good preparation for the controversy over Anglican Orders, *Edward VI and the Book of Common Prayer*.[25] This was chiefly Bishop's work, though it bore the names of both men. Bishop was a man of vast erudition in the field of liturgical history. A convert from High Anglicanism in his youth, he was loved and cherished by a small circle of friends for his encyclopedic knowledge and the generosity with which he dispensed it, and despite his possession of a temperament at once cantankerous, hypersensitive, and suspicious, which was both the result and a contributory cause of his chronic ill health. Bishop's huge stores of liturgical and historical knowledge were placed at Gasquet's disposal for a number of years, thus bringing the latter a measure of fame which he could never have attained on his own.[26] But not even Bishop could prevent Gasquet from

[24] London 1888; followed by volume ii in 1889.

[25] London 1890. This work did not mention the Orders question directly.

[26] Bishop's share in Gasquet's scholarly success did not escape the shrewd eye of the Revd T. A. Lacey, whom we have already met as the joint author of *De Hierarchia Anglicana* (cf. p. 63 above), and who was to be one of the two Anglican clergy present in Rome during the investigation of Anglican Orders in 1896. Following the publication of his *Roman Diary* at the end of 1910, Lacey wrote to Lord Halifax: 'No, Gasquet will not have learnt anything. He is not a learner; nor ever was, I should say; ergo, not learned, which is evident to all men diligently reading his books written without the help of Edmund Bishop. He is always admiring the sunrise of the day before yesterday.' (Letter of 17th January 1911, HP A4.223.) For Bishop's learning, on the other hand, Lacey had the highest regard.

filling his books with innumerable errors and misstatements. Gasquet's habitual inaccuracy, and even more his refusal ever to correct his errors or to take any notice either of criticism or of any other work inspired by his own, caused him, after two decades of scholarly success, to become generally discredited even before his death in 1929. Gasquet played a leading role in the condemnation of Anglican Orders, and his standards of accuracy will be dealt with in detail in the course of our narrative. Meanwhile the reader should bear in mind that Gasquet's statements must be treated with critical reserve. Edmund Bishop was at Gasquet's side during these winter months of 1895, and the diary notes later worked up by Gasquet into the *Leaves from My Diary, 1894–1896* are partly in Gasquet's hand, and partly in Bishop's.[27]

Gasquet was in full accord with Cardinal Vaughan's views about the reunion movement which Lord Halifax was trying to promote, and he vigorously supported these views in his own audiences with the pope. Amongst Gasquet's papers at Downside are two drafts of a memorandum which he submitted to Leo XIII on 20th April 1895.[27a] In this document the pope was informed:

> The Ritualists are uneasy both about their past history and about their *Orders*. This explains the desperate efforts they have made of late to obtain some recognition of the validity of their Orders first from the Oriental schismatic Churches, then from the German and Swiss Old Catholics, and finally from the Dutch Jansenists. It is now confidently hoped through the influence of foreigners to obtain something which may be regarded as a recognition of their Orders from Your Holiness. This they desire not with any design of bringing about a reunion with the Catholic Church, but to enable them to quiet the minds of many who are

This comes out in a characteristic passage in a letter he wrote to Halifax on 22nd September 1910, in which he first refers to the antiquary and liturgiologist Francis Carolus Eeles (1876–1954): 'Eeles is one of those tiresome men who are always attaching importance to things that don't matter. You can't look at the shape of his head without seeing that he will do so. And he is one of the three men in England most learned in liturgics. The others are Wickham Legg and Edmund Bishop. Curious that all are laymen' (HP A4.223).

[27] It has not been possible hitherto to find amongst the Gasquet Papers at Downside the original diary notes subsequent to 1895.

[27a] Cf. Gasquet's letter to Edmund Bishop cited in n. 61 below.

now gravely disturbed with doubts. It is rather a matter of practical politics than of religion.[28]

A fatal delusion

These statements were as plausible as they were untrue, and reflected chiefly Gasquet's ignorance of the true condition of the Anglican Church—a result, as Wilfrid Ward put it, of 'the isolated intellectual life so many of our men lead (in England).'[29] Cardinal Vaughan and his supporters were completely mistaken in supposing that large numbers of Anglicans had doubts about the validity of Anglican Orders. We shall see that the Holy See was told that a formal condemnation of the Orders would usher in 'a period of grace' in the form of a flood of conversions of people eager to receive genuine sacraments in the place of bogus imitations. This proved in the event to be wishful thinking. Wilfrid Ward warned Vaughan about the folly of clinging to this illusion. He wrote subsequently:

> I disagreed . . . with his view that a formal condemnation of Anglican Orders would at once lead many to leave the Church of England. I believed, on the contrary, that it would turn away from all thought of Rome many more than it brought nearer to us.[30]

Cardinal Vaughan chose to ignore all such warnings. As late as 1910 Wilfrid Ward could write of Vaughan's policy of working for a solemn and public condemnation of the Orders and of the reunion movement:

> . . . I still venture to think that a movement towards the Church was checked by Cardinal Vaughan's action. His logic was sound; but logic does not always persuade.[31]

Portal and Halifax were actually far more realistic in this matter than Cardinal Vaughan, blinded as he was by his *idée fixe* of individual conversions at all costs as the only way

[28] GP.
[29] Letter of Ward to Lord Halifax, September 1894, *Leo XIII* 110.
[30] *Leo XIII* 444f. [31] *Morning Post*, 16th August 1910, 4.

to reunion compatible with the claims of truth. They realised that many potential converts to the Roman Catholic Church were held back from taking the final step by the conscientious conviction that Anglican Orders and sacraments were valid, and by the fear that submission would involve repudiating this conviction. A declaration by the Holy See that Anglican Orders were valid or even possibly valid would have obviated the need for any such repudiation and so have removed what was for many the last remaining conscientious obstacle to conversion.

Halifax stated this consideration in late February 1896 in an address to a large gathering of leading Roman Catholic clergy and journalists in Paris. In a letter which he wrote to the Archbishop of York immediately after this meeting he summarised his remarks as follows:

> I honestly believe *justice* being done us on the question of Orders would do much to help forward the cause of peace, that no doubt from *their* point of view it might stop some individual conversions, but that from another it was very likely to facilitate them, since the one thing members of the English Church never would or could do was to deny their spiritual past, and seem to cast a doubt upon their communions, absolutions, etc.[32]

It is worth stating in this connection that of the large number of Anglican bishops who wrote to Halifax about his efforts for reunion not one contradicted his view that recognition of Anglican Orders by the Holy See would remove an obstacle to reunion with Rome, though several pointed out that his was merely one obstacle amongst many, and that others were more serious. This was a position with which Halifax was in full agreement: we have already seen that he wanted the pope, in the proposed letter to the English archbishops, to 'hint gently that there are grave questions between us quite apart from the matter of the validity of

[32] Letter of 19th February 1896, HP A4.270. This account is somewhat clearer than that Halifax gave of his remarks on this occasion in *Leo XIII* 252. Cf. also Macmillan, *Portal* 59.

Anglican Orders'.[33] The Anglican bishops who corresponded with Halifax during his efforts for reunion all agreed that recognition of Anglican Orders could only be greeted with gratification by Anglicans, and a number added that this was a necessary pre-condition of any serious theological discussion looking towards ultimate reunion.[34] It should be borne in mind that hardly any of these correspondents could have been called Anglo-Catholics, and that none of them shared the very advanced Anglo-Catholic views of Halifax himself.

Some time after the final condemnation of Anglican Orders, Fr David Fleming, who had been one of Cardinal Vaughan's three representatives on the papal commission which investigated the Orders in 1896, was forced to take cognisance of the fact that the decision for which he had laboured so zealously had created an additional barrier to conversions.

> I am sorry to hear [Fleming wrote to a correspondent] that so many are kept back by the mistaken notion of the validity (even probable) of their Orders.[35]

'We desire peace with all our hearts'

On 14th February 1895 Lord Halifax delivered a speech on reunion to a meeting of the English Church Union in Bristol. It was a skilful utterance, thoroughly eirenic in tone, and calculated to appeal to as broad a body of opinion as

[33] Cf. Athelstan Riley's account of his conversation with Cardinal Vaughan in early January 1895 on p. 67 above.

[34] The view has been expressed by Anglican spokesmen many times since. Cf. p. 3 above.

[35] *The Tablet* 169 (1937), 189. The Roman condemnation of Anglican Orders remains a serious obstacle to conversion even today. Cf. the statement of Mgr H Barton Brown in 1955: 'The real difficulty which I have found in the minds of those who have found their way to the faith has been their tenacious belief in the validity of their ordination' (*The Tablet* 205 [1955], 482). Mgr Brown also reminded his readers in this letter that the same tenacious belief had been a serious obstacle to the conversion of Archdeacon (later Cardinal) Manning (cf. E. S. Purcell, *Life of Cardinal Manning* i, London 1895, 619). See also the important letter of 'Anglican chaplain' *The Tablet* 222 (1968), 234. It is remarkable that proselytisers never seem to consider the possibility that this 'tenacious belief' might have its roots not in mere stubbornness or theological obtuseness but in a scruple for truth.

possible in the Church of England, and not merely to High Churchmen. Halifax mentioned 'the hostility of large sections of English feeling' towards any talk of reunion with Rome. But he urged

> that all this was no reason for not doing all in our power to leaven public opinion, for not striving to dispel prejudice, or for not endeavouring by mutual explanations to prepare the way for reunion on both sides in the acknowledgement of the same truth.[36]

Anglicans, he said, were quite willing to admit their share of blame for the schism of the sixteenth century: it remained for Roman Catholics to admit theirs, for there had been fault on both sides. The only constructive policy was one motivated by a mutual desire to see things in their most favourable light, and to take the other side at its best and not at its worst. The recent controversy about Anglican Orders had shown that this generous spirit did in fact exist in the Roman Catholic Church, though it was rare in England. Halifax emphasised, however, that the question of orders in itself was of secondary importance.

> Certainly the recognition of the validity of the Orders conferred by the English Church would not of itself bring about reunion: many other grave and difficult questions would remain behind. At the best it would only put the Anglican Communion in the same position as regards the Roman Church as that occupied by the great communions of the East; but no one can doubt that such a recognition, though it would not be everything, would be a step, and a great step, in the direction of unity.[37]

The denial by Rome of the reality of Anglican Orders and sacraments was a source of continual irritation to Anglicans.

> That question out of the way, the whole relation between the two Communions would be put on quite a different footing—a footing which would facilitate other negotiations in their turn.[38]

Even from the point of view of Roman Catholics whose sole interest was in individual conversions, the recognition of the Orders would be, on a long-term view, a gain.

[36] *Leo XIII* 185. [37] *The Tablet* 53 (1895), 299. [38] Ibid.

> It is precisely the denial of the validity of the Orders conferred by the Church of England, and of the sacraments which she administers, which acts as a powerful deterrent in many cases to joining the Roman Communion. There are persons who are keenly alive to the scandals they see at home. They are attracted by much in the Roman Communion, but one thing they cannot do, and that is to deny the spiritual experiences of their whole lives. They can do nothing which seems to cast a doubt upon the validity of the Orders or of the sacraments of the Anglican Communion.[39]

At the same time, recognition of the Orders could not be expected to bring about reunion between the two churches.

> . . . for it is folly to suppose that we can hope to sign a concordat between Lambeth and the Vatican tomorrow. A new national attitude in regard to the relations of Christian bodies has to be taken up. The misunderstandings and prejudices of three centuries have to be dispelled.[40]

The duty of Anglicans was to pray for reunion unceasingly, and to speak of it and work for it at every opportunity.

> Let us say boldy we desire peace with Rome with all our hearts. Public opinion will never be influenced if we hold our tongues.[41]

This speech aroused a surprisingly broad and positive response. The letters of appreciation which Halifax received, and of which he printed excerpts in his book, show that even amongst many who could by no stretch of the imagination have been called Anglo-Catholics there was a longing for reunion, and a willingness to consider things in a fresh light, if only some sign of such willingness could be discerned on the Roman side—a likelihood which several of Halifax's correspondents discounted with expressions of regret.[42] A

[39] *The Tablet* 53 (1895), 299. [40] Ibid. [41] Ibid.

[42] Cf. *Leo XIII* 185–94. As it was very difficult for Halifax ever to believe that anyone *really* disagreed with him (he preferred to think that apparent disagreement was due simply to the fact that he had not yet been able to explain his point of view adequately to his interlocutor), it might be suspected that in his book Halifax merely quoted the portions of the letters he received which indicated agreement, while omitting many criticisms of his views. The original letters, preserved in the Hickleton Papers, do not support such a suspicion. Had Halifax quoted his correspondents more fully the impression of substantial sympathy for his views, even in the most unexpected quarters, would have been strengthened. Thus, to cite but one example from amongst many, the Bishop of Brechin, from whose letter Halifax quotes only two sentences, wrote that he had prayed daily since childhood for reunion, and that he had been inwardly moved since the election of Leo XIII to the papacy to pray for him every day.

number of letters came from Anglican bishops, and there were positive comments too from Roman Catholics like Wilfrid Ward, who found the speech 'very remarkable in its breadth of sympathy and the power it shows of seeing many points of view',[43] as well as from the Abbé Duchesne, who wrote:

> May God grant that the good sense and the truly Christian spirit [of your speech] may overcome these unhappy schisms. I do not doubt that Mr Lacey's book[44] will do much good. . . . Your visit to Rome will have no small importance. It is to be wished that it should not be too long delayed. I understand that the good Cardinal Vaughan and his advisers are very active in what they believe, alas! to be a good cause. But I have great hopes in the deep intelligence and large heart of Leo XIII.[45]

Halifax visits the pope

The visit to Rome referred to in this letter took place in March. Halifax was received by the pope in private audience on 21st March. He explained all that he and Portal had done, and reinforced this explanation by one of his lengthy memoranda, written in French for the benefit of the pope and his advisers.[46] Halifax made the following points:

1. He and Portal had acted solely from a sincere desire for reunion. 'In order to unite, the two sides must get to know one another.' He and Portal believed 'that the question of Orders offered the best terrain' for this mutual process of deeper acquaintance which was a prerequisite to reunion.

2. The Archbishop of Canterbury, though expressing his desire to do everything in his power for the cause of reunion, did not conceal his misgivings. He feared that the Abbé Portal had seen only one side of the Anglican Church, and that Lord Halifax did not fully appreciate the strength of anti-Roman prejudice in England or the

[43] *Leo XIII* 185.
[44] *De Hierarchia Anglicana*, cf. p. 63 above.
[45] *Leo XIII* 193f.
[46] Halifax printed this memorandum in full in his book: *Leo XIII* 202–7.

magnitude of the difficulties in the way of agreement between the two churches on all outstanding questions of doctrine and discipline. It was most important that nothing be done which should stir up prejudice and passions in England.

3. The Archbishop of York and the Bishop of Lincoln, although agreeing about the necessity of avoiding anything which might arouse popular prejudice, had spoken far more encouragingly than the Archbishop of Canterbury.

4. The Archbishop of Canterbury's misgivings had been greatly increased by the public utterances of Cardinal Vaughan.

5. The attached letters to Lord Halifax from English bishops and others, including a letter from the Archbishop of Canterbury, showed that a generous approach by the pope to the English archbishops proposing conferences between theologians of the two churches on the subject of orders and other outstanding matters would meet with a positive response. If the question of Anglican Orders were settled to the full satisfaction of Anglicans this would not lead necessarily to reunion; but it would be a great step in this direction.

6. In view of the public attitude of Cardinal Vaughan to Anglicans, as well as the loyalty of the English people to their archbishops and to the national church, it was essential that the suggested letter proposing theological conversations should be sent to the archbishops direct, and not through Cardinal Vaughan.

Halifax's audience with the pope, at which he presented this memorandum and the letters referred to under number 5, took place in an atmosphere of great warmth and cordiality, and both Pope Leo and Cardinal Rampolla, who was also present, promised to give full consideration to all that Lord Halifax had said and suggested.

Drafting the pope's letter

Halifax could not have known it, but in urging on the pope the desirability of a friendly letter to the Anglican archbishops suggesting theological conferences, he was talking to a man who had already decided on a different course of action, and was even then engaged in carrying it out. The Gasquet papers preserved at Downside Abbey reveal that on 15th February, long before Halifax reached Rome and a full five weeks before he was received in audience, Cardinal Rampolla had sent for Dom Gasquet and had asked him, at the pope's request,

> to draft a letter in conjunction with Cardinal Vaughan which the Pope intended to write to the English bishops.[47] It was specially to be guarded in its language so as not to excite opposition or provoke an answer. The point of it was to be prayer for unity. This (he said) was to be kept as a profound secret. It was to be done as soon as possible and was to be taken to him [Rampolla] either in French or Latin.[48]

This was the origin of the papal letter *Ad Anglos*.[49]

The first rough draft was written by Cardinal Vaughan and given to Gasquet on 21st February. He and Edmund Bishop worked over it for the next two days, and the new version was then read to Vaughan on the 24th. He made some suggestions of insertions, which the two friends then tried to incorporate as far as possible, 'but some didn't go at all,' Bishop wrote. Work on the document continued all the next day, and about 5 p.m. on the 25th Gasquet and Bishop went to the English College and, finding Vaughan absent, left their work on his table. Various drafts are preserved amongst Gasquet's Papers at Downside. On 27th February Gasquet records:

> Wrote to Cardinal Rampolla suggesting that the letter should be

[47] i.e. the Roman Catholic bishops.
[48] This is recorded in the handwriting of Edmund Bishop.
[49] For a detailed account of the events related briefly below cf. Kentigern Connelly, *An Unheard of Thing: An Historical Study of the Apostolic Letter* . . . Ad Anglos . . . (unpublished master's dissertation, University of Louvain 1967). The account given here was written independently of Dom Connelly's.

> addressed to Cardinal Vaughan *only* and not to English bishops and through him to English people.[50]

On 2nd March, the pope told Cardinal Vaughan according to Gasquet's account,

> that he had read the document which we had prepared, was much pleased with it and had directed that it should be translated into Latin at once.[51] On Sunday (3rd) Cardinal Vaughan . . . dined with Cardinal Rampolla who had said same and that they had adopted my suggestion as to addressing it to Cardinal Vaughan alone.[52]

Gasquet's 'Leaves from My Diary'

These original diary notes had to be carefully edited before publication sixteen years later. A comparison of Gasquet's book, *Leaves from My Diary: 1894–1896* (London 1911), with the notes by himself and Edmund Bishop from which the book was compiled, shows not only the omissions implied in Gasquet's reference in his preface to 'extracts from my diaries', but much new matter as well as a number of alterations in the original account. The *Leaves from My Diary* was not what it purported to be, but actually a more or less free composition based only loosely on the original diary notes. In his preface Gasquet stated the reason for this composition: it was to meet the exigencies of controversy.

> The following extracts from my diaries . . . are printed at the request of several friends, in consequence of the publication of *A Roman Diary and other Documents* by the Rev T. A. Lacey.[53]

Lacey was one of the two Anglican priests who, as we shall see, was in Rome at the time Anglican Orders were investigated. He was thus able to be in close touch with the work of the investigating commission through two of its members, the Abbé Duchesne and Mgr Gasparri. Lacey's account in his diary of the investigation contained, along with a certain

[50] GP.

[51] The draft had been submitted in French.

[52] GP, recorded in Gasquet's hand.

[53] Op. cit. 2. The reference is to T. A. Lacey, *A Roman Diary and other Documents relating to the Papal Inquiry into English Ordinations, 1896*, London 1910.

amount of misinformation reflecting his partial and imperfect knowledge of events, a number of revelations seriously embarrassing to those who had worked for the condemnation of the Orders. Gasquet doubtless chose to reply to Lacey in diary form because Lacey's book had also been in that form, and had been all the more effective for containing expressions written in the heat of the moment, and not always entirely creditable to their author. Lacey apologised for such passages,[54] but felt that in fairness to his readers he must let them stand.

> Some things I should like to omit on my own account, but they are retained in order that the evidence may be entire. The Diary . . . must be produced as a whole; excerpts would be useless. Severe demands are therefore made on the patience of the reader.[55]

Lacey revealed his motive as well as his integrity as editor of his own diary in a letter which he wrote to Lord Halifax on 29th June 1910, during preparation of the book for the press.

> There are reasons for printing [my diary] intact, with all its personalities —sometimes rather unpleasant—and trivialities. Unless it is produced verbatim, it will be open to anyone to say that the memories of the time are being cooked.[56]

Gasquet was untroubled by any such considerations.

On 17th March, just four days before Halifax was to be received in audience by the pope, Gasquet wrote:

> Dined at Irish College. Cardinal Vaughan told me that he had had a most satisfactory interview with the Pope the day before. The *Letter* was getting on well and was expected to be ready about the 25th or so. . . . The Pope asked how he was to receive Lord Halifax and referring to *Anglican Orders* said he had satisfied himself that there were grave difficulties in the way of any change in the practice of the Church and that he had had the opinions of the best authorities that they were *invalid*. He said that he

[54] Cf. Lacey, op. cit. x, and the footnotes on pp. 42, 61, and 80.
[55] Lacey, op. cit. x.
[56] HP A4.223. The anonymous reviewer in *The Tablet*, disarmed by Lacey's apology and unable to claim that the diary notes had been 'cooked', as Lacey wrote, claimed that the passages for which Lacey apologised were in bad taste and should have been omitted for this reason (*The Tablet* 84 [1910], 1015).

Sunday 17 Dined at Irish college. Card. V. told me that he had had a most satisfactory interview with the Pope the day before. The Letter was getting on well & was expected to be ready about the 25th. or so. The Pope told him that "Questo padre Benedictino Inglese" had written him a letter containing reasons why he should not address the letter to the Bps generally & that he approved of those reasons. The Pope has quashed the decree of H. Off. as to Primrose League. Pope asked how he was to receive Lord Halifax & referring to A. Orders said he had satisfied himself that there were grave diffic^s in the way of any change in the practice of the Church & that he had had the opinions of the best authorities that they were invalid. He said that he had on his table there the opinions of those best qualified to speak & they show him they could not be considered valid.

Leaves from my Diary 23

told me he had had an interview with the Pope the day before. Amongst other matters, the Holy Father referred to the Anglican Orders question, saying that he had satisfied himself that there would be grave difficulties in the way of any change in the practice of the Church as regards re-ordination. He further said that he had had the best authorities consulted, and that there (pointing to his table) he had the opinions of men qualified to judge; from these, he added, it was clear that without a full examination, no change in the present attitude of the Church would be possible.

Gasquet's diary: the original manuscript (*left*) and the published version (*above*). For explanation of the discrepancies cf. pp. 83–4

> had on his table there the opinions of those best qualified to speak and they show him they couldn't be considered valid.[57]

Stated as baldly as that, this was too damaging for publication in 1911. For Anglicans would immediately have seized upon this account as proof that a full year before the investigation of the Orders had begun the pope was already convinced of their invalidity; and that therefore no serious investigation was ever intended. Gasquet might have solved this difficulty by simply omitting any reference to the pope's conviction in 1895 that the Orders were invalid. Instead he chose to rewrite the passage. The version given to the public as an 'extract' from Gasquet's diary has the pope saying:

> . . . there would be grave difficulties in the way of any change in the practice of the Church as regards re-ordination. He further said that he had had the best authorities consulted, and that there (pointing to his table) he had the opinions of men qualified to judge; from these, he added, it was clear that without a full examination, no change in the present attitude of the Church would be possible.[58]

This version, that no change could be made without a full examination, was a far cry from Gasquet's original version of what the pope had told Vaughan: that no change was possible at all because the best authorities in the church had already shown him that the Orders 'couldn't be considered valid'.[59]

Any doubt as to whether Gasquet's original account of what the pope had said to Cardinal Vaughan on 16th March was correct is dispelled by Gasquet's contemporary account of his own audience with the Holy Father on 20th April.

> His own opinion he told me after his studies was that the Orders were certainly *invalid*. 'They tell me the English Reformers did not believe in the *sacerdotium or sacrifice*, how then could they consecrate priests?'[60]

[57] GP, emphasis in original.
[58] Gasquet, *Leaves from My Diary* 23.
[59] See illustration.
[60] This question admits of a simple answer. The English reformers could 'consecrate priests' despite their disbelief in the '*sacerdotium or sacrifice*' in the same way in which catholic bishops who did not believe in these things (and perhaps not even in God) have been able to confer valid orders. Duchesne reminded readers in 1894 that a good portion of the French clergy derived its orders from the apostate and

My strong impression was that the Holy Father is clear about the matter. . . . Other points that have come back later. The Holy Father . . . implied that the result of any commission must in his opinion be to confirm the practice of the Church and its practical judgement of the *Invalidity* of the Anglican Orders. He said that most people had told him the same.[61]

In the extensive account of this audience printed in *Leaves from My Diary* Gasquet omitted all reference to this part of the conversation.

Final work on the pope's letter

If the pope and Cardinal Rampolla thought that in asking Vaughan and Gasquet to draft a letter to be sent to England they would merely get helpful suggestions about what could usefully be said in a situation of which they had no direct knowledge, they got more than they bargained for. For when Gasquet and Bishop saw the Latin translation of the draft which they had submitted, they found that changes had been made, and felt bound to object. There are two different proof copies of the Latin text amongst Gasquet's

---

unbelieving bishop, Talleyrand. It is a fundamental principle of sacramental theology that neither orthodox ideas about the sacrament being conferred nor even faith of any kind are necessary in the minister for the validity of the sacrament he confers. Leo XIII's remark is also an excellent illustration of the limitations of the doctrine of papal infallibility. Whatever the doctrine means, it affords no ground for believing that the pope will never make a mistake about the principles of catholic theology in a private conversation.

[61] GP, emphasis in original. Further confirmation of the fact that the pope was convinced early in 1895 that Anglican Orders were invalid is provided by an undated letter from Gasquet to Bishop, which bears in the latter's hand the pencilled notation 'c. 21.4.95':

'Last afternoon at 4 o'clock the Pope sent for me to be there at 5.30. I was rather in a flurry as you may suppose but pleased that it had come from him proprio motu and without my asking for any audience. I took with me the memorandum on the reasons why Anglicans want their Orders confirmed by the Holy See [cf. pp. 73–4 above]. I was admitted to the Pope's private work room about 20 to 6 and was at once put at my ease by his extreme kindness. He made me get a chair and bring it quite close to him. I cannot of course tell you all that passed in the 50 minutes I was with him and this must wait till your return; but I had the chance of saying all and everything I wanted and that fully. *Entre nous* he told me he was quite satisfied that any enquiry must result in a confirmation of the present practice of the Church and when he asked me what I thought were the Orders valid or invalid and I said that everything seemed to me to show their invalidity, he added 'sento anche io'. . . . Finally he has set a room apart in the Vatican where all the H[oly] Ofc papers I want are to be put and I am to be allowed to work at them at my own sweet will' (Bishop Papers, Downside; henceforth cited as 'BP').

Papers, as well as manuscript material in Gasquet's handwriting pointing out things which must be eliminated. Gasquet warned of the danger of arousing the strong protestant temper of the English public and calling forth another 'No Popery' campaign by insisting too much on the prerogatives of the pope and the Church of Rome. It would be more prudent to appeal to the catholicity and universality of the church, especially since a section of the Anglican Church was keenly aware of its isolation from the rest of christendom. In so far as Englishmen were drawn to catholicism at all, it was to the church's universality that they were attracted, and not to the pope or to Rome. These objections were embodied in a memorandum written in French and given to Cardinal Vaughan on 1st April.[62] The two friends then went with the cardinal to see Mgr Merry del Val at the Vatican. The memorandum was presented and discussed, and Merry del Val saw the point of the suggested changes.[63]

The second proof of the papal letter was delivered to Gasquet and Bishop on 7th April. Although their suggested changes had been incorporated, the two friends thought they discerned in an exhortation to English catholics to live in concord with their fellow citizens an implied rebuke. This would never do. The next day they again visited Merry del Val at the Vatican.

> The chief thing we insisted on was that we would have nothing implying blame on English Catholics nor any recommendation for them to leave Anglicans alone. M. del V. quite understood our points.[64]

Lord Halifax persists

While all these negotiations were going on with regard to the pope's letter, Lord Halifax was seeing people in Rome and innocently hoping that the pope might be induced to

[62] A pencilled draft of this French memorandum is preserved amongst Gasquet's papers.
[63] GP. [64] GP diary note in Gasquet's hand.

write a friendly letter to the English archbishops suggesting theological conversations on disputed points. He was also urging a change in the practice of re-ordaining convert Anglican clergy absolutely. He felt that Denny and Lacey's Latin work on the Orders, which had come out in January, had made a *prima facie* case in favour of conditional ordination, and urged that such a change would be greeted in England as a sign of goodwill on the part of Rome.

During these weeks there were a number of meetings between Halifax and Portal, on the one side, and Vaughan, Gasquet, and Bishop, on the other. These encounters were polite and friendly, and Halifax was indefatigable in trying to win support for his point of view. He met with no more understanding than he had previously. On the contrary, Gasquet 'begged him earnestly to pause before trying to raise the thorny question of Anglican Orders', which Gasquet felt sure 'would infallibly bring about condemnation'.[65] Gasquet's diary notes show that there was never even the beginning of a meeting of minds between the two sides.

> Sunday, March 24th: I dined at the English College with Cardinal Vaughan. Amongst the guests was Lord Halifax, who, after dinner came and talked to me. He was very earnest about reunion, and said that he thought the first step would be taken if only the Pope would write his letter to the Archbishop of Canterbury. I told him that, in my opinion, such a thing would be absurd, as neither the Archbishop, nor, for that matter, any other Anglicans that I had come across, had shown any desire to make their submission to the Holy See.[66]

No one had ever suggested that the archbishop wished to 'make his submission to the Holy See'. Halifax wanted the pope to write a letter which might lead to theological conversations and thus to a way out of the impasse of 'submission'. This was a position which people like Gasquet and Vaughan could not grasp. In fact, Gasquet's original diary entry shows that he still thought the real reason why

[65] Gasquet, *Leaves from My Diary* 21.
[66] Gasquet, op. cit. 23. Gasquet seems to have written this account in 1911; his original diary note is much briefer (see p. 88 below).

Halifax was agitating the Orders question was to obtain re-assurance for his own or others' doubts.

> Lord Halifax . . . buttonholed me after dinner and harks back to the Pope writing to the Archbp. of Cant. Told him it was absurd and that if they had doubts about their Orders they should beg to have the question examined. He replied that they had no such doubts.[67]

The memorandum which Gasquet submitted to the pope at his audience on 20th April[68] shows that Halifax's assurance was never accepted.

Although he failed to take Gasquet's advice, Halifax did not completely disregard his warning. In a letter which he wrote to Cardinal Rampolla two weeks after this conversation,[69] Halifax repeated some of the points he had made in his lengthy memorandum to the pope, which he had submitted at his audience on 21st March. Perhaps influenced by Gasquet's arguments against raising the question of Anglican Orders at all, Halifax emphasised to Cardinal Rampolla that this question had been chosen solely because it seemed the only one which could lead the Church of England 'to resume her rightful relations with the Church of Rome' by means of 'friendly conferences . . . to elucidate the questions that divide us, in particular the question of Orders'.[70] Replying to the argument that a change in the practice of re-ordaining convert clergy absolutely would encourage Anglicans to believe that Rome, having given way on this point, would surely yield on others, Halifax wrote:

> If the Roman Church were to recognise its errors, as its superiority easily permits it to do, it would be adopting the best means of leading us to recognise ours.[71]

Such a change, Halifax added, would also silence the hostile critics in England who were insisting that since Rome never changed all hope of reunion was vain.

[67] GP. [68] Cf. p. 73f. and n. 61 above.

[69] The undated French text of the letter is in *Leo XIII* 207 ff. Halifax says that it was written at the beginning of Holy Week. Easter fell on 14th April in 1895, so the letter must have been written about 7th April.

[70] *Leo XIII* 208 f. [71] Ibid.

Despite the repetition in this letter of earlier statements both by Portal and himself that the Orders question was being agitated not for its own sake but merely as a means to an end, it is clear that Halifax seriously underestimated the strength of the opposition with which he was faced. A few days after his arrival in Rome he had written to his wife, for instance, that Cardinal Vaughan did not have much importance in Rome, and 'will do us no harm (*because he can't*)'.[72] The explanation for Halifax's over-confidence is not far to seek. Quite apart from his inveterate optimism, without which he never could have achieved the real measure of success he did, there was the great friendliness and encouragement displayed by Cardinal Rampolla. It is only natural that Halifax considered Rampolla's attitude to be more important than Gasquet's. We may reasonably assume that Halifax considered Gasquet's warning not to press the Orders question as merely another example of the bitter hostility of Cardinal Vaughan and his followers to the catholic claims of the Church of England. And Halifax was neither mistaken nor alone in maintaining that there could be real progress towards reunion only to the extent that this hostility was overcome.

It is easy to say that the Orders question was singularly ill chosen as a point of contact between the two churches. But this is hindsight. In fact there were in the mid-nineties a number of serious and responsible Roman Catholic theologians whose views on the matter were favourable to Anglican claims. We shall see that in 1896 Cardinal Vaughan's three representatives in the papal investigating commission were able to convince only one of their five colleagues of the invalidity of the Orders—and this despite the fact that these three English commissioners were far better prepared than the five others, and submitted an incomparably greater mass of evidence. It was arguments of expediency more than theological considerations which

[72] Lockhart, *Halifax* ii, 62.

finally dictated the wholly negative decision of *Apostolicae curae*. Those who believe that the Orders question was unhappily chosen for the purpose of promoting theological discussions must say what question would have been better. Cardinal Vaughan's suggestion was to start with the papacy, 'the question which would have to be settled in the end, [so] that it was therefore better to begin with it'.[73] In view of the prevailing 'No Popery' sentiment in England, Vaughan's proposal was tantamount to admitting that no theological conferences between the two churches were possible—or desired.

The papal letter 'Ad Anglos'

The pope's letter, *Ad Anglos*, was printed in *The Times* on 20th April. It emphasised the pope's benevolent interest in England and its people, paid tribute to British justice and public morality, but contained no reference at all to the Church of England. The pontiff appealed for goodwill and prayers for unity, and said that difficulties in the way of reunion were no reason for refusing to labour in so holy a cause. The letter closed with an appeal to Roman Catholics in England to recite the rosary and other prayers for reunion, and attaching indulgences to these pious practices. This final paragraph had been added to the text prepared by Gasquet and Bishop and against their advice by the thirty-year-old Mgr Merry del Val, who had acted as liaison man between the authors of the letter and the pope, and who was to play an increasingly crucial role in future events.[74]

[73] Cf. p. 38 above.

[74] A pencilled note in Edmund Bishop's hand on a letter written to him by Gasquet on 26th April 1895 enables us to identify Merry del Val as the author of the final paragraph of *Ad Anglos*, which was not in keeping with the tone of the rest of the letter, and which gave offence in England. Gasquet wrote in his letter to Bishop:

'A letter from the Card. [Vaughan] says "Everybody seems much pleased with the translation, which reads uncommonly well. You and Mr Bishop have rendered a great service. In the clubs I hear people are speaking highly of the letter but saying that prayer isn't their line."'

A pencilled note in the margin in Bishop's hand reads: 'It was Merry del Val's: and against the wish of . . .' (the dots are in the original and presumably were used by Bishop to indicate himself and Gasquet): BP.

The papal letter had a surprisingly good reception in England. One of those who was not edified, however, was Archbishop Benson, who was deeply offended by the fact that the communication ignored the existence of the Anglican Church. Benson acknowledged 'the sincerity of an appeal which was transparently sincere', but deplored the indulgences referred to at the end of the letter as 'rewards of worship . . . totally alien to the feelings of a nation which had become readers of the Bible, and who could never admit that such things had any attractions for them'.[75]

[75] A. C. Benson, *E. W. Benson* ii, 618 f.

5
DOVES VERSUS HAWKS

We must insist on everything which is really necessary, and allow great latitude on all matters which can be considered to lie in the realm of private opinion. We must also abstain rigorously from all reproaches which, mutatis mutandis, *could be directed equally against ourselves. We on our side, for example, should leave aside all our criticisms of you, and apply ourselves to correcting our own faults. And you in turn must leave the most difficult points on one side for the moment, and try to reach agreement in those areas where ignorance and prejudices have created differences that have no basis in truth and could be cleared up by explanations. . . . After all there is only one Church—I do not believe in the three-branch theory of the Church—and if we on our part are convinced that despite the exterior separation we are really part of the same body with you then everything which concerns you concerns us too. In view of the past we can for the moment well endure patiently the denial of our position on the part of the authorities of the Roman Church, such as Cardinal Vaughan.*

—Lord Halifax to the Abbé Portal[1]

It would be blasphemy to say that God is the author of Anglicanism or Ritualism, or of any sect or society at all outside the unity of the Body of Christ, which is the Church governed by his Vicar. . . . We can permit ourselves to smile at the ambition of a dying heresy setting itself up as the rival of blessed Peter and usurping a mission which is entrusted to him alone.

—Cardinal Vaughan[2]

Platform oratory

During the spring and summer of 1895 Lord Halifax circulated to a large number of bishops and other interested people in England another of his lengthy memoranda, this one recounting the events connected with his visit to Rome. This led naturally to a large correspondence on the topic of Anglo-Roman reunion.[3] At the end of June, Halifax delivered an important speech on the occasion of the celebration of the thirty-sixth anniversary of the English Church Union. After recounting his meeting with the Abbé Portal in Madeira five years previously, and their conversations and

[1] Letter of 8th January 1894, *Leo XIII* 72.
[2] Preface to P. Ragey, *Anglo-Catholicisme*, Paris 1897, xiii and xv.
[3] Cf. *Leo XIII* 217–42.

correspondence about Anglo-Roman reunion, he said that the question of Anglican Orders had been chosen for public discussion merely as a means of promoting conferences and conversations between the theologians of the two churches. Halifax described the visit which Portal had made to England in August of the previous year, with a view to seeing Anglicanism at first hand.

> It will be obvious that, for a variety of reasons, I could only give him a one-sided view of the Church of England. The fact that this visit took place in August, when so many of the clergy are away for their holiday, was to some extent responsible for this; but I took pains to impress upon him that there was another side to the Church of England besides the one with which I had made him acquainted, and, further, that it was one which could not, and ought not, to be neglected.[4]

Halifax mentioned Cardinal Vaughan's hostility to the reunion movement: he had taken 'an extremely narrow and unhistoric view'. But Halifax was glad to record his 'great personal affection' for the cardinal, and the hope that he might change his view. Halifax added that he expressed such sentiments the more readily 'because of the unjust statements sometimes made against [Cardinal Vaughan] by Anglicans'.[5]

Halifax spoke of the opposition which he and the Abbé Portal had encountered. It had been represented at Rome

> that there was nothing to be done in the direction indicated by the Abbé Portal; that it was intolerable a foreigner should interfere in matters about which he had been completely misinformed; that the practice of the Roman Church in regard to the re-ordinations of Anglican clergy without any condition, had, in fact, already settled the question; and that what was wanted, in view of the action of the Abbé Portal, the Abbé Duchesne, etc., whose action had been already stopping individual conversions, was a definite and distinct utterance from the Holy Office absolutely condemning the validity of Anglican Orders; . . . that such a decision would accelerate and increase . . . conversions; that people in England had to be told clearly that they had nothing to do but submit, and that such plain speaking would repel no one who was inclined to the truth and disposed to be favourable to Roman claims. . . . It was doubtless in order

[4] *The Tablet* 54 (1895), 39. [5] Ibid.

still further to formulate and fix these views that Dom Gasquet and Mr Bishop were sent for to Rome. . . . It was perhaps thought that they could be able to supply the materials for . . . a condemnation [of Anglican Orders] and the reasons upon which it could be based.[6]

If Halifax underestimated the strength of the opposition with which he was faced, he was quite clear about its nature. The subsequent narrative will show that this part of the speech was accurate in every particular.

In view of this opposition, Halifax said, it was more than ever necessary for Anglicans to prove the sincerity of their desire for reunion.

The Pope and the Roman authorities must be convinced that members of the English Church, in putting forward the question of the validity of English Orders, are actuated by an honest and sincere desire to remove an impediment out of the way of future union, and are not merely desirous of strengthening their own position. . . . The obstacles in the way of all attempts in the direction of union would be enormously lessened if both sides could be convinced, first, of each other's sincerity in wishing to arrive at an agreement, and in the next place that the agreement contemplated was not a mere alliance, or a federation of independent churches, professing divergent creeds, but a union founded upon the profession of one faith, with only such differences in regard to matters of discipline and practice as might rightly be acquiesced in.[7]

At present there was a fear at Rome that Anglicans merely wanted to bolster their own position against the Roman Catholic Church. And Anglicans could not believe that any explanations of distinctively Roman Catholic doctrines were possible, and were convinced that Rome insisted upon 'absolute submission to the most exaggerated statement of her claims'. This Halifax termed

a conviction which is as unjust as it is uncharitable, [and it] makes English Churchmen so slow to express the hope, which nevertheless they do entertain, that it may please God in his own good time and in his own way to heal the schisms which now divide his church.[8]

Halifax concluded with an eloquent tribute to Leo XIII's desire to reunite Christ's church, and a plea to all Anglicans

[6] *The Tablet* vol. cit. 39, col. 2–40 col. 1.
[7] *The Tablet* vol. cit. 40 col. 2.
[8] Ibid.

to work and pray with the pope for the great end he had at heart.

This speech was answered by Cardinal Vaughan in a lengthy address to the meeting of the Catholic Truth Society at Bristol in September 1895. Vaughan told his hearers that Halifax's suggestion of theological conferences and explanations of Roman Catholic doctrine in terms calculated to be as acceptable as possible to Anglicans was in reality a suggestion that the pope could and should compromise with the faith. This, he explained, was quite impossible. And while he would be glad to lay down his life for the return of England to union with the Holy See, this could only come about by absolute submission to the papal claims, and the abandonment of that right of private judgement in religious matters which had been so dear to the hearts of their countrymen since the reformation. In view of the existing religious situation in England such submission must take the form of individual conversions. Referring to the spread of catholic doctrines and practices in the Church of England, the cardinal said that these things were useless to Anglicans who lacked the bond of union with Rome; but they gave reason to hope that conversions would continue and increase. The question of Anglican Orders had nothing at all to do with reunion. It was impossible for catholics, looking at the facts of history, to admit that the Orders were valid.

> Nevertheless, so far from desiring that the question of Anglican Orders should be left where it is, I have earnestly pleaded that it be thoroughly re-examined in Rome.[9]

He was convinced that a new investigation would only confirm the church's present practice. But he was in favour of Anglicans having every opportunity to bring forth new historic facts and arguments in support of their orders.

This characteristically fervent and intransigent utterance was robbed of some of its effect by the Bishop of Clifton, the

[9] *The Tablet* vol. cit. 413.

Right Revd, William Robert Brownlow, who, in thanking the cardinal for his address immediately after its conclusion, remarked pointedly that 'he did not think the position in regard to reunion so hopeless as it might seem to some to be'.[10]

A meeting of the Church Congress at Norwich in October provided Lord Halifax with a platform for a reply to the cardinal. Halifax assured Vaughan that he had never suggested doctrinal compromise. Anglicans had always acknowledged that the pope had, from Christ, a certain primacy over the whole church; what they needed to be reassured about was the nature of this primacy. In particular they could not admit that the pope and not Christ was the source of episcopal jurisdiction. Halifax quoted the seventeenth-century, Anglican theologians Bramhall and Thorndike, as well as his contemporary, Canon Everest, in support of this position. This speech brought an enquiry from Cardinal Vaughan as to whether the primacy which Halifax had said that Anglicans were willing to concede to the pope was one of honour or of jurisdiction. Halifax entrusted the answer to the Revd T. A. Lacey, a first-class theologian who was quite equal to the task. After complaining that 'the looseness of the Cardinal's expressions makes it difficult to answer him without either spreading into a regular thesis, or, on the other hand, evading his real point', Lacey pointed out that the term 'primacy' was in itself equivocal. His answer was based upon a careful distinction between *auctoritas* and *potestas*.[11] What Cardinal Vaughan made of this answer is not recorded.

Halifax also received support at the October meeting of the Church Congress already mentioned from the Archbishop of York, who preached a sermon speaking positively of the growing interest in reunion and expressing the 'hope that the day will come when another Pope may be the instrument of reconciliation'.[12]

[10] *The Tablet* vol. cit. 416. [11] Cf. *Leo XIII* 233 ff. [12] *Leo XIII* 231.

Opposition moves behind the scenes

The opponents of the reunion movement in Rome and England were active in these summer months in pursuit of the two goals which Cardinal Vaughan deemed essential for the welfare of the Roman Catholic cause in England: the destruction of the reunion movement, and the public and solemn condemnation of Anglican Orders. The method chosen to achieve these goals was to take advantage of Halifax's demand for joint theological conversations, beginning with orders but going on to other questions, and turn it into a demand for a closed and secret Roman investigation of Anglican Orders, with the hope that this would result in a public condemnation of the orders. A crucial role was played by the half-English, half-Spanish Mgr Raphael Merry del Val, then thirty years old and a special protégé and favourite of the eighty-five-year old Pope Leo XIII, who saw Merry del Val daily and placed special trust in his opinion, especially in regard to English affairs. A number of letters written by Merry del Val and preserved amongst the Gasquet Papers at Downside Abbey show the invaluable assistance he was able to render to Cardinal Vaughan.

On 21st July 1895 Merry del Val wrote to inform the cardinal of a long conversation he had just had with the pope in which he had explained how much harm Lord Halifax was doing with his talk of corporate reunion, and how he was keeping back conversions, 'as I am assured from all sides'.

> The Holy Father was much impressed [Merry del Val wrote], I will almost say displeased and said that something must be done to stop this.

The letter goes on to recount various measures which the pope was considering to correct the 'confusion' which Halifax was sowing in England: a letter from the pope to Cardinal Vaughan, or one from Cardinal Rampolla to Lord Halifax 'stating what the Pope means when he speaks of reunion'. The Holy Father had also spoken of sending for Portal 'and giving him a letter and a warning to convey to Halifax, setting things right'. Before deciding on a course of action the pope wanted Cardinal Vaughan's opinion as to what should best be done. Merry del Val added his opinion that it was the Holy Father's intention to appoint a 'Commission of Cardinals' in the following winter to investigate Anglican Orders: 'indeed it is to be hoped he will and that a definite decree will be issued, now that it has been so much talked about'.[13]

Three days later Merry del Val wrote at even greater length and with obvious despondency to inform the cardinal; 'I have no good news for you tonight and I am rather out of spirits'. The pope had sent for him on the morning of 24th July to continue the conversation reported in the previous letter. Everything was going fine, the Holy Father saying 'he could not possibly allow a misunderstanding to subsist as to the real basis of reunion or a misrepresentation which would delay or prevent conversions', and he was contemplating writing a letter to Halifax setting things right—'when Cardinal Rampolla was announced and there began a rather painful time for me'. Rampolla was an earnest upholder of Halifax and had in Merry del Val's mind 'been completely hoodwinked by him'. Rampolla was 'full of Halifax' and had assured the Holy Father that the English peer 'quite understands and intends reunion in the true catholic sense as we understand it', that he believed in the infallibility of the pope, in the church, 'in everything in fact'. Rampolla had told the pope there was simply a difference of opinion between Halifax and Vaughan as to how the reunion desired by both could best be achieved, Halifax advocating corporate reunion, the cardinal insisting on the necessity of 'individual secessions'. Merry del Val had done all he could to contradict the unhappy impression produced by the cardinal's assurances, and 'the H[oly] F[ather] saw my

[13] For the full text of this letter see Appendix, p. 295, below.

point and said something must be done'. He had asked Merry del Val to prepare translations of the recent oratorical exchanges in England between Halifax and Vaughan. But, Merry del Val told the Cardinal,

> with Cardinal R[ampolla] against me it is hard work. I am alone entirely and I am nobody, and he is the Card[inal] Sec[retar]y and has numberless Italian and French Portals to back up his impressions. We must pray God most earnestly to help or there will be some dreadful blunders made.

Developments with regard to the Anglican Orders question were a further source of despondency. Various papers in favour of the validity were being circulated in Rome, making it most desirable to print a translation in Latin, French, or Italian of Canon Moyes' *Tablet* articles attacking the Orders. Merry del Val added that he saw

> a growing conviction on the part of the H[oly] F[ather] and of course of Cardinal R[ampolla] that any concession that could be made on the point of A[nglican] O[rders] would be a step towards reunion and help on conversions!! I may be taking a doleful view, but the discussion this morning has produced a sad impression upon me and seemed to show that we have gone back.[14]

Five days later, on 29th July, Merry del Val wrote once again, reporting a further attempt to enlighten the pope about the true nature of Halifax's reunion talk. The Holy Father had been at a loss to realise 'how people could call themselves Catholic, apostolic without meaning exactly what we mean' and had remarked 'that this was not the case some years ago to his knowledge, and that when a person said Catholic they meant Roman Catholic'. Once again, however, Rampolla had queered the pitch by seizing on a reference in one of Vaughan's speeches to Anglicans as 'rebels', which Rampolla had maintained was irritating and unbecoming, and showed that there was a harshness between Vaughan and Halifax.

> We must pray hard, very hard, that our Lord may turn the question of A[nglican] O[rders] into the right channels. I am not without anxiety, from

[14] For the full text of this letter see Appendix, p. 296f, below.

> different things I have heard. I am more convinced than ever that a treatise in Latin or Italian putting things in their true light and distributed here might prevent endless mischief.[15]

On the same day Merry del Val wrote briefly to Gasquet repeating his apprehensions about the course of future events, and emphasising that 'we must pray hard'.[16]

On 7th August Cardinal Vaughan informed Gasquet that he had written to the pope insisting that 'mischief beyond words' would be done if any change in the 300-year old practice of the church on Anglican Orders were to be made without the fullest investigation or without the co-operation of English catholics. He had asked for a full investigation and a decision, but had protested against this being done behind his back. A letter from the catholic hierarchy in England could come later, if needed. Meanwhile, Vaughan wrote, he was proposing to summon a commission after the Assumption to begin to prepare the English case against Anglican Orders and so to 'be prepared for Rome in the winter'.[17] On 20th August Merry del Val was able to write to Gasquet that things had 'taken a more favourable turn' at Rome, and that 'though there is some danger still I think we are pretty sure now by hook or by crook of getting the question properly sifted, when it does come on'. His last interview with the Holy Father had been satisfactory:

> I think he quite reckons with *you* now at all events and I am most thankful you came to Rome for this has been the corner of the wedge. Thank God for it all.[18]

In September Cardinal Vaughan announced publicly that a special commission was to be appointed at Rome to investigate the validity of Anglican Orders.[19] He had already formed his own English committee to prepare the English case against the Orders, as he had told Gasquet he intended

[15] For the full text of this letter see Appendix, p. 298f, below.
[16] For the full text of this letter see Appendix, p. 299, below.
[17] For the full text of this letter see Appendix, p. 299f
[18] For the full text of this letter see Appendix, p. 300
[19] Cf. Snead-Cox, *Cardinal Vaughan* ii, 194.

to do in his letter of 7th August.[20] Through Merry del Val the cardinal attempted to obtain for this committee's use a copy of the Abbé Duchesne's favourable report to the pope on Anglican Orders, the existence of which Vaughan had learned about through Lord Halifax. This attempt was not successful. Merry del Val was told by the pope's private secretary, Mgr Angeli, that since Duchesne's report had been prepared without reference to English arguments, Cardinal Vaughan's theologians should draw up their report independently of any statements already submitted by others. The time for comparing all the arguments, and threshing the matter out in direct confrontation, would come later.[21] The *votum* prepared by Cardinal Vaughan's special committee will be considered in Chapter 7 below.

The 'Revue Anglo-Romaine'

While Cardinal Vaughan's theologians were preparing the English case against Anglican Orders, the Abbé Portal was collecting articles and other material for an ecumenical journal to propagate the ideas of the reunion movement. Portal had first proposed this scheme to Halifax in a letter dated 1st July 1895. The principles laid down by the abbé are identical with those which guide responsible ecumenical action today.

> This review [Portal wrote] should always proceed by means of expositions and never by polemic. If polemic should be deemed necessary it would be undertaken elsewhere. The articles should have the goal of making the other churches better known amongst us and of explaining

[20] Cf. James Moyes, 'An Anglican Diarist at Rome' *The Tablet* 85 (1911), 47f, 48 col. 1. Cardinal Vaughan's letter is on p. 299f below.

[21] The correspondence between Merry del Val and Mgr Angeli is printed in Pio Cenci, *Il Cardinale Raffaele Merry del Val*, Roma–Torino 1933, 58ff, and in English transation in Viglio Dalpiaz, *Cardinal Merry del Val*, London 1937, 33–6. Cf. also E. C. Messenger, 'The Condemnation of Anglican Orders' *The Tablet* 137 (1937), 118f and Messenger's work, *The Reformation, the Mass and the Priesthood: a Documented History with Special Reference to Anglican Orders* ii, London 1937, 529 n. 2. It is characteristic of Messenger's attention to detail that he calls the pope's secretary 'Mgr Angelo' in his *Tablet* article and 'Mgr Angeli' in his book, cf. RMP ii, 529 n. 1.

> certain obscure and controverted points in our own dogmatic teaching, such as the role of the popes in the first centuries, for instance. . . . There must be room for historical documents of interest to different churches. These documents are to be found only in libraries. They should be made available to all.[22]

Thus was born the *Revue Anglo-Romaine*, the first number of which appeared at the beginning of December in Paris. It was edited by Portal, and during the short time in which it was in existence it published a large number of articles by scholars of the calibre of Gasparri, Duchesne, and Loisy.[23] There were also contributions from Anglicans, and a mass of documentary material, most of it made available for the first time to continental readers. Although it was to be suppressed by authority in less than a year's time, the issues published comprise three bound volumes, each more than 800 pages in length: a testimony to Portal's energy and efficiency as editor. The *Revue* was taken up at once and read with interest by catholic theologians all over the continent, as well as by English subscribers, and was bitterly resented by Cardinal Vaughan, who was scandalised by the sight of a Roman Catholic publication opening its columns to representatives of heresy and schism to spread their errors. All attempts to obtain contributions to the magazine from Roman Catholics in England were frustrated by the cardinal, who then complained that the *Revue* was too much in the hands of the Anglicans.[24]

[22] HP A4.213.

[23] Loisy was to write much later in his memoirs: 'M. Portal was not sorry to show the Anglicans that there were some scholars in the Catholic Church interested in the study of the Bible, and able to treat it in a scholarly way. He thought that I would be able to give his English readers a good idea of the liberal spirit with which the Catholic clergy could approach exegetical questions' (Alfred Loisy, *Mémoires pour servir à l'histoire religeuse de notre temps* i, Paris 1930, 390).

[24] Cf. *Leo XIII* 272 n. 1 and 298, where Halifax prints the text of a letter he wrote on 1st May 1896 to Portal reporting that Cardinal Vaughan had told Wilfrid Ward not to contribute to the *Revue*, a matter on which Halifax said he felt Ward should have been able to make up his own mind. On 29th December 1895 Portal wrote to Halifax: 'I have written to D. Gasquet to tell him I would like to publish in the Revue an analysis of the remarkable work which appeared in the Tablet and suggesting that he undertake this himself. This seems to me to be a wise policy. In this way we prevent the English Catholics from going elsewhere. We have them with us where they will be less free. Finally we centralize the whole current of ideas. If he does not accept we shall still have the advantage of having put the right

Numerous letters and memoranda of Merry del Val, Gasquet, and Cardinal Vaughan are preserved amongst the Gasquet Papers testifying to the bitterness and resentment felt by these men towards the *Revue* and its editor. Merry del Val first mentioned the paper in a letter he wrote to Gasquet on 15th December 1895, only a fortnight after the first issue of the magazine had appeared. Early in February of the following year a memorandum by Gasquet records that Merry del Val had written to Cardinal Vaughan that he

> thought the *Revue Anglo-Romaine* was a scandal and ought not to be allowed. The Holy Office would certainly censure it if it were any other matter, here they are tied. This revue was doing a lot of harm.[25]

On 2nd March Merry del Val wrote to Gasquet 'that the publication ought to be discountenanced in every way', and in the same month we learn from another of Gasquet's memoranda that

> the Cardinal wrote to say that if he did not denounce the *Revue* it was only because his action would be misunderstood. Rome had approved it and therefore on Rome be the responsibility.[26]

Merry del Val's complaints about 'that mischievous magazine'[27] reached a crescendo by the summer of 1896, when he wrote to Gasquet that Portal was 'positively heretical in his statements'.[28] Merry del Val's official biography contains letters he wrote to Leo XIII's secretary, Mgr Angeli, in an attempt to get the *Revue* suppressed and Portal severely reprimanded.[29]

---

foot forward' (PP). Amongst Gasquet's Papers at Downside there is a letter in Portal's handwriting to 'Mon Réverend Père' (not further identified) dated 24th October 1895, asking permission to print in the *Revue* an abridgement of 'the remarkable work on Anglican Ordinations which appeared in the *Tablet*'. There are also two drafts, in French and unsigned, of an affirmative reply to this letter in an unknown hand. No such article ever appeared in the *Revue*. Portal's reference was presumably to the long series of articles by Canon Moyes which appeared in *The Tablet* in the course of the year 1895 (cf. p. 297 n. 5 below).

[25] GP: memorandum in Gasquet's hand dated 6th February 1896.

[26] GP: memorandum dated 'March 1896'.

[27] Letter from Merry del Val to Gasquet, 10th March 1896, GP.

[28] Letter of 10 July 1896, GP.

[29] Cf. Cenci, *Merry del Val*, 55f, 65, 66f; and Dalpiaz, *Merry del Val*, 31f and 39.

So much bitterness and resentment could not be concealed from those against whom they were directed. Writing to Portal in March 1896 about a conversation he had had with Cardinal Vaughan, Halifax told his friend:

> The Cardinal doesn't like the *Revue* at all: it is clear that he detests it. . . . The obvious irritation which the *Revue* is producing proves that they feel that they are under attack and that their position is none too strong.[30]

So far as Cardinal Vaughan was concerned, this judgement was wishful thinking. Vaughan's confidence in the impregnability of his own theological position could hardly have been greater. The cardinal was genuinely grieved and shocked at seeing what he regarded as the most dangerous heresies being propagated under catholic auspices. The indignation felt by Vaughan and his supporters at the *Revue Anglo-Romaine* survived even the publication of *Apostolicae curae* and did not come to an end until 13th November 1896, when Canon Moyes was able to telegraph Gasquet:

> EMINENTISSIMO PERVENIT BREVIS PONTIFICIA REPROBANS EPHEMERIDEM ANGLO-ROMANAM MOYES[31]

The *Revue* was a pioneer venture in the ecumenical field with articles of a high quality on a considerable variety of subjects which can still be read today with profit. More than half a century was to elapse before anything similar could be attempted.

[30] *Leo XIII*, 272f.

[31] PAPAL LETTER REPROVING REVUE ANGLO-ROMAINE HAS REACHED HIS EMINENCE (GP).

6

THE PAPAL COMMISSION TO INVESTIGATE ANGLICAN ORDERS

The Roman Court does not understand English. It is only informed as to your affairs by a small number of interpreters who, from all I know of them, are far from being of open mind.

—The Abbé Duchesne to the Revd T. A. Lacey[1]

They want to create another Galileo case!

Fr de Augustinis to the Abbé Duchesne[2]

In February 1896 Cardinal Vaughan sent Mgr Merry del Val a letter which the latter at once passed on to Mgr Angeli to be shown to the pope. The letter included the following passage.

> Conversions are numerous [Cardinal Vaughan wrote] and if it weren't for the idea which has been spread abroad that the Holy Father believes in the validity of Anglican Orders, and that the Holy See will make a concession in the end, the number of conversions would be greater. Facts are confirming more and more my conviction that it is a tremendous trick of the devil to lead the Holy See to some sort of recognition of Anglicanism and of the Orders—not a formal recognition, but sufficient to keep people in heresy.[3]

This view, the fruit of Vaughan's fervent and *simpliste* piety, was to be pressed upon the Holy See ever more strongly in the months to come. Combined with its corollary, that a condemnation of the Orders would bring about a flood of conversions, it was to produce a situation in which it was very difficult for the pope and the cardinals of the Holy Office, with whom the ultimate decision about Anglican Orders rested, to avoid a step which, they were assured, was

[1] Letter of 25th February 1895, *Leo XIII*, 196.
[2] Cf. p. 111 below.
[3] Cenci, *Merry del Val*, 64. I am indebted to Dom Kevin McGuire of Downside Abbey for assistance in translating this and several other passages from Mgr Cenci's book.

so clearly in the interest of the church and as such desired, surely, by God himself.

Cardinal Vaughan's representatives on the commission

In March 1896 the members of the papal commission were announced. There were three English commissioners, Gasquet, Canon James Moyes, and a Franciscan, Fr David Fleming. The continental members were Duchesne, Mgr Pietro Gasparri, and a Jesuit professor of dogmatic theology at the Collegio Romano, Fr A. M. de Augustinis.

The three English commissioners were appointed on Cardinal Vaughan's nomination. They were the leading members of Vaughan's committee to prepare the English case against Anglican Orders, a project upon which they had been engaged since September 1895. All the remaining correspondence and other papers show that their co-operation was harmonious and close. None of the three was a professional theologian. Moyes' speciality was controversy. He was a frequent contributor of controversial articles to the columns of *The Tablet*, and was later to become editor of the *Dublin Review*, a position which he held for many years. He was a close associate of Cardinal Vaughan, with whom he lived for twenty-seven years.[4] Like many men who live in an atmosphere of constant controversy, Moyes' primary concern was to have an answer ready to hand in every situation with which he could annihilate his opponent. Inevitably this led him into inconsistencies. We shall have occasion in the course of the subsequent narrative to take note of several such controversial lapses. They will show that despite a certain flair for polemic Moyes was essentially second rate even as a controversialist. This fact is reflected in a letter written by Merry del Val to Gasquet in January 1896 concerning the choice of members for the coming commission

[4] Cf. *The Tablet* 88 (1912), 8 col. 1.

> I quite feel as you do about Moyes. But it has been a case of taking what we could get, and of prudence.[5]

Fr David Fleming was the linguist of the team. He was primarily responsible for putting into Latin the material prepared by Cardinal Vaughan's English committee. A number of letters and notes from the autumn of 1895 refer to material being 'sent on to Fr David to be Latinised'. His linguistic abilities proved to be especially useful in Rome, from whence Gasquet wrote to Edmund Bishop after the investigation had got under way:

> Fr David is invaluable: he has a first rate head—keeps his hair on always and speaks Latin and French fluently—quite as well the former as these Italian beggars.[6]

But it was Gasquet who was the leader of the team, and in view of the central role he played in the condemnation of Anglican Orders we must pause to consider his historical methods in some detail. Reference has already been made to Gasquet's flexible standards of historical accuracy in connection with the publication of his own *Leaves from My Diary*. The mass of inaccuracies which disfigure his serious historical works have long since caused him to be generally discredited in the scholarly world. The contemporary English catholic historian Professor David Knowles has assembled the shattered pieces of Gasquet's reputation in a brilliant lecture, 'Cardinal Gasquet as an Historian'.[7] After paying full tribute to Gasquet's virtues and achievements, which have often been overlooked, Knowles gives a lengthy list of Gasquet's defects. These are all the more striking when placed in contrast to the positive features of Gasquet's work. Knowles writes that Gasquet was 'unusually inaccurate' (253); 'from c. 1900 Gasquet's pages crawl with errors and slips' (254); 'towards the end of his life . . . Gasquet's capacity for carelessness amounted almost to genius' (254); 'Gasquet never

[5] Letter of 12th January 1896, GP.
[6] Letter of 4th April 1896, BP.
[7] In David Knowles *The Historian and Character and other Essays*, Cambridge 1963, 240–63.

revised' (255). Knowles notes further Gasquet's 'inability to grip a problem or argument and to shed light on dark places', and writes that a work published in 1912 gives the reader

> the mental impression of being lost in a maze or engulfed in a nightmare. . . . Yet in spite of that the booklet settles from documentary sources problems of identity and chronology that had led astray the editors of Dugdale, Froude and James Gairdner himself. You have in it an epitome of the splendours and distresses of Gasquet's achievement. [255]
>
> More serious still perhaps, was a lack of fidelity as an editor . . . of the Acton correspondence. . . . Besides technical inaccuracies of many kinds Gasquet consistently omitted or even altered without indication passages or phrases which might, he felt, cause personal offence. . . .
>
> Something in Gasquet . . . led him to ignore even the most cogent evidence against anything he had written. [256]
>
> For many of Gasquet's mistakes, and still more for his failure to admit and correct them, no defence can be offered. . . . he rarely approached an historical topic with an open mind . . . Either he wrote to convince others of what he believed to be the truth, or he set out a discovery which he held to be significant. In other words, he started with a conviction or a fact, and went to other documents to find confirmation. [260]

But on the other hand Gasquet's achievements, Professor Knowles writes,

> are not small achievements, and they cannot be cancelled out or reduced to zero by an enumeration of his numerous errors and failings. If it is perilous to accept Gasquet uncritically, it is foolish utterly to neglect or despise him. [262]

At the same time Knowles admits that

> in any appraisal of Gasquet's work one unknown factor, one *x*, remains to perplex the calculator. How much did he owe to Edmund Bishop? That the debt was great was common knowledge to all who knew the two men personally, and Gasquet both in print and in private letters acknowledged it. It was, however, felt, even at the time, that this ackowledgement was less explicit and less generous than might have been expected. Gasquet was not a humble man, nor was he in personal relationship a notably generous man. [251 f.][8]

[8] What Edmund Bishop thought of Gasquet's irresponsible scholarship may be gathered from a brief note in Bishop's hand in Gasquet's *England under the Old Religion*, London 1912. Inside the front cover of this volume, now amongst Bishop's books at Downside, there is pasted a scathing review of the work from the *Nation*

Perhaps the gravest of Gasquet's many lapses from the narrow path of historical accuracy occurred only a year before the investigation of Anglican Orders. In May 1895 Gasquet had, by his silence, deceived the Holy See in the beatification of three English martyrs who are now known to have suffered death not for their steadfast allegiance to the pope but for less creditable reasons. It is certain that Gasquet knew of the evidence against the martyrdom in one case; and his knowledge of the adverse evidence in one and perhaps both other cases is probable. Although it was common knowledge that the beatification was based upon Gasquet's published statements,[9] and that a word of caution from him would have stopped or delayed the beatification proceedings until a full investigation of the historical facts could be undertaken, Gasquet kept silent and thus permitted the Roman authorities to commit a blunder which was to be an acute embarrassment later on when the facts became generally known.[10]

---

of 30th November 1912, in which a host of the most egregious errors and false statements in this and previous works of Gasquet's is laid bare, and Gasquet is castigated for repeatedly refusing to take any notice of previously published corrections by critics of the misstatements with which his books were filled—and for republishing these falsehoods unchanged after attention had been drawn to them publicly. Alongside this review Bishop has written in his unmistakable spidery hand and in his characteristic style, reminiscent of Queen Victoria's: 'This is "surely" a *pity*. But *I* cannot be *surprised*—alas!'

[9] Cf. F. A. Gasquet, *Henry VIII and the English Monasteries* ii, London 1889, 379–84, and further references in Knowles, op. cit. in n. 7 above, p. 237. Dom Alberic Stacpoole of Ampleforth Abbey has put me in his debt by drawing my attention to the additional evidence published by J. E. Paul, 'The Last Abbots of Reading and Colchester', *Bulletin of the Institute of Historical Research* 33 (London 1960), 115–21.

[10] Knowles writes: 'Gasquet was at the time the one man in England qualified to enter a firm caveat for the sake of historical truth, and to warn his readers of his earlier ignorance. Instead, he persisted to the end in a *suppressio veri* which in the circumstances carried with it more than a trace of *suggestio falsi*' (op. cit. 257). Knowles is mistaken, however, in claiming that Dom Bede Camm admitted in 1904 that the evidence published in 1895 by Gairdner (Abbot Marshall's confession and retraction, written in his own hand) 'rendered Abbot Marshall's claim to the title of martyr unprovable, if not positively disproved' (Knowles, loc. cit.). Camm concluded that despite Marshall's retraction of anything he might have said in favour of the papal claims, which had been published by Gairdner for the first time in 1895, it was 'sufficiently clear that the last Abbot of Colchester died a true martyr for the unity of Christ's Church'. Camm added the qualifying statement, however: 'Nevertheless, I frankly own that more positive evidence on the matter is much to be desired' (Bede Camm, *Lives of the English Martyrs declared Blessed by Pope Leo XIII in 1886 and 1895* i, London 1904, 411).

This was the man who, in the words of his biographer, 'led the English team which signally defeated the distinguished French clergy, who believed or hoped it was possible for Anglican Orders to be recognized as the genuine brand'.[11]

The continental members of the commission

The Abbé Duchesne's positive opinion about the validity of Anglican Orders has already been discussed above in connection with Portal's pamphlet on the question.[12] Gasparri was a canonist. He had already attained distinction as a professor at the Institut Catholique in Paris, and was later to direct the vast labour of compiling the present code of canon law and become Cardinal Secretary of State under Popes Benedict XV and Pius XI. Gasparri had published two closely reasoned articles on Anglican Orders

Knowles also slips in stating that Marshall and the two other abbots were beatified in 1897, two years after documentary disproof of Marshall's martyrdom had been published by Gairdner. In acknowledging this error Professor Knowles has been kind enough to communicate the following supplementary information:

'It is fairly certain that Gasquet knew of Abbot Marshall's recantation long before 1895. Gairdner did not really "discover" any document, he merely printed it. Abbot Marshall's recantations are only a few folios farther on in the bundle which contained the accusations against him which Gasquet knew well. He and Gairdner were for a long time sitting more or less side by side at the Public Record Office, and were on very good terms, and for many years Gairdner saw eye to eye with Gasquet in all ways. It is hard to see how Gasquet would not have been familiar with that page: at no time did he suggest that he had not seen it till it was printed. . . . And it was common knowledge that the decree of beatification rested on Gasquet's work' (Letter to the author, cited by permission).

It seems clear that although the beatification of Abbot Marshall came in the same year that Gairdner published Marshall's recantation, and not two years later, no injustice has been done to Gasquet. It is morally certain that he knew of the recantation long before it was printed by Gairdner; and to the end of his life Gasquet continued to ignore the recantation, and to maintain that Marshall had died a martyr for opposing the Royal Supremacy. Gasquet's personal interest in the beatification of the three abbots is shown by a postcard he wrote to Edmund Bishop (who never threw away *anything*, and was even capable of saving a postcard bearing the single word 'Yes!') on 21st May 1895: 'Today I hear that the Pope has approved of the decree *re* martyrs and nothing remains but to publish it' (BP).

[11] Shane Leslie, *Cardinal Gasquet, A Memoir*, London 1953, 53. There is a certain poetic justice in the fact that such an inaccurate historian and scholar as Gasquet should have received such a disorganised and gossipy biography.

[12] Cf. p. 48 above.

in the *Revue Anglo-Romaine* in which he concluded that the Orders were doubtfully valid—a conclusion which would have justified a change in the existing practice of re-ordaining convert clergy absolutely. If Anglican Orders were doubtfully valid such clergy must receive conditional ordination.[13]

De Augustinis was convinced, like Duchesne, that Anglican Orders were valid. His *votum* on the question concluded:

> The English ordinations, on which the Holy See has not yet given a doctrinal judgement, are valid by reason of their being effected by a competent minister, with a valid rite, with the intention of doing what the Church does.[14]

Coming out of one of the commission's meetings at which he had been particularly annoyed by the arguments of Cardinal Vaughan's representatives, de Augustinis turned to Duchesne and said: 'They want to create another Galileo case!'[15] De Augustinis told the English commissioners the same thing. Moyes wrote to Cardinal Vaughan on 18th April 1896:

> Fr de Augustinis called here during the week, and I had a long conversation with him, and endeavoured to put before him the actual position in England, but he is narrow-minded and *entêté* and thinks that if the Holy

[13] Gasparri's conclusions in detail were as follows:

(1) Barlow's consecration could be considered historically certain, so that the material succession was intact.

(2) There was a probable, but not a certain, defect of intention.

(3) The sacramental form was doubtful, the degree of doubt varying with each of the three orders.

(Cf. RAR i, 481–93, 529–57.)

[14] Lacey, *Roman Diary* 46. Lacey printed an extended summary of de Augustinis' *votum*; cf. op. cit. 42–6.

[15] This incident is reported in two letters from Portal to Halifax. The first, written 19th September 1896, may be found in *Leo XIII*, 357; the second, dated 3rd September 1910, is in the Hickleton Papers (HP A4.213). De Augustinis seems to have repeated his remark frequently. It was first reported by Portal in a letter written to Halifax from Rome on 14th April 1896: 'P. de Augustinis is excellent. He cannot get over the stupid prejudice of Moyes etc. His whole fear is that the question will be taken to the Holy Office. "These gentlemen," he said the other day speaking of the Triumvirate, "are preparing another Galileo case"' (PP). De Augustinis' remark very probably lies behind Halifax's comment in a letter he wrote to Bishop Mandell Creighton of Peterborough on 21st September 1896, in which Halifax wrote that though he had not yet been able to read the text of the Bull, one of the things which occurred to him was 'the famous words in a not dissimilar case: *E pur si muove*' (HP A4.254).

> Father gave a decree affirming the nullity, the evidence for the sufficiency of the Ordinal would probably go on increasing and the Church would find herself in the same predicament as over the decree against Galileo.[16]

Gasquet published an entirely different version of this conversation, at which he was also present.

> Wednesday, April 15th: This morning we had a long talk with Padre de Augustinis in our room. He appears to think that we shall all agree as to the invalid nature of the *Form* used in the Anglican rite . . . [17]

De Augustinis' conviction that the Anglican form of ordination was *valid* is as certain as anything can be. Portal and Moyes testified independently of one another to his remark about the danger of another Galileo case; de Augustinis stated his positive opinion about the Anglican form in his *votum*; and we shall see that he voted for validity at the end of the investigation.[18] Gasquet's published statement, allegedly an extract from his contemporary diary notes, that de Augustinis had told him and his colleagues that they would all agree about the *invalidity* of the Anglican form, speaks volumes for Gasquet's reliability as a witness to the events in which he participated. De Augustinis was a professional theologian who had taught both in the United States and in Rome, and who had published his lectures in dogmatic theology.[19] Compared with him Moyes and Fleming were rank amateurs. Gasquet was no theologian at all (nor did he claim to be), but a self-taught historian of extremely dubious accuracy.[20]

Although the commission appeared to be balanced evenly between the proponents and opponents of Anglican Orders, it was in fact heavily weighted on the negative side by the appointment of a president and secretary who were as strongly opposed to Anglican claims as Cardinal Vaughan's three representatives, with whom they co-operated closely

[16] Cited from Messenger, art. cit. in Chapter 5, n. 21, above, *The Tablet* 137 (1937), 153 col. 1.

[17] Gasquet, *Leaves from my Diary* 53f.

[18] Cf. p. 162 below.

[19] Aemilius M. de Augustinis, *Re Sacramentaria, praelectiones scholastico-dogmaticae* 2 vols., Rome 1887 and 1889.

[20] Cf. pp. 217–23 below.

throughout the investigation. The president of the commission was the Jesuit Cardinal Mazzella. He was assisted by Mgr Merry del Val as commission secretary.

Two members are added to the commission

The commission met for the first time on Tuesday 24th March 1896. The six commissioners already mentioned were present, as well as the president and secretary. The meeting transacted no business, and was devoted entirely to procedural matters. Gasquet recorded in the published version of his diary[21] that 'some question was raised' as to the possibility of admitting Anglicans to the commission's meetings. Cardinal Mazzella ruled at once that the suggestion was out of order: the question was 'entirely a domestic one', and in any case it was impossible to say who could properly claim to represent the Church of England.[22] This was a faithful echo of the line which had been adopted more than a year previously by Gasquet in a conversation with Portal in Rome.[23] It is not unreasonable to presume that the question of Anglican participation had already been the subject of private conversations between the English representatives, Merry del Val, and Cardinal Mazzella, and that the latter's remarks on this subject in this first meeting of the commission represented the line which it had been agreed to adopt in case the question should come up. We shall see in the next chapter that the character of the *votum* submitted to the commission by Cardinal Vaughan's representatives made it essential to exclude Anglicans from the discussion.

Easter fell on 5th April in 1896, and the second meeting of the commission did not take place until Easter Tuesday, 7th April. Two additional commissioners were now present, the Revd T. B. Scannell and Fr Calasanzio de Llaveneras.

[21] The original diary notes for the 1896 period cannot be found. Cf. Chapter 4, n. 27, above (p. 73).

[22] Gasquet, *Leaves from My Diary* 46f.

[23] Cf. p. 147f below.

How they came to be named to the commission at this late date was related by Gasquet to his friend Edmund Bishop in a letter written on Easter Eve.

> You were quite right about your supposition as to Scannell. It was evident that some of the very few busybodies were at work to get Scannell sent for. Von Hügel par exemple, I heard, had put in a petition to Rampolla and that Gasparri (who evidently is using this to make his own name) had represented that there was a body of men who did not believe in our view. The Pope finally gave way (and I think wisely) and had the Cardinal Vaughan written to that it would be better to have this view represented. But (and here is the indication that the Pope fully is determined, whilst giving no chance for the French beggars to have cause of complaint, to back us up) the Pope appointed one Padre Calasanzio Llaveneras OSF who is considered the best consultor of the Holy Office, proprio motu to join in the discussions of the commission. He is more than we could have expected—is thoroughly up in his subject—a first rate speaker and quite in accord with us. He has seen our *Votum*, the Pope having given it to him, and he says it is unanswerable and the best *votum* he has ever set eyes on.[24]

Fr Scannell was at that time a parish priest in Sheerness, Kent. In the autumn of 1895 he had written several letters to *The Tablet* concerning the meaning of certain disputed papal documents on Anglican Orders during the Marian restoration.[25] These letters revealed the keen intelligence and exact theological knowledge of their author, and showed that he was independent enough not to support polemical claims advanced by his side in a controversy when the weight of evidence was against them. The English catholic layman Baron Friedrich von Hügel had written to Halifax towards the end of October 1895 drawing his attention to Scannell's letter in *The Tablet* for October 19th:

> That is a man worth cultivating. I had him up to Hampshire and delighted in him. I want him on the Orders commission. . . . A capital theologian.[26]

Scannell's appointment to the commission has been interpreted by both Vaughan's biographer and by Halifax's as

[24] Letter dated 4th April 1896, BP.
[25] Cf. *The Tablet* 54 (1895), 633 col. 2; cf. also pp. 305, 473, 552, and 594.
[26] HP A4.253.

evidence of the cardinal's impartiality and generous spirit.[27] This is a misunderstanding. Scannell was appointed only after the pope had asked Vaughan to send to Rome an English theologian who would represent a point of view different from that of the three men he had already nominated. To such a request Cardinal Vaughan was bound to accede; generosity and impartiality had nothing to do with it. Nor should the significance of Scannell's participation be exaggerated. Unlike his three English colleagues he was quite unprepared for discussion of the complex matters to which he was so hastily and unexpectedly summoned. And he would have been less than human if he had not reflected that too great a measure of deviation from the 'official' English line in the commission could cost him dearly for many years to come. During the investigation he told the Revd T. A. Lacey, one of the two Anglican priests who were in Rome at this time in a purely private capacity, that he did not believe in the validity of the Orders, and was working for no decision at all.[28] Even this amount of independence was to cost Scannell dear. On 23rd May Lacey noted in his diary:

> In the afternoon Scannell called, a priest of the English College accompanying him. He explained that he had been keeping out of our way because of the fashion that he was spied upon.[29]

Fifteen years later Scannell was still regretting that he had ever got involved in the affair. In a letter dated 4th September 1911, von Hügel told Lord Halifax:

> I have incontrovertible, abundant proofs that Scannell has been, and continues, *most* anxious, since the miscarriage of that affair, *that his share in it should be completely ignored.*[30]

Finally, we have already seen that Scannell's appointment was counter-balanced by the appointment of a 'safe' man,

[27] Snead-Cox, *Cardinal Vaughan* ii, 196, and Lockhart, *Halifax* ii, 87.
[28] Cf. Lacey, *Roman Diary* 38. [29] Lacey, op. cit. 70.
[30] HP A4.253, emphasis in original.

committed in advance to support the case submitted by Cardinal Vaughan's three representatives against the Orders.

Lacey and Puller

The appointment of a purely Roman commission was of course not at all what Halifax and Portal had worked for. They had envisaged joint conversations between Anglican and Roman Catholic theologians, at which the question of the Orders would result in mutual explanations by both sides, and so lead on to a discussion of the wider theological issues separating the two churches. Even on the particular question of Anglican Orders the presence on the commission of theologians sympathetic to Anglican claims did not assure that the Anglican case would be adequately represented.

Although de Augustinis submitted a *votum* in which he maintained the certain validity of Anglican Orders, it is unlikely that as an Italian and a dogmatic theologian he would have felt at home in a discussion of details of English reformation history. Much the same might be said about Gasparri, who suffered from the additional handicap of not being able to read English, the only member of the commission who had no acquaintance with the language at all. Although Duchesne was a church historian, the sixteenth century was not his field, and he was at a disadvantage in dealing with a man like Gasquet, who had been doing scholarly research into the history of the English reformation for years, and whose published works show that he was capable of unusual carelessness in the presentation and interpretation of historical evidence.

Even before the commission met, Gasparri and Duchesne realised that they would need expert assistance if they expected to hold their own in argument with English representatives. Gasparri sent a plea for help to England, asking if he might have information during the investigation from the joint author of *De Hierarchia Anglicana*, T. A. Lacey. This request placed the Anglicans in a difficult position: they did not wish to do anything which might give the impression of having asked the Holy See to investigate and recognise Anglican Orders. However, after consultation it was decided that the Macedonian call must be answered, and Lacey was sent to Rome immediately after Easter accompanied by Fr F. W. Puller, a member of the Society of St John the Evangelist,[31] who had contributed a long article on Anglican Orders and the sacrifice of the mass to the *Revue Anglo-Romaine*, and who had read Portal's original pamphlet on the Orders before it was published.[32] Thomas Alexander Lacey was at that time vicar of the parish of Madingley, near Cambridge. His biographer in the *Dictionary of National Biography* writes:

> He became one of the most accomplished Latinists of his time, and it is related that when he was in Rome in connection with the inquiry into Anglican ordinations Pope Leo XIII said that he wished that he had a cardinal who could write such Latin as Mr Lacey.[33]

Not only Lacey and Puller themselves but all those concerned with their trip to Rome were careful to emphasise that they went in a purely private capacity and not as representatives of the Anglican Church. Lacey wrote later:

> My own bishop would not even grant me formal leave of absence. The benison of the Archbishop of York, which we valued highly, was purely personal.[34]

The two men lost no opportunity to demonstrate that they were in Rome solely at the invitation of certain members of the commission, to supply information as requested, and that neither they nor the Anglican Church was asking the Holy See for any kind of judgement about Anglican Orders.

[31] An Anglican monastic order for men with its mother house at Cowley, outside Oxford.
[32] Cf. RAR i, 395–414, 433–51, 494–507, and Chapter 3, n. 2, above.
[33] DNB 1931–10, Oxford 1949, 519.
[34] Lacey, *Roman Diary* xii. Both of the prelates mentioned approved of Lacey and Puller's mission to Rome.

It was for this reason, for instance, that Lacey and Puller made no request to be received by the pope, though they made numerous visits to other ecclesiastics in Rome and to communities of religious.

The storm of indignation in England following the condemnation of the Orders caused the defenders of Cardinal Vaughan to put upon Lacey and Puller's trip to Rome the very construction they had tried to avoid; it was claimed that Anglicans had sued for recognition of their orders and had now got what they deserved, and indeed what they should have expected all along.[35] Some years later Cardinal Vaughan's biographer wrote that the two Anglicans had acted with one side of the commission 'much as solicitors who work with counsel'.[36] Lacey answered this charge in his characteristically forceful style.

> We were not solicitors, we were managing the affairs of no clients; we were promoters of no cause, we had engaged no advocates. . . . From more than one side we were represented as going to Rome with a petition for the recognition of our Orders. . . . A more complete misconception there could hardly be. We did desire a favourable decision at Rome, we worked for it and we prayed for it;[37] but we did not desire it for our own assurance. Nothing of that kind was needed. What we desired, what we worked for and prayed for, was the removal of a practical obstruction hindering the concord of Christians. It was not on our side alone that the need of this relief was felt. There were others, eager advocates of Christian union, whose efforts were hampered by their uncertainty about our Orders. They could not ignore, as we could, the practice actually current in the Roman Church. For their sake, no less than for our own, the obstruction must, if possible, be demolished. The Pope was willing to examine the obstruction. That was enough for us; we would give our help. . . . We worked as solicitors work, but not always. It is not a solicitor's business to furnish the court with evidence that tells against his own client: he leaves that to the other side. Father Puller and I did furnish the commission with some evidence that told against

[35] Cf. *The Tablet* 56 (1896), 690, where this charge is made at length in a leading article.

[36] Snead-Cox, *Cardinal Vaughan* ii, 195.

[37] Was Lacey's memory playing tricks on him? Before his departure for Rome he wrote to his Ordinary, the Bishop of Ely: 'The object which Fr Puller and I set before ourselves is not to obtain a favourable decision, but to hinder the giving of any decision at all' (Letter of 27th March 1896, *Roman Diary* 90).

our own contention.[38] It annoyed us a little when men praised us for this. It did not seem to us a remarkably virtuous act. We were engaged in an honest investigation and we could not have acted otherwise.[39]

Lacey and Puller did not reach Rome until the commission had already held three of its twelve meetings. Since they were not present at the commission's deliberations they had no opportunity of intervening in response to weak points in the arguments of the other side, or to correct misstatements or misunderstandings. We shall see in the next chapter that the case against the Orders presented by Cardinal Vaughan's three representatives offered a host of opportunities for such intervention. Lacey and Puller had to depend for their knowledge of their opponents' arguments upon what Gasparri and Duchesne, hampered by an oath of secrecy, felt able to tell them or ask them. This was subsequently admitted by *The Tablet*, which wrote of Lacey's *Roman Diary* in 1910:

These pages make it evident that those who were prompting [Gasparri and Duchesne] were much in the dark as to what was really going on, and from time to time themselves blundered badly.[40]

This blundering, the inevitable consequence of the conditions under which Lacey and Puller had to work, shows that the Anglican case was never properly or fairly presented. It is true that after the commission had terminated its deliberations Fr Puller wrote to Lord Halifax:

Duchesne frankly said that he could not have answered some serious objections raised by the opponents if we had not been there.[41]

[38] During the investigation of the Orders Lacey and Puller heard that evidence of a few re-ordinations of Ordinal clergy during the Marian restoration (1553–58) had just been discovered in England. Although this information told against the Anglican contention that the Orders of Ordinal clergy had been recognised in the Marian period, Lacey and Puller at once communicated this information to Duchesne and Gasparri (cf. Lacey, *Roman Diary* 57f).

[39] Lacey, *Roman Diary* 8ff. This statement should be weighed carefully in assessing the charge repeatedly made by Cardinal Vaughan and his representatives in Rome that the Anglicans were insincere, and that their only interest was in obtaining some recognition of their orders in order to strengthen their position against Rome.

[40] *The Tablet* 84 (1910), 1056 col. 1.

[41] Letter of 8th June 1896, HP A4.243.

But what of the objections and misstatements never submitted to Lacey and Puller because Duchesne assumed that they must be true? That the existence of such flaws in the English case against the Orders was not a merely hypothetical possibility will become evident in the pages which follow.

7
THE ENGLISH CASE AGAINST THE ORDERS

The English Catholics have presented an enormous memorandum, *but not really very formidable. Duchesne merely shrugs his shoulders significantly whenever he speaks of it. Gasparri finds certain historical points in it that are worthy of note.*

—The Abbé Portal to Lord Halifax, 31st March 1896[1]

The 'enormous memorandum' referred to in the above quotation from a letter written by the Abbé Portal in Rome to Lord Halifax in England was the work of Cardinal Vaughan's special committee, which had been formed in the late summer of 1895 and worked away through the autumn drawing up and documenting the English case against the Orders. The resulting work, *Ordines Anglicani*, was privately printed and bears the names of Vaughan's three representatives on the commission, Fleming, Gasquet, and Moyes. Although not secret, the contents of this work have never been divulged, and the number of people who have read it in the seven decades since its appearance is probably very small. A brief table of contents was printed some thirty years ago by Dr E. C. Messenger in his vast and confused polemic against Anglican Orders.[2] And Fr Francis Clark cites a brief passage from the work in *Anglican Orders and Defect of Intention*, and makes considerable use of its arguments, but fails to mention material in immediate juxtaposition to his citation which directly contradicts one of the central arguments of his book.[3]

This virtually unknown work is an important and revealing document, for it was the brief from which Cardinal Vaughan's representatives in the commission argued against

[1] A copy of this letter in Halifax's hand, enclosed in a letter of his to Athelstan Riley, is in the Hickleton Papers, A4.215.

[2] RMP ii, 549f.

[3] Cf. pp. 138–9 below.

Anglican Orders. It is written throughout in strongly polemical terms. The reformation is constantly referred to as 'the so-called Reformation',[4] and Anglican Orders are always 'so-called Orders'. Normal and neutral terms are seldom used for the Anglican reformers when abusive ones can be found. Thus the work speaks in a number of places of Cranmer's 'henchmen'[5] rather than of his associates or allies. There are numerous other instances of such abusive language which will become evident in the course of the summary of contents which follows. The entire effort was to see how much could be said against the Orders, not how much could be said for them. In this the authors were loyally carrying out Cardinal Vaughan's wishes.

The brief begins with a Prologue which claims that the Holy See has already declared Anglican Orders to be invalid on no less than eight occasions. As only four of these precedents are mentioned, the reader is left wondering how the total of eight was arrived at.[6] In any case the decision to reopen the question showed that existing precedents could not be regarded as decisive. After this appeal to precedent the brief argues that to change the practice of treating Anglican Orders as null and void, which has been consistent and well known ever since 'the so-called "Reformation"', would have the gravest consequences. It would encourage the 'absurd heresy' that the Anglican Church is a branch of the true church, co-equal with the Greek Church. In the 'almost unanimous' opinion of the clergy and laity of the British Isles and indeed of the whole English-speaking world such a change in the church's practice would be a most serious obstacle to conversions, would assist the Anglican heresy, and encourage people to say that since the Holy See had been proved wrong on one matter, it was only

[4] 'sic dicta Reformatio'.

[5] The Latin term is *assecla*, a word found only in larger Latin dictionaries.

[6] J. Moyes, A. Gasquet, D. Fleming, *Ordines Anglicani: Expositio Historica et Theologica, Cura et Studio Commissionis ab Em.o et Rev.o D. D. Herberto Cardinali Vaughan ad hoc institutae*, London 1896 (privately printed), 1–7. This work is cited hereafter as 'OA'.

a question of time before it would have to admit its errors in others.[7]

Two comments may be made about these arguments. First of all, it is worthy of note that the authors did not claim unanimous agreement amongst English-speaking catholics about the negative results to be expected from a recognition of the Orders. In fact Roman Catholic opinion on this matter was divided, even in England. We have already seen that Halifax had drawn attention to the fact that the existing non-recognition of Anglican Orders was frequently an obstacle to the conversion of Anglicans, and that a Roman Catholic like Wilfrid Ward was convinced that a formal condemnation of the Orders 'would turn away from all thought of Rome many more than it brought nearer to us'.[8] Second, the argument about the inexpediency of admitting that the Holy See had been wrong about Anglican Orders implied logically that it was inexpedient to admit that the Holy See had ever been wrong about any important question at all—a claim for which there is no justification either in the dogmatic teaching of the Roman Catholic Church or in the history of the Holy See.

After arguing these considerations of expediency the brief then proceeds to turn to a consideration of the facts of the case on their own merits, giving first a highly tendentious account of the teachings of the English reformers[9].

Cranmer and the other English reformers were in constant contact with the continental reformers and adopted their ideas. They denied that ordination was a sacrament, or that it conveyed an indelible character or grace. They considered it merely the institution of a civil ministry. They did not even consider ordination necessary at all, but retained it merely for the sake of seemliness and order. Since they believed that all christians were priests, they held that the presbyter's only function was to administer the Lord's Supper to others. They held that Christ's sacrifice had ceased completely, and that the eucharist was not a sacrifice, save in the sense of a sacrifice of praise or a commemoration of Christ's sacrifice

[7] OA 7ff.

[8] Cf. pp. 74ff above.

[9] The following passage and others similarly printed are summaries. Throughout this chapter direct quotation is indicated by quotation marks.

on the cross, which was finished once and for all. For this reason they maintained that any propitiatory sacrifice in the mass was a blasphemy and injurious to Christ. Since the English reformers held Christ to be the only sacrificing priest, there were no other priests in the church at all except in the sense in which all christians may be called priests. They denied any objective presence of Christ in the eucharist, and taught a real presence only through grace in the soul of the recipient. They denied that the power of forgiving sins imparted by Christ to his apostles existed in the sacrament of penance, and said that there was only a preaching of forgiveness in the church. The power of the keys they interpreted as applying solely to the church's disciplinary authority in the external forum. They believed in justification by faith alone, excluding good works. They said that the sacraments had their effects not *ex opere operato* but by stirring up the recipient's faith. The sacraments were simply vivid representations of Christ's passion, and there was no need for the minister to have any intention at all.[9]

The reformers changed the liturgy in the entire land and removed the Catholic rites in order to inculcate these new heresies. They eliminated all references to sacrifice in both the Ordinal and the eucharist, retaining in the Ordinal only those ceremonies which signified the administration of commemorative sacraments, a ministry of preaching, and of the forgiveness of sins by the preaching of God's word. These changes were introduced under the pretext of wanting to return to primitive purity of doctrine and worship. But this pretext was in fact completely unfounded, for the greater part of the new prayers consisted of novelties taken over from the writings of the German reformers, and not of primitive elements as claimed. The reformers' true mind may be most clearly seen in the rite for the priesthood, in which they dropped the tradition of the instruments and the accompanying words which refer to sacrifice. They retained the words, 'Receive the Holy Ghost,' which they were able to understand in an heretical sense; moreover these words were not primitive, but just as recent as the things which were eliminated. In the form for the episcopate the reformers mutilated the eucharistic preface because it referred to the priesthood, but kept the words, 'Receive the Holy Ghost,' which were a medieval addition. It is clear that the intention of the reformers in all these changes was to deny the priesthood and sacrifice in the catholic sense, and to substitute for these things a non-sacrificial ministry and a purely commemorative eucharist in which Christ was present not objectively, but merely through the faith of the recipients, and in which there was no eucharistic sacrifice, save in the sense of a recollection of Christ's sacrifice, and a sacrifice of praise and thanksgiving.[10]

[10] OA 11ff.
[10a] OA 13ff.

For three centuries it was hardly possible for any other doctrines to penetrate into England at all. The reformers threw down altars and replaced them with tables, often placing the altar stones where they would be walked on. The eucharist was celebrated mostly once a month; or only three to four times a year. Only communicants were permitted to attend, and the remainder of the consecrated elements was given to the curate for profane use. All signs of reverence for the sacrament were suppressed. The practice of confession was abandoned. At most a dying person might be urged to confess his sins to the minister. But sacramental confession was denounced as an abuse and a blasphemy. Mass was forbidden under pain of cruel death, and even the harbouring of priests was a capital crime. Catholicism was so thoroughly rooted out that for almost three centuries it is impossible to find a single clear admission of the priesthood in the catholic sense. Even the few authors, such as Laud and others, who seem to be more catholic, are really of no weight. For they speak merely of a commemorative sacrifice, or of a sacrifice of praise and thanksgiving. And when their doctrine is properly assessed it is seen to differ *toto caelo* from the catholic doctrine, and to be nothing more than a rare aberration 'in the vast abyss of the burning desert of the Protestant Reformers' doctrine'.[11]

Even today the Low Church bishops continue the rankest protestant denial of catholic doctrines. Lightfoot, than whom no bishop in the nineteenth century has been more eminent, has written: 'The Anglican Church has *no sacerdotal system*, and places no sacrificial caste between God and man.'[12] 'Neo-Anglicanism' started fifty-five years ago. Its principal tenets are the following: there is a visible church to which all should belong; all are members of this church who are baptised, and who accept the teaching of the first four or six councils. Hence this church includes the Roman Catholic, Orthodox, and Anglican Churches, all as equal constituent parts. All bishops are equal and the pope has no jurisdiction over national churches. The Neo-Anglicans are grateful to the reformers for freeing the Anglican Church from Rome, but otherwise they want to believe all catholic doctrine (in the above sense), while rejecting the papacy and all the councils since the Fourth Lateran Council inclusive, as well as the modern dogmatic definitions. These Neo-Anglicans hope to increase their following, and they constantly assert that they are in continuity with the pre-reformation church. They claim that the power held by the popes in England prior to the reformation was usurped. They say that Henry VIII wanted merely to restore the previous and primitive independence of the English church. In order to maintain their claim to be a church equal to Rome and the oriental

[11] OA 16ff. The original of this citation: 'in gurgite vasto aestuosae et arenosae Protestantium Reformatorum doctrinae' (OA 18).

[12] OA 19, emphasis in original. Source not given.

churches, but independent of them, it is absolutely necessary that they have valid orders, and they therefore bend all their efforts towards obtaining recognition of their orders. They leave no stone unturned to obscure the reformers' teaching. They try to explain the Articles of Religion and the liturgy in the most ingenious ways and even adopt pious frauds[13] in their attempts to explain these things in a catholic sense. They assert that the changes were introduced merely to combat errors and superstitions! But it is obvious that this denial of the reformers' monstrous (*nefarius*) work conflicts with the most well-known facts.[14]

These Neo-Anglicans have a very small following. But the idea of an independent national church appeals to the pride and vanity of people who would like to see a church which is ancient and catholic, but English and independent of Rome, pre-eminent amongst all churches in the world as the British Empire is pre-eminent among all nations. It is only the rise of this new school of Anglicanism which has made any dispute about Anglican Orders possible at all. For the older Anglicans did not care about this question, and their definitions of the priesthood, sacred orders, and the apostolic succession were totally different from ours.[15]

Critique of these arguments

Now whatever may be thought of this presentation of Anglicanism—intended, it will be remembered, for those who had no independent knowledge of it—it cannot be denied that statements as undifferentiated as these are a gross oversimplification of highly complex facts and circumstances. Evidence for most of the statements summarised above can be found, but there is scarcely one of them for which a great deal of contrary evidence cannot be produced as well. Almost all of these assertions are debatable, and several of them are quite simply false. Thus the claim that pre-Tractarian Anglicans had no interest in arguing about the validity of their orders in the catholic sense is belied by a mass of controversial literature on this subject, beginning in the sixteenth century, and widening into a flood in the seventeenth and eighteenth centuries. And the further claim that until the Oxford Movement Anglicans defined the priesthood and apostolic succession in a sense totally dif-

[13] 'etiam adhibita quadam piae fraudis *saltem specie*'.
[14] OA 19–22.
[15] OA 22f.

ferent from that of catholic theology is difficult to reconcile with the fact that Anglicans have always treated Roman Catholic Orders as identical with their own by receiving Roman Catholic clergy in their orders. Protestant clergy, on the other hand, have regularly been required to receive episcopal ordination before being permitted to administer Anglican sacraments. The argument that the reformers' professed desire to return to primitive models in their liturgical changes was a mere pretext, since in fact they did not return to the liturgy of the early ages of the church but retained medieval elements, assumes that the reformers had a scientific knowledge of liturgical history which was in fact not available to anyone in the sixteenth century.[16] The statements about the English reformers believing merely in a commemorative sacrifice ignore the fact that St Thomas Aquinas, Peter Lombard, and a host of earlier theologians all speak of eucharistic sacrifice in terms of representation and commemoration. The assertion that the reformers denied that the church had any power to forgive sins, and could merely preach forgiveness, cannot be reconciled with the retention in both the First and Second Prayer Books of the indicative formula of absolution:

> Our Lord Jesus Christ, who hath left power to his Church to absolve all sinners, which truly repent and believe in him, of his great mercy forgive thine offences: and by his authority committed to me, I absolve thee from all thy sins, in the name of the Father . . . etc.[17]

Since the authors of the brief refer to the Prayer Book office for the Visitation of the Sick,[18] they could hardly claim to be ignorant of this form of priestly absolution,[19] though it is

[16] This argument also appears in *Apostolicae curae*: '. . . under a pretext of returning to the primitive form [the authors of the Ordinal] corrupted the liturgical order in many ways to suit the errors of the Reformers' (AO[E] 11). But the authors of the Ordinal did not act 'under a pretext' of returning to the primitive forms: they honestly thought they were doing so.

[17] Gibson, 262 and 419.

[18] Cf. p. 125 above: 'At most a dying person might be urged to confess his sins to the minister.'

[19] Nor of the rubric which precedes it: 'Here shall the sick person make a special confession, if he feel his conscience troubled with any weighty matter. After which

morally certain that those for whom they were writing were.

Finally, even if this highly tendentious account of the doctrine of the English reformers and their successors were correct, this would not prove that those who held these doctrines had succeeded in imposing them upon the Anglican Church, any more than the definition of papal infallibility by the First Vatican Council proves that Cardinal Manning and other extreme infallibilists succeeded in imposing their doctrine of the papacy upon the Roman Catholic Church. In the latter case it is clear that the definition was actually very moderate[20] and represented a defeat for the extreme infalliblist party which most people at the time considered to have won. But again, even if the Anglican Church *had* committed itself to every one of the doctrines alleged in this document to have been those of the English reformers, this would not of itself make its orders invalid. For the validity of orders does not depend upon the orthodoxy of those possessing or transmitting them, nor even upon their orthodoxy with regard to the sacrament of order itself.

The history of the English reformation

The brief next proceeds to deal with the history of the English reformation. It states that Henry VIII brought about organic and constitutional separation from the Holy See, but that doctrinal and liturgical changes came only after his death in 1547.[21]

confession the Priest shall absolve him after this sort' (Gibson 419). The 1549 Prayer Book added at this point the words: 'and the same form of absolution shall be used in all private confessions' (Gibson 262).

[20] The First Vatican Council said that the Roman pontiff, when speaking *ex cathedra*, 'enjoys that infallibility with which the divine Redeemer willed that his Church should be endowed for defining doctrine of faith or morals' (DS 3074 [1839]). The nature and limits of the infallibility which Christ willed that his church should possess for those purposes were not defined, and are thus left to the free discussion of theologians. It is this (undefined) infallibility which the pope possesses, and that only under very narrowly defined, and correspondingly rare, circumstances.

[21] Roman Catholic apologists in England have since become bolder, and claim that Henry VIII's break with the papacy was a change in doctrine and thus formally heretical. Fr Philip Hughes takes this position in his well-known work *The Reformation in England* 3 vols., London 1951–54.

> The principal part in the abominable work of the reformation is to be attributed to Cranmer and his associates. Cranmer had been in Germany and had there become infected with protestant doctrines. Although he was a priest, Cranmer secretly married the niece of Osiander. As Henry VIII's Archbishop of Canterbury, Cranmer managed to bring about a weakening in doctrine, and to get reforming bishops appointed to vacant sees. Henry's death in January 1547 enabled the reformers to carry out their aims: the removal from the liturgy of all vestiges of catholicism which were contrary to Cranmer's heresies; and the production of a vernacular liturgy which expressed these heresies. Cranmer's method was to take his material from the Sarum breviary, missal, and ritual, so far as it did not conflict with the doctrines of the reformers. Where this was the case he adopted material from the continental reformers. In December 1547 communion in both kinds was introduced and in March 1548 a vernacular Order of Holy Communion was interpolated into the mass. Cranmer gained the leadership in the work of liturgical revision. He had already given evidence of his heretical principles in his book, *Of the True Doctrine of the Sacrament.*[22]

This work was in fact not issued until 1550, and its title was not that given by the authors of *Ordines Anglicani*, but rather *A Defence of the True and Catholicke doctrine of the sacrament of the body and bloud of our saviour Christ.*[23] The problem of explaining to French and Italian theologians how such an arch-protestant as Cranmer could have written a book in defence of the 'true and catholic doctrine' of the sacrament was avoided by the simple expedient of changing the title of Cranmer's book.

A good deal of material follows about Cranmer's heresies, repeating what has already been said in the first section of the work summarised above. Cranmer is alleged to have been Lutheran until the First Prayer Book of 1549.

> The 1549 Prayer Book was devised to express Cranmer's heresies. The daily offices (which correspond to the breviary) eliminated the invocation of saints, and the collects referred only to the saints' examples, not to their prayers and merits. There were no intercessions for the souls in purgatory. The terms, 'host', 'oblation', and 'sacrifice', were excluded in

[22] OA 23–6.

[23] London 1550. Cranmer incorporated this work entire in his *Answer . . . unto A crafty and sophisticall cavillation devised by Stephen Gardiner . . .*, London 1551, which is most readily available in the first volume of the Parker Society edition of Cranmer's works.

> the eucharistic rite, but 'sacrifice of praise' was retained. Everything signifying the real and objective presence of Christ in the Eucharist was dropped, as were also the rubrics connected with the real presence: ablutions, elevation, joining of the celebrant's thumb and forefinger, etc. The celebrant was ordered to celebrate so that the people could hear his words and see his actions. This agreed exactly with the Zwinglian heresy, which holds that communion gives grace not *ex opere operato* but *ex opere operantis*, and that it is therefore important to stir up the people's faith by allowing them to see the representation of the Lord's death. Only communicants were permitted to remain for the canon. This new book was subscribed by all the bishops save Day of Chichester. Thirlby later protested that the subscription had not been free, and that the word 'oblation' had been removed after the bishops had signed. This First Prayer Book came into force on 15th January 1549, and Cranmer at once set about introducing a new Ordinal, retaining the three ancient orders, but divesting them of their catholic sense. He did not even believe that ordination was necessary at all, but kept it for the sake of seemliness.[24] Almost five-sixths of the Ordinal is taken from Bucer, the main difference being that Cranmer has different forms for the three Orders, where Bucer had only one.[25]

This was obviously a difference of no little theological significance, as it showed that the English reformers, in contrast to Bucer and the continental reformers in general, desired to retain the three-fold apostolic ministry of bishops, priests, and deacons.

The brief continues by stating that the Second Prayer Book of 1552 swept away even the few tenuous vestiges of catholic doctrine in the 1549 book, and that it is this very protestant Second Prayer Book which must be borne in mind, since it was restored with a few changes under Elizabeth. The most important of these changes, we are told, was a conflation of the words of administration in the First and Second Prayer Books, and the removal of the Black Rubric. As neither of these statements is explained, the reader without independent and exact knowledge of the history would never guess that both of these changes were of considerable theological importance, and that they were made in order to make it possible for those who believed in

[24] This statement now appears for the third time. [25] OA 27–31.

the real presence to accept the Second Prayer Book when it was restored under Elizabeth in 1559[25a].

> Altars were then ordered to be destroyed and tables were substituted for them. The Articles of Religion were also introduced, denying the catholic doctrine of the mass and ordering the extremely anti-catholic homilies to be publicly read in churches. 'These Articles, defiled with the aforesaid errors, were adopted by Queen Elizabeth and by the Anglican sectarians, and all Anglican bishops and ecclesiastics must subscribe them up to the present day.'[26]

This statement, as it stands, is false. The Articles issued in the closing weeks of Edward VI's reign were not adopted by Queen Elizabeth, as here claimed, but were in fact carefully revised, changes being made in a catholic direction in the hope that Roman Catholics in England would assent to them. In particular the previous condemnation of the phrase *ex opera operato* was withdrawn, as was the previous denial of the real presence.[27]

> The few bishops who resisted these changes, such as Gardiner and Bonner, were either imprisoned or removed from their sees.[28]
>
> When Edward VI died in the month of July 1553 the catholic faith was restored and the English Church was reconciled by Cardinal Pole, the Papal Legate, on 30th November 1554.

The fact, so embarrassing to English catholic apologists, that the restoration of catholicism was carried through by act of parliament and the Royal Supremacy prior to Pole's arrival in England, is passed over in silence.

> During Pole's legacy all heretical bishops were deprived, bishops consecrated with the Pontifical rite were restored after doing penance, '*but no bishop consecrated with the Ordinal was restored.*'[29] On the contrary, Taylor of Lincoln was deposed '*propter nullitatem consecrationis*'.[30]

[25a] cf. p. 11 above. [26] OA 33.

[27] For a history of the Articles of Religion and a detailed analysis of the changes made in Elizabeth's reign and later see E. J. Bicknell, *A Theological Introduction to the Thirty-Nine Articles of the Church of England* (ed. H. J. Carpenter), London 1950, 12–23.

[28] OA 31ff. [29] OA 34, emphasis in original.

[30] At the second meeting of the commission on 7th April Fr de Augustinis argued that *nullitas* in sixteenth-century canonical usage simply meant 'illicit', and that the terms of Taylor's deposition thus meant only that his orders had been given him by heretics. Cf. Gasquet's diary account cited by Leslie, *Cardinal Gasquet* 64.

> Pontifical priests were restored in their orders after doing penance, but up to now '*no single case could be found* of the recognition of orders conferred with the Ordinal'.[31] When clergy were deprived, enquiry was made as to how long ago the man had received orders, and if he had been ordained with the Pontifical rite he was first degraded from his orders before being deprived. The instructions brought back from Rome by Bishop Thirlby in *Praeclara carissimi* [21st June 1555] said that all those ordained by a bishop who was not himself ordained *rite et recte* were to receive their orders again. The Bull *Regimini* [30th October 1555] explained who had not been consecrated *in forma Ecclesiae*. Those ordained by such bishops had not received true orders, and must be ordained again.

The brief says nothing about the other statement in this Bull *Regimini* that *all* those ordained by properly consecrated bishops *had* received valid orders. Since the Bull omits any reference to the rite used by such a bishop in conferring orders, it implies that the criterion of validity was the credentials of the ordaining bishop, and not the rite which he used: if *he* was properly consecrated, then *all* those whom he had ordained, whether with the Pontifical or the Ordinal, had received valid orders.[32]

> After receiving this Bull, Cardinal Pole held a synod and declared that the form of Holy Orders was that contained in the Roman Pontifical. Hence the Orders were condemned both by the Holy See and by the Papal Legate, the ground for this condemnation being the insufficiency of the Ordinal form and not the 'Nag's Head Fable', which was not published for another fifty years.[33]

This description of Pole's action at the Lambeth Synod of 1555–56 is somewhat misleading. What the Legate actually did was to promulgate as the standard of sacramental doctrine the provisions of the Decree for the Armenians of Pope Eugene IV. This states that the essential form of the sacrament of orders is the words accompanying the tradition of the instruments. For the priesthood these words are:

[31] OA 34, emphasis in original.

[32] At the time of the Marian restoration there were a number of bishops in England themselves consecrated with the Pontifical who had conferred orders both with the Pontifical and Ordinal rites. cf p. 216f below.

[33] OA 34ff.

'Receive power to offer sacrifice in the Church for the living and the dead.'[34] In so far as the Anglican form of ordination was considered insufficient by Pole and his colleagues, their condemnation appears to have been based upon the failure of the Ordinal rite to contain these words or their equivalent. Since no ordination rite for more than a thousand years contained words of this kind, it is clear that a condemnation of the Anglican form based upon the omission of a feature not found anywhere until the Middle Ages would be equally fatal to Roman Catholic Orders.

> Shortly after Elizabeth's accession [in November 1558] she and her Council decided to revive the laws abolishing papal authority, which shows that the blame for the separation does not rest on the pope, as the Anglicans claim.

The later papal excommunication and deposition of the Queen and the liberation of Roman Catholics from their allegiance to her are passed over in silence. The brief again mentions that Elizabeth restored the Second Prayer Book, 'with a few changes', but these are not specified, nor does the reader learn that they were all in a catholic direction.

> Bishops and clergy resisted this return to protestantism, and all but one of the bishops were deprived. Elizabeth appointed Matthew Parker to be Archbishop of Canterbury, but the catholic bishops refused to consecrate him. The consecration was entrusted to schismatical or heretical bishops who had conformed under Henry or Edward, and who had now returned from their exile under Mary. Hodgkin is the only one of the four consecrators who is known to have received valid consecration. The substantial accuracy of the account of Parker's consecration given in the Lambeth register may be assumed. Parker is the sole source of the Anglican episcopate; for other consecrators, such as De Dominis,[35] did not repeat any part of the form with the consecrating bishop and were therefore not ministers of the sacrament. So that even if the assistant bishops in the Roman rite could be considered as co-consecrators, which we do

[34] Cf. *Reformatio Angliae ex Decretis Reginaldi Poli Cardinalis*, Rome 1562, fol. 9^{v}; English translation by Henry Raikes, *The Reform of England by the Decrees of Cardinal Pole*, Chester 1839, 19. For the *Decretum pro Armenis* incorporated by Pole in his decrees cf. DS 1310–28 (695–702).

[35] Cf. p. 25 above.

not admit, it is impossible to take this view of the role of the co-consecrators in the Anglican rite.[36]

Extensive arguments are then presented to show that the consecration of Barlow, Parker's chief consecrator, must be considered gravely doubtful. These arguments are expanded in Appendix IX, so that the work devotes four pages in all to a topic which Canon Moyes said in several *Tablet* articles afterwards was always considered by the commissioners to be a minor and very unimportant point.[37] This first part of the brief then concludes with a summary of the 'crime' (*facinus*) perpetrated by Cranmer and the other reformers. This material repeats what has already been said on this subject.

The heresies and motives of the reformers exclude even the slenderest and most remote analogy between the Ordinal and ancient Greek or oriental rites whose formal motive and structure are most plainly consistent with orthodox doctrine. Any vagueness in these rites may be attributed to their antiquity, whereas the vagueness of the Ordinal is due to the pertinacious and heretical denial of the priesthood and eucharistic sacrifice on the part of its compilers, and to their destruction of the old catholic rites. When we consider the grave doubt about Barlow's consecration, and the *silent* and secondary role given to the assistant bishops in the Anglican rite, it is impossible to be morally certain that any defect in Barlow was remedied by Hodgkin.[38]

This statement overlooks the fact that the role of Parker's co-consecrators was not silent, but that all four bishops repeated the essential form of consecration together while laying on hands.

Theological arguments

Having thus dealt with the history of the English reformation after the manner of the popular pamphleteer, the authors of

[36] OA 37ff. The use of the argument that the assistant bishops in the Roman rite could not be considered co-consecrators was somewhat disingenuous. A diary note in Gasquet's hand records that on 1st March 1895 he had been told in Rome of a decision of the Holy Office in the case of a consecration in Malta 'that all three bishops were *Episcopi consecrantes* and not merely *assistentes* to the principal consecrator, and so would make up for any defect' (GP).

[37] Cf. *The Tablet* 85 (1911), 47f, and 87 (1912), 801–4.

[38] OA 41ff.

Ordines Anglicani proceed in the second part of their work to deal with the theological issues in themselves. They first lay down certain general principles which they assert are fulfilled by all known forms of ordination, despite the great diversity of these forms in non-essential points.[39]

> Had the reformers, despite their bitter hostility to the catholic cause, used the Pontifical forms of ordination it would be impossible to question the material sufficiency of their rite. But they introduced new forms which neither signified Holy Orders nor made any distinction between them.

The Preface to the Ordinal, which has always been appealed to by Anglican apologists because of its clear statement that the new rites were issued 'to the intent that' the Orders of 'bishops, priests, and deacons' which had been in the church 'from the Apostles' time' might be 'continued, and reverently used, and esteemed, in this Church of England', is dismissed in the following terms:

> But although the Preface of the aforesaid Ordinal mentions deacons, presbyters, and bishops as orders of ministers which have existed in Christ's church from the apostles' time, it preserves a profound silence as to the nature and origin of these orders, so that the error of the Sacramentarians might be reconciled with this Preface.[40]

Turning to the Ordinal form for the priesthood, the brief states that the words accompanying the laying on of hands cannot be the essential form, since they are lacking in many rites, and are a late innovation.[41] And the words which follow, 'Be thou a faithful dispenser of the word of God and

[39] OA 44–7. This argument was greatly expanded in a separate *votum* by the authors of *Ordines Anglicani* which bears the date 5th May 1896: 'Brevis conspectus ritualium ordinationum in oriente et occidente adhibitorum quoad formam consecratoriam cum manuum impositione coniunctam.' In this work it was claimed that all known forms of ordination contained three essential features not found in the Edwardine Ordinal. The three criteria were unhappily chosen: the essential forms of the present Roman Pontifical as defined by Pius XII in 1947 fail to fulfil two of them.

[40] OA 48.

[41] The essential form for the priesthood in the Edwardine Ordinal was: 'Receive the Holy Ghost: whose sins thou dost forgive, they are forgiven: and whose sins thou dost retain, they are retained: and be thou a faithful dispenser of the word of God and of his holy sacraments. In the name of the Father and of the Son and of the Holy Ghost. Amen.'

of his holy sacraments', would be just as suitable for the other two orders as well.

> The form for the priesthood is thus wholly inadequate, and the fact that the Anglicans have improved it by the addition of the words, 'for the office and work of a priest in the Church of God, now committed unto thee by the imposition of our hands', shows that they themselves realised the insufficiency of the earlier form.[42]

This is the kind of argument which proves too much. The additions to the Roman rite of ordination through the centuries have been far more numerous than this single addition to the Anglican Ordinal. The authors of *Ordines Anglicani* would have had no difficulty in dealing with the argument that each of these additions to the Roman rite betrays an awareness that the rite in its previous form was insufficient. Moreover it is clear that the words in question were added to the Ordinal in 1662 because of controversy with the Puritans, who were trying to maintain that there was no difference between priests and bishops.[43]

The brief then states that the form for the episcopate is equally invalid.[44]

> Nowhere does it mention the *summum sacerdotium;* the words, 'Receive the Holy Ghost,' are a late innovation and thus cannot be the essential form; and the subsequent citation from 2 Timothy 1:6 refers to the grace of Orders already received and cannot be a form for conferring this grace. Moreover the form could just as well refer to ordination to the presbyterate: it contains nothing about episcopacy. It is thus clear that the Ordinal forms of ordination are 'new, unheard of, defective, and mutilated', that they differ substantially from the church's forms, and that the Holy See has rightly rejected them as wholly invalid.[45]

Having thus demonstrated what they call the material inadequacy of the Ordinal forms of ordination, the authors

[42] OA 49f.

[43] This point was dealt with by the Anglican archbishops in their Reply to the Bull in 1897; cf. AO(E) 45 and Gregory Dix, *The Question of Anglican Orders*, London ²1956, 65f.

[44] The form for the episcopate in the Edwardine Ordinal was: 'Take the Holy Ghost, and remember that thou stir up the grace of God, which is in thee, by imposition of hands: for God hath not given us the spirit of fear, but of power, and love, and of soberness.'

[45] OA 60.

go on to prove the formal invalidity of these forms: the meaning of the words, as seen from the public teachings of those who wrote them, is insufficient, and does not signify orders in the catholic sense. What follows is merely a repetition of what has already been said twice over about the doctrines and actions of Cranmer and his 'henchmen'.[46] Once again we are told that the Anglican Church has always acted upon these doctrines until the advent of the Ritualists or Anglo-Catholics in modern times.

> They have borrowed many doctrines and ceremonies from the Catholic Church and think that the Anglican Church is an integral part of the Catholic Church. They make tremendous efforts to prove that they have valid orders, leaving no stone unturned and producing the most far-fetched and subtle arguments in the hope of obtaining some sort of recognition from the Holy See. They urge all kinds of nonsensical arguments (*tricas omnigenas*) to try to cover up the heretical origins of their church—as if orders which were originally invalid could become valid merely by the passage of time.[47]

This section of the brief concludes by saying that it is easy to see that those who consecrated Parker used a form which was invalid both materially and formally, and that they did not intend to do what the church does.

> They denied not only certain *effects* of Holy Orders, but also that these orders were a sacrament or that they were in any way instituted by Christ; and they taught that orders consisted in an *external* calling and admission *only*.[48]

The Appendices

Almost three-quarters of the brief consists of supplementary evidence on specific questions in the form of three *scholia* and eleven appendices. Scholion I quotes several scholastic theologians to the effect that the laying on of hands and not the tradition of the instruments is the essential matter of ordination.[49] This was to rebut the criticism that Anglican

[46] OA 51ff.
[47] OA 54f.
[48] OA 55, emphasis in original.
[49] OA 55ff.

Orders had been rejected in the past merely because of the omission of the tradition of the instruments in the Ordinal. Nothing was said, however, about the corollary of this view, that the essential form consisted of the words *accompanying* the tradition of the instruments, in the case of the priesthood the words, 'Receive power to offer sacrifice for the living and the dead.' The charge that Anglican Orders had been rejected because these or equivalent words (which are not found in any rite till the Middle Ages) were lacking in the Ordinal is thus left unanswered. The charge is supported by a great deal of historical evidence.

Scholion II argues that the accessory parts of the rite cannot supply the necessary determination or signification to a vague and indefinite essential form which is inadequate in itself. Apologists for Anglican Orders were accustomed to answer the argument that the Ordinal forms could mean everything or nothing, and specifically that they did not identify the order being imparted, by saying that if one took the rite as a whole, including the rubrics, the title, and the Preface, there could be no doubt about which order was being conferred. In his book *Anglican Orders and Defect of Intention* Fr Francis Clark quotes the first part of this scholion.[50] He says nothing about the passage immediately following, which says that the defenders of Anglican Orders illustrate their argument by a reference to the sacrament of matrimony, in which catholic theologians admit that words and signs too indefinite in themselves to express the consent of the contracting parties can be given the necessary signification by reference to the whole context of the rite. The authors of *Ordines Anglicani* deny the legitimacy of this argument emphatically.

> We utterly deny the analogy between matrimony and the sacrament of Order.[51]

It was impossible for Fr Clark to quote this sentence, though it stands in immediate juxtaposition to the passage

[50] AODI 181 n. 1. [51] OA 58.

which he does cite; for it directly contradicts the central argument of his entire book, which is based upon an unsound theory of ministerial intention which assumes the very analogy here denied.[52] Clark's abrupt termination of his citation, and the omission of any reference to what immediately follows, is even more significant than might at first sight appear. For having carefully by-passed his predecessors' vigorous denial of any analogy between the sacraments of matrimony and orders, which would have made a shambles of his whole carefully constructed argument, Clark again adopts exactly the argument of this scholion as soon as it becomes safe for him to do so. The brief continues that even if the context of the rite *could* give the necessary signification to a vague and inadequate form, which the authors vigorously deny, the appeal to the whole context of the rite would be fatal to Anglican Orders. For the historical context shows that the very tenuous analogy between the words of the Ordinal and the catholic description of orders is wholly deceptive: in fact the reformers intended to *exclude* orders in the catholic sense. Readers familiar with Fr Clark's works will recall that this is precisely the argument used by him in Chapter IX of *Anglican Orders and Defect of Intention*, and in many places in *Eucharistic Sacrifice and the Reformation*.[53] Clark uses everything in this scholion except the categorical denial that there is any analogy between the sacraments of matrimony and order, concerning which, to adopt the language of *Ordines Anglicani* in a number of places, 'he maintains a profound silence'—*altum silentium tenet*.[54]

[52] For a brief preliminary discussion of this point cf. the articles cited on p. 47 n. 3 above.

[53] London and Westminster, Maryland, 1960.

[54] Scholion II also argues that the addition of a clause to the Preface to the Ordinal in 1662 shows that the Anglicans themselves realised that the Preface in its original form was inadequate. This argument parallels that dealt with on p. 136 above concerning the additions to the forms of ordination in 1662, and like that argument it would be fatal, if granted, to the rite of the Roman Pontifical, which has had far more things added to it than the Anglican Ordinal. The real reason for the addition made to the Preface in 1662 was the contemporary situation, and not the controversy with Rome over Anglican Orders. It was necessary to say that foreign

A 'Note A' follows listing sixteen features of the eucharistic rite of the First Prayer Book of 1549 which manifest the anti-sacrificial animus of its authors. The second part of this note lists the changes made in this rite in the Second Prayer Book of 1552 in order to destroy any vestiges of similarity with the old Latin mass which remained in the first book. The changes in a catholic direction made in 1559 are not mentioned, so that the reader with no independent knowledge of Anglican history is left with the impression that the 1552 Prayer Book contained the Anglican liturgy in its definitive form.

There follow eleven appendices. Appendix I argues that the work of liturgical reform in Edward VI's reign was entirely dominated by Cranmer and his 'most crafty associates' (*socii vaferrimi*),[55] and that others with more catholic views played a negligible role. There are four tables classifying bishops and other leading ecclesiastics of the time according to the categories: 'reformers', 'schismatics', and 'opportunists'. These tables as well as three similar ones in Appendix II show a detailed knowledge of English reformation history which is in marked contrast to the greatly oversimplified account of the same events and personalities given immediately following the close of the commission's sessions by Gasquet and Moyes in an Italian pamphlet printed for distribution to the pope and cardinals with whom the decision lay. In the latter work the complexities of English reformation history were completely disregarded. The story was told in black-and-white terms as a struggle between the good catholics and the bad protestants.[56] In each case arguments were used which seemed for the moment to be most sure of success.

clergy would be admitted to minister in the Church of England only if they had had episcopal ordination or consecration. Far from being evidence against the Orders, this is strong evidence for them, for it shows that the restoration Anglicans did not equate episcopal and non-episcopal ordination.

A Scholion III follows, arguing that a supposed decision of the Holy Office that the words 'Receive the Holy Spirit' in the Abyssinian rite of ordination cannot be cited in favour of the Anglican rite.

[55] OA 70.

[56] Cf. pp. 169–78 below.

Appendix II illustrates the theological opinions of over seventeen English reformers by means of brief, carefully selected quotations from their writings.[57] These quotations were not placed in the context of their authors' whole thought, nor seen against the background of the eucharistic theology and the practical mass system familiar to the reformers. The result was inevitably to subject the aged Pope Leo XIII and the Roman cardinals, for whom these pages were written, to a theological chamber of horrors, and so prejudice them gravely against the Anglican case.

An Appendix III sets out the eucharistic rites of the Sarum Missal and the First and Second Prayer Books in parallel columns, and draws attention to indications of heretical intent, either by omission of catholic features or inclusion of protestant ones. The material presented is selective, with a view to putting the Anglican rites in as bad a light as possible. Thus whereas the rubrics of the Sarum Missal are given in full, the 1549 rubrics ordering certain manual actions in the canon, and the two crosses at the words 'bless and sanctify these thy gifts and creatures of bread and wine', are omitted, thus making the contrast between the rites of Sarum and 1549 appear greater than it actually is. Crosses are printed in the Sarum rite wherever they occur. On the other hand, the 1549 rubric forbidding the elevation of the consecrated elements *is* printed, because it strengthens the impression the authors are trying to create. The so-called Black Rubric, illegally inserted at the last minute into the 1552 Prayer Book and saying that the kneeling at the reception of communion does not imply any adoration, is printed in full, and the altered version of this rubric inserted in 1662 is given in a footnote.[58] Nowhere does the reader learn that the Black Rubric was suppressed entirely from 1559 to 1662; and only the most careful reading of the footnote reveals that the rubric in its 1662 form is so worded as not to exclude the catholic doctrine of the eucharistic presence.

[57] OA 71–86. [58] OA 112.

Appendix IV sets out in parallel columns the forms for Holy Orders in the Sarum Pontifical and in the Ordinal. Nothing is said about the fact that the first Ordinal in use from 1550 to 1552 (with which five of the six Edwardine bishops were consecrated) contained a tradition of instruments. Appendix V attacks the argument that the English reformers did not deny the catholic doctrine of eucharistic sacrifice, but only popular superstitions and perversions of the truth. The arguments closely parallel those used by Fr Clark in *Eucharistic Sacrifice and the Reformation*, save that nothing at all is said about the existence of popular errors and superstitions.[59] By the time Clark's book appeared in 1960 it was no longer possible to ignore the existence of superstitious aberrations in medieval religious life. Clark discusses medieval errors, but dismisses them as unimportant.[60]

Appendix V criticises the argument that the English reformers did not intend to deny the true doctrine of eucharistic sacrifice, but only perversions of this doctrine. The material in this appendix has been laid under contribution by Fr Clark in *Eucharistic Sacrifice and the Reformation*. One statement in this appendix is especially worthy of note. Cranmer and his associates, we are told, 'asserted over and over again that Christ had never given anyone the power to offer him'.[61] As a statement of historical fact this is unexceptionable, for the rejection of any idea that in the mass Christ is 'offered by the priest to the Father' was one of the fundamental principles of the reformers' doctrine. Where the authors of *Ordines Anglicani* were in error was in supposing that such a rejection is necessarily incompatible with catholic dogma.

An Appendix VI discusses the treatment of clergy who were deprived during the Marian restoration. Cases are cited of clergy who had been ordained with the Pontifical rite being degraded from their orders before deprivation,

[59] OA 160–72. [60] Cf. ESR Chapter 4. [61] OA 163.

whereas the orders of Ordinal clergy were simply disregarded. It is asserted that Ferrar, who was consecrated Bishop of St David's on 9th September 1548, was consecrated with the Ordinal,[62] though this rite was not authorised until 1550.[63] This unqualified assertion should be contrasted with Moyes' more cautious statement of the case in a *Tablet* article in September 1895 (at the very time he was engaged in preparing *Ordines Anglicani* with his colleagues), that 'the consecration of Ferrar was carried out with some modifications of the Catholic Pontifical, made in the direction of the coming changes'.[64] If the English commissioners thought that on such a minor point the caution necessary in England could be dispensed with in a confidential document written for foreigners, they were to receive a rude awakening. For at the fourth meeting of the commission on 11th April 1896 Duchesne challenged the statement about Ferrar's consecration in the English brief, and was satisfied that he had established that Ferrar had been consecrated with the Pontifical rite.[65]

Of greater significance is the less than frank statement of this appendix about John Scory, the Edwardine Bishop of Chichester. We are told simply that he was 'deprived, did penance, and fled the realm'.[66] Nothing at all was said about a document in the register of Edmund Bonner, Marian Bishop of London, restoring 'our well-beloved brother, John, lately bishop of Chichester' to the 'public exercise of his ecclesiastical ministry and his pastoral office'.[67] Messenger has since argued that this document does not refer to Scory at all, and that 'John . . . of Chichester' is a copyist's error for 'John of Chester'. This would mean that the document is actually the rehabilitation of John Bird, who had been consecrated by the Pontifical rite in the reign

[62] OA 174.
[63] For further discussion of Ferrar's consecration and its significance for the controversy over Anglican Orders cf pp. 266–8 below.
[64] *The Tablet* 54 (1895), 459 col. 2 note.
[65] Cf. Lacey, *Roman Diary* 33.
[66] OA 174.
[67] Burnet-Pocock v, 389f.

of Henry VIII.[68] But in 1896 everyone assumed that it *was* Scory whom Bonner had rehabilitated, and that in so doing he had recognised the validity of Scory's Ordinal consecration. The case had long been a serious embarrassment to Roman Catholic apologists, who had resorted to special pleading of various kinds to get round it. Canon Moyes had devoted an entire article to this subject in *The Tablet*. He concluded that Bonner had in fact rehabilitated Scory, but that he had acted quite illegally in so doing; his action was purely personal, and thus could not compromise either the pope or his legate, Cardinal Pole.

> This act of Bonner's seems almost ludicrously *ultra vires*. A simple bishop has no power to rehabilitate an excommunicated fellow bishop who happens to live in his diocese than he has to involve him in excommunication. . . . That Bonner perpetrated the eccentricity of such an absolution, his Register bears witness. That he did so in the teeth of all Canon Law, past, present, and future, is equally evident. But then he was Bishop Bonner.[69]

This article appeared on 2nd November 1895, at the very time when Moyes was engaged with his colleagues in the preparation of *Ordines Anglicani*. In Appendix VI of the latter document the supposed rehabilitation of Scory, so damaging for the Roman Catholic claim that Edwardine Orders were consistently disregarded during the Marian restoration, was passed over in complete silence.

An Appendix VII discusses at great length the 'true opinion' concerning Anglican Orders of the seventeenth-century Franciscan convert from Anglicanism Christopher Davenport (known in religion as Francis a Sancta Clara), whose eirenic treatment of Anglicanism has been an embarrassment for successive generations of Roman Catholic polemicists in England.[70] The arguments in this appendix have been utilised by Fr Clark in his own discussion of Davenport's work in *Anglican Orders and Defect of Intention*.[71] Appendix VIII argues that an opinion of de Lugo

[68] Cf. RMP ii, 68–72.
[69] *The Tablet* 54 (1895), 702 col. 2.
[70] OA 182–91.
[71] Cf. AODI 92–7.

about the moral unity of all elements in the rites of ordination cannot be appealed to in support of the sufficiency of the Ordinal rite.[72] Appendix IX deals once again with the doubts concerning the consecration of Barlow, Parker's chief consecrator.[73] And the last two appendices present evidence of the irreverent treatment of the consecrated eucharistic elements by some Anglican clergy, and of the failure of a few clergy to follow the Anglican baptismal rubrics which could mean that now and then a man may have been ordained in the Anglican Church whose baptism was invalid. Both these arguments had been used by Newman three decades previously, and had been devastatingly refuted by a fellow clerical convert of his (probably Oxenham), who pointed out that they could just as easily be turned against Roman Catholic Orders, and that people in glass houses should not throw stones.[74]

Evaluation

This case against the Orders was exceedingly thorough and thoroughly partisan. It did not pretend to be anything else. The document was a lawyer's brief for his client, and nothing more. There would have been nothing illegitimate in this if full opportunity had been given for the presentation of the Anglican case by experts equally familiar with the details of English reformation history. In this way the matter could really have been argued out with some prospect of arriving at a true and fair judgement. This was not done. For despite the presence in the commission of members favourable in varying degrees to the Anglican case, they were, as we have already seen, largely unfamiliar with the history of the English reformation, and thus no equals for their English opponents. The very fact that the English *votum* was by far

[72] OA 191ff. [73] OA 194f.

[74] Cf. the present author's 'Two English Cardinals on Anglican Orders', JES 4 (1967), 1–26.

the longest of those submitted to the commission shows how unequally matched the two sides were, and how much better prepared the three English commissioners were than any of their colleagues. De Llaveneras, to whom the pope had shown the English *votum* before the commission met, told Gasquet that in his opinion 'it is unanswerable and the best votum he has ever set eyes on.'[75] This is frequently the impression given by a skilfully drawn up lawyer's brief. Such an impression can, however, be changed by an equally telling statement of the case from the opposite side. The manner in which the investigation was conducted prevented any such statement of the Anglican case being presented. Inevitably the result was unsatisfying.

One of those who foresaw this result was Dom Cuthbert Butler, the future Abbot of Downside, who wrote in February 1895 to Edmund Bishop, then in Rome with Gasquet gathering material against the Orders and helping to write the papal letter *Ad Anglos*:

> I do hope nothing will be decided until the Anglicans have been given a full opportunity of presenting their own case themselves. A decision in which one of the parties has not been heard for himself will never be satisfactory. I should like a commission to be appointed to sit in England wherein three Catholics could confer and discuss the question with three Anglicans, and then each side send in a report to Rome.[76]

In the storm of indignation in England following the condemnation of the Orders there was naturally a good deal of criticism of the fact that Anglicans had not been represented on the commission. Canon Moyes undertook to reply to this objection in *The Tablet*. He argued that the two Anglican clergymen sent to Rome had in fact had every facility to present arguments to the commission through their friends who were members of it, and said they had made full use of this opportunity. He did not mention, however, that Lacey and Puller could hardly know what arguments would be most effective, since they were largely in the dark as to

[75] Cf. p. 114 above. [76] BP.

what the other side was saying. Moyes concluded patronisingly:

> Personally we doubt whether the Anglican Community could have found . . . any exponents more able or qualified for the presentment and handling of their case than those members of the Commission upon whom they relied for its advocacy. These Catholics were not only eloquent and earnest, but possessed that expert knowledge of theology and Canon Law which enabled them to give every argument its most accurate and effective presentment and application, unmarred by misconception of Catholic principles, and by non-Catholic obliquity.[77]

At the time, however, Gasquet recorded that he and his colleagues had a rather different opinion of the eloquence and earnestness of their opponents, and of their expert knowledge of theology and canon law. After the eighth session of the commission on 25th April Gasquet wrote in his diary:

> On the way home we asked ourselves, Was it possible that what we had so far heard was all that had to be said? Have these Frenchmen, acting on behalf of the Anglicans, nothing more to say than has been so far brought up and discussed at our eight meetings?[78]

Moyes was never noted for his consistency, and just for good measure he supplied in *The Tablet* article cited above an additional reason for the exclusion of the Anglicans from the commission's deliberations.

> The Anglican clergymen who came to Rome had nothing which could be called a mandate to speak in the name of the Church of England, nor were they officially commissioned by the Anglican authorities. They could have no claim to be treated as representatives.[79]

Moyes did not reveal, nor could he have revealed, that it was himself and his two colleagues who had insisted on the exclusion of any Anglican representatives. A full year before the commission met, Gasquet made it clear in conversation with Portal and Halifax in Rome that he was determined to exclude Anglicans from any investigation of their orders.

[77] *The Tablet* 57 (1897), 246 col. 1. [78] Gasquet, *Leaves from My Diary* 59.
[79] Art. cit. in n. 77 above, 245 col. 2.

> The group around Gasquet was manoeuvring at that time [Portal wrote later] to obtain a radical condemnation, and second to prevent mixed conferences. When I met him Gasquet was not yet certain that they would win on this last point. He said to me: 'If necessary we shall go to these conferences, but in our opinion the question of the Orders is a domestic question, and concerns us Catholics alone.'[80]

To anyone familiar with the details of the controversy over Anglican Orders it is obvious, reading the arguments of Moyes, Gasquet, and Fleming in *Ordines Anglicani*, why it was essential for them to exclude Anglican theologians from participation in the investigation. Had they been present they could have driven a coach and four through the 'enormous memorandum' presented to the commission by Cardinal Vaughan's three representatives.

[80] Letter of Portal to Halifax, 17th October 1911, HP A4.213. Halifax confirms this remark in *Leo XIII* 285 n. 1. Portal's letter clarifies a statement in Mr Nigel Abercrombie's biography of Edmund Bishop: 'With the Abbé Portal [Bishop] and Gasquet, together and separately, wrestled for the same object of restraining Lord Halifax and company, and to aim at conferences in plain English between the Catholics and Anglicans as a more practical step towards "reunion" than what was contemplated' (op. cit. 214). Conferences in plain English between qualified representatives of the two sides were precisely what Halifax and Portal desired. Mr Abercrombie has been kind enough to explain that theological conferences 'were nothing to do with Edmund Bishop or Gasquet, who were not theologians'. They were interested in non-theological conferences for purely practical aims. This clarification, for which I am grateful, is based upon Mr Abercrombie's unique knowledge of the huge deposit of papers left by Edmund Bishop. It confirms the statements of Portal and Halifax that Gasquet and Bishop were working to prevent mixed theological conferences.

8

THE COMMISSION AT WORK

Nothing here seems to be more difficult than to get on with anything, and the Holy Office has successfully resisted all efforts; the only known case was of a German who for historical purposes wanted to see certain definite documents but was only allowed to do so on the condition that Cardinal Franzelin accompanied him and stood over him whilst he looked at the particular volume.

—Edmund Bishop[1]

It is quite impossible to get at the archives of the Holy Office. One might as well ask to see Rothschild's books.

—T. A. Lacey[2]

The function of the commission was to investigate the existing practice of treating Anglican Orders as null and void, and to say whether there were any compelling reasons for a change of policy. The commission was to report its finding to the Holy Office, of which the pope himself is prefect. It was at this level, and not in the commission, that the power of decision lay. The commissioners laboured under an oath of secrecy. The records of the commission's meetings are in the archives of the former Holy Office, now the Congregation for the Doctrine of the Faith. These papers are still secret more than seventy years after the events which they record and a good three decades after the death of the last of the participants. All those who have attempted to obtain access to these important documents testify to the extreme sensitivity of curial officials whenever they are mentioned. My own request for permission to study these papers, which was supported by leading members of the hierarchy in Germany and England, including two cardinals, one of them himself a member of the Holy Office, was not granted. It is still impossible, therefore, to give anything like a complete report of the commission's work, and the investigator

[1] Diary note, 12th February 1895, GP.
[2] Letter to the Revd E. G. Wood, 24th May 1896: Lacey, *Roman Diary* 129.

must piece together partial disclosures and veiled references in the published and unpublished writings of the participants and those with whom they spoke or corresponded about their work.

The available sources of information

The oath of secrecy imposed upon the commissioners was modified by the permission granted by Cardinal Rampolla to Gasparri and Duchesne to communicate with Puller and Lacey and to ask them for information.[3] Fifteen years later the Abbé Portal, who, though not on the commission, was in Rome during its sessions and in close contact with Gasparri and Duchesne, explained the scope of this permission to Lord Halifax.

> Cardinal Rampolla did not release them from the *secretum pontificium*, and I do not believe that either Gasparri or Duchesne broke it.[4] But it was possible to conclude with fair accuracy from their questions and requests for information what was going on within the Commission. The English party—since this is the language adopted—would have liked to prevent any relations at all. They wanted you to be treated *as if you did not exist*.[5]

The publication of Lacey's *Roman Diary* in 1910 was the first breach in the wall of secrecy which had surrounded the

[3] Lacey wrote in his diary at the time: 'Apr. 15th 1896: Gasparri has seen Cardinal Rampolla, spoken about us, and obtained permission to show us anything and consult us. Apparently some one had been objecting' (*Roman Diary* 35). And Portal wrote to Halifax on 15th January 1911: 'Gasparri and Duchesne were formally authorised by Cardinal Rampolla to communicate with Puller and Lacey and to ask them for information. Their requests for information were necessarily connected with the work of the Commission' (HP A4.213).

[4] Remarks in Lacey's diary lend support to this statement. Cf. the entry for 6th May, reporting a conversation with Duchesne: 'About Mazzella his mouth is shut. He had learnt what he knows in the Commission, and so can say nothing' (*Roman Diary* 59f). Cf. also the following, referring to a telegram received from England regarding the supposed discovery of new documents showing that Barlow had received episcopal consecration: 'Apr. 30: In the morning Gasparri came. We could get nothing out of him about the effect of the telegram at the meeting of the Commission yesterday' (*Roman Diary* 51). Baron von Hügel wrote to the Abbé Loisy on Palm Sunday 1896 that he had seen Duchesne the afternoon of the commission's first meeting (the previous Tuesday, 24th March) and that the Abbé was full of Anglican Orders and would talk of nothing else, but that he could not say anything of interest on the subject because of the Pontifical secret (cf. A. Loisy, *Mémoires* i, 398f).

[5] Letter of 12th March 1911, HP A4.213. Emphasis in original.

commission's work. Lacey's information was incomplete, and he sometimes drew false conclusions from what he heard. But many of his revelations were embarrassing nevertheless to those who had acted for Cardinal Vaughan. Vigorous attempts were made in the columns of *The Tablet* to discredit Lacey,[6] but it was felt that something more was needed.

> It seems imperative [*The Tablet* wrote] that an answer to this exposition of the case should be forthcoming from the Catholic side. Is it possible for one and all of Cardinal Vaughan's representatives and delegates to obtain the needful permission for their lips to be unsealed? Nothing short of this can satisfy our just curiosity, and our right to be in possession of such facts as may enable us to arrive at the truth.[7]

This proved in the event not to be possible. But within a few months of the appearance of Lacey's book, Dom Gasquet, by this time Abbot President of the English Benedictine Congregation, entered the lists with his *Leaves from My Diary*. We have already seen that this was not what it purported to be, but that it was carefully composed to meet the controversial requirements of the hour. Both Gasquet and *The Tablet* implied that whereas the English commissioners had adhered strictly to the oath of secrecy, it had been flagrantly broken by Duchesne and Gasparri. The available evidence does not support this charge. Both sides appear to have interpreted the obligation of secrecy somewhat loosely. The English commissioners communicated the contents of Fr de Augustinis' *votum* to Cardinal Vaughan, who disclosed in a speech at St Joseph's College, Mill Hill, that de Augustinis had pronounced in favour of validity.[8] Vaughan's representatives might have justified their action in this case by claiming that the obligation of secrecy applied only to what was said at the commission's meetings, and not to *vota* submitted by its members. But

[6] Cf. *The Tablet* 84 (1910), 1014ff, 1056f; 85 (1911), 47ff, 87ff, 163ff, 287f.
[7] *The Tablet* 84 (1910), 1057 col. 1.
[8] Cf. *Leo XIII* 284 and Lacey's report of the impression made at Rome by the news of Vaughan's indiscretion, *Roman Diary* 99f.

on the other hand they had no permission to consult with outsiders, whereas Gasparri and Duchesne had been granted this permission by the Secretary of State. On the whole the oath of secrecy was well kept. This is shown by the fact that our knowledge of the commission's work remains fragmentary and uncertain.[9]

Apart from the diary notes published by Lacey and Gasquet there are a few small revelations in *The Tablet* articles referred to in this chapter. Additional diary notes published by Gasquet's biographer, Sir Shane Leslie,[10] add further details, as do fragmentary scribbled notes taken by Canon Moyes during the meetings.[11] Portal's letters to Lord Halifax are, like Lacey's diary, a secondary source of information. The account of the commission's meetings given by Messenger[12] appears to be based on the published sources already mentioned, though in view of Messenger's chaotic documentation this must remain conjecture. Some of the details reported by Messenger conflict with the evidence of the original sources to which he refers—an example of the carelessness evident throughout his work. Finally, there are the important letters from Merry del Val which will be cited below.

[9] During the meetings of the commission Portal, who was in Rome and in close daily contact with Duchesne and Gasparri, wrote frequently and sometimes daily to Lord Halifax. Copies of these letters are preserved in the Portal Papers (the originals cannot be found amongst the Hickleton Papers). Portal appears to have passed on to Halifax as much information as he was able to obtain. The fact that these letters shed no light on the commission's deliberations is strong evidence that Duchesne and Gasparri were close-mouthed. The closest that Portal comes to reporting anything substantial about the commission's work is in a letter he wrote to Halifax on 10th April 1896, in which he says: 'The Commission has resumed its meetings. It meets three times in the week. D. Gasquet says nothing. David [Fleming] thinks after he speaks. Moyes plays the role of the orator and theologian, he is surly and angry. Duchesne has the impression that they are not always in good faith. He took issue with Canon Moyes on this point coming out of the Commission the other day and said some rather hard things. P. de Augustinis and Mgr Gasparri conduct themselves well and fight like true scholastic theologians, in good Latin and in good form' (cf. also the letter cited on p. 166f n. 65 below).

[10] The original notes from which Sir Shane quotes could not be found amongst the Gasquet Papers at Downside despite lengthy searches.

[11] Preserved amongst Moyes' papers in the archives of the Archdiocese of Westminster, and consulted by kind permission of Cardinal Heenan. These notes, obviously scribbled during the commission's meetings, are in part illegible.

[12] Cf. RMP ii, 555ff.

The commission's meetings

Reference has already been made to the commission's first meeting on 24th March at which procedural matters were dealt with, and Cardinal Mazzella ruled that Anglican representatives could not be admitted.[13] The commission began its deliberations at the second meeting on Easter Tuesday, 7th April, when Scannell and de Llevaneras were present for the first time. Mgr Gasparri spoke at considerable length on the meaning of the disputed Bull and Brief of Pope Paul IV about Anglican Orders in 1555. These documents are complicated and their interpretation obscure. As a canonist, Gasparri was uniquely qualified to voice an opinion about them. He had already written in the *Revue Anglo-Romaine* that these papal documents of the Marian period were more favourable to Anglican Orders than the reverse.[14] The length of Gasparri's remarks in this meeting moved Gasquet to complain in his diary that the investigation would take years if pursued in this manner.[15] De Augustinis supported Gasparri's position and argued that the use of the term *nullitas* in documents of this period meant nothing more than 'illicit': the documents said that Anglican Orders had been given by heretics, but not necessarily that they were invalid.[16]

The third meeting of the commission followed two days later, on Thursday 9th April, the day on which Lacey and Puller reached Rome.[17] This meeting continued the discussion of the Bull and Brief of Paul IV.[18] The three English commissioners distributed their reply to the *votum* submitted by de Augustinis.[19] Canon Moyes noted that the tone of this meeting was 'better', implying that the tone of the previous one had left something to be desired.

The commission met for the fourth time at 10 a.m.[20] on

[13] Cf. p. 113f above.
[14] Cf. pp. 263ff below.
[15] Leslie, *Cardinal Gasquet* 64.
[16] Ibid.
[17] Cf. *Roman Diary* 30.
[18] Gasquet, *Leaves* 52.
[19] Cf. Moyes' letter to Cardinal Vaughan, *The Tablet* 137 (1937), 152 col. 2.
[20] Moyes' note, Westminster Archives (WAr).

Saturday morning, 11th April. There was a considerable argument as to whether Ferrar, Edward VI's Bishop of St David's, had been consecrated in 1548 with the Pontifical rite or not. Duchesne insisted that he had been; Cardinal Vaughan's representatives asserted that essential changes in the rite had been introduced, and that it was for this reason that, at his trial for heresy under Mary, Ferrar had been degraded from his priestly order but not from the episcopate before being condemned. In Appendix VI of their *votum* the three English commissioners had stated that Ferrar was consecrated by the Ordinal, although this did not appear until eighteen months after Ferrar's consecration.[21] Moyes' notes record that the discussion moved on from Ferrar to the cases of 1684 and 1704.[22] He and his colleagues insisted against opposition from other members of the commission that Anglican Orders had been formally condemned by the Holy See on both occasions. Moyes found the French attitude towards the decisions of the Holy See 'carping', and Gasquet complained that 'the French people have no respect at all to the decisions of the Holy See and freely reject and criticise.'[23]

The fifth meeting took place two days later, on Monday 13th April. The discussion returned to the treatment of Anglican Orders during the catholic restoration under Queen Mary (1553–58). Gasquet complained in the published version of his diary:

> A good deal of time wasted by an attack upon us led by Mgr Gasparri. Cardinal Mazzella tried several times to put a stop to this which he had really invoked . . . Duchesne was about as captious and nasty as it was possible.[24]

Moyes records the reason for this attack: 'for using Cardinal Pole's Acts and Synods in proof of the idea of *forma ecclesiae*'. These documents said that the essential form of

[21] Cf. Lacey, *Roman Diary* 33, confirmed by Moyes' notes. For the significance of this point cf p. 266f below.
[22] Cf. Chapter 13 below.
[23] Leslie, *Cardinal Gasquet* 64.
[24] Gasquet, *Leaves* 53.

ordination to the priesthood was the words accompanying the delivery of chalice and paten to the ordinand: 'Receive power to offer sacrifice in the church for the living and the dead.'[25] We have already noted that these words were a medieval innovation so that they cannot be considered a *sine qua non* for valid ordination. Cardinal Mazzella asked the commissioners to say at the next meeting whether there was any *gravissima ratio* to change the existing practice of treating Anglican Orders as null and void.[26] This was in line with Mazzella's policy of insisting that the question be considered solely from the point of view of the existing practice of the Holy See.[27]

The answers to Cardinal Mazzella's question were read at the sixth meeting on Saturday 18th April, which Gasquet tells us lasted from 10 a.m. to 1 p.m.[28] Nothing further is known about this meeting. The next day Gasquet wrote to Edmund Bishop back in England:

> Our difficulty, entre nous, has been the having to deal with a set of men who haven't in the least any idea of the circumstances of the time or of the state of things in England, added to a firm belief that we are all a set of ignorant fools who can't be trusted to give a fair account of anything and that at the same time every word men like Puller, Denny and Lacey write and say must a priori be true. It really has made me sick to sit opposite Duchesne and see the kind of thing he calls *criticism.* After my experience here I feel sure neither Moyes, David nor self will ever believe a single thing that Duchesne thinks fit to assert. This between ourselves of course. Still I am quite satisfied we have stood our ground I think well on the *Historical* part, which closed yesterday. I am more than satisfied and so I know is Cardinal Mazzella.[29]

Gasquet's closing remark indicates that he and his colleagues were working in close co-operation with the commission's president, an impression which is confirmed by a

[25] This point has been briefly discussed on pp. 132ff and 138 above.
[26] Gasquet, *Leaves* 53. [27] Cf. pp. 165ff below.
[28] Cf. Gasquet, *Leaves* 55.
[29] Letter of 19th April 1896, BP. On 26th April Gasquet wrote to Bishop: 'I am perfectly convinced that Duchesne is an absolute charlatan and hope that you will get ahead with your work on Liturgy and prick that inflated humbug once for all' (ibid.).

letter from Merry del Val to be cited below. That Gasquet mentions only two of his three English colleagues indicates that Scannell was taking an independent line in the commission.

The seventh meeting was scheduled for the following Monday, but was postponed until Tuesday 21st April.[30] Gasquet's remark in his letter of the 19th to Bishop that the historical part of the investigation was ended proved to be an error, for a good part of this meeting was devoted to a discussion of the evidence for and against Barlow's consecration.[31] Gasquet noted that the question of co-consecrators was also treated, which indicates that it was pointed out that even if Barlow had not been consecrated, the co-consecrators of Parker would have made good the defect. This would have led naturally to a discussion of the role of the assistant bishops at an episcopal consecration. We have seen that in their *votum* Cardinal Vaughan's representatives had refused to admit that the assistant bishops were true consecrators, despite the fact that Gasquet had been informed in Rome in 1895 that they were so treated in practice by the Holy Office.[32]

The discussion about Barlow was continued at the eighth meeting of the commission on Saturday 25th April, which Gasquet reports lasted from 10 a.m. until 12.15 p.m.:

> For most of the first hour the discussion on the Barlow case was renewed. After that the whole of the session was devoted to the question of the Form *in se*, and the arguments were not finished when we had to rise. Fr David has to take his turn at the next session.[33]

Moyes noted that the discussion of the form was initiated by Gasparri, who as a monsignor was the most senior member of the commission and always spoke first.[34] According to Moyes' notes, Gasparri said that the prayer following the

[30] Cf. Gasquet, *Leaves* 55.
[31] Cf. Gasquet, *Leaves* 55, and Leslie, *Cardinal Gasquet* 64. Moyes notes: 'All about Barlow' (WAr).
[32] Cf. Chapter 7, n. 36, above.
[33] Gasquet, *Leaves* 58.
[34] Cf. also Lacey, *Roman Diary* 54f.

litany in the Ordinal was morally united with the rest of the rite. This indicates that Gasparri had accepted the argument of Cardinal Vaughan's representatives that the words accompanying the laying on of hands in the Ordinal could not be the essential form because they were 'not a prayer', and that he was seeking the essential form in another part of the rite. This argument that the essential form must be a prayer was a red herring introduced into the discussion unnecessarily. It created a host of additional difficulties.

The discussion of the form was continued at the ninth meeting on Wednesday 29th April, 'Fr David [Fleming] leading off as arranged'.[35] Lacey's diary entry for the following day records a visit from Gasparri, who continued to argue on the assumption that the essential form of the Ordinal must be sought in one of the prayers, and not in the words accompanying the laying on of hands. Gasparri contended that the Ordinal prayers were sufficient as ordination forms, and that they were morally united with the laying on of hands, so that the rite as such was valid.[36] Thus to interpret the Ordinal according to principles foreign to its structure was a needless complication of the argument.

An undated letter from the commission secretary, Merry del Val, which appears to have been written on 1st May, shows the close and cordial co-operation between Cardinal Vaughan's representatives and the president and secretary of the commission.

Friday night

My dear Canon Moyes,

I was with Card: Mazzella this evening and he bids me make a suggestion for tomorrow's discussion, in case by any chance the point should escape your attention. It is that when you come to show the various omissions 'ex industria' which of course are most important and furnish a powerful argument, you should proceed to point out also how even in those portions of the old Pontifical which are retained in the Ordinal, changes have been made with heretical intent. This would destroy once more and very forcibly any attempt at pretending that the only aim of the

[35] Gasquet, *Leaves* 61.

[36] Lacey, *Roman Diary* 51f.

Reformers was to abolish those portions of the old Pontifical which may be considered as additions and developments of the *primitive* rite. Si opus fuerit! For indeed it is too foolish.

The Cardinal is very pleased with the way in which the 'Accipe Sp.Sm' and the 'Memento ut resuscites *gratiam*', were disposed of last time.

Yours devotedly in Xt
Raph Merry del Val[37]

The tenth meeting was held on Saturday 2nd May. Cardinal Mazzella's suggestion, if followed, seems not to have met with the anticipated success. Gasquet wrote in his diary:

Gasparri held that *formaliter consideratus* the Anglican rite was quite susceptible of a Catholic interpretation and that there was nothing on this side to make Orders received invalid! Duchesne believed that the *Preface* made it quite clear that the authors intended to perpetuate Orders in the Catholic sense! On the whole it was the most painful meeting we have had. It was impossible to believe that four Catholic priests could have calmly accepted full-blown Protestantism as they did today. Mazzella spoke with great emotion and evidently from Gasparri's attitude afterwards the speech created consternation.[38]

Gasquet's mention of 'four Catholic priests . . . calmly accepting full-blown Protestantism' is significant. Moyes' notes record that de Llevaneras condemned the Ordinal form at this meeting, so he cannot have been one of the four. This means that Fr Scannell sided with Duchesne, Gasparri, and de Augustinis.[39] This disposes of the oft-repeated claim that the only people favourable to Anglican Orders in 1896 were continental theologians unacquainted either with Anglicanism or the history of the English reformation.[40] Moyes recorded that Duchesne contended the Ordinal rite had probably been used by bishops who were quite catholic in intention, and that the Preface to the Ordinal showed that the rite was intended to convey catholic orders. De Augustinis accepted the rite as 'quite Catholic, and [he] would be glad

[37] GP. [38] Leslie, *Cardinal Gasquet* 64f.

[39] This is confirmed by Moyes' notes on this meeting, which indicate that Scannell's opinion of the rite was favourable (WAr).

[40] Cf. the letter of Merry del Val reproduced pp. 164f below.

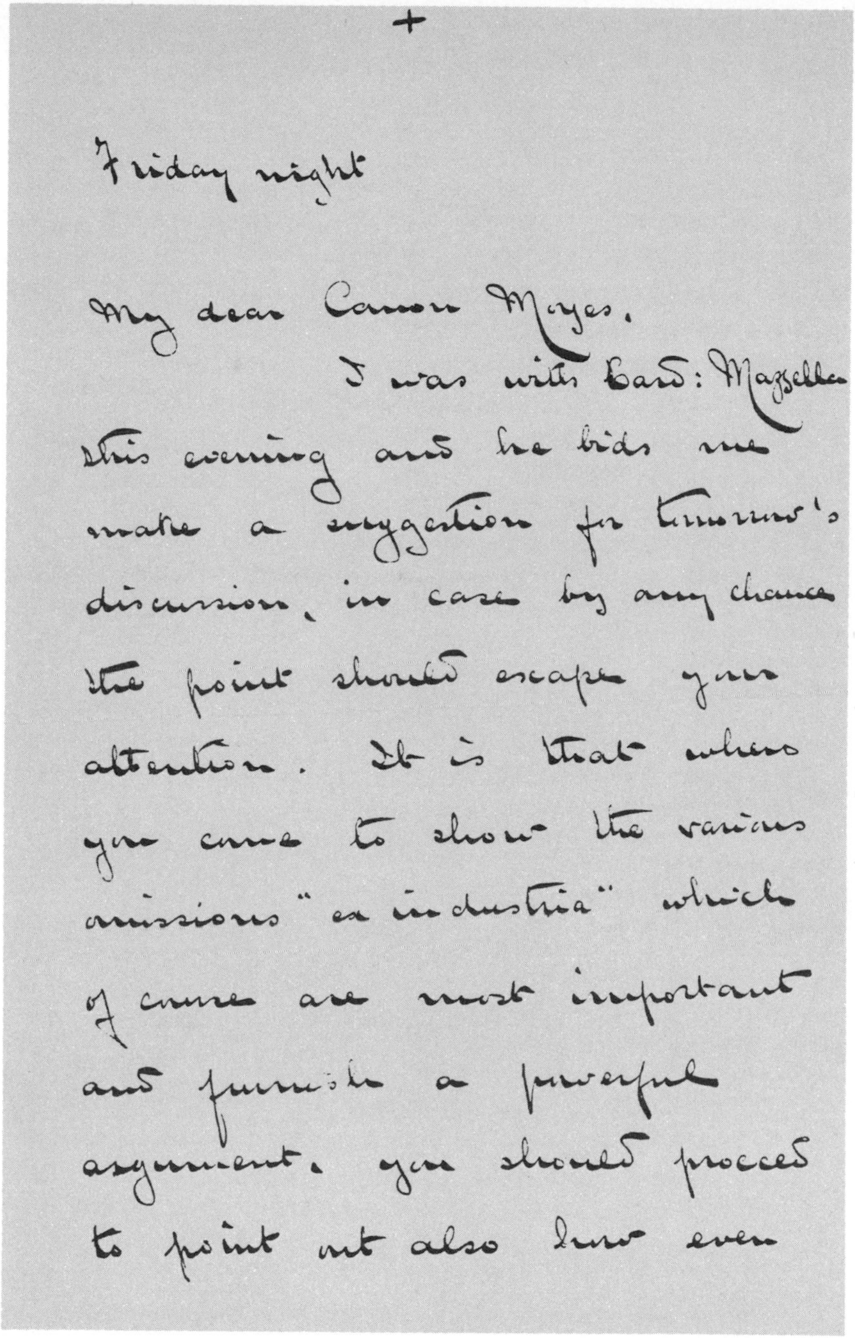

+

Friday night

My dear Canon Moyes.

I was with Card: Mazzella this evening and he bids me make a suggestion for tomorrow's discussion, in case by any chance the point should escape your attention. It is that when you come to show the various missions "ex industria" which of course are most important and furnish a powerful argument. you should proceed to point out also how even

Merry del Val's letter to Canon Moyes (see page 157)

Gasquet Papers

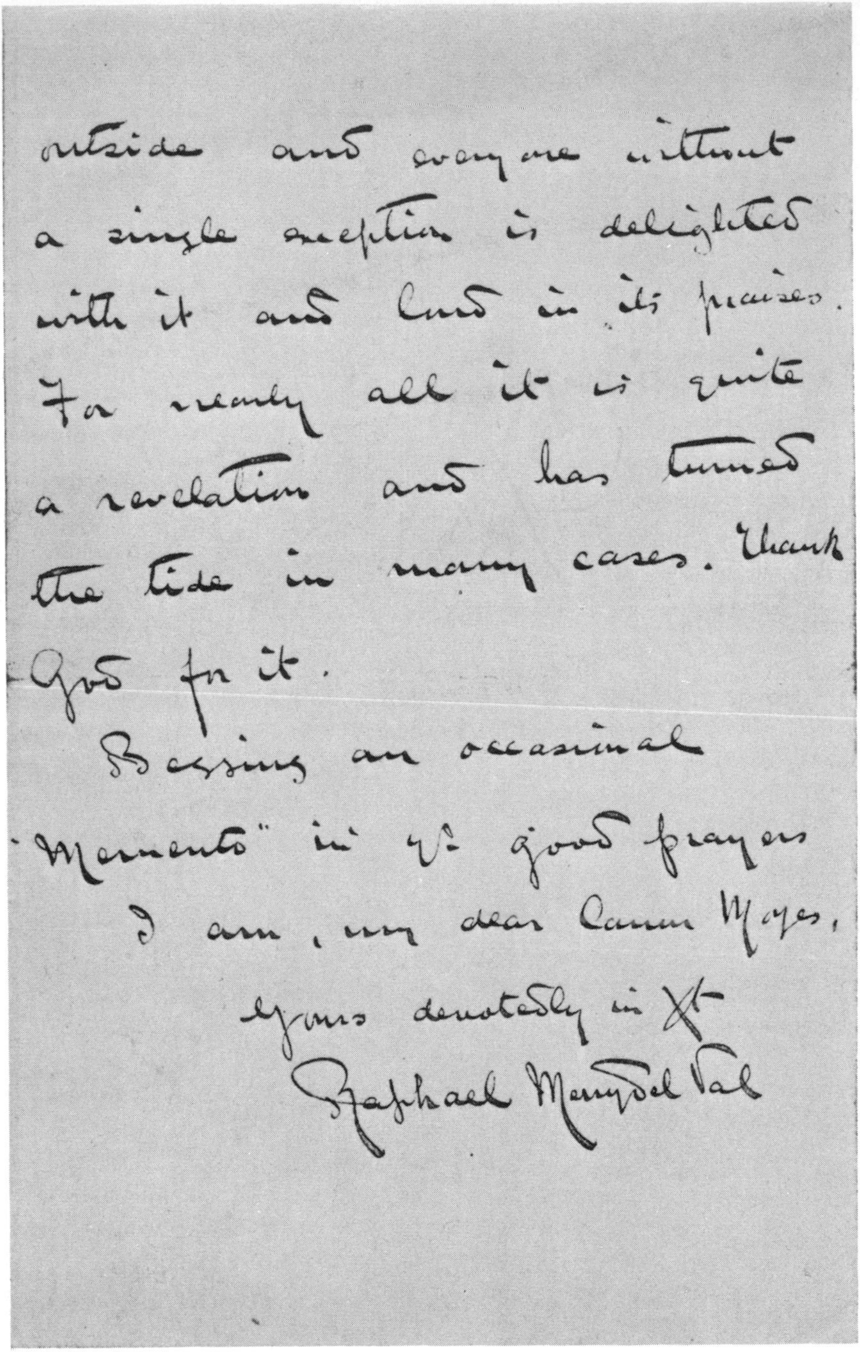
outside and everyone without
a single exception is delighted
with it and loud in its praises.
For nearly all it is quite
a revelation and has turned
the tide in many cases. Thank
God for it.
Begging an occasional
"Memento" in yr good prayers
I am, my dear Canon Moyes,
Yours devotedly in Xt
Raphael Merry del Val

Merry del Val's letter to Canon Moyes (see page 184)

Gasquet Papers

to see it used as Pontifical'.[41] At the close of this meeting Cardinal Mazzella dictated seven questions to which written answers were to be submitted at the next meeting.[42] Moyes recorded that it had been a 'stormy session'.

The commission is terminated

The commission had now held ten meetings. The first had been concerned with procedural matters only, and need not concern us. We know that the fourth, sixth, and eighth meetings began at 10 a.m., and it is reasonable to assume that this was the regular time for the sessions to start. The eighth meeting was over by 12.15,[43] the sixth lasted until 1 p.m.[44] If we assume that the average length of the sessions was three hours, a generous estimate in view of the above evidence, this would mean that twenty-seven hours had been spent in discussion to date. Of these twenty-seven hours at least nineteen had been devoted to historical arguments: the treatment of Anglican Orders in the Marian period, the alleged precedents of 1684 and the Gordon case of 1704, and Barlow. Only in the second hour of the eighth meeting did the discussion reach what Canon Moyes later claimed was felt by the commissioners to be 'the main and decisive issue':

[41] Moyes' notes (WAr).

[42] Moyes recorded these questions as follows (WAr):

'1. An ad validitatem consecrationis episcopalis necesse sit, ut forma exprimat ordinem seu potestatem quae confertur?

'2. An id exprimatur in ordinale Anglicana ex quibius verbis.

'3. An haec verba sint explicita et clara vel quadamtenus ambigua quorum significatio ulteriore determinatione indigeat?

'4. An et unde habent certam et definitam significationem?

'5. An verba quae absoluta vim et significationem formae Catholicae habere, aut ad eam trahi possent; si in sensum contrarium notorie detorquentur, facta etiam ad hoc immutatione ritus, catholicam significationem in hoc novo ritu, adhuc retinere merito censeantur?

'6. An constat ab auctoribus et promotoribus ordinalis Anglicani repudiatam fuisse doctrinam catholicam de ordine deque iis quae ad hoc sacramentum spectent atque huic innovationi conformes immutationes inductas fuisse in ritum?

'7. Quid consequenter iudicandum de forma intentione sit[?] in hoc novo ritu?

'NB: Eadem quaeri possunt de ordinatione presbyteriali si opus fuerit.'

[43] Cf. Gasquet, *Leaves* 58. [44] Ibid. 55.

the question of the adequacy of the Ordinal rite as a sacramental form for the conferral of Holy Orders.[45] This topic had now occupied the commission for only eight of the total twenty-seven hours which it had sat. There is no evidence that the question of intention, which has figured so prominently in polemical works against the Orders, and which was to be one of the grounds of condemnation, had played more than an incidental role in the discussions. It is clear that the commission had not finished its work with the conclusion of this tenth sitting on 2nd May. Just a little over a fortnight previously, on the day after the fifth meeting, Portal had written to Lord Halifax that 'the Commission has work for a month and a half at least',[46] a report which presumably reflects the opinion of Gasparri or Duchesne, or of both together. A letter written by Canon Moyes to Cardinal Vaughan on the eve of the eleventh meeting on 5th May betrays no expectation of an imminent termination of the commission's work.

> We have a meeting tomorrow [Moyes wrote on 4th May], and then, I think, two meetings more, or at most three, ought to conclude the work of our Commission.[47]

In fact the eleventh meeting on 5th May was to be effectively the last, for the twelfth meeting, like the first, was devoted to formalities.

The eleventh meeting on Tuesday 5th May began as expected, with the answers to the questions put by Cardinal Mazzella at the end of the previous session. The president's announcement which followed must have taken the commissioners by surprise.

> After the *responsa* . . . had been read [Gasquet wrote], the Cardinal made an address, summing up the discussion we had been engaged upon. He concluded by saying that the opinions we had been asked for by the Holy Father had been sufficiently made known and debated, and that he would only request us to meet once more on Thursday, to pass the *acta*.[48]

[45] Cf. Snead-Cox, *Cardinal Vaughan* ii, 206.
[46] Letter of 14th April 1896, *Leo XIII* 289.
[47] *The Tablet* 137 (1937), 153 col. 2. [48] Gasquet, *Leaves* 62.

This account should be compared with Moyes' statement that 'the Commission itself agreed, by its own vote, that nothing more remained to be added, and that its work was complete'.[49] Is it fanciful to suppose that the commission's vote for this abrupt termination of the discussion came only in response to the statement of its president, who as a cardinal far outranked all those present, that further expressions of opinion were not desired? Portal's informants in the commission obviously had the impression of haste, for Lacey wrote in his diary on 6th May, the day after Cardinal Mazzella had made his unexpected announcement in the commission:

> After breakfast M. Portal came with important information. The Commission will probably finish its work to-morrow . . . They hardly touch at all on the question of intention, merely stating a few general truths. *Apparently things have been hurried.* All graver considerations are to be reserved for another Commission of Cardinals . . . [50]

The impression that the termination of the commission's work was hasty and abrupt, the result of intervention by a 'higher authority', is strengthened by the pains taken by Canon Moyes to deny it. Having stated in 1897 that 'the Commission itself agreed, by its own vote, that nothing more remained to be added, and that its work was complete', he felt compelled to repeat this statement twice more, in 1911 and in 1912.[51]

The twelfth and last meeting of the commission took place on Thursday 7th May. Duchesne managed to create a last flurry of excitement by producing a telegram from England announcing that supposed evidence of Barlow's consecration had at last been found.[52] But the English

[49] *The Tablet* 57 (1897), 284 col. 1.
[50] Lacey, *Roman Diary* 59, emphasis supplied.
[51] Cf. *The Tablet* 85 (1911), 89 col. 1, and 87 (1912), 803 col. 1.
[52] This proved to be a misunderstanding. In a supplement to his *De Hierarchia* which was issued in Rome later in May, Lacey put matters straight by saying that in fact no new evidence had been found. Merry del Val tried to make out later that Lacey had been deliberately dishonest and admitted the truth only when 'found out'. There is no evidence to support this charge, which may be viewed as an indication of how heated tempers had become (cf. p. 194 below).

commissioners indicated that the matter was unimportant, and it was dropped.[53] The minutes of the commission's sessions were read and signed. Cardinal Mazzella again reminded all those present, as he had at the first meeting, of the obligation of secrecy, and the meeting was closed.[54] The investigation of Anglican Orders was over.

The final vote on validity

It remains to report an important fact which has been a carefully guarded secret for more than seventy years: the final vote of the commissioners on the validity of Anglican Orders. When Lacey's book was published in November 1910 Canon Moyes wrote to Merry del Val, who was then Cardinal Secretary of State, asking him to verify certain details of the commission's work. In the course of his reply, which is dated 13th December 1910, Merry del Val wrote:

> I have asked Fr David [Fleming] to look up my minutes and it will be easy to settle the point of the votes. My impression is that they were as follows: Gasquet, Moyes, David and Llevaneras voted for the invalidity. Duchesne and de Augustinis for the validity. Gasparri and Scannell for a doubtful validity and therefore a 'sub conditione'. If, as Fr David thinks, Scannell voted for the validity with Duchesne and de Augustinis, in a sense, the validity was lost by one vote.[55]

In an investigation dominated by the massive and well-documented *votum* of Cardinal Vaughan's representatives, and in which the Anglican side was never adequately represented, the opponents of the Orders had been able to convince only one of their five colleagues of the soundness of their arguments. Only four of the eight experts appointed by the Holy See to investigate Anglican Orders in 1896 returned a verdict of invalidity. Three of these four had been sent to Rome for the express purpose of obtaining a formal

[53] Leslie, *Cardinal Gasquet* 65. [54] Gasquet, *Leaves* 62.

[55] Moyes Papers, WAr. Merry del Val goes on to explain that the decision did not rest with the commission, but with the cardinals of the Holy Office and the pope, as has been stated at the outset of this chapter (cf. p. 149 above). The full text of this letter is reproduced on pp. 300–04 below.

condemnation of the Orders; and the fourth was appointed to the commission at the last minute because he was known in advance to support the negative view.

Six weeks after receiving Merry del Val's letter cited above, Canon Moyes published a long article in *The Tablet* in which he contrived to create the impression that no vote on the question of validity was ever taken in the commission.

> Naturally, at the close of the Commission each of the members was asked to state (in writing, if I remember right) his *votum* upon the main issue, and these *vota* were sent up to speak for themselves to the Holy Father and the Cardinals. . . . Undoubtedly, the members could informally and for themselves count these *vota*, and form their conclusion as to where the majority lay, and whether it was great or small. . . . It has been stated that the majority in the Commission, counted thus informally, but *de facto*, representing the mind of the commissioners, was but a narrow one unfavourable to Anglican Orders. But, be that as it may, from the very constitution of the Commission, such a result was surely to be expected. . . . Equality of *pro* and *contra* was the very basis of the Commission.[56]

Moyes went on to explain that a change of opinion on the part of the members of the commission could not have been expected, due to the sincerity with which each held his view. This was an argument thought up only after all attempts at persuasion had failed. At the time, Moyes had been more sanguine about the possibility of winning over some of his colleagues. In two undated letters from the late autumn of 1895, when Vaughan's committee was completing work on *Ordines Anglicani*, Moyes told Dom Gasquet:

> It will be a great point won if you can put Gasparri in the right path, and open his eyes to the vitiation of the Anglican rite. He does not seem to be half bad, and ought to be open to conviction.

And another letter from this period says:

> If you succeed in converting Gasparri, or even in enlightening him on the historical issues, it will be a great point gained.[57]

[56] *The Tablet* 85 (1911), 164f.

[57] Both letters from Gasquet Papers.

On the 4th April, between the first and second meetings of the commission, Moyes wrote to Cardinal Vaughan:

> Gasparri called again yesterday, and we were able to explain to him many points contained in our case, and additional evidence which we have found since coming out.[58]

Moyes' report to the cardinal on 11th April, when the commission had held four meetings, showed him still hopeful that some of the other commissioners could be won over by the English arguments.

> The good feeling between ourselves and the opposite side is decidedly improved, and we have hopes of conciliating some of them, while holding firmly to our own position. . . . Cardinal Segna . . . is very sound upon the Orders question, and we think he is likely to influence Gasparri, who was his pupil in former years. Padre Llevaneras has proved a valuable acquisition, and speaks remarkably well.[59]

The care taken to conceal the result of the commission's final vote is illustrated by a letter written in 1930 by the then Cardinal Merry del Val to the English Jesuit Fr Francis Woodlock. Although the letter contains no direct misstatements of fact, it could only be seriously misleading to someone who did not possess the writer's inside knowledge. The letter ignores Fr Scannell's view by implying that the only commissioners dissenting from the verdict of invalidity were those ignorant of the history of the Prayer Book and Ordinal. Especially noteworthy is the implication that dissenting views in the commission were limited to the opinion of doubtful validity. In 1910 Merry del Val had written that two and perhaps three of the four dissenters had voted for validity. The letter is reproduced in its entirety.

> January 26th 1930
>
> My dear Father Woodlock,
>
> It is a daring and groundless misstatement, to put it mildly, on the part of White and Knox to assert that 'The argument of the competent theologians of His [*sic*] own Communion were on one side' and that 'He followed them [Card. Vaughan and English Catholics] against the advice

[58] *The Tablet* 137 (1937), 152. [59] Ibid.

of his competent theologians'. That one or other member of the Commission may have held to the opinion of a doubtful invalidity of A.O. especially considering, as was notoriously the case, that several of them had a scant knowledge of the history of the Prayer Book and Ordinal, cannot justify the assertion that such was the opinion of the Commission. Of course, if White and Knox choose to say that theologians who pronounce A.O. to be invalid are incompetent, it is impossible to argue with them. Battifol was not on the Commission. If they quote him, we are entitled to quote the array of practically all theologians past and present outside the Commission. Duchesne was a member of the Commission. As is notorious he made no secret of his usual sceptical criticism, whilst never pretending to be a theologian or to care for theology.[60] The Commissioners were given all the material and all the documents available and were asked simply to examine them and express their individual opinion, leaving it to the Holy Father to consider their discussions and draw his conclusions. The Pope had before him the arguments and verdict of the theologians, his theologians past and present, not to speak of the Cardinals of the Holy Office who examined the whole case and were unanimous as the Bull declares. It is contrary to fact to assert that the Commission pronounced a different verdict, though it may not have been unanimous in the individual opinions expressed.

Many thanks for your excellent article, so clear and convincing.

Yours devotedly in Xt

R. Card. Merry del Val[61]

The appeal to precedent

One of the aspects of the commission's work which will remain unclear until the records of the investigation are made available for scholarly research is the role played by the Gordon case of 1704.[62] Gordon was supposed (almost certainly erroneously) to have received episcopal consecration according to the Anglican Ordinal. On 17th April 1704 his orders were declared invalid by Pope Clement XI, presiding personally over a meeting of the Holy Office on a 'Feria V'. Ordinary meetings of the Holy Office take place in the absence of the pope and on Wednesday (Feria IV). The

[60] The latter statement was equally true of Gasquet; cf. pp. 216f below.
[61] Reproduced from photographic copy kindly supplied by the Most Revd John A. Murphy, Archbishop of Cardiff.
[62] Cf. pp. 280–83 below.

meetings on Thursday (Feria v) in the presence of the pope are extremely rare, and the decisions of such meetings possess corresponding solemnity. There were many in Rome in 1896 who held that the decisions of a Feria v meeting of the Holy Office were irrevocable. *Apostolicae curae*, while refraining from a statement concerning this disputed question, mentions that the decision in the Gordon case was reached on a Feria v, and implies that this decision settled the question of Anglican Order once and for all.[63] Portal was convinced that the Gordon case had played a decisive role in the commission's deliberations. And in his *Roman Diary* Lacey charged that the ultimate decision about the Orders had been determined not so much by the theological issues as by the unwillingness of the Holy Office to reverse the 1704 decision.[64] Portal commented as follows about this charge and about Moyes' indignant reply in *The Tablet*:

> Cardinal Mazzella's personal opinion was that the Gordon decision was definitive, since it had been made by the Pope on a Feria v. The Bull itself certainly says that this was the fact. For after recounting the Gordon case it says: 'Hence it must be clear to everyone that the controversy lately revived had been already definitely settled by the Apostolic See.'
>
> The Commission on the Orders was not permitted to deal with the value of this decision. The members received all the documents relating to the case. They were charged with developing the reasons which led them to adopt whatever opinion about your Orders they held. But they were not charged with saying whether in view of the evidence the decision of 1704 was well founded or not. Likewise when a member advanced a reason which was discussed there was no vote on the value of this discussion nor on the conclusion to be drawn from it. Everything went into the dossiers which were passed on to the commission of cardinals. And it is there in my opinion that the question of the value of the 1704 decision was raised.
>
> Duchesne and Gasparri wanted everything to be discussed with complete openness; and they also wanted the Commission to express its opinion on each disputed point by a vote. This was not done. And you see how right Lacey is as well as how Moyes can say what he says. But his angry tone shows clearly that he had been hit in a sensitive spot.[65]

[63] Cf. AO(E) 8.
[64] Cf. *Roman Diary* 135f.
[65] Letter of 27th January 1911, HP A4,213. The statements made in the final paragraph of this letter are confirmed by Portal's contemporary account. On 18th

In a later letter Portal furnished further corroborative detail.

> Cardinal Mazzella told me himself with regard to the decision of 1704 that he is one of those who holds that the pope himself is not entitled to question a decision of this nature. And the Assessor of the Holy Office said to me at the same time (1896): 'You cannot say that the Holy Office has made a mistake.' 'But, Monsignor, I have never said anything of the kind.' 'People say that the Holy Office made a mistake in the Galileo case.' 'Yes, Monsignor, they do . . . '[66] I have always thought that this was meant as a warning to me. Duchesne was saying on every hand that the Holy Office had made a mistake, and these statements were accompanied by joking remarks which were terribly irritating to everyone.[67]

Further clarification of the role played by the Gordon case, and the freedom or lack of freedom of the commissioners to go behind it, must await the opening of the commission's records. We have seen that the commission had no authority to make a decision. But its final vote, in which only four of the Holy See's experts voted for invalidity, with two and perhaps three giving a verdict of valid, and one and perhaps two declaring for doubtful validity, would more naturally have justified a decision of doubtful validity than the unqualified condemnation of *Apostolicae curae*. How this condemnation was obtained will be the subject of the next two chapters.

April 1896 he had written to Halifax: 'Duchesne is very dissatisfied, and Gasparri also, with the manner in which the discussions are conducted. He complains that there is not a proper critical examination of each proposition or assertion. He would like to see the members required to say whether a given proof is good or not, whether an assertion is destroyed by the adversary's attack or whether it remains. As it is each side gives its opinion and when both are finished there is not a single conclusion but two conclusions' (PP).

[66] The dots here do not indicate an omission; they are in Portal's letter.

[67] Letter of Portal to Halifax, 1st December 1911, HP A4.213.

9

PRESSING FOR A CONDEMNATION

My belief is that Cardinal Vaughan and his band will omit no opportunity and will not greatly scruple any means of defeating the Pope in his present purpose.
—W. E. Gladstone to Lord Halifax[1]

The day after the commission's final meeting Cardinal Rampolla told the Abbé Duchesne that he wanted Lacey and Puller to remain in Rome for the time being,

> to hold ourselves in readiness [Lacey wrote in his diary] to give information to the Commission of Cardinals which is now appointed. He wishes us to wait upon him but before this to see some other cardinals also.[2]

The round of visits to cardinals suggested by Cardinal Rampolla showed how ignorant Italian prelates were of the true state of the Anglican Church. Lacey had been working night and day on a Latin supplement to his previous work, *De Hierarchia Anglicana*, dealing with points of interest to the cardinals of the Holy Office, with whom the decision now lay. This work,[3] on which Lacey had laboured no less than sixty hours in five days, was completed on Friday 5th May. Portal immediately charged him with yet another task: 'a brief outline of the present state of the Church of England, with a clear explanation of *parties*'.[4] Lacey at once set to work afresh and completed the pamphlet in two days. He

[1] Letter 20th May 1896, *Leo XIII* 305.

[2] Lacey, *Roman Diary* 63. Cf. also the letter Lacey wrote on 10th May 1896 to the Revd E. G. Wood: 'Well, we thought of packing up our traps, but a message from Duchesne stayed us, and on Friday he went to see Cardinal Rampolla to talk about us. The Cardinal told him that a Commission of Cardinals was nominated to take over the question, and it was most important that we should stay to give our help. So now, if you please, we are here not by invitation of Gasparri and Duchesne, but by the command of the Cardinal-Secretary. He added that he wanted to see us, but we must call on some other Cardinals first' (Lacey, op. cit. 114).

[3] T. A. Lacey, 'Dissertationis apologeticae de Hierarchia Anglicana Supplementum', Romae ex typographia Pacis, Philippi Cuggiana, 1896; cf. *Roman Diary* 66.

[4] Lacey, *Roman Diary* 66.

reckoned that the two works, both of them in Latin and written in a single week, had taken him not less than ninety hours in all.[5] The second work, *De Re Anglicana*,[6] contained a brief historical sketch of the Church of England, emphasising the nineteenth-century developments in the wake of the catholic revival initiated by the Oxford Movement. An Appendix set forth statistical information from *The Church Year Book*. Lacey was to admit in an article published less than five months later:

> The statement was obviously an *ex parte* one; it pretended to be nothing else. But I am not afraid to claim that it was composed with careful moderation and candid truthfulness.[7]

Gasquet and Moyes responded by mounting an all-out attack on Lacey's work and motives.

> In a secret paper I was accused of deliberate fraud, of saying things in the ears of Cardinals at Rome which I should not dare to say in the open air of England. It was a charge of conscious and intentional falsehood, and it was delivered as a stab in the dark. . . . As soon as the accusation came to my ears, and before it was made public, I placed [copies of my pamphlet] in the great public libraries in England. It was myself, indeed, who made the accusation public.[8]

Gasquet and Moyes' 'Risposta'

The attack on Lacey's work was contained in an Italian pamphlet more than twice the length of the original, and entitled *Risposta all' Opuscolo 'De Re Anglicana'*.[9] The work is dated 6th June 1896. The first part of the *Risposta* quotes individual statements from Lacey's work, and then refutes them. The second part is an embittered attack upon the

[5] Lacey, *Roman Diary* 67.
[6] Privately printed, Rome 1896; reprinted in *A Roman Diary* 195–209. An English translation was printed in *The Tablet* 56 (1896), 741–7.
[7] *Guardian*, 7th October 1896, 1514; reprinted in *Roman Diary* 240–9.
[8] Lacey, *Roman Diary* 20f.
[9] Printed privately, Rome 1896; reprinted in *Roman Diary* 210–39; English translation in *The Tablet* 56 (1896), 768ff and 823–7; excerpts in English translation in the *Guardian*, 30th September 1896, 1488. All citations from this work are from the original edition printed privately in Rome, which I have examined in the library at Downside Abbey.

motives of the Anglicans, who are accused of seeking the recognition of their orders from the Holy See merely in order to bolster their own position as an independent church in rivalry with Rome. The pamphlet closes with an impassioned plea to the cardinals of the Holy Office to repel this subtle and insidious plot against the faith and the true church by declaring once and for all that Anglican Orders are completely null and void.

Lacey's pamphlet was written from the High Anglican point of view. Although it contained nothing but what was said day in and day out by Anglo-Catholics in England, a number of its statements were bound to be misleading for the Roman cardinals for whom it was intended. In particular, the use of the term 'catholic' was ambiguous. The most misleading statement in the work for those unacquainted with the religious scene in England was the following:

> The English Church, delivered from so many dangers, has differed in nothing from the other national Churches included in Catholic unity, save that she has lacked communion *in sacris* with the Holy See.[10]

Gasquet and Moyes quite naturally felt that such statements must be explained if they were not to lead to wholly false conclusions. Unfortunately their *Risposta* contained a number of factual and historical half-truths and misrepresentations which went beyond anything in Lacey's pamphlet. Gasquet and Moyes claimed that the Anglo-Catholic position represented by Lacey was the work of the devil, and as such a foe of true catholicism even more dangerous and insidious than outright protestantism. Their charge that Anglicans were seeking recognition of their orders from the Holy See only in order to mount a stronger attack upon the Roman Catholic Church was especially unjust, for Gasquet and Moyes had every reason to know that the charge was false. They were aware that only a few weeks previously

[10] Lacey, *Roman Diary* 198. 'Delivered from so many dangers' was a reference to the struggles with the Puritans. The original Latin reads: 'Ecclesia Anglicana tot periculis elapsa ab aliis ecclesiis nationalibus in unitate catholica comprehensis nihil distulit nisi quod communione sacrorum cum Sancta Sede careret.'

Lacey and Puller had themselves supplied the commission with newly discovered evidence of a few re-ordinations of Anglican clergy during the Marian restoration. Since this evidence told against the Anglican contention that the Orders had been accepted under Mary, the action of the Anglican representatives was incompatible with the charge of seeking recognition of their orders from Rome from motives of mere self-interest.

Quotation of a few representative passages will illustrate the methods used by Gasquet and Moyes to obtain the condemnation of Anglican Orders from a group of Roman cardinals entirely dependent upon their English co-religionists for their knowledge of Anglicanism. Lacey had written that although under Edward VI many partisans of the reformation were given ecclesiastical preferment, the Henrician bishops of catholic sentiments retained their sees, accommodating themselves to the new state of affairs as best they could. He went on to explain that a few of these catholic-minded bishops were expelled from their sees, and that there was no doubt that some of the reformers would have gone further in a protestant direction if their plans had not been thwarted by Edward's premature death.[11] This last statement is a typical example of the pains which Lacey had taken, even in his admittedly partisan statement of the case, to be fair. He could legitimately have omitted the purely conjectural statement about the course religious affairs in England would probably have taken had Edward lived longer. It would have been quite sufficient, and in view of his purpose in writing fully understandable, had he contented himself with the simple statement of what the reformers actually had done, and said nothing about what they might have done in the event of an hypothesis which was in fact not realised.

Gasquet and Moyes had both written extensively about the history of the English Reformation, and could hardly

[11] Cf. Lacey, *Roman Diary* 196.

claim ignorance of the details of the subject which they were now describing as self-avowed experts. They replied to Lacey's fair statement of the facts:

> In no sense could those who retained their sees under Edward be called Catholic. . . . On the contrary, all the bishops who in some way retained a Catholic feeling or a vestige of veneration for Catholic dogmas were driven from their sees under Edward.[12]

They then proceeded to list six catholic-minded bishops expelled from their sees in Edward's reign. They said nothing in this section about the fact that there were nine Henrician bishops who remained in undisturbed possession of their sees throughout the whole of Edward's reign, and who were considered catholic enough upon Mary's accession to be left in office. Two of them were even promoted to new sees by Mary: Parfew was translated from St Asaph to Hereford in 1554, and Thirlby went from Norwich to Ely[13] as well as being chosen to be Cardinal Pole's ambassador to the Holy See in the spring of 1555. Thirlby's case is especially interesting, for it illustrates how complex the episcopal changes were in England under the four Tudor monarchs, and how little susceptible to the kind of black-and-white presentation made by Gasquet and Moyes. Thirlby had first been named by Henry VIII to the see of Westminster, newly created when the Abbey of Westminster was suppressed. He was translated to Norwich under Edward VI, which shows that he was not merely tolerated but enjoyed preferment in this reign when, according to the *Risposta*, 'all the bishops who in some way retained a Catholic feeling or a vestige of veneration for the Catholic dogmas were driven from their sees'. And upon Mary's accession Thirlby was *again* preferred, this time to the see of Ely, and sent on a special mission to Rome.

[12] *Risposta* 6.

[13] Cf. the 'Table of Episcopate' in W. H. Frere, *The Marian Reaction*, London 1896, facing p. 162, which shows the episcopal changes for twenty-six English and Welsh sees from 1549–61. Consultation of this table will save the student lengthy searches in numerous other works for information about the English episcopate during these twelve crucial years.

In the section following, Gasquet and Moyes dispute the account Lacey had given of the episcopal changes under Mary. Lacey's statements were quite correct, and the criticisms of them in the *Rispota* are mere linguistic quibbles. It was Gasquet and Moyes who slipped on the facts. They wrote that six bishops 'were rehabilitated after having done penance and made their abjuration to Cardinal Pole'.[14] The number was incorrect: we have already seen that not six but nine bishops remained in office. There was a canonical process of reconciliation, and it was this to which Gasquet and Moyes referred. But whereas the reader unacquainted with the complicated history of the time might easily gain from the word 'rehabilitated'[15] the impression that these bishops were restored to offices from which they had been expelled, the fact of the matter is that they were simply left where they had been during the whole of Edward's reign. And two of them were even promoted, as we have seen. About these two promotions Gasquet and Moyes were entirely silent.

Having contended that catholicism was destroyed root and branch by the deprivation of all catholic-minded bishops under Edward, Gasquet and Moyes then proceed, in dealing with the events subsequent to Elizabeth's accession, to contradict their previous contention. The new regime, we read, 'was not content with restoring the reformed religion as it was introduced under Edward VI, *when it retained at least some remnants of Catholic belief*'.[16] This statement is supported by reference to the fact that it was the second and more protestant Prayer Book which formed the basis of the Elizabethan settlement of religion. Gasquet and Moyes mention that 'some few alterations'[17] were made in this liturgy. They do not say that these changes were all in a catholic direction.

In short, the account given by Gasquet and Moyes of the

[14] *Risposta* 7.
[15] Italian: 'restituti'.
[16] *Risposta* 8, emphasis supplied.
[17] 'alcune poche mutazioni' *Risposta* 9.

highly complicated events of the English reformation was considerably more misleading and partisan than Lacey's description of the same events. The *Risposta* was written in the black-and-white terms of popular polemic, and entirely failed to do justice to the complexities of the history. Gasquet and Moyes were quite familiar with the historical details and their significance. Appendix I of the lengthy brief against the Orders which they had prepared and submitted in Rome contains no less than four lists of sixteenth-century English bishops and other reformers carefully analysing their positions and classifying them as reformers, schismatics, and opportunists.[18] The accuracy of this classification is irrelevant in this connection. But it shows that Gasquet and Moyes were not at all averse to making careful distinctions between the leading figures of the English reformation when it suited their purposes to do so.

Lacey's pamphlet had emphasised the role of the Tractarians and of the catholic revival which they started in bringing new spiritual life to the Anglican Church. Gasquet and Moyes countered by minimising the effect of the catholic revival within Anglicanism, and by saying that in any case it was a complete innovation and false to the whole previous three centuries of Anglican history. This was identical with the line taken by a small wing of extreme protestants in the Church of England, correctly referred to by Lacey in his work as 'Puritans'. And it was in its own way quite as false and misleading as anything that Lacey had written.

This attack on the catholic revival in the Anglican Church revealed its authors' ignorance of prominent aspects of contemporary Anglican life. This may be illustrated by the *Risposta*'s statement about the infrequency with which the Eucharist was celebrated in the Church of England. Lacey had written that one of the effects of the catholic revival had been an increase in the celebration of the Eucharist, which was now celebrated regularly (*iugiter*), with a corresponding

[18] OA 68ff.

increase in devout communions.[19] The authors of the *Risposta* informed the Roman cardinals that this was quite untrue, and that in fact the Holy Communion was celebrated only once a month in the ordinary parish church in England.[20] It was this statement, rather than Lacey's, which was false.

Fifteen years later Moyes made a belated admission of this error, saying that he had subsequently discovered that the Eucharist was in fact celebrated every Sunday in Anglican churches. This correction first appeared in the small print of a footnote.[21] When he repeated it in 1912 Moyes placed the correction in the body of his article, but played down the importance of the error by referring to it as a 'statistical mistake in one particular', and saying that it could not possibly have had any material effect upon the question of Anglican Orders in any case.[22] It was disingenuous for Moyes to hide behind the convenient excuse of a 'statistical mistake'. The difference between a church which normally celebrates the Eucharist weekly and one which celebrates it only once a month is that between a body which regards the sacraments as the normal channels of grace, and for which the celebration of the Lord's Day is incomplete without the sacramental memorial of his atoning work, and a body whose normal worship is non-sacramental and in which the celebration of the Eucharist is exceptional. This distinction is a fundamental one, separating churches of the catholic from those of the protestant type. That Moyes and Gasquet could be ignorant about a matter of such importance shows how little English catholics in the 1890s knew about the most ordinary features of Anglican religious life. For there was nothing secret about what services were held in English parish churches: the schedule of services appeared on public notice boards and in the press for all to see and read. This ignorance could of course have been paralleled on the other

[19] Lacey, *Roman Diary* 200.
[20] *Risposta* 17.
[21] Cf. *The Tablet* 85 (1911), 164 col. 1.
[22] Cf. *The Tablet* 87 (1912), 883 col. 1.

side.[23] Its existence was one of the strongest arguments for the joint theological conversations which Halifax and Portal had tried to promote.

The second part of the *Risposta* is not concerned directly with statements in Lacey's pamphlet. It proceeds independently to give a view of Anglicanism and of the catholic revival in the Church of England which does little credit to its authors. An anonymous 'Catholic bishop in England' is quoted as ascribing the catholic revival in the Anglican Church to demonic influence.

> From the time of the Reformation the devil has constantly combatted the Catholic faith in England by means of heresy, and by OPEN AND VIOLENT HOSTILITY. Having now obtained his intention, he has changed his tactics since that year (1830), and combats the Catholic Church by IMITATING her and by using against her a travesty of her doctrine; and by usurping her practices he attracts simple souls. These tactics are more to be feared than the others, although we hope by the grace of God to frustrate them.[24]

Such language cannot be excused by saying that after all it was a pre-ecumenical age, and that no other view was possible for Roman Catholics in 1896. The attitude of Cardinal Rampolla, of numerous French clergy, and of a number of English catholics whose views will be discussed below[25] proves the contrary. And even such a militant opponent of Anglicanism and especially of Anglo-Catholicism as Cardinal Vaughan had, two years previously, concluded a glowing picture of the catholic revival in the Church of England with a different evaluation:

[23] Cf. the letter written by Halifax to Portal on 6th May 1894: 'There is much prejudice amongst our people, and much ignorance—things which cannot be done away with all at once. It seems to me that there is also a certain amount of ignorance amongst your people' (*Leo XIII* 83). The Bishop of Peterborough, Dr Mandell Creighton, also referred to this ignorance when telling Portal in August 1894 that 'he often told his own people that they did not understand what they were saying when they talked about the Pope' (*Leo XIII* 98). Cf. also Archbishop Benson's erroneous understanding of the papal claims, p. 61 n. 45 above.

[24] *Risposta* 29, capitalisation in original. The error of three years in the beginning of the Oxford Movement (1830 instead of 1833), while unimportant in itself, illustrates the authors' ignorance of the matters they were discussing as self-avowed experts.

[25] Cf. pp. 232ff below.

> Has there ever been seen a more marvellous change, and this within half a century! I know that it has been called Popery, or the Mass in masquerade—not without some reason. St Jerome speaks of the devil as the *Simia Dei*, the ape of God, so clever is he in counterfeiting the works and ordinances of God. . . . It may be so still. But, for my part, I prefer to hope and believe that we are witnessing, at least in a very large measure, an instance of the marvellous ways of Divine grace, and that if Satan be apeing God he is outwitting himself.[26]

Lord Halifax thought that it was from this speech that the quotation of the anonymous 'Catholic bishop in England' which appeared in the *Risposta* was taken.[27] It is more than likely that Gasquet and Moyes were quoting Vaughan, but that they had in mind what he was accustomed to say in private conversation. Moyes had lived in the same house with the cardinal for many years, and was intimately familiar with his views.[28] Fr B. W. Maturin, who left the Anglican Society of St John The Evangelist in 1897 to become a Roman Catholic, writes that when he first paid his respects to Cardinal Vaughan

> he asked me whether I thought the [catholic] movement in the English Church came from the devil or the Holy Spirit.[29]

In his preface to Père Ragey's *L'Anglo-catholicisme* Vaughan wrote that demonic inspiration was part of the explanation for Anglo-Catholicism, but not the whole explanation.[30] It

[26] Cardinal Vaughan, *The Re-Union of Christendom*, 37f. With this statement should be compared Cardinal Wiseman's assessment of the Tractarian revival in 1841: 'I know what some will say—that all this interest is of an *interested* character; that they wish to take so much from us as may serve to give consistency to their own Church, but have no idea of advancing further, or aiming at reunion with us. The suspicion is, I conceive, unjust and ungrounded: it is based upon ignorance of the true character and feelings of these writers. Their admiration of our institutions and practices, and their regret at having lost them, manifestly spring from the value which they set upon everything *Catholic*; and to suppose them (without an insincerity which they have given us no right to charge them with) to love the parts of a system, and wish for them, while they would reject the root, and only secure support of them,—the system itself,—is to my mind revoltingly contradictory' (Nicholas Wiseman, *A Letter on Catholic Unity, addressed to the . . . Earl of Shrewsbury by Nicholas, Bishop of Melipotamus*, London 1841, 14).

[27] Cf. *Leo XIII* 111 n. 1.

[28] Cf. Moyes' statement to this effect in *The Tablet* 88 (1912), 8 col. 1.

[29] Basil W. Maturin, *The Price of Unity*, London 1917, 203f. Lord Halifax referred to this incident without identifying the 'distinguished convert' to whom Vaughan had addressed his question; cf. *Leo XIII* 363 n. 1.

[30] Vaughan's preface is dated 12th April 1897.

seems most probable that Vaughan could never make up his mind what to think of Anglo-Catholicism, and wavered between those who told him that it was the work of the devil and the desire, expressed in his 1894 speech quoted above, to believe that it was in some dim way beyond his comprehension the work of God. Wilfrid Ward wrote to Halifax at the time of this speech:

> I think that the passage about 'the ape, etc.' which I regretted, was simply the echo of what some men living with the Cardinal say, not about your representative men, but about a comparatively small group of ritualists, as they are called.[31]

A danger to the church?

The closing pages of the *Risposta* bring to a climax the attempt to arouse the Roman cardinals to a realisation of the terrible danger threatening the church and the faith in the proposal to extend any recognition whatsoever, even a doubtful one, to Anglican Orders and sacraments. Only a fortnight before the appearance of the *Risposta*, a very favourable impression had been created in Rome by a lengthy and characteristically long-winded open letter from the eighty-six-year-old William Gladstone to the Archbishop of York, which contained expressions of great friendliness and respect towards the pope.[32] Anxious to damage the Anglican cause in every possible way, Gasquet and Moyes refer to the author of this letter as 'the celebrated chief of English Liberalism' who 'sought to destroy the work of the Vatican Council under Pius IX, and who today under Leo

[31] *Leo XIII* 111. Is it fanciful to discern the figure and view of Moyes himself in Ward's reference to 'some men living with the Cardinal'? If so, we have in the *Risposta* the phenomenon, not unknown in polemical writing, of a writer quoting his own words and views, but giving them greater importance by placing them in the mouth of a superior.

[32] Text in *Roman Diary* 139–49. Portal informed Halifax that the translation of this document, with which Lacey and Puller had assisted him, had occupied twenty-eight hours in all (*Leo XIII* 308). Fr Puller wrote to Halifax on 8th June 1896 that this letter 'has produced a profound and most excellent impression' in Rome (HP A4.243).

XIII would render it absolutely useless'.[33] This reference to 'English Liberalism' was quite as ambiguous as Lacey's use of the term 'catholic'. To the Roman cardinals in 1896 'liberalism' was the avowed enemy of true religion, specifically condemned as such by Pius IX in his Syllabus of Errors.[34] They could hardly have been expected to be aware that British liberalism was quite different from the continental variety, and that Gladstone himself was a devout High Church Anglican. It is not even likely that all of them could have been persuaded of this difference. The unexplained use of the term was disingenuous.

The pamphlet then quoted the London *Times*, which had said in a leading article commenting on Gladstone's letter only a fortnight previously that the recognition of Anglican Orders might well '*serve to weaken rather than to fortify the position of the Pope and of his Church*'.[35] Moreover the cardinals were reminded that this 'great English newspaper . . . represents more than any other the mind of the English people'. Just how representative *The Times* of this era was in matters affecting relations between the Church of England and Rome is shown by the fact that it had consistently championed Cardinal Vaughan's militant and intransigent line in commenting on the discussions of reunion between the two churches. Lord Halifax complained of this repeatedly,[36] and Archbishop Benson had noted the same bias in the newspaper and commented on it caustically. Thus he wrote in his diary on 29th June 1895, after consecrating five bishops in St Paul's Cathedral, London:

> *The Times* gave three small print lines to this consecration in the Metropolitan Cathedral of five bishops for all parts of the world and Edgar Jacob's striking sermon. It gave same day two columns to the foundation

[33] *Risposta* 31f. [34] Cf. DS 2977–80 (1777–80).

[35] *Risposta* 32f, emphasis in original citation. The leading article quoted here appeared in *The Times* on 1st June 1896.

[36] Halifax complained, for instance, that *The Times*' treatment of the pope's letter, *Ad Anglos*, on 22nd April 1895 'was a complete transcript of Cardinal Vaughan's mind, and gave exact expression to his wishes' (*Leo XIII* 20; cf. also 215f, 323–7, and 355f).

> of a new Romish Cathedral for Westminster. There are now two Romanists on the staff of *The Times* and this is the result. They miss no chance.[37]

Such facts could not be known to Roman cardinals, to whom the voice of *The Times* was quite simply the voice of imperial England, as Gasquet and Moyes knew full well.

The promised fruits of a condemnation

Finally, the authors of the *Risposta* held out for the cardinals who were shortly to judge of the validity of Anglican Orders a glowing prospect of the fruits to be reaped from a stern condemnation:

> Throughout England conversions are numerous. There is no doubt that the already large number of converts will increase if it is made more evident that the Roman Catholic Church is the only one in England which has a right to the prerogatives and name of *Catholic*.[38]

This was a faithful echo of a letter sent to the pope only a few weeks previously by Cardinal Vaughan with the endorsement of the entire catholic hierarchy in England.[39] This letter, which had just been printed for distribution to the cardinals, pleaded for the final and complete condemnation of Anglican Orders, alleging that any recognition would be a 'scandal to the faithful' in the British Isles, and that a condemnation 'would bring about a number of conversions'.[40] Cardinal Vaughan arranged for letters in the same sense to be sent by Irish and Scottish bishops. The abridged texts of these letters published for the first time by Messenger confirm the charge made by numerous Anglican commentators on the Bull that the Holy See had been subjected to very heavy pressure from the English hierarchy to give a negative decision on the Orders. Canon Moyes had frankly

[37] Diary, Trinity College Cambridge 1895, p. 180. For further expressions of Benson's view about the pro-Roman bias of *The Times* cf. A. C. Benson, *E. W. Benson* ii, 725 and 727.

[38] *Risposta* 33, emphasis in original.

[39] Abridged text in Messenger, RMP ii, 567ff.

[40] RMP ii, 568.

pleaded for such pressure to be brought to counter-balance the urgings from the other side that if the verdict on the Orders were negative it should not be published, so as not to destroy the goodwill which the reunion movement had built up.[41] Moyes had written to Cardinal Vaughan on 31st March 1896:

Mgr Merry del Val thinks, as we all think, that a firm and outspoken manifesto and representation of the English bishops (associated, if possible, *ad hoc*, with some of the Scottish and Irish), will be essential if we are to succeed. Your Eminence might, if it shall seem good to you, avail yourself of the Low Week meeting to secure this representation. The moment for submitting it to the Holy See could be chosen later on, and at the time when such pressure would be most likely to carry its purpose.[42]

The arguments in the letter of the English hierarchy closely parallel those used in the *Risposta.* The motives of the Anglicans were misrepresented in both documents, which stated that recognition of the Orders was being sought so that Anglicanism could, for the first time, claim the title of 'Catholic', and thus oppose the Roman Catholic Church in the English-speaking world more effectively. This ignored the fact that Anglicanism had claimed the title of 'Catholic' from the very start; the claim did not originate with the Tractarians, though they naturally gave it fresh emphasis. But they found ample support in the writings of earlier Anglican theologians.

[41] A great deal was subsequently made by Moyes and *The Tablet* of the pressure allegedly brought on the Holy See from the Anglican side. 'We have been accused [Lacey wrote subsequently] of trying alternately to bully and to cajole the Pope into giving a decision favourable to our claims. Our aim, it is hinted, was to frighten him by representing an adverse decision as fatal to hopes of union, so that he should at the worst keep silence. The memorandum with which Mr Gladstone intervened was 'a magnificent bribe', an attempt to move the aged Pontiff by holding out the prospect of what was nearest to his heart—the reconciliation of England to the Holy See' (*Roman Diary* 18). Lacey pointed out that this charge was inconsistent with another that was just as commonly made, both before and after the condemnation of the Orders: 'how [this charge] is to be reconciled with the supposition that we were timorously seeking a resolution of our own doubts, I will let others determine.' (ibid.). Most of the charges brought against the Anglicans were cancelled out in this way by other charges. Moyes especially was indifferent to any considerations of consistency (cf. also pp. 214ff below).

[42] RMP ii, 565.

Both the *Risposta* and the letter from the English hierarchy argued that the condemnation of Anglican Orders would result in an increased number of conversions.[43] It is certain that Cardinal Vaughan was convinced, despite Wilfrid Ward's warning to the contrary,[44] that a condemnation would bring many into the Roman Catholic Church. Ward wrote to the Duke of Norfolk after the Bull, reporting a conversation with the cardinal:

> He says numbers told him that if such a Bull was issued they would become Catholics, but that they have shown no sign of it since the Bull came out.[45]

When the anticipated wave of conversions did not materalise Moyes had no hesitation in informing the world, on the basis (as he wrote) of his twenty-seven years' residence in the same house with Vaughan and the intimate knowledge of the cardinal's mind thus afforded him, that no increase of conversions had ever been expected.

> It was said that Cardinal Vaughan seriously expected that hundreds of Anglican clergy would enter the Church if Anglican Orders were condemned. There was certainly a rumour to that effect, but, as far as I know, the Cardinal never attached importance to it, nor treated it as anything more than a rumour 'much too good to be true'.[46]

Just for good measure Moyes added that anyway there *was* a greater number of conversions after the condemnation than before: 'not notably greater, but still distinctly greater'.[47] The modesty of this claim is the surest measure of its significance.

Vaughan's expectation that the condemnation would usher in a 'period of grace and conversion'[48] does more credit to his piety than his intelligence. The Birmingham Oratorian Fr Humphrey Johnson was to write much later:

> A solemn pronouncement by Rome meant so much to [Vaughan] that he may well have felt that, once Peter's voice had sounded, numbers of his

[43] Cf. RMP ii, 568. [44] Cf. p. 74 above.
[45] Maisie Ward, *The Wilfrid Wards and the Transition*, London 1934, 294.
[46] *The Tablet* 88 (1912), 8 col. 2. [47] Ibid.
[48] Cf. Snead-Cox, *Cardinal Vaughan* ii, 227f, and *Leo XIII* 368f.

> truant children would cast themselves in loving submission at his feet. Had the Cardinal understood the Church of England better, he would have expected no such result. To the bulk of her clergy, the condemnation of their Orders was but one example of that never-failing *gaucherie* which the Popes showed whenever they meddled in English affairs; while to the minority who held a doctrine on the subject of Orders closely akin to the Catholic one, the belief that the sacraments of the Church of England had been to them vehicles of divine grace weighed more than all the arguments which Leo XIII's theologians could adduce.[49]

Despite the glowing assurances made to the pope that a condemnation would bring an increase of conversions, Moyes felt able to write afterwards that the condemnation had been dictated only by stern necessity. The recognition of the Orders would, he said, have gained for the pope

> the deep gratification [of] by far the most large and influential section of the English nation . . . the favour of the most powerful of Empires . . . popularity beyond all [the Pope's] predecessors in the estimate of the English-speaking press and people, . . . and a species of canonisation by the Anglican press and people. Above all . . . he would have done much . . . to conciliate souls, and to break down . . . prejudice. . . . As a set off to these gains, the Catholics of England could offer him nothing.[50]

In fact they had offered him a great deal, and no one was in a better position to know this than Moyes. The letter from Vaughan and the English hierarchy in May 1896 had assured the pope that a condemnation of the Orders

> would bring about a number of conversions [and be] nothing more than what Catholics universally in [English-speaking] countries, and Protestants, and the general public, expect. The astonishment would be extreme were the decision otherwise, and it would be rejected by a large number of the Low Church party with indignation.[51]

When it was a case of securing the condemnation, the pope was told that nothing but good would come of it, that it would increase conversions, and that the consequences of a positive decision would be disastrous. When the time came to justify the condemnation to the public, which had not reacted in the way predicted in these private communications

[49] H. J. T. Johnson, *Anglicanism in Transition*, 149f.
[50] *The Tablet* 57 (1897) 285 col. 1. [51] RMP ii, 568.

to the Holy See, people were told that only stern duty had dictated the decision, that the pope knew he had nothing to gain from a condemnation and much to lose.

In short, the *Risposta*, especially taken in conjunction with the letter of the English hierarchy which had preceded it by a few weeks, and which advanced the same arguments put forth in the concluding pages of Gasquet and Moyes' pamphlet, placed the matter before the pope and the cardinals in such a light that a vote in favour of even the most doubtful recognition of Anglican Orders was a vote against the faith and the church. The effect of the *Risposta* in Rome was reported by the indefatigable Merry del Val in a letter to Canon Moyes on 30th June 1896:

> I have distributed the *Risposta* to every prelate in the Vatican and to many outside and everyone without a single exception is delighted with it and loud in its praises. For nearly all it is quite a revelation and has turned the tide in many cases. Thank God for it.[52]

The indignation expressed by Halifax and Lacey in their books is entirely understandable. Of greater significance are the opinions expressed by two men identified with Halifax. The scholarly Bishop of Peterborough, Dr Mandell Creighton, wrote to Halifax:

> The production of Moyes and Gasquet is unworthy: it is purely political and founded on nothing but temporary expedient.[53]

And only a fortnight before his death Archbishop Benson wrote to Halifax:

> I am extremely obliged to you for sending me the Memorandum of your correspondence and for the Italian document, *Risposta* . . . I can scarcely understand how so shameless a document as the latter can have been put out and accepted.[54]

[52] GP. [53] *Leo XIII* 367.

[54] Ibid. 368. In the original of this letter (HP A4.219) the archbishop referred to *Apostolicae curae* as 'the Encyclical [*sic*] with its infallible fallacies', thus anticipating by more than a half a century the anonymous authors of a polemical Anglican tract. [Eric Jay *et al.*], *Infallible Fallacies*, London 1953.

10
THE CONDEMNATION

How shocking to adore as very God elements that are but bread and wine, and to bend down after auricular confession in order to receive a mere human and useless absolution!

—Cardinal Vaughan[1]

Three days after the abrupt and unexpected termination of the commission's work on 7th May Canon Moyes wrote to Cardinal Vaughan:

> The Commission held its final sitting on Thursday, and the whole matter now passes into the hands of the Holy Office. The preparation of the statement for the use of the Holy Office and résumé of the results of the Commission has been put into the hands of a Dominican Father, a friend of Mgr Merry del Val, and of P. Llevaneras, whose opinion is quite upon our side.[2]

In a subsequent letter to the cardinal, written on 3rd June, Moyes identifies the Dominican here referred to as 'Fr Pierrotti, who is altogether sound upon the question, and has stated the case excellently'.[3] It will be recalled that de Llevaneras had supported Vaughan's three representatives in the commission throughout, and that he was probably the only one who joined them in voting at the end for invalidity. When the dossier was entrusted to two strong opponents of the Orders to be put into shape for submission to the cardinals of the Holy Office, who were to make the decision, it was clear which way the wind was blowing. Even in the commission itself the balance had been weighted against the Anglicans by the appointment of a president and secretary who acted throughout in close co-operation with the three original English members and de Llevaneras against the Anglican claims. With the abrupt termination of the

[1] Snead-Cox, *Cardinal Vaughan* ii, 227f. [2] *The Tablet* 137 (1937), 153 col. 2.
[3] *The Tablet* art. cit. in previous note, 154 col. 1.

commission's work on 7th May the principle of parity of representation between the two sides was abandoned completely. Gasquet had already written during the commission's meetings that the final decision would not depend on the results of the commission's work.

> I expect a decree against the validity is a certainty. Luckily it does not depend on the result of our meetings, and I have a much higher idea of the utility of the Holy Office than I had, and I have no doubt that the consideration of the question will be put into the hands of some good man.[4]

This prediction proved to be considerably more accurate than many of Gasquet's statements about facts and events of past history.

Fleming, Gasquet, and Moyes were received by Leo XIII in farewell audience on 18th June. Although the final meeting of the Holy Office was still a month off, the pope obviously had little doubt as to what the decision would be when it came. He asked the three English priests whether a condemnation of the Orders, which, so far as he knew, would be the ultimate outcome of the affair, would not cause annoyance to the British government, or whether the Anglican bishops would not urge the Queen and her government to resent a condemnation of their church and their orders.

> We assured him [Moyes wrote to Cardinal Vaughan the next day] that neither Her Majesty nor her Government would dream of taking any steps in the matter, and that the Anglican archbishops had no such influence. To which the Holy Father said, 'Yes, that is my belief, for those bishops are only *employés* and creatures of the State.'[5]

[4] Letter of Gasquet to Vaughan, 24th April 1896, *The Tablet* art. cit. 153 col. 1. On 4th April 1896 Gasquet had written to Edmund Bishop: 'Heaven only knows how long *our* discussions are likely to last; but the result of them really doesn't matter, because they are only preliminary to the examination of the question by the Holy Office' (BP).

[5] RMP ii, 572. Typical of Messenger's carelessness with regard to even the most important details is his statement that this audience occurred 'two days after the final decision of the Holy Office' (loc. cit.), which he has stated on the previous page (571) was held on 16th July. And yet on p. 573 n. 1 he can write that the letter from Moyes to Vaughan reporting this audience was written on 19th *June*. This confusion of June and July is an excellent example of the errors which fill Messenger's two ponderous volumes, and make it very difficult to place any confidence in their contents, despite the vast amount of labour that has obviously gone into their production.

This last statement was taken directly from the *Risposta*, which had appeared less than a fortnight previously. Gasquet and Moyes had obviously done their work well. The audience closed with the three English priests telling the pope there was not the slightest chance of corporate reunion, but that they had

> every reason to hope that there would be a steadily increasing influx of converts. . . . But for that result it is essential that we should make it absolutely clear that Anglicanism has no vestige of title to call itself Catholic.[6]

Frs de Llevaneras and Pierrotti appear to have taken the better part of a month working over the documents, and then to have submitted them to the cardinals of the Holy Office early in June. On 8th June, the day of his departure from Rome, Fr Puller wrote to Lord Halifax:

> The commission of Cardinals begins its sittings this week. They have got a month to study the matter, before they report.[7]

He added that this information had been given to him confidentially and 'must not at present be given to the public'.[8] Lacey records that he and Puller went to see Cardinal Rampolla at 1 p.m. on the day that Puller wrote this letter, so it is possible that this information was given them by Rampolla himself. Lacey says they found him 'curiously nervous in manner, but most encouraging'.[9] Lacey's diary also reports that Fr Puller had called on Cardinal Serafino Vannutelli on Saturday 6th June and was told

> that a commission of Cardinals was forthwith to take up the question of the Ordinations. He would receive the dossier on Monday 8th June, and the first meeting would be on Wednesday or Thursday.[10]

The day following this inteview the same cardinal told Portal 'that the instruction to the Commission was to study the documents for a month'.[11]

[6] RMP ii, 572f. [7] HP A4.243. [8] Ibid.
[9] Lacey, *Roman Diary* 81. [10] Ibid. 80. [11] Ibid. 81.

Cardinal Rampolla's absence from the Feria V meeting

The cardinals of the Holy Office met in the presence of the pope on Thursday 16th July 1896. A Feria v meeting under the personal presidency of the pope was chosen in order to lend greater authority to the decision which was to be taken. An unusual effort must have been made to procure a full attendance, for Cardinal Mertel, who was ill, had himself carried into the meeting. There was one absentee: the Secretary of State, Cardinal Rampolla.[12]

That the leading cardinal in curia should absent himself from such an important meeting is most interesting. Both Lord Halifax and Canon Lacey make it clear that Rampolla had been unusually sympathetic and friendly towards the Anglicans and the reunion movement from the start. It will be recalled that it was he who first sent for Portal in the summer of 1894, and who at once took him to see the pope after hearing Portal's report about his recent visit to England. During the meetings of the commission it was Rampolla who had given Gasparri permission, despite the oath of secrecy imposed upon the commissioners, to consult freely with Lacey and Puller. Rampolla's friendliness towards the Anglicans was the subject of constant complaints in Merry del Val's letters to his friends in England. On 15th December 1895 he wrote to Gasquet:

> You are quite right in saying that the mischief has been done here and is almost exclusively due to Cardinal Rampolla, who has acted without seeking and very often in spite of information and warnings received. It is all the more sad that it is difficult to speak too highly of his right intentions and high qualities. But facts are facts. Still I can assume that we have to be thankful that matters are not worse, for we have had some hairbreadth escapes in the last few months. I wonder that my hair has not

[12] Cf. Gasquet, *Leaves* 75. A manuscript memorandum in Gasquet's hand reports under the date of Thursday 10th September 1896: 'Merry del Val gave me an account of the meeting of the Holy Office on July 16th. He says that the Cardinals were all present, including even Card. Mertel who had to be carried in. There was an absolute unanimity of all the members (Card. Rampolla did not attend)' (GP).

turned white, for it has only been at the last minute and by speaking directly to the Holy Father that some things have been stopped.[13]

Two letters written by Merry del Val to Gasquet after the meeting of 16th July, at which the decision to condemn Anglican Orders was taken in Rampolla's absence, show that the cardinal's friendliness to the Anglicans continued to the end. On 29th July 1896 Merry del Val cabled to Gasquet in London:

ABSOLUTE RESERVE MORE NECESSARY THAN EVER. TELL CARDINAL [Vaughan]
MERRY DEL VAL[14]

Merry del Val followed this up with a letter of explanation to Gasquet on the same day.

I telegraphed today by way of extra precaution commending absolute reserve on all that concerns Anglican Orders. Every effort is being made to save Portal and his mischievous work, and unfortunately he has still the favour of Card. R[ampolla]. If anything transpires of what the Pope is doing or preparing in the matter of a decision on Anglican Orders we shall have a deal of trouble. They will move heaven and earth to stop an adverse decision.[15]

Five days later Merry del Val again lamented Rampolla's continuing friendship towards Portal and Halifax and the cause they had been promoting.

Halifax is using every means in his power, fair and foul, to protect the *Revue* and defend Portal here, and alas! there is one here as you know who is only too ready to listen to him and believe in him.[16]

[13] Leslie, *Cardinal Gasquet* 59f; original letter in GP.
[14] Original telegram in GP. [15] Letter of 29th July 1896, GP.
[16] Letter of 3rd August 1896, GP. The 'fair and foul' means adopted by Halifax consisted of a letter to Cardinal Rampolla protesting at the misrepresentations of Portal's work by English catholics both in private communications to the Vatican and in public attacks in the columns of *The Tablet*, which reached a climax of vituperation in August 1896. (For the text of this letter cf. *Leo XIII* 346f.) In particular Portal was charged with ignoring the claims of the papacy in a speech to a private gathering in London on 14th July 1896, at which he had pleaded for corporate reunion as a better and more christian way of ending the divisions between christians than proselytising for individual conversions, with all the spiritual dangers involved for those whose whole religious lives and convictions were thrown into turmoil and doubt by such proselytism. Portal's speech also included an impassioned proclamation of loyalty to the papacy. *The Tablet*, which published repeated attacks on Portal for this speech in the weeks following, completely ignored the Abbé's defence of the papal claims and concentrated entirely on the passages of the speech which dealt with corporate reunion. The full text of the speech can be read in English translation in Macmillan, *Portal* 66–74.

It is clear that Rampolla, who was fifty-three in 1896 and at the height of his powers, was a man of independent and, for those days, progressive views. To the Anglican layman Sir Walter Phillimore, Rampolla spoke of 'the necessity that the Church should be democratic (not demagogic), the "plebs sancta", and so forth'[17]—views which have a startlingly modern ring to them. And a remark made by Rampolla to Lord Halifax in the winter of 1895 gives further evidence of the cardinal's independent views. Halifax related the conversation shortly afterwards to Archbishop Benson, who was staying with friends in Florence, and Benson recorded it in his diary.

> Halifax told me that he had expressed to Rampolla his own (not very English) liking for the office of Benediction. To which R. replied: 'I don't know about that. The multiplication of such rites is not to be desired. We must never forget that the central word of our Lord's command is *Eat*.' Rather a striking reproof. [18]

Weighing all this evidence, and putting it together with the full attendance at the Feria V meeting of 16th July, for which even a sick cardinal appeared, it is difficult not to suspect that Cardinal Rampolla deliberately absented himself in order to avoid association with a decision which he knew was inevitable but regretted. It was a device for which there was excellent precedent at Rome.[19]

[17] Letter of Phillimore to Halifax, *Leo XIII* 288. Cf. also the letter of Baron von Hügel to the Abbé Loisy, written from Rome towards the end of 1894, in which von Hügel described Rampolla as a 'friendly, forthcoming, good and holy man, who desires the welfare of the Church', and contrasted him with Cardinal Mazzella, whom the Baron characterised as 'very absolute and very irritable in all matters' (cf. A. Loisy, *Mémoires* i, 367).

[18] Diary, Trinity College, Cambridge: entry for 19th April 1895, p. 112. Halifax was such an irrepressible enthusiast that he cannot always be relied on when he reports that people agreed with him. But in this case be is reporting that he was contradicted, and his account may be accepted. Halifax's views about the people he was dealing with reveal him as a shrewd judge of character. Benson records: 'He finds Vaughan stupid but honest—Rampolla good—Gasquet nobody, Moyes violent—Gaspari [*sic*], von Hügel, Duchesne the real able... [illegible]' (Diary, 18th April 1895, p. 109).

[19] The most notable precedent being the action of the minority at the first Vatican Council, which departed before the final vote on papal infallibility in order to avoid being compelled to vote *non placet*.

The decision

The meeting of the pope and cardinals was lengthy. Fourteen years later Merry del Val, who was by then Pius X's Secretary of State, wrote to Canon Moyes:

> I can testify that the Feria V lasted at least two hours and a half. I was in attendance on the Holy Father and I spent all that long time in the Holy Father's private chapel, saying my office and praying for the blessing of God on the meeting. I remember coming out from time to time wondering at the length of the proceedings and rejoicing that the matter should be so fully discussed. It did not take five or six Cardinals two hours and a half to say 'affirmative' or 'negative' or 'dilata'. Each one must have spoken at length and you know that their verdict was unanimous.[20]

Portal informed his Anglican friends at the time that in his opinion it was this meeting which discussed the value of the previous decisions in 1684 and 1704, which Cardinal Mazzella would not permit the original commission to debate.[21] Portal's conjecture is supported by the account of this Feria V meeting printed by Gasquet, who got his information from Merry del Val. In his *Leaves from My Diary* Gasquet says that two questions were submitted to the cardinals:

> 1. whether the question of the validity of Anglican Orders had been previously submitted properly to the Holy See, and fully determined;
>
> 2. whether the recent enquiry had shown that the previous decision was just and wise, or whether it called for revision.

The answer of the cardinals was unanimously affirmative in both cases: the question *had* been fully determined already,

[20] Letter of 13th December 1910, Westminster Archives; cited by kind permission of Cardinal Heenan. 'Dilata' is the technical term for voting to take no action on a pending question. The full text of this letter is printed on pp. 300–4 below.

[21] Cf. Lacey's letter of 26th September to the Revd W. D. Frere: 'As Portal says, the only question for [the cardinals] was, *whether there were grounds for revising the decision*' in the Gordon case (*Roman Diary* 135f; emphasis original). Cf. also the letter of Portal to Halifax cited on p. 166 above.

and the recent enquiry had shown the previous decision to be just and wise.[22]

'Apostolicae curae'

The drafting of the Bull embodying this decision was entrusted to the secretary of the commission which had investigated the Orders, the thirty-one-year-old Mgr Merry del Val. He was aided by Mgr Vincenzo Tarozzi, of the Secretariat for Latin Letters, who was responsible for putting Merry del Val's draft into acceptable Latin. Merry del Val found his task no light one, and he turned increasingly for information and assistance to Gasquet. The letter of 29th July cited above emphasising the need for secrecy also contained the first of Merry del Val's questions.

> Can you let me know as soon as possible whether the quotation in the foot note of page 4 of 'Documenta ad legationem Card: Poli spectantia'[23] taken from Queen Mary's decree is textually copied or not. It differs from the version given by Gasparri on page 9 of his work No. 18: e.g. he has 'juxta novum ordinandi modum' and 'cum non vere ordinati sint', whereas in your version the decree is made to say 'secundum modum ordinandi noviter fabricatum' and then 'quod vere et de facto ordinati non fuere'. I require to settle this point and to be sure of the original text.[24]

Gasquet's published works show that he was not a trustworthy authority on questions of this sort. Merry del Val did not know this, however, and continued to appeal to Gasquet for the information he needed in drafting the Bull. On 1st August another lengthy letter from Merry del Val posed fourteen questions with regard to the faculties issued by Pope Julius III to Cardinal Pole.[25]

Two days later a similar but shorter letter followed with

[22] Cf. Gasquet, *Leaves* 75.
[23] Privately printed, Rome, 5th May 1896. This was one of the documents submitted by Cardinal Vaughan's three representatives to the commission.
[24] GP.
[25] GP. For the full text cf Appendix, pp. 304–5.

supplementary questions of the same sort, Merry del Val assuring Gasquet:

> I have been asked to write to you and of course a word from you will do away with all doubts on this point.[26]

Gasquet was flattered by this deference, and took an early opportunity of informing his friend Edmund Bishop of the important role he was playing behind the scenes. He wrote on 8th August:

> I had to rush back from Stanbrook to look up some papers for the authorities in Rome. They kindly offered to take my word for the facts; but I thought it worth breaking into my rest to give them chapter and verse.[27]

There is no part of the controversy over Anglican Orders which is so confusing as these lengthy legal documents from the Marian period, and anyone who has wrestled with their intractable and endless sentences will be able to sympathise with Merry del Val, trying to find his way through this maze of sixteenth-century legal terminology in the heat of the Roman summer, with Francis Aidan Gasquet as his guide. The extent of Merry del Val's dependence on Gasquet, as well as the perplexities that the work of drafting the Bull were causing him, come out clearly in the following letter:

✠ *Private*

10.viii.96

My dear Fr Gasquet,

Many thanks for your letters duly received. They furnish me abundantly with all I wanted and now I think it will be straight sailing. There can be no doubt that the 8th of March document 'Dilecte fili' and 'sub annulo piscatoris' is a '*Brief*' including and extending faculties contained in the previous Bulls and Briefs you mention. The three documents 'Si ullo unquam tempore, 2) Cum nos hodie and 3) Post nuntium nobis—must be Bulls. You do not give the form in which they wind up nor the countersignatures, but the servus servorum from the Pope to the Legate leaves no doubt as to the nature of the documents. These latter are what I particularly wanted to be able to quote in order to establish the progression authoritatively.

[26] Letter of 3rd August 1896, GP. [27] BP.

I am entirely at one with you on the advisability of not being too explicit as to the reasons; and in fact I have done a great deal already in the way of pruning on the first draft. Some things were too absolutely asserted, others left open to misunderstanding; others on the contrary were omitted which had to be referred to, or our Anglican and French friends might say that such or such position had not been met and that a basis had been left for further discussion. It is difficult to know exactly where to draw the line. It is wished that the document should be reasoned out and there seem two extremes to be avoided: saying too much, and saying too little. One argument naturally suggests another and there are so many that it is not easy to select what should be put in and what should be left out. If one had not to deal with such absurdly sophistical opponents, there would not be much trouble. I have pleaded, and I hope with success, that the document or at all events a portion of it should be submitted to you. In a matter so serious every precaution should be taken, and you will be able to give a valuable judgment.

I have not said anything to you as yet of the famous Fer.v: a great day for us. I am waiting to do so until I see you which I hope may be before very long. The secrecy of the H.O. has not been laid upon me, but I felt that under the circumstances and in view of the confidence shown me, I ought to be able to say that I had not even spoken to you, to whom I should have communicated what I knew before any one else. The reserve maintained by the Cardinals of the H.O. is a blessing: but in this case there is something providential in the general way in which the whole thing has passed unnoticed. Nothing, not even the fact of the meeting was realised or mentioned. The local press and chatterboxes were silent, and yet considering the solemnity of the meeting, it would have been natural to notice it and not very difficult to guess what was going on. But nothing transpired even amongst the attendants.

I am glad you have been getting prayers. We want them so much to steer us thro' this last phase.

Believe me
Yrs affec[ly]
Raph. Merry del Val

How innocent Lacey makes himself out in the Tablet!![28]

[28] GP. The reference in this postscript was to Lacey's explanation in letters to *The Tablet* of his action in submitting to the commission the previous May in Rome a document which purported to be a record of Barlow's consecration. Lacey explained that this document had just been found in England, and news of it telegraphed to him. For a few days he thought it was something new, and that it proved Barlow's consecration. He soon discovered that this was not the case, and stated in his 'Supplementum', which, it will be recalled, he had written in Rome immediately after the close of the commission's meetings, that the document in question was not new and did not prove Barlow's consecration (cf. *The Tablet* 56 (1896), 140 and 218). After Lacey's first letter of explanation in *The Tablet* at the end of July Merry del Val had written to Gasquet in his letter of 29th July: 'What falsehood and dis-

On 19th August Merry del Val was able to send the full text of the Bull as he had drafted it, together with the following letter:

✠

J.M.J.

Private

19.viii.96

My dear Father Gasquet,

I am instructed to forward to you these two copies of the Bull on Ang: Ord[s]. for you to remark on. I send two copies in case Can: Moyes may be within easy reach and you may like to consult with him. You are requested not to take more than two or at most three days to look through the document, and to forward your criticism and suggestions to me as soon as possible.

There is no need to return the copies, as we have others: it will be sufficient if you refer to the pages. When you have sent off your remarks, the orders are, that these copies are to be destroyed without delay.

Do not hesitate to say quite freely what you think might be taken off, added or corrected in the document.

I hope Can: Moyes will not be angry at his old friend Barlow being left out in the cold.

I have not been at all well these days. I hope to start for England very soon after receiving your answer.

Yrs affect[ly] in X[t]

Raph. Merry del Val[29]

By the time this letter, with the two copies of the Bull mentioned in it, reached England, Gasquet was cruising up the Seine aboard the yacht *Alvina*, which belonged to his wealthy English friend Mr Cave. There was considerable excitement, therefore, when a large packet arrived at Mr Cave's country house in Hampshire from the Vatican addressed to Dom Gasquet, and this occasioned a flurry of telegrams back and forth to Rouen, where the French post office managed to make contact with the yacht. Merry del Val's letter and the two copies of the Bull were sent over to

---

honesty after being found out!' (GP). The evidence does not support Merry del Val's interpretation of Lacey's motives: he appears to have acted in good faith throughout. This did not prevent *The Tablet* from printing the charge of bad faith and fraud in a number of articles attacking Lacey.

[29] GP.

France, and reached Gasquet at Rouen on 24th August. Two days previously Merry del Val had wired Gasquet that he was to send his remarks to Mgr Tarozzi at the Vatican and not to Merry del Val. A letter written on the same day explains this change of plan.

> I have got so knocked up that the Holy Father has settled that I should leave at once for England without waiting for yr. answer. By his wish I have sent you a telegram telling you to forward yr. remarks on the Bull in Latin or French to Mgr Tarozzi, Vatican. If you have anything further to communicate on the subject after that you can let me know as I shall be in correspondence with Tarozzi. We have been working together at the document and there will be no difficulty in understanding each other. In fact I think it would be well if you were to let me know what corrections etc. you have sent him in order that I may be able to see that he has not misunderstood them.[30]

As soon as he received the draft of the Bull Gasquet sat down on the yacht and wrote out a memorandum summarising its contents. His comments show that he was delighted at the document, as well he might have been, for it followed closely the arguments advanced by himself and his two colleagues in their *votum Ordines Anglicani*, which has been analysed in Chapter 7 above. In the letter which he sent to Mgr Tarozzi from Rouen on 24th August, copies of which in both English and French are preserved amongst Gasquet's papers,[31] he suggested only one change. It was inaccurate, he wrote, to say that 'the new form and manner of ordaining and consecrating' was presented to Pope Paul IV at the time of Thirlby's mission in 1555.

> This is hardly correct, since the document referred to is not a *full* account of the form of ordination but gives what it takes to be the essential parts

[30] Letter of 22nd August 1896, GP. This letter shows that Mgr Tarozzi was unfamiliar with the complexities of the question itself, and confirms that his contribution was primarily linguistic.

[31] The French translation is in an unknown hand on letter paper headed 'Alvina, R Y S' (i.e. Royal Yacht Squadron), and bears the notation in Gasquet's hand: 'Letter sent *re* Bull to Mgr Farozzi [*sic*] from Rouen Aug. 24.' Merry del Val's telegram of 22nd August had been garbled in transmission, and gave the name of his colleague as 'Farozzi' instead of 'Tarozzi'. (Original telegram in GP.) The initial letter of the name in Merry del Val's letter to Gasquet of 22nd August was also unclear.

only, amongst which is the Accipe Spiritum Sanctum. That being so I should suggest that the clause be omitted.[32]

On 30th August Merry del Val, who was by now in England, wrote to acknowledge Gasquet's comments on the Bull, and to assure him that the change he had suggested would be made. This letter is particularly important, for it shows that up to this point no one but Merry del Val and the Latinist Tarozzi had worked on the draft of the Bull.

✠ Writtle Park,
Chelmsford.

30.viii.96

My dear Fr Gasquet,

I was delighted to get yr. letter of yesterday; the other no doubt will be duly forwarded. It is such a relief to think that the work of these last weeks has not been useless, as it gave some trouble and I was awaiting yr. opinion with some anxiety. Tarozzi had at first expressed the point you mention even more explicitly. I objected to it, but I thought there was sufficient evidence, tho' not documentary, to admit of our saying 'forma et ratio' as a general expression.[33] But of course if you think it had better be changed, it will be quite easy to do so. No doubt by this time Tarozzi will have expressed it differently.

The document so far has only been in his and my hands. It is to go to Cardinals Mazzella, Serafino Vannutelli, and Di Pietro and possibly (?) to Card R——. I do hope it will not be spoiled. But I am to see it again I was told before it is published and we are to have it here for the translation, so that if there is something to correct or suggest there will still be time.

I am very much better since I left Rome and above all since I came here. I shall be in town one day soon and *of course* I will pay you a visit. It will be such a pleasure to see you again.

Yrs affec^{ly}

Raph Merry del Val[34]

Since Gasquet destroyed both copies of Merry del Val's draft, as instructed, it is impossible to compare this version with the one published three weeks later. But any changes

[32] Letter of Gasquet to Mgr Tarozzi, 24th August 1896, GP. This suggestion of Gasquet's was adopted, and in the Bull as finally issued it was stated simply that 'the pertinent parts of the new Ordinal were submitted to the Pope' (AO[E] 5).

[33] The phrase criticised by Gasquet had said that Pope Paul IV was given the 'forma et ratio nova ordinandi et consecrandi'.

[34] GP.

must have been minor, for the Bull as published corresponds in all particulars to the summary made by Gasquet of the draft he received on 24th August. Subsequent letters between him and Merry del Val, as well as memoranda of events in Gasquet's hand, show that the work of translating the Bull into English was done jointly by Merry del Val and the three English commissioners between 9th and 15th September. Cardinal Vaughan was not involved in these final stages. The work which he had so much at heart was done for him by others more competent in such things than himself. Gasquet recorded in one of his memoranda:

> At Downside on Monday, 14th [September], where I was for Fr Jerome's funeral, I gave the Cardinal a copy of the Bull to read. He hadn't seen it before.[35]

The Bull was dated 13th September 1896, and was issued in Rome on Friday 18th. The news was in some of the London evening papers on that date, and the full story appeared in all the morning papers on 19th September. The Bull's conclusion is well known:

> We pronounce and declare that Ordinations carried out according to the Anglican rite have been and are absolutely null and utterly void.[36]

[35] GP. 'Fr Jerome' was a brother of Cardinal Vaughan, and died on 9th September 1896. I am indebted for this information to Dom Daniel Rees of Downside.

[36] AO(E) 14.

11
POST-MORTEM

It was really the love of souls which motivated us, we wanted nothing else. We wanted to do something to put an end to the divisions between those who love our Lord Jesus Christ, those divisions which keep so many souls from him. . . . We have tried to do what God, as I believe, inspired us to do. We have been checked for the moment, but if God wills it, his will will be accomplished; and if he allows us to be broken, it is because he wants to accomplish things himself. It is not a dream. The thing is as certain as ever. There are afflictions which are worth all earthly joys, and it is a thousand times dearer to me to suffer with you in such a cause than to triumph with the whole world.

—Lord Halifax to the Abbé Portal[1]

It is not for us to judge what we have done, but it does seem to me that it will be clear to all that we were inspired solely by Christian motives in beginning our work, and that we carried it out with Christian methods. . . . I certainly do not think the same can be said of our adversaries.

—The Abbé Portal to Lord Halifax[2]

Apostolicae curae naturally marked the end of the reunion movement which the Abbé Portal and Lord Halifax had initiated. Within a few weeks the *Revue Anglo-Romaine* had been suppressed. And 'the lynx-eyed Merry del Val', as Gasquet's biographer calls him, told Gasquet, Moyes, and Fleming at a 'happy and exciting dinner' in Gasquet's house in London celebrating the great victory over the Anglicans:

> The unfortunate Abbé has at last been shut up. [Halifax] is very angry at Portal being sent to other spheres of usefulness'.[3]

Lord Halifax

Thus the reunion movement ended in total and abject failure—as the world judges failure. And Lord Halifax has generally had a rather bad press since. In fact, it has become

[1] Letter of 21st September 1896, *Leo XIII* 357f.
[2] Letter of 14th March 1912, commenting on receipt of Halifax's book, *Leo XIII and Anglican Orders*: HP A4.213.
[3] Leslie, *Cardinal Gasquet* 70f.

fashionable to dismiss him as a hopelessly unrealistic visionary and dreamer, and a mischievous interferer into the bargain. Gasquet's biographer refers to 'the charming and irresponsible Lord Halifax, half a saint and wholly a busybody'.[4] And even as sober and responsible a writer as the Anglican Bishop G. K. A. Bell of Chichester refers to Halifax as being 'on fire for the unity of the Church' but not 'skilled in ecclesiastical statesmanship', adding that he possessed

> not only an astonishing vivacity, but an ardent belief that if only the Pope and the Archbishop of Canterbury would write one another the sort of letters he drafted for their consideration, everything would be well.[4a]

The principle charge brought against Halifax is that he never realised that he spoke for only a tiny minority in the Church of England.[5] There is, however, a surprising amount of evidence for Halifax's realism. Despite his soaring enthusiasm, Halifax realised in his soberer moments that he was far in advance of public opinion, and that not even all the members of the English Church Union were prepared to go as far as their president in conceding the primacy of the Bishop of Rome. We have already noted Halifax's statement that 'reunion could not be the work of today or tomorrow, inasmuch as I and those who sympathised with me only represented a comparatively small party in the Church of England'.[6] To this may be added a letter which Halifax wrote to Portal in March 1896 defending himself against the criticisms of another French priest, the Abbé Klein.

> It is true [Halifax wrote] that if one considers the Church of England as a whole the proportion of those who desire reunion with Rome is small [*peu nombreuse*]. We do not need the Abbé Klein to inform us of this; but it is also true, and the Abbé Klein does not say this, that, numerous

[4] Leslie, *Cardinal Gasquet* 53f.
[4a] G. K. A. Bell, *Christian Unity, The Anglican Position*, London 1948, 68ff.
[5] 'Halifax overestimated the influence of the Anglo-Catholics . . .' (J. P. Michael, art. 'Halifax', LThK iv, 1331).
[6] Cf. p. 70 above.

> or not, circumstances, or, as I should rather say, God's providence allows the partisans of reunion, thanks to you, to stir people's minds in England and to push this question to a point which it has never reached hitherto.[7]

In season and out Halifax maintained that 'great movements were generally the result of determined action on the part of resolute minorities',[8] and he could point to the history of the catholic revival in the Church of England in support of this statement. The documents published by Halifax in 1912 show that what he was able to achieve in forming and leading public opinion was astonishing, considering the temper of the times and the opposition with which he was faced. No one is entitled to pass judgement upon Halifax who has not carefully read and considered these documents.

Halifax himself placed the blame for the failure squarely upon the shoulders of Cardinal Vaughan and Archbishop Benson. Halifax's biographer has pointed out that these two men

> from their conflicting points of view, were closer to each other than either was to Halifax. They, at any rate, spoke the same language and lived on the same plane. The language was that of common-sense, the plane that of practical politics. It was no more possible for their minds to meet the mind of Halifax than it is for two parallel straight lines to meet each other.[9]

Halifax's judgement about both men was severe:

> I say it with regret: the whole of Cardinal Vaughan's conduct, as I think the correspondence makes sufficiently clear, was unworthy of him; and it is no less painful to have to admit that what is true of Cardinal Vaughan is true in its degree of Archbishop Benson. . . . Few men have ever had so great an opportunity offered to them as the Archbishop; no man, I think, ever so completely threw it away. On Cardinal Vaughan's shoulders rests the chief responsibility for the failure of all that was attempted, but a share of that responsibility must also rest on the shoulders of Archbishop Benson.[10]

By the time he came to write these lines in 1911 Halifax had obviously forgotten a more generous judgement of the

[7] PP. [8] *Leo XIII* 385; cf. also ibid. 101 and loc. cit. in n. 7 above.
[9] Lockhart, *Halifax* ii, 90. [10] *Leo XIII* 386ff.

archbishop which he had expressed fourteen years previously in a hitherto unpublished letter to Benson's son and biographer A. C. Benson, a copy of which is preserved amongst the archbishop's papers in the library of Trinity College, Cambridge. Referring to Benson's suspicious and negative attitude at the time of Portal's second visit in September 1894, when Cardinal Rampolla's letter was produced and discussed, Halifax had written on 17th December 1897:

> I was very much disappointed on [*sic*] the attitude of the Archbishop then and later. As things have turned out, in the light of subsequent events I am by no means sure I did not do him an injustice. I think now the check was providential and that though what I wanted was right in itself, men's minds were not ready for it, and that the *shock* would have been too great if the Archbishop had done what I wanted.[11]

If Halifax's subsequent judgements were severe, his conduct was magnanimous and generous throughout. Even after the final humiliating defeat, while Cardinal Vaughan was publicly taunting the fallen foe, Halifax did not waver from the magnanimity he had shown from the start. On 28th September Vaughan made a speech at Hanley in which he alleged that interest in the pope's condemnation of Anglican Orders was confined to 'an extremely small minority of the English people, and even to a minority amongst Anglicans'. No effort and skill had been spared by this minority, he said, to convince the Holy See of the validity of the Orders.

> They now find themselves shivering in their insular isolation, condemned by the Catholic Church, disowned within their own communion, as well as by the immense majority of the English people. . . . The close of the

[11] Typed copy of letter from Lord Halifax to A. C. Benson at the back of volume, 'Private Letters of Abp. Benson 1895 to 1896', unpaginated; Trinity College, Cambridge. Emphasis in original. Halifax was to go on finding prelates in both churches disappointing people for most of his life, men strangely unaware of the responsibilities and opportunities of their high calling. A letter he wrote to his friend Athelstan Riley, in 1919, contains a typical judgement:

'What you say about the Bishop of Winchester is exactly what I said to Edward [his son] last week: everything that was good in his letter could have been put into one sentence, but that is a prelate with whom I find it extraordinarily tiresome to have to do—all that one can say is that he is not wicked like the Bishop of Carlisle' (Letter of 22nd September 1919: HP A4.215).

controversy for those who face reality . . . will usher in a period of grace and conversion. . . . How shocking to adore as very God elements that are but bread and wine, and to bend down after auricular confession in order to receive a mere human and useless absolution![12]

Only a few days after this speech Halifax wrote to Vaughan:

I have a great regard and affection for your Eminence, and I like to say so because your Eminence compels me to fight, instead of, as I had hoped and prayed, helping us to peace. Thank God, gentlemen can fight and be friends, that they can do so is a great happiness, and your Eminence will see that despite everything I feel your Eminence to be my friend by my sending you the letter I wrote to the Abbé Portal when I got his letter announcing the Bull. Your Eminence will see from it that above all things I want to be loyal and true, for indeed I could not bear to say behind your Eminence's back what I did not say to your face.[13]

Cardinal Vaughan replied with a long letter of which Halifax reproduced only a small part in his book. The cardinal thought Halifax would agree with him in rejoicing at the Bull's decision, since it meant that

men have not had the power to profane and dishonour Our Lord in the Blessed Eucharist during the last three centuries which they would have had were their Orders valid. Think of how shocking it would be if men were actually producing Our Lord, not to be honoured and adored, but in truth to be disowned and dishonoured by themselves and the people.[14]

The remainder of the letter, not printed by Halifax, is a

[12] Snead-Cox, *Cardinal Vaughan* ii, 227f; cf. *Leo XIII* 368f. It was of this speech that Wilfrid Ward wrote fourteen years later, in what may be termed a classic example of English understatement: '. . . the language was not persuasive' (Ward, 'Cardinal Vaughan, A Personal Appreciation', *Morning Post*, 16th August 1910, 4.)

[13] *Leo XIII* 371.

[14] Ibid. Apart from the theological crudity of the expression 'producing Our Lord', to which Halifax took exception in his book (372), Vaughan's language showed no awareness of the truth stated by his contemporary Cardinal Rampolla to Lord Halifax in 1895: 'We must never forget that the central word of our Lord's command is *Eat*' (cf. p. 190 above). Vaughan's language on this occasion was neither a slip nor an example of his careless and loose use of words: it was really the way he conceived of the eucharistic mystery. Commenting on the Anglican archbishops' Reply to the Bull in March 1897, Vaughan asked whether Anglicans claimed 'the power to produce the actual living Christ Jesus by transubstantiation upon the altar according to the claim of the Eastern and Western Churches'? Commenting on this statement, the Anglican theologian R. C. Moberly wrote that Vaughan had 'done his best to reduce the spiritual mysteries of the Christian Eucharist and priesthood to the level of a merely vulgar thaumaturgy; and many a thoughtful Romanist must have writhed under the naive recklessness of his polemics' (Moberly, *Ministerial Priesthood*, London [2]1905, 351 n. 1).

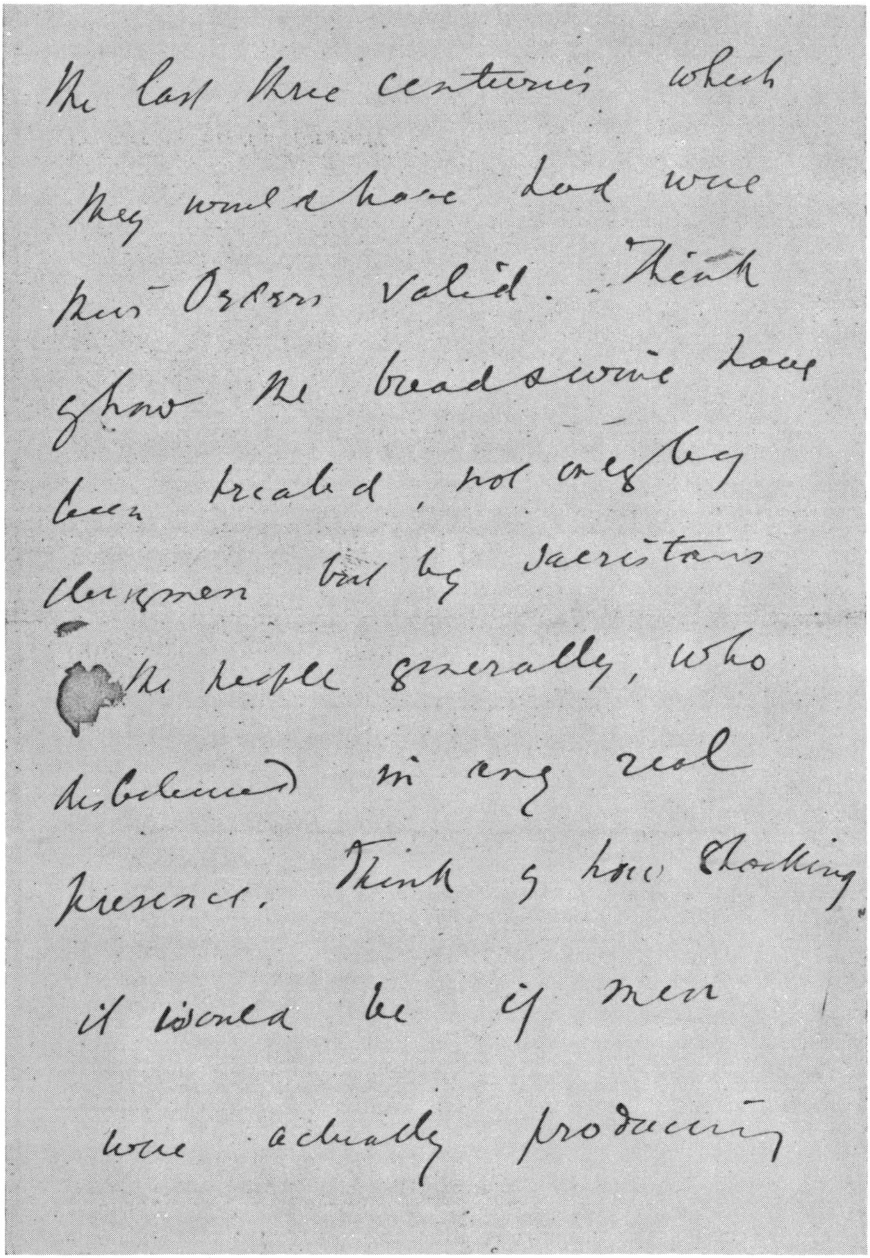
the last three centuries which they would have had were their Orders valid. Think of how the bread & wine have been treated, not only by clergymen but by sacristans & the people generally, who disbelieved in any real presence. Think of how shocking it would be if men were actually producing

Cardinal Vaughan's letter to Lord Halifax (quoted p. 203)

Hickleton Papers

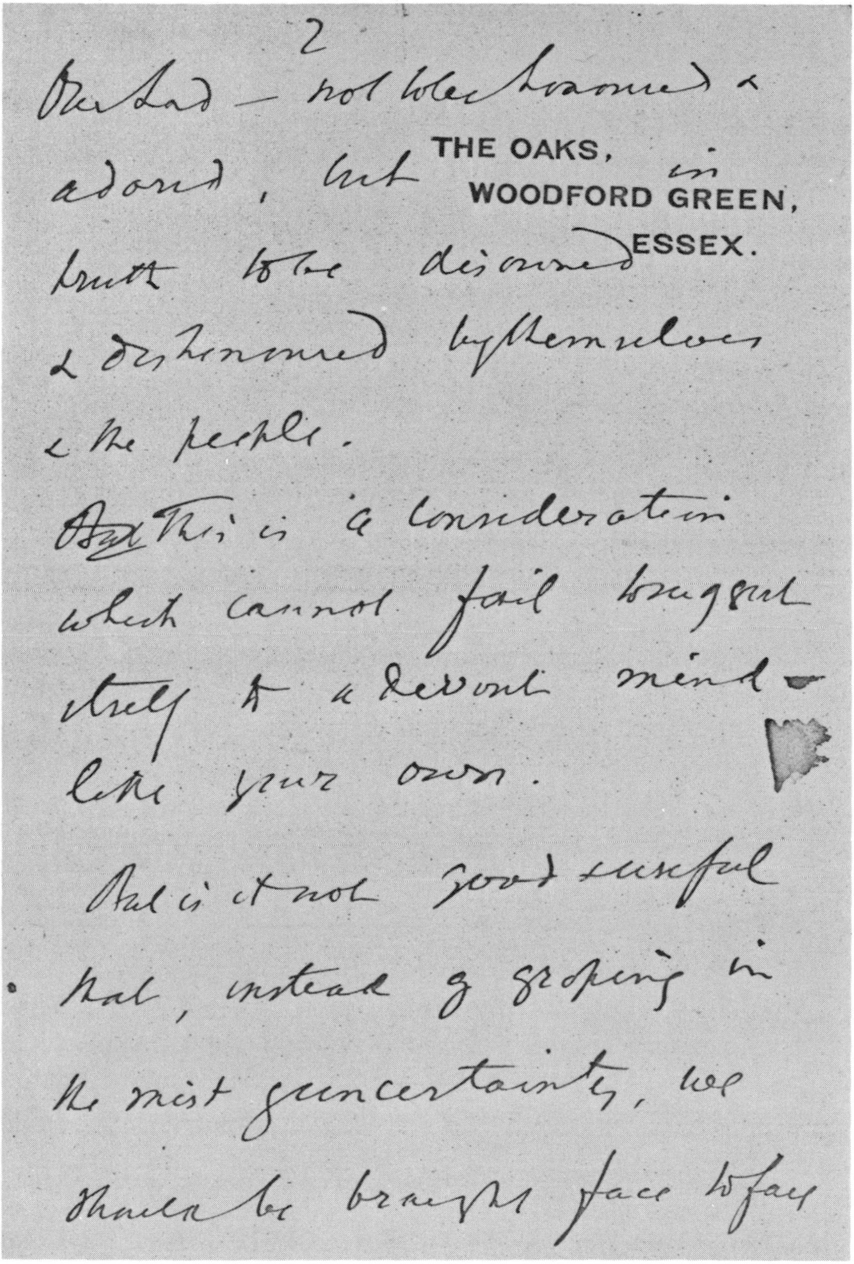
2

THE OAKS,
WOODFORD GREEN,
ESSEX.

the Lord — not to be honoured & adored, but in truth to be disowned & dishonoured by themselves & the people.

And this is a consideration which cannot fail to suggest itself to a devout mind like your own.

And is it not good & useful that, instead of groping in the mist of uncertainty, we should be brought face to face

Cardinal Vaughan's letter to Lord Halifax (continued from opposite page)

Hickleton Papers

thinly veiled plea for Halifax's conversion to the Roman Catholic Church.[15]

Halifax was certainly a man before his time. But so was Newman, and no small part of Newman's sufferings as a Roman Catholic was due to the fact that so few of his contemporaries were able to understand and appreciate his ideas. Today we honour Newman for his ideas. Is it just to condemn Halifax for his, or for trying to put them into practice? The reunion Halifax conceived and worked for was right. If his vision of that reunion was faulty this was not because it was too vast, but rather too narrow. For Halifax reunion meant simply healing the breach between Canterbury and Rome: protestants did not come within his ken, and his interest in eastern Orthodoxy was slight. Edmund Bishop remarked once about the poet Swinburne:

> He made English musical, and you can't ask more than one thing of a man.[16]

Halifax raised the great and noble vision of Anglo-Roman reunion, and kept it alive when it required supernatural courage to do so. Is it fair to ask for more?

A French writer said of Halifax in 1937:

> . . . he did not reach his goal, the object of his desires, and he could not reach it: the time was not ripe. Like Mount Everest this spiritual summit of reunion with Rome continues to remain inaccessible. But that is no reason for failing to recognise the courage of those who attempt the ascent.[17]

Moreover, the methods which Halifax advocated and himself used in working for the limited goal of Anglo-Roman reunion would prove to be equally useful for all ecumenical work. For Halifax's methods, and indeed many of his utterances, were strikingly similar to those of Pope John XXIII.

In July 1894, in response to a request from the Abbé

[15] Letter of Vaughan to Halifax, 5th October 1896, HP A4.240. For complete text cf. Appendix, pp. 305–6 below.
[16] N. Abercrombie, *Edmund Bishop* xv.
[17] Joseph Huby, 'Lord Halifax', *Études* 230 (1937) 596–610 and 756–73, 610.

Portal, Halifax put down on paper a summary of his thoughts and ideas about reunion. The result was a very long letter, which, though written in French and in haste,[18] is a closely reasoned statement of ecumenical ideals and methods, strikingly modern in tone. Most of the leading ideas advanced by Halifax in this letter have been fulfilled since the election of Angelo Roncalli to the see of Peter.[19]

Halifax begins by saying that the world is obviously drawing closer together: the spread of newspapers, railroads, and the telegraph all tend to eliminate divisions and bring nations together by helping people to know one another better. Even the increasing social and economic difficulties seem to indicate that God is preparing something tremendous for Europe: either a frightful cataclysm, or a return to religion on a mass scale. It could even be, he writes, that a coming time of troubles could be God's means of bringing about christian reunion.[20]

> The first thing is for us to get to know one another; the second, to desire union with all our hearts, to judge everything that has been said or done in the past, as well as everything that is said or done now on one side or the other, in the most generous manner possible without sacrificing anything of the truth. Above all we need explanations.

Halifax writes that he is convinced that dogmatic unity could easily be reached on all outstanding points, if only there were a firm determination to insist only on what was of faith, and a readiness to allow the greatest liberty beyond this minimum.

> Greeks and Latins both use the term 'transubstantiation' to express the doctrine of the Real Presence. The way in which they treat the Blessed Sacrament *extra usum* is completely different. Permit other matters to be treated in a similar manner, and one would have banished with a single stroke three quarters of the difficulties which prevent peace. Obviously

[18] 'Je vous adresse cette lettre à la hâte', *Leo XIII* 92.
[19] The complete French text of Halifax's letter is in *Leo XIII* 88–92; the excerpts printed in translation below are not further identified.
[20] These words may be considered prophetic in view of the impetus given to the ecumenical movement by Nazism and by other enemies of christianity in our century. They may yet prove to be more prophetic still.

no part of the Church can contradict directly what it has said. But with the passage of time we can see that certain words, certain formulas, have not always the precise force that was once attributed to them, and that there is room for explanations which permit a *rapprochement* formerly thought impossible. . . .

But for all this we must get to know each other. People are led much more by their hearts than by their heads; and above all you must try to understand our position. Rightly or wrongly we hold that there is much to be said about the sixteenth century schism, and that the wrongs are not all on one side. If they are not all on one side, the responsibility for the schism and its consequences cannot be placed entirely on our shoulders. . . .

No doubt there are innumerable difficulties in the way of peace. We have a thousand things that would shock you terribly. But with God everything is possible, and if Leo XIII really wanted to work seriously for a *rapprochement*, who could foretell the result? But, as we have said, we must begin little by little, and the consideration of the validity of our Orders is the point at which to start. However, you will easily understand that there would be a great deal of reluctance here about submitting the question of our Orders to those who would declare them invalid for reasons like those which are deduced from Eugene IV's decree for the Armenians, or because the Roman Church has always treated them as invalid. Your people here, or a number of them at least, would like nothing better than to do everything in their power to declare our Orders invalid, since they would find this an easy and expeditious way of terminating a controversy which is not particularly easy to conduct otherwise. . . .

If, for example, Leo XIII (you will permit me, my dear friend, to ascend into the clouds a bit) were to write a letter as the Father of Christendom to the Archbishops of Canterbury and York and to the English bishops, as the *de facto* representatives of the ancient national episcopate, reminding them of the happy times before the schism when all were united under the Primacy of him who, from the Anglican point of view, is at least the Patriarch of the West and the first bishop in the Catholic Church, and assuring them that there is nothing in the world that he desires as much as the ending of the schism; if he were to give an assurance that for the moment every consideration of the bond that ought to exist between the Holy See and the rest of the Church would be put aside, and that the Orders would be considered solely with regard to the teaching of the entire Church about the matter and essential form and the historical fact of the succession; if his language bore witness to the strongest desire of recognising the Orders, then I am convinced that the effect produced on all sides would be magnificent, and that it is impossible to foretell the result which such a *démarche* might have.

It is easy to poke holes in such a plan in detail. To take but one example: many people in England in the 1890s would not have responded at all as Halifax supposed and hoped to a letter from the pope reminding them of how happy things had been before the schism, when all were united with Rome. They would have insisted long and loud that conditions before the reformation were far from happy, and that the breaking of a bond which had been illegitimately forged in the first place was an unparalleled national blessing. And yet such a criticism, as well as many others which might be made, and indeed have been made very extensively, pale into insignificance beside the fact that with the visit of the one hundredth Archbishop of Canterbury to Rome in March 1966 the pope *has* begun to deal with the Anglican hierarchy in England as the *de facto* representative of the ancient episcopate. And those who witnessed the historic meeting, and saw Dr Ramsey being invited by Paul VI to join in imparting the blessing at the end of their common act of worship in St Paul's without the Walls, and receiving the episcopal ring which the pope removed from his finger and placed on the finger of his departing guest, did not have the impression that the successor of St Peter and St Gregory the Great was treating the successor of St Augustine like an unordained layman.[21] Moreover, it is agreed today on all sides that the method of working for reunion proposed by Lord Halifax is the only one which promises success: joint theological conferences, with mutual readiness to explain and to listen, to take the most generous and not the most unfavourable view, and to allow as great a liberty as possible beyond the absolute essentials of faith.

[21] In a speech delivered on 5th October 1966 Bishop Jan G. M. Willebrands of the Vatican Secretariat for Promoting Christian Unity said of the meeting between the pope and the archbishop the previous March: 'Has there ever been a meeting at Rome so official and so solemn in character which in so limited a space of time gave rise to events of such great importance? I remember that in preparing for this meeting the Pope wished that a very special protocol be worked out which would characterize the event as a visit of one Church to another, and not as a meeting of Heads in a consecrated spot . . .' ('The Ecumenical Significance of the Visit of the Archbishop of Canterbury to the Holy Father', *Unitas* 19 [1967], 8–17, 14).

Halifax's concluding words can stand without comment, for they have been fulfilled in Pope John XXIII. Those who still dismiss Halifax as a hopelessly unrealistic dreamer should recall that he wrote these words in 1894.

> Have a little imagination, a little faith. We must be daring if we expect great results. To save the world God became man. It seems to me that for the sake of reunion the Holy Father could take steps that could be demanded of no one else. What won't a father do for the good of his children? Oh! we must cast aside conventions, fetters, everything that hinders those steps that people like to call folly, but which are the true wisdom. The age of miracles is not dead, and if ever a Pope had the right to act in this way it is certainly Leo XIII, who has had such magnetic influence on souls everywhere.

No less impressive than Halifax's prophetic ecumenical vision in the nineties is the courage with which he and Portal sustained hope in the years following the collapse of all they had worked for. It is moving to read the unpublished letters exchanged by the two friends in those years.

> It is winter now for our ideas [Portal wrote in 1912]; probably we shall not see the new spring. There is nothing for us to do but to work at home like the peasants. Your book [*Leo* XIII *and Anglican Orders*] closes the series of acts which my brochure began. It is an end. Let us hope that it is only the end of the first stage.[22]

> As we have said so often, we have sown a seed. Your book will guarantee that it is not forgotten in the church, and perhaps the book will bring the seed to fruition one day. You certainly deserve this. I congratulate you very sincerely at having finished this tremendous work so happily, and I have rejoiced, both for the work and for yourself, to see it done in such a christian manner. . . . I cannot tell you how grateful I am to our Lord for the grace of working with you.[23]

In another letter from the same period Portal turns again to the future which he was sure would come some day.

> There is nothing to do but to work in the shadow and to form a few men for the future. That is what I am trying to do with as much patience as possible.[24]

[22] Portal to Halifax, 4th April 1912, HP A4.213.

[23] Portal to Halifax, 14th March 1912, HP A4.213. This letter was written immediately after Portal had received Halifax's book. In letter after letter the Abbé mentions his gratitude for the privilege of having been permitted to work with his dear friend for reunion.

[24] Portal to Halifax, undated but probably about 1911–12, HP A4.213.

Quietly Portal did just that, imparting his ideas to a few younger men, preparing them to go out and reap the harvest when the spring which he never expected to see should arrive at last after the long, hard winter. The letters between the two men show how Portal would send his young friends to England, to stay with Lord Halifax at Hickleton, where they were entertained as only Halifax could entertain, given the run of the library, and talked to by the hour.

One of these young men was the future journalist, author, and lay auditor at the second Vatican Council Jean Guitton. He recalls that in his many conversations with Lord Halifax there was one ever-recurring theme.

> He dreamed of seeing a Pope who 'would speak to humanity like a father, without sacrificing anything of his rights', who would summon those who are in fact, if not of right, the heads of the dissident churches, and who would say to them: 'Let us see what our differences really are, let us see if there is not some way for us to understand one another.' That was the whole problem for Lord Halifax. He longed for a sort of Hildebrand who would cast off old habits, who would launch out into the deep: *duc in altum.*[25]

> Oh! if only a great Pope would come and say: 'Let us forget the past . . . Let us launch out into the deep!'[26]

When he was Nuncio in Paris Angelo Roncalli told Jean Guitton that Lord Halifax's efforts for reunion had attracted his attention to this problem.[27] And Mgr Loris Capovilla, private secretary to Pope John XXIII, has written that on 3rd October 1959 he found the pope reading a letter by Cardinal Saliège, Archbishop of Toulouse, on the subject of christian reunion. 'With a trembling and solemn voice,' Mgr Capovilla records, the pope read aloud these sentences of Cardinal Saliège, themselves so reminiscent of Halifax.

> This union has not yet been achieved. But it will come. It is in the designs

[25] Jean Guitton, *Dialogue avec les précurseurs*, Paris 1962, 61f.
[26] Ibid. 139.
[27] Private correspondence with the author; information revealed by kind permission of M. Guitton, who adds that Cardinal Roncalli also spoke of the Malines Conversations and his admiration for Cardinal Mercier.

of God. It has been the object of prayer on the part of so many fervent Christians.[28]

Cardinal Saliège too had been influenced by Halifax, whose ideas and work for reunion he had often discussed with Jean Guitton. In M. Guitton's words: 'It all fits together.'[29] The seed sown more than half a century before was not sown in vain.

The Abbé Portal

If it has been fashionable to speak and write patronisingly of Halifax as an unrealistic visionary and dreamer, the criticism of Portal has been much more severe. Portal has been the victim of innumerable bitter attacks by the supporters of Cardinal Vaughan and his policy. Numerous conversations and a large correspondence with Roman Catholics in England during the preparation of this book have revealed that the bitterness against Portal is not yet dead. No opportunity has been lost by those who favour an uncompromising and rigid approach to Anglicanism to vilify him as a traitor to the catholic cause, and a meddler and busybody with no understanding of the religious situation in England. To these charges has been added that of disloyalty to the church's hierarchy, for it is claimed that he deliberately went behind the backs of the only people capable of understanding Anglicanism, and those entrusted by the pope with the care of souls in Britain: Cardinal Vaughan and his successor, Cardinal Bourne.[30]

Before quoting the judgement of an English catholic of different views from Vaughan and Bourne, it will be interesting to let Portal speak for himself. The Abbé could

[28] Loris Capovilla, *Giovanni XXIII, cinque lettere*, Rome 1961; cited from Guitton, op. cit. in n. 25 above, 228.

[29] Letter of M. Guitton to the author, cited by permission.

[30] It must be remembered that Portal is also hated for his role in the Malines Conversations of the 1920s, which were resented quite as bitterly by Vaughan's successor, Cardinal Bourne, as were the earlier attempts of Portal and Halifax to promote a *rapprochement* in the 1890s by Vaughan himself.

never have achieved what he did had he not possessed tremendous optimism. But he was a man of shrewd judgement as well. This comes out clearly in a letter he wrote to Halifax in 1911 about the events in which they had been involved fifteen and more years previously.

> We got Leo XIII into a bad scrape, there is no doubt about it. And if he did not manage to get out of it this was not entirely his own fault. He was too old and too weak. As to Cardinal Rampolla, if he did not have the decision and the energy that we could have wished at certain moments he was faithful to us, and that is something at any rate.[31]

In the same letter Portal criticises Wilfrid Ward for writing that

> It was essential that Rome should . . . be accurately informed as to how comparatively small was the section of the Established Church who at present desired reunion with the Holy See—this was a point on which Abbé Portal was himself, I think, under a not quite accurate impression.[32]

Portal replied to this charge:

> W. Ward knew very well that this was not true, because I told him myself that we had no idea at all that union was going to come about today or tomorrow. I told him that I knew you and your friends were a minority. But what I maintained was that all great movements were produced by minorities. And the whole question was whether the elements which existed within the Church of England were strong enough to give birth to a movement of real importance capable of achieving some result within a given time. We said they were. W. Ward was not able to give any answer to this question. Cardinal Vaughan and his friends went further and maintained that the reunion movement was bad in itself. Cries of utopianism were raised on every side. And to make doubly sure that the newborn child would not be capable of life, they strangled it or had it strangled by others.
>
> What you accomplished, along with your friends like Lacey, Puller, the Archbishop of York and others, proves that our opinion about the possibility of creating a large movement was correct. In spite of all the difficulties you met with you stirred up public opinion. What might you have done if you had received encouragement?[33]

[31] Letter of 7th November 1911, HP A4.213. [32] *Leo XIII* 444.

[33] The claim made by Portal in this paragraph is fully documented by the correspondence published by Halifax in *Leo XIII and Anglican Orders*. Portal's question was rhetorical and does not admit of an answer. But it should be weighed carefully none the less.

As to my 'not quite accurate impression', there was no need to take a census of the parties in the Church of England. It was enough to say that you were a minority, but that this minority was capable of moving the mass. I did not have to undertake a profound study to make known the differences existing on your side, even amongst those who were closest to us. Obviously the Archbishop of Canterbury and yourself did not give the same impression. And Wilfrid Ward knew very well what I thought on that score.[34]

After Portal's death the following appreciation of the man and his work was written by an English catholic who had taken some pains to understand the Abbé, and who was no less ardent in the cause of reunion than Portal himself. Since this judgement does not appear to have been published hitherto, it is worth giving here in full.

It was in the spring of 1913 that I first made the acquaintance of the Abbé Portal, to whom I was presented by one of those Anglican friends of whom so many loved and venerated him. One was immediately struck by his understanding of the Anglican position, and the extraordinary tact with which he referred to points at issue. This, as from closer knowledge of his mind I afterwards realised, was due firstly to his thoroughness and sense of justice, to a temper which made him feel that, in all things, one must spare oneself nothing in examining a difficulty, and, secondly to what had arisen from this, an extraordinarily profound knowledge of the Church of England, and of her claims, especially as they appeared to those in the advanced Anglo-Catholic position of Lord Halifax. It was naturally with Lord Halifax and his friends that the Abbé had been in the closest touch, but he was well aware of the existence of other parties in the Church of England, and the suggestion that his knowledge was partial or superficial was fantastic.

The foundation of the Abbé's position was that if the Church of England made Catholic claims, she must try herself, and allow others to try her by Catholic standards. If she claimed to be a daughter church of Rome, she must cultivate a filial regard. Rome is indeed the Mother Church of Christendom, as the Pope is the father and teacher of Christians. It was this point to which, with infinite tact and patience, the Abbé tried to accustom his English friends. How could they use their Catholic principles to consummate unity? How could they fulfil the promise of their Catholic heritage?

In convincing members of the Church of England that Rome regarded them with benevolence, in encouraging and sustaining Lord

[34] Letter cited in n. 31 above.

Halifax in his apostolate of Catholic unity, in the perseverance with which he continued his campaign through the conversations of Malines to the last day of his life, the Abbé Portal performed a work of unity which was both heroic and unique. He commenced his work at a time when English Catholics did not moderate their bitterness and scorn in their references to the Church of England. The warnings of Cardinal Manning that they were alienating the feelings of those nearest to the Church, the charitable appeal for sympathy which had been made by Cardinal Wiseman as the only way to use a great opportunity, had been drowned in the jealousy and suspicion which the English Catholic families felt of converts, and by the political and racial animosities of an Irish element which grew ever stronger. In these circumstances, the very virtues by which the Catholics had through centuries of persecution maintained their sacrosanct principles, and the peculiar prerogatives of their Church, tempted them to take up a sectarian and exclusive attitude, when by more tact, more courtesy and more charity, they could have advanced the thesis that Catholic Christianity was the religion in which England's peculiar gifts and traditions would attain their fulfilment. It was just this opportunity that the Abbé Portal saw and seized, which he demonstrated not without success at the Vatican, and which he continued to assert through good report and evil report. The benefit was immense.

When I last saw the Abbé Portal, it was five days before his death. He talked to me alone for two hours, discussing the difficulties of the situation, dwelling on the need of courage, giving warnings against the malevolence which from time to time charity or courtesy would arouse, and speaking not without feeling of the sufferings he had himself to undergo from unprincipled detractors.

The attacks which were made upon him were first, as has been suggested, that he did not understand the position in England. This was absurd. Few scholars knew it more thoroughly. The second form of attack was that he wavered in his loyalty or orthodoxy. But this was almost more absurd. A profound Thomist and theologian, his defence of Catholic principles, as I attempted to show in *Theology* in July 1926,[35] won the approbation of the ecclesiastical authorities best qualified to judge. It was indeed his peculiar excellence to combine an undeviating loyalty to the Holy See with a sympathetic understanding of the points that needed correction, so that, instead of alienating those he wished to convince, he kept them well disposed. And this showed the depth and delicacy of his charity.

It was never shown more clearly than in the negotiations of 1894 to 1896. Their object was to establish such conversations as have since been held at Malines. But at the instance of certain English priests, it was

[35] Cf. R. E. Gordon George, 'The Church in France in its Relation to Christian Unity', *Theology* 13 (1926), 21–30; the section on Portal is on pp. 22f.

narrowed down to the question of the validity of Anglican Orders. Now like Leo XIII, the Abbé saw that if those Orders were recognised by Rome as valid, it would be much easier to allay Anglican prejudices against renewing unity with Rome. But, never drowning his reason in sentiment, he always kept facing the difficulties of the Anglican claim, and in a brochure on the subject, he actually anticipated the decision of *Apostolicae curae*. But he did not allow that decision to weaken either his interest, or his sympathy.

In his wide fairness, the Abbé Portal felt, like Cardinal Wiseman, how much his own side had been to blame. Almost his last words to me were to warn me of the immense difficulties the past had raised. It was, he said, the conviction of Cardinal Mercier that the past had been so full of mistakes on both sides that only a new beginning could offer sound foundations. His one object in the work of Church unity was to lay some of the stones of that foundation. Courage and fairness were the mainstays of his charity. His hope was equal to his faith. He never wearied in presenting to Anglicans an example of the attitude taken by the Holy See, and in him the apostles of unity found a *point d'appui* when every other seemed to fail them on the Catholic side.

That, at the moment of the Abbé's death, he had won his battle, is too much to be said. But he had gathered an indomitable company around the standard. He saw also arising a small but fervent band of English Catholics who were prepared to carry on his work, and pray for Catholic unity, recommending it as he had done by Christian virtues. And he had aroused an interest in France, a sense of responsibility which could not be said to be less important. For it is the Church of France that most happily presents to the English mind the characteristics and advantages of Catholicism, and if the Church of France once turns her luminance and fervour towards the triumph of the spirit of peace, then we are in sight of that victory for which in the darkest days the Abbé Portal so heroically fought, and which makes real for him the promise which sustained him: 'Blessed are you when men revile you and persecute you and utter all kinds of evil against you falsely on my account. Rejoice and be glad, for your reward is great in heaven, for so men persecuted the prophets who were before you. You are the salt of the earth; but if salt has lost its taste, how shall its saltness be restored?' (Matt. 5: 11–13).[36]

Canon Moyes

Although for the public at large, including Lord Halifax, it was Cardinal Vaughan who had fought for and obtained the

[36] PP.

condemnation of the Orders, we have seen that most of the work was done by others, who worked behind the scenes in accordance with Vaughan's wishes and in pursuance of the goals which he had set. Dom Gasquet and Mgr Merry del Val were easily the most important of these lieutenants. A man much more in the public eye, though the role which he played was comparatively minor, was Cardinal Vaughan's friend and close associate Canon James Moyes, who published a series of thirty-one articles on Anglican Orders in *The Tablet* between February and December 1895, and who undertook the task of explaining and defending the Bull of condemnation in nineteen articles in the same paper between February and July 1897. We have seen that both Gasquet and Merry del Val had misgivings about Moyes' qualifications to serve on the commission.[37] The controversial lapses which we have already noted in Moyes' writings were not an asset to the cause. Nor were his apologetic efforts after the condemnation such as to commend what had been done to any save those who were already convinced. Even as staunch an opponent of Anglican Orders as Fr Francis Clark has written that Moyes' interpretation of the defect of intention alleged in Leo XIII's Bull

> offers no important contribution to the understanding of *Apostolicae curae*. It cannot be the intention in question.[38]

It is worthy of note that a man considered at the time to be a theologian could have been as closely associated as Moyes was with the investigation and condemnation of Anglican Orders and still fail to understand one of the two main arguments upon which the condemnation was based.

Moyes' subsequent defence of what had been done in 1896 was no more helpful than his explanation of the defect of intention. In 1910 he wrote, apropos of Lacey's pamphlet *De Re Anglicana*:

> It is very doubtful if Mr Lacey's picture would have seriously deceived anyone—least of all the Cardinals—even if our *Risposta* had not dealt

[37] Cf. pp. 106ff above. [38] AODI 199.

> with its misrepresentations. . . . Rome, as a historic centre of communication in Christendom, has its living tradition—its traditional memory—of Reformation facts in England as elsewhere. In its archives lie the process of Elizabeth, the dispatches of its agents, the letters of its missionaries and martyrs, and a body of authentic testimony to show what was the character and scope of the religious changes effected in this country. Rome, moreover, is constantly in touch with men of all conditions whose eyes and ears are open to the facts of religious life of England of today. Hence Mr Lacey's task of substituting what was really a purely subjective version of Anglicanism, for the historic and actual one, was one which not even his sincerity and ability could save from failure.[39]

Two years later, however, Moyes was off on another tack, and his view of the competence of the Roman authorities to form a judgement about religious conditions in England was considerably less sanguine.

> It was not grasped in Rome, as fully as it might have been [Moyes wrote in 1912], that the English nation is not, and is never more likely to be, coterminous with the Church of England—that anything which Lord Halifax could promise or pledge would never affect, except by exciting a deeper hostility, the millions of Dissenting Englishmen who stand outside the pale of the Establishment—that even if every Anglican in the land were won over to Rome, it would mean the capture of a half-England—that the dissenting masses lying outside our net would form, both religiously and politically, if not a majority, at least a minority so strong and so numerous and so vehement that it would be unthinkable that the power and resources of the nation, as such, could be used in behalf of Catholicity.[40]

These two passages are not only a striking illustration of the inconsistency which we have already seen in the pages of the *Risposta*. The arguments advanced by Moyes are typical of his controversial methods. By a great show of superior wisdom, and patronising references to his opponent, or sometimes to the opponent's argument, combined with flattering references to the adversary personally—the implication being that he was a good, sincere, likeable chap, who ought not to be held responsible for the patently absurd arguments he had advanced—Moyes contrived to give the impression of having made his point, whereas in fact he had merely

[39] *The Tablet* 85 (1910), 164 col. 2. [40] *The Tablet* 87 (1912), 963 col. 2.

made a lot of noise. The logical implication of the argument advanced by Moyes in the second of the two passages cited above is that English catholics could not possibly have anything to do with any movements for corporate reunion with the Church of England, because even if successful such a movement would still leave half the nation outside the pale of the true church. To prove his point, Moyes would have had to show that the method of proselytising for individual conversions which he advocated held out greater prospects of bringing into the fold not only the large body of faithful Anglicans but the mass of nonconformists as well, who he complained would be left out in any movement of corporate reunion. Demonstration of this proposition was beyond the powers of even so practised a controversialist as Moyes, and it is hardly to be wondered at that he never attempted it.

Dom Gasquet

A far more important role in the condemnation of Anglican Orders than that of Moyes was played by Dom Francis Aidan Gasquet. Gasquet had been involved in the affair from the start, and his work in the Vatican archives with Edmund Bishop in the winter of 1895 had given him a better preparation for the discussions than that possessed by either of his two English colleagues. It is not easy to place Gasquet on the theological map. He was no theologian, and made no pretence of being one. His theological studies had been only such as the struggling English Benedictine Congregation of his youth had been able to give him: a few house lectures by amateur and overworked teachers, and the reading of standard textbooks of the day. Like his great friend and mentor Edmund Bishop, who was vastly superior to Gasquet in intellectual power and learning, Gasquet frankly despised theology. If this is an attitude difficult to understand today, when we are witnessing the greatest revival of theological studies since the thirteenth century, it must be remembered that theology in Gasquet's formative years was a very different thing from what it has since become. Professor David Knowles has written of the theological situation in the 1870s, when Gasquet was nearing thirty:

> Speculative, scholastic theology was then but slowly recovering from the all but complete extinction of the schools during the period of the French Revolution and the Napoleonic Wars. When, as the Catholic revival began to gain ground, theology began again to flourish, it was for long kept occupied with fighting a defensive war against liberalism, positivism and the so-called higher criticism in all its forms. Thus positive theology, Christian origins and scripture studies were . . . absorbing the energies of the most distinguished Catholic scholars and teachers. The epoch-making recall to St Thomas in the encyclicals of Leo XIII was about to be heard, but the theologians and text-books then in vogue were either eclectic or at best represented only formalised scholasticism, which seemed, above all in England, to have no connexion with and shed no light upon the burning questions raised by Mill, Huxley, Darwin, and the agnostic, idealist or materialist schools in general.[41]

Gasquet displayed great impatience with the controversy over Anglican Orders: this is evident in virtually all his correspondence and notes. He was unable to see that there was any problem at all, and regarded the whole discussion as an irritating waste of time, rather like being forced to have a long and involved argument with people who were trying to prove that the world is flat. Those who have tried to carry on a theological discussion with the members of one of the more agressive modern sects will have experienced the same sense of frustration which took hold of Gasquet as he found more and more of his time being taken up with the problem of Anglican Orders—a 'general *cui bono* feeling' Gasquet called it in a letter to Edmund Bishop at the end of April 1896, when the investigation was at its height.[42]

> I am much too occupied with the wretched Anglican Orders business [Gasquet wrote to Edmund Bishop in the summer of 1894] and feel

[41] David M. Knowles, 'Abbot Butler: A Memoir' in the same, *The Historian and Character and Other Essays* 264–341, 270f. Knowles is writing about the period of Butler's 'youth and young manhood'. Butler was born in 1858, Gasquet in 1846, so that what is true of Butler's formative years applies *a fortiori* for the corresponding period in Gasquet's life.

[42] Letter of 26th April 1896, BP.

> quite sure that we ought to attack the question from its commonsense side of cold-blooded fact.[43]

By 'cold-blooded fact' Gasquet meant a purely historical and non-theological approach. His unwillingness to take the theological side of the question seriously had disastrous consequences. Again and again in his extensive notes on the question he writes that the English reformers 'did not intend what the Church intends'. The following is a typical quotation:

> It is obvious when dealing with the doctrine of intention that we are unable to enter into the secret recesses of the mind, but we may and indeed we must judge of intention by the acts and words of the persons concerned. In this case the acts and words of those who made and used the new forms of Ordination cannot be doubtful. Their intention was deliberately to exclude the ancient idea of a sacrificing priesthood as they had already banished that of the eucharistic sacrifice. The character of their acts or words can consequently neither be explained away or minimised by even the most liberal interpretation of the phrase *intendit quod intendit ecclesia.*[44]

From the point of view of sacramental theology the gaffe was vast. To intend what the church *intends* is precisely what is *not* required in the minister of a sacrament.[45] Such a requirement logically entails a correct theology about the sacrament being administered as well as a belief in its supernatural character. Neither are required of the minister, for such a requirement would be the end of all certainty. A moment's reflection will show that large numbers of clergy have had entirely wrong-headed and unorthodox ideas about the sacraments they have administered; and it is impossible to deny that there have also been clergy who did not believe in what they were doing. Yet neither fact, however regrettable in itself, can have the slightest effect upon the validity

[43] Letter of 8th August 1894; cited from Leslie, *Cardinal Gasquet*, 153.
[44] Undated memorandum in Gasquet's hand, GP.
[45] St Robert Bellarmine points out that the Council of Trent 'does not say that a minister must intend what the Church *intends*, but what the Church *does*' (Bellarmine, *De sacramentis in genere* lib. i, cap. 27 n. 13). This passage was cited by the Holy Office in its 1872 decision about Methodist baptisms in Oceania, which has figured prominently in works about Anglican Orders (cf. DS 3102).

of the sacraments administered by such clergy. All that is necessary is that the minister intend to *do* what the church *does*—a far more modest requirement, and the only one which can be maintained without undermining the whole sacramental system. There is no evidence that Gasquet ever grasped this elementary principle of sacramental theology. Not once, but over and over again, he insists on the phrase *quod intendit ecclesia*. Gasquet's error arose from his entirely non-theological treatment of the question.

Although Gasquet's approach to the question of Anglican Orders was ostensibly purely historical, it was in reality quite unhistorical. For Gasquet the fact that the English reformers rejected what he always called 'the sacrifice and sacerdotium' as understood and practised in the sixteenth century meant that the reformers rejected the ministry instituted by Jesus Christ. Had Gasquet been a better historian he would have been bound to ask whether the sixteenth-century understanding of 'the sacrifice and sacerdotium' was in fact identical with the New Testament and patristic understanding of these things. This identity was never investigated, but simply assumed. It is only fair to add in Gasquet's defence that the same assumption has been made by virtually all opponents of Anglican Orders.

It is tempting to place Gasquet in the same category with Cardinal Vaughan, Moyes, and Merry del Val—all men of a narrowly apologetic and polemical cast of mind, whose concern was to defend every aspect and detail of contemporary ecclesiastical teaching and practice, and whose presentation of the faith was invariably an integralist one. Though Gasquet was at one with these men on the question of Anglican Orders, his views on other questions were, for his day, what would now be called 'progressive'.[46] He disliked continentals and other foreigners, whom he regarded as

[46] In the spring of 1896 Gasquet was involved, with Edmund Bishop and Fr David Fleming, in a plan to invite the Abbé Loisy, who was already under suspicion because of his radical views on biblical criticism, to give some lectures on this subject at Cambridge. Nothing ever came of the plan. (Cf. Loisy, *Mémoires* i, 402ff).

'lesser breeds without the law', and he made no exception for those who happened to profess the same religion as he did. His references to 'these French and Italian beggars', which have been quoted above, are characteristic.[47] Gasquet was no enthusiast for Roman ways, Roman rules, or Roman prelates—differing strongly in this respect from Merry del Val, whose Romanism had all the fervour and intensity of the expatriate convert to foreign ways and ideas. Gasquet was sharply, and often indiscreetly, critical of churchmen and their doings. A letter he wrote in 1900 to his erstwhile colleague on the Anglican Orders commission, Fr David Fleming, shows that Gasquet did not hesitate to criticise even such a sacred cow as the 'First Friday' devotion.

> I wish something could be done to condemn the practice of the Nine First Fridays, as I am sure harm will come from what is rapidly becoming a superstition. I have a letter from a mother whose son died of a long illness and who refused to see a priest or do anything on the ground that he had made the Nine Fridays—that our Lord had promised that anyone who did so should be saved and that he expected Him to keep His promise.[48]

It is difficult to imagine this letter being written by Vaughan or Merry del Val, both of whom, one suspects, would have been scandalised by the suggestion that something as beautiful and edifying as the First Friday devotion could ever be condemned, or that it could be productive of anything but the greatest spiritual good. And whatever Moyes may have thought privately about such a matter, his controversial bent suggests that he would have defended the First Friday devotion to the uttermost, if only to avoid letting the side down.

Gasquet's intransigence on the question of Anglican Orders arose not so much from principle (as in the case of those with whom he was associated) as from his conviction that any discussion of the question would focus attention upon the wrong point—and a point about which, in his

[47] Cf. pp. 107 and 114 above.

[48] Leslie, *Cardinal Gasquet* 198.

view, it was impossible for right-thinking and informed people (intelligent, historically knowledgeable English catholics like himself and Edmund Bishop) to discuss at all. With Edmund Bishop, Gasquet felt that careful, painstaking historical research could gradually persuade his fellow-Englishmen that the English reformation had been a complete and illegitimate break with the good old days of England's catholic past. He knew that a condemnation of Anglican Orders would only offend and alienate the very people from whom he was trying to get, and increasingly getting, a hearing: men, for instance, like the Anglican historian James Gairdner, with whom Gasquet was for a number of years on terms of friendship, until Gairdner could no longer swallow the historical errors and falsehood with which Gasquet's books were filled, and began to point them out in print. It was this desire not to offend and alienate those whom he hoped to influence that made Gasquet try in March 1895 at Rome to persuade Lord Halifax to abandon the question of Anglican Orders. Gasquet's notes and correspondence show clearly that he wished to avoid the bad feeling which a public condemnation of the Orders was bound to create. In view of the major part he played in obtaining the condemnation, it is only fair to Gasquet to state this. He deprecated the raising of the question, but felt that once it had been raised it was essential for the pope to speak out clearly (and of course negatively) on the matter, so as to remove all doubt as to what the church's attitude was.

Finally, it must be stated that neither as an historian nor as a theologian did Gasquet possess the expertise necessary to deal successfully with the problem of Anglican Orders. He had never passed through a demanding intellectual school. Even his historical knowledge was entirely self-taught. Professor Knowles writes that Gasquet's mind

> was not naturally clear enough to compensate for his lack of training. He felt no inclination to get at the roots and difficulties of a problem; he never shook it out, so to say; instead he tended to tangle the skein beyond

hope of unravelling. Evidence, whether old or fresh, did not impinge upon his consciousness with the cogency which it in fact possessed. In his later writings he sometimes dismissed a critic with rotund avuncular platitudes which exasperated those who had pointed to undoubted mistakes.

. . . Gasquet was not an intellectually humble man and he showed little insight into his own limitations of knowledge and training. . . . He lacked that passion for absolute intellectual chastity, which is desirable in any man, but in an historian is as much an occupational requirement as is absolute integrity in a judge. He did not primarily seek for truth without fear or favour. He held obstinately to what he thought and when he should have recognised the force of fresh evidence he ignored it, probably quite unaware that a great issue was at stake.[49]

Merry del Val

None of those who worked so hard for the condemnation of Anglican Orders—not Gasquet, nor Moyes, nor even Cardinal Vaughan himself—could have achieved the outstanding success which ultimately crowned their efforts without the invaluable assistance and support of Raphael Merry del Val. From the day in 1885 when Leo XIII first set eyes on this tall, handsome young seminarian of twenty (as he then was), and personally decided after a few minutes conversation that Raphael was not to enter the Scots College as planned, but to go to the Academy of Ecclesiastical Noblemen, entrance to which was normally reserved to priests, there was a relationship of unusual warmth and trust between the aged pontiff and his young protégé. Made a monsignor while still a sub-deacon, sent on diplomatic missions to the courts of London, Vienna, and Berlin before his ordination to the priesthood at the early age of twenty-three, Merry del Val was clearly marked out by fate and his superiors for an unusual and brilliant career. Unlike many to whom dazzling honours come before they have quite left

[49] Knowles, *The Historian and Character* 260f. I am indebted to Abbot (now Bishop) Christopher Butler of Downside and to Professor Knowles for assistance in assessing Gasquet's theological position. For the opinions expressed above I take sole responsibility.

their youth, Merry del Val fulfilled this youthful promise and the hopes which were so early set upon him. He was an archbishop at thirty-five and Cardinal Secretary of State at thirty-eight.

Through force of character and his own intense piety, Merry del Val managed to avoid having his head turned by the honours which were thrust upon him so early in his life. Only if he had been superhuman, however, could he have remained wholly unaffected by the heady atmosphere in which he lived and moved from earliest manhood. Gratitude for the favour shown him in such abundant measure combined with his own loyal and generous nature to stifle his critical faculties with regard to the institution of the papacy or the person, policies, and utterances of the current incumbent of that office. And by an inevitable corollary Merry del Val was quick to see a dangerous heretic in anyone who suggested plans or ideas which seemed to threaten, however remotely, his own exalted view of the papacy. Cardinal Vaughan's emphasis on the need for individual 'submission' to the Holy See, and his claim that the chief obstacle to such submission amongst non-catholic Englishmen was human pride, found a ready response in the ardent and devout soul of Merry del Val, whose attitude of adulation for Leo XIII was, in the circumstances, as natural as it was unfortunate.[50]

[50] Merry del Val achieved a more balanced view of the papacy comparatively late in life, as the result of having to experience the slings and arrows of outrageous fortune at the hands of a pope whom, only three months previously, he had deemed unworthy of the cardinalate: Benedict XV, the former Giacomo della Chiesa. Della Chiesa was a disciple of Cardinal Rampolla, whose views, as we have seen, differed from those of Merry del Val as night differs from day. When Merry del Val became Pius X's Secretary of State in 1903 he fired della Chiesa from his post at the Secretariat of State, and ordered him to vacate his apartment in the Vatican. The pope named him Archbishop of Bologna in 1907, but Merry del Val steadfastly refused to place della Chiesa's name on the list of candidates for cardinal's hats. Only three months before his death Pius X personally added della Chiesa's name to the list of creations at the consistory of May 1914 at which Gasquet finally received the hat of which there had been recurrent rumours since the great victory of 1896. By the end of the summer Pius X was dead and 'della Chiesa had the satisfaction of murmuring that the stone which the builders rejected had been made the head-stone of the corner: and more practically asked Merry to vacate his rooms in the Vatican in the same terms which Merry had once served on him. "We forgive but we cannot forget," said Benedict XV. Only the President of the Academia had stood

Leo XIII treated Merry del Val like a son. He summoned the young priest at the age of twenty-seven to live in the Vatican, and for a number of years Merry del Val was in daily attendance on the aged pontiff. Leo's confidence in his young protégé's judgement was unbounded, and nowhere more so than with regard to English questions, which have always baffled and perplexed Italian ecclesiastics. Merry del Val was thus an invaluable ally for Cardinal Vaughan. As early as August 1895, while on a brief visit to England, Merry del Val wrote to the pope's secretary, Mgr Rinaldo Angeli, that 'if, as is to be expected, the English ordinations are again declared to be invalid, a great many Ritualists will leave the Anglican Church.'[51] Mgr Angeli communicated the contents of this letter to the pope, as its writer intended. The assurance which this letter contained was followed in the months to come, as we have already seen, by many others from the same source as well as from others.[52] These assurances could not fail to have a considerable effect.

Merry del Val's letters to Gasquet, Moyes, and Vaughan are filled with stern denunciations of the reunion movement. Merry del Val reserved his most intense indignation for Portal, who, as a catholic priest, should in Merry del Val's eyes have known better. By the summer of 1896 Merry del Val was convinced that Portal was 'spreading heresy and poisoning people's minds'.[53] For Merry del Val this was one of the worst sins of which a catholic priest was capable. He was quite unable to appreciate any other view of the question but his own. That Anglicans like Lord Halifax really suffered because of their separation from Rome, that it was possible for a catholic priest, like Portal, to combine complete

---

by della Chiesa in 1903 and to him the new pope gave his first audience. Only the American cardinals visited the fallen Merry, who cried out to O'Connell: "Here we have no abiding city"' (Leslie, *Cardinal Gasquet* 190).

[51] Letter of 29th August 1895; cited from Viktor von Hettlingen, *Raphael Kardinal Merry del Val*, Einsiedeln/Köln 1937, 23.

[52] Cf. Cardinal Vaughan's letter of February 1896 cited on p. 105 above, and the letter of the English hierarchy in May 1896 referred to on p. 180.

[53] Letter of Merry del Val to Canon Moyes, 30th June 1896, GP.

loyalty to the Holy See with a genuinely eirenical and sympathetic attitude towards non-Roman Catholics without trying at all costs to convert them—these things were inconceivable to Merry del Val. There can be little doubt that he would have regarded such suggestions as heretical. His entire conduct throughout the reunion movement, which he was largely instrumental in diverting into the blind alley of a secret Roman investigation of something labelled in advance as 'a purely domestic matter'—how to treat convert Anglican clergy who wished to become Roman Catholic priests—reads like a dress rehearsal for the treatment of the modernist crisis in the decade following, when Merry del Val was Secretary of State and in a position to exercise an influence which cannot be said to have been either helpful or constructive. In both cases there is the same extreme narrowness of view, the same unshakeable conviction that anyone who differed from his view (which he was confident was the church's) was in bad faith, the same readiness to see a heretic in anyone who was making an honest effort to rethink traditional catholic answers which had clearly outlived their usefulness.[54]

One of the great 'ifs' of modern church history is posed by the veto against Cardinal Rampolla's election to the papacy in the conclave of 1903. When one reflects that in the question of Anglo-Roman reunion and Anglican Orders he represented a standpoint diametrically opposed to that of Merry del Val, and displayed great sympathy and understanding for the genuinely ecumenical aims of Portal and Halifax, it is more tempting than ever to speculate upon what might have been if Rampolla, and not Pius x (with Merry del Val as his almost worshipful lieutenant), had directed the

[54] The position of extreme modernists was certainly incompatible with the profession of the catholic faith. What was regrettable was the failure of the authorities, of whom, next to Pius x, Merry del Val was the chief, to see that there were many who were making an honest, and not in all cases misguided, effort to present catholic teaching in a form which would be both meaningful and acceptable to a world which had read Darwin, Huxley, and Marx, and which had tasted the fruits of liberal democracy.

church's policy in the crucial and tragic decade before the First World War.[55]

Cardinal Vaughan

The leading public figure in the events we have described was Cardinal Vaughan. The cardinal's attitude was representative of the sentiment of many Roman Catholics in England in his day and for a long time thereafter. An explanation, though not necessarily a justification, of Vaughan's views and actions is to be found in the history of Roman Catholicism in England since the reformation.

> It is not so very long [wrote Mr Gordon George in 1926] since Roman Catholics were placed under very grave disabilities in Great Britain and Ireland, and the tradition of a persecuted but orthodox Church in a country where once few cared even for the name of Catholicism still survives amongst English Roman Catholics. Their feelings towards the Church of England are very often of distrust rather than of hope, of contempt rather than of sympathy.[56]

There were many Roman Catholics in England in the 1890s who were more than content to continue living in the complete spiritual and intellectual isolation which had been forced upon their ancestors in the seventeenth and eighteenth centuries. Lord Halifax himself, in reviewing the events which led to the condemnation of Anglican Orders, reminded his fellow Anglicans of their own responsibility for Roman Catholic hostility towards the claim of the Church of England to be a church in the traditional sense of the term.

> Let us remember how the Roman Catholic body in England has been treated under the Penal Laws till comparatively recent times. Only so

[55] The lack of a scholarly, critical biography of Merry del Val is greatly to be deplored. The six biographies consulted in the preparation of this work seldom rise above the level of hagiography, much of it of a singularly vulgar and tasteless kind. Since Merry del Val's cause of beatification has been introduced a prospective biographer would presumably find it difficult, if not impossible, to obtain access to the relevant documents. Moreover, issues arising out of the modernist crisis continue to be so controversial in certain quarters that anyone wishing to write a serious and critical assessment of Merry del Val would have to bring to the task unusual qualities of courage and perseverance.

[56] R. E. Gordon George, art. cit. in n. 35 above, 22.

late as the year 1786 a Benedictine, Dom Anselm Botton, was tried at York for his life on a charge of High Treason for converting a girl to the Roman Catholic faith. What would members of the Church of England have said if their Prayer Books had had to be disguised as the works of Horace or Virgil, or if they had been compelled, like a Lord Arundel of Wardour, to sell their carriage horses for five pounds apiece to their nearest neighbour, or, like Mr Constable Maxwell of Everingham, to pay double land tax, for the sake of their religious convictions? What would we have said if these things had been done to us, and what would have been our feelings towards those in any way responsible for them? Yet, did the Anglican clergy as a body protest against them? Did those clergy as a body advocate, or oppose Roman Catholic Emancipation?

We have to bear in the present the results of such conduct in the past. The sins of the fathers are visited on the children, and we have no right to expect that we shall at once be taken at our word, and an entirely different view of our position be accepted from what we have, many of us, been accustomed to take.[57]

Cardinal Vaughan lost no opportunity of maintaining, both in England and, more importantly, at Rome, that the Church of England was a radically anti-catholic body, with no fixed or definite standard of belief, and with little or no interest in sacramental life and worship. Although evidence for each of these statements could be found, this view of Anglicanism was in fact a travesty of the truth. Of the realities of contemporary Anglicanism Cardinal Vaughan was quite simply ignorant. This ignorance was even more widespread amongst his co-religionists in England than the narrow and suspicious sectarian spirit produced by the history of persecution and referred to above.

Fr B. W. Maturin, who left the Anglican Society of St John the Evangelist to enter the Roman Catholic Church in 1897, testifies how totally ignorant he found English catholics to be concerning the fruits of the catholic revival in the Church of England, for the aims of which Maturin had worked as an Anglican priest and religious for many years.

I remember well my astonishment, shortly after I was received, at finding that most Catholics knew little or nothing about [the Catholic movement in the Church of England]; they did not even give us the credit

[57] *Leo XIII* 418f.

of being sincere. One learned priest, occupying an important position, told me he had once seen an Anglican clergyman in a cassock! But about other developments he was absolutely ignorant. . . . Of the inner life that had been developed by the revival they know little or nothing.[58]

After many years as a Roman Catholic priest in England Fr Maturin could write to an Anglican priest:

I am sorry to say that the ignorance and lack of interest which English Catholics display towards the English Church is difficult to imagine. They think *nothing* of it and care nothing for it; it surprised me when I was received. If they come across an ordinary moderate High Churchman who talks of the Real Presence or Confession, they express and feel amazement that he remains where he is. . . . Very few Catholics in this country give [Anglicans] the credit of being serious.[59]

Cardinal Vaughan shared to the full the ignorance of his fellow catholics in England about Anglicanism of which the erroneous statements of the *Risposta* furnish a conspicuous example.[60]

But if it was ignorance that caused Vaughan to misrepresent the Church of England to the pope, the same cannot be said of his constant charges that the Anglican promoters of the reunion movement were acting from interested motives, and that they were merely trying, in cynical fashion, to manoeuvre themselves into a better position from which to attack the Church of Rome. Vaughan was convinced that the reunion movement was insincere, and that the real motive behind it was the desire to save the Church of England, which he imagined to be reeling under the blows of conversions to Rome. Apart from the injustice

[58] Basil F. Maturin, *The Price of Unity*, London 1917, 203f. Shortly after Fr Maturin's entry into the Roman Catholic Church Halifax wrote to Portal: 'I have written to Fr Maturin but have not yet had a reply, probably the letter has not reached him. At the moment he is with the Cardinal . . . It appears, according to what Maturin says, that the Cardinal is perfectly ignorant about everything which concerns the internal life of the Church of England, about which he does not understand the first thing; it is really what I expected' (Letter of 8th April 1897, PP).

[59] Maisie Ward, *Father Maturin, A Memoir*, London 1920, 164f. The present writer can testify from personal experience that the situation was not greatly improved in the English-speaking countries on the eve of the second Vatican Council.

[60] Lord Halifax wrote that 'a distinguished convert' had said that 'of the internal affairs of the Church of England the Cardinal was absolutely ignorant' (*Leo XIII* 361). Elsewhere Halifax used the phrase 'a distinguished convert' to refer to Fr Maturin; cf. op. cit. 363 n. 1 and p. 177 n. 29 above.

of attributing such cynical motives to anyone as transparently sincere as Halifax, such an explanation was, on the face of it, highly illogical. For it assumed that those who were doing all they could to move Anglicans in a Romeward direction, and to convince them that the papacy was the divinely appointed centre of unity, were doing so in order to keep them from accepting the pope's authority. Even on his own principles it might have been expected that Vaughan would have welcomed the movement, recognising that at most it could hold back conversions only temporarily, and that in the long run it was doing his work for him. But nothing would shake the cardinal's conviction that the reunion movement was a 'snare of the evil one'. And when it was impossible to impute bad faith to Halifax, the line adopted by Vaughan and his supporters was that Halifax was being duped by Satan, acting through other Anglicans (who were never identified) whose motives *were* cynical. It was impossible for Vaughan to believe that he was dealing with people who deeply regretted their separation from Rome. He was convinced that Anglicans were obstinate heretics, and that the reunion movement was an attempt to bolster up a faltering church[61] by tactics as clever as they were devious. Halifax used the language of gentle persuasion. He spoke always of the desire for 'peace'; he pointed out, for instance, that if the choice lay between the Privy Council as the supreme authority in the Church of England, and Leo XIII, there was everything to be said for choosing the pope, who was at least sure to be a christian, and whose authority was entirely spiritual. Vaughan's utterances were filled with polemic and attacks: Anglicans had to sign, not a treaty of peace, but an unconditional surrender. They must admit their awful heresies and submit their proud wills and intellects to the authority of the church.[62]

[61] Cf. Vaughan's reference to Anglicanism as 'une hérésie expirante' in the passage from his preface to Père Ragey's *L'anglo-catholicisme* cited on p. 92 above.
[62] Cf. P. Thureau-Dangin, *Le Cardinal Vaughan*, Paris 1911, 82f.

Vaughan's attitude and actions can be explained, even if they cannot ultimately be excused. Like any man, Herbert Vaughan was a product of the training he had received. Theology had been presented to him as a series of logical propositions to be learnt by heart ('theses'). Each of these propositions was thoroughly 'proved' by quotations from scripture, the fathers, and the church's tradition, and by logical arguments which showed that the truth under consideration must command the assent of any honest man with a modicum of intelligence. Moreover, the objections were considered one by one and carefully refuted. To a certain kind of mind this sort of theology is very impressive. None other than the son of the Archbishop of Canterbury, Robert Hugh Benson, who left the Anglican priesthood for the Roman Catholic Church and priesthood after his father's death, was delighted by the kind of theology here described when he first encountered it during his theological studies at Rome in the winter of 1904.

> I am getting through a quantity of solid theology [Benson wrote]. My goodness! The scheme of it all is tremendous; every possible objection dealt with![63]

If Herbert Vaughan had been the kind of person who did not find such proofs convincing, and his biography shows that he was not, and that he never had any intellectual difficulties with regard to the faith at all, his training would have taught him to seek the solution to the difficulty in the moral sphere. Doubts against the faith, he was told, came from the devil, and should be met by acts of faith in the infallible teaching authority of the church. This attractively simple solution appealed to an ardent and devout nature like Vaughan's. It is most unlikely that anyone over pointed out to him that the vast majority of theses in the manuals of dogmatic and moral theology rested not upon the church's infallible *magisterium* at all, but upon the human authority

[63] C. C. Martindale, *The Life of Monsignor Robert Hugh Benson* i, London 1916, 338.

of fallible theologians.[64] And Vaughan was certainly far too humble and obedient to authority to have entertained such a thought on his own.

It is very difficult for anyone trained in this way to regard those who do not accept all these obviously true propositions ('non-catholics') as anything except fools (too stupid to understand the proofs) or knaves (insincerely maintaining their errors despite the fact that they have been shown how false these errors are).[65] Is it, in the circumstances, surprising that Cardinal Vaughan believed the Anglican proponents of reunion to be cynical and insincere?

And yet, when everything has been said in explanation of Vaughan's attitude, it remains true that many of his contemporaries, who had been trained in the same intellectual tradition, and who, if they were Englishmen, were heirs of the same historical situation, were able to take, and did take, a more positive view of the reunion movement—a view which one can only call more christian. Reference has already been made to the views of Cardinal Rampolla and the French clergy who acted with Halifax or sympathised with him. But even in England there were many Roman Catholics who did not think as Vaughan did. One should always be suspicious of the claim that there is one single view on this or that question amongst Roman Catholics, and that deviation from this view is impossible—either because nonconformity is ruthlessly suppressed by a draconic system of

[64] This was pointed out, however, by James Duggan in his *Steps Towards Reunion*, London 1897 (cf. p. 234 below).

[65] In 1929 Fr Henry St John OP wrote that Roman Catholics in England seldom understood the Anglo-Catholic position. 'The result is an inevitable feeling, generally inarticulate, that an Anglo-Catholic must be either a knave or a fool' (H. St John, 'The Anglo-Catholic Problem', *Blackfriars* 10 (1929), 1176–83, 1176). Cf. also the following passage from Karl Rahner, *Theological Investigations* v Baltimore and London 1966, 318:

'The present author himself can still remember vividly a conversation with an old parish priest in Lower Bavaria who took it for granted that a Protestant theologian cannot possibly adhere to his beliefs in good faith, since he is surely in a position to recognize the truth of the Catholic Church.' Rahner also refers to Boswell's meeting with a Jesuit at Mannheim in 1764 who told the Scottish traveller that he must count him among the damned: 'It may sound hard, but it is absolutely necessary for me to believe this to be the case. The extenuating circumstances present in the case of a poor country yokel are not valid in your case. You are educated' (ibid.).

discipline or automatically eliminated by the natural unanimity of catholic opinion. Roman Catholics are united in their common assent to the church's dogmatic teaching; and the body of doctrine officially taught by the church is considerably smaller than is often supposed, even by catholics themselves. The myth of a monolithic unity of catholic opinion on other matters is fostered by two classes of people: those who wish thus to discredit the church by showing that Roman Catholics have no intellectual freedom; and those who mistakenly suppose that by encouraging the myth of catholic unanimity in all questions they are doing the church a service. The freedom and intensity of debate at the second Vatican Council were a shock to both classes of people, and there is evidence that many in both groups have not yet recovered from the shock.

The Roman Catholic Church in England in the 1890s could no longer be called tiny. But it was still a very small body. This did not make it a particularly united body. Small as it was, it contained a number of highly diverse elements: the 'old catholic families', which had produced men as different as Lord Acton and Vaughan himself; a rapidly increasing Irish element; and the large group of converts, themselves a very mixed lot, as may be indicated by mentioning a few representative nineteenth-century names: Newman, Manning, Simpson, Faber, and Oxenham. There were not a few Roman Catholics in England in the nineties who understood and sympathised with Halifax's efforts and deplored the *simpliste* and intransigent position of Cardinal Vaughan. If published expressions of such opinions are comparatively rare, this merely testifies to the effectiveness of ecclesiastical censorship. As late as 1934 this system of censorship was still in full working order in England. This was clearly stated by the English Jesuit Fr Albert Gille in a book which argued that the method of joint theological conversations between Anglicans and Roman Catholics advocated by Halifax and Portal in the nineties and finally begun at Malines in the 1920s under the protection of Cardinal Mercier (to the intense displeasure of Vaughan's successor in the see of Westminster, Cardinal Bourne) was the only reasonable way of seeking reunion between the two churches.

> There are many English priests [Fr Gille wrote], both secular and religious, who . . . firmly hold that Cardinal Mercier's move was the only sane, sensible, and hopeful effort towards regaining the Anglican Church; only these priests are not allowed to express their opinions in print. The censors see to that.[66]

> The scheme of reconciliation which [Cardinal Mercier] read out at the Malines conversations, though possibly not his own, yet fairly represented his own views on the subject, and still embodies the secret ambition of many a Catholic priest in England.[67]

No Imprimatur could be obtained in England for the public expression of such views in 1934, and the author was forced to publish them anonymously. Tongue in cheek, he called the book 'a secret and friendly message from the beleaguered city of God, the Catholic Church, to the besieging armies of Protestantism'.[68]

The same censorship also withheld its approval in 1897 from a remarkable and little noticed book by the parish priest of the Roman Catholic church at Maidstone, James Duggan, entitled *Steps Towards Reunion.* The author's approach to the problem of reunion was markedly different from that of Cardinal Vaughan:

> If we want reunion, it will never do for us Catholics to say absolutely that we have all along been right in everything, and that we cannot give in in anything. . . . Contrary to what is commonly said by Catholics, we can surrender a vast body of doctrine. We can surrender all that is taught not by the Church but in the Church by theologians.[69]

[66] Fr Jerome [Albert Gille], *A Catholic Plea for Reunion*, London 1934, 31.

[67] Ibid. 73. The reference is to a paper by Dom Lambert Beauduin, 'L'Église anglicane unie non absorbée', which enraged Cardinal Bourne by suggesting a Uniate status for Anglicans in case dogmatic unity with the Roman Catholic Church could be achieved (cf. Lord Halifax, *The Conversations at Malines, 1921–1925*, London 1930, 241–61).

[68] Op. cit. 15.

[69] Op. cit. 3f.

The book consists mainly of a trenchant exercise in catholic self-criticism somewhat in the manner of a modern work like *Objections to Roman Catholicism.*[70]

Another dissenting voice was that of the Revd William Francis Barry, who had taught in the seminaries at Birmingham and Oscott, and who was pastor of the Roman Catholic church in Dorchester from 1883 to 1908. He was the author of a large number of essays and articles, and of many books, including a biography of Newman.[71] Barry wrote to Lord Halifax upon the publication of the Reply of the Anglican Archbishops to *Apostolicae curae* in March 1897:

> Do not lose heart because the first steps are difficult or disappointing. They *are* steps, and must open the path to something further and better Even such a softening of tone as we observe in the Pope's documentary language, on the one hand, and in the Archbishops' reply on the other, proves, as I often say, that a feeling of spring is in the air. But we want much more interchange of thought and personal acquaintance. This will be helped by the opening to our own students of Oxford and Cambridge. It would also be much advanced if the devotional and catechetical works, published by members of the Church of England for their own people, could be brought under the direct notice of the Holy See. Why should not a selection of them, with an appropriate letter, be offered to Cardinal Parocchi or to Cardinal Mazzella, both of whom read English? This, I think, would enable the Roman authorities and the Holy Father to see how deep is the spiritual life which so widespread a literature nourishes. And the more conspicuous the persons that made such an offering, so much the better.
>
> . . . It may be said, who is to begin? I know. But a great recompense is awaiting the members of your Church who will take on themselves in Rome this embassy of *explanation*, and will keep on supplying needful light to the persons there charged with the duty of Propaganda.
>
> For myself, I am always happy when doing what in me lies to interpret the genuine thoughts and convictions of one side to the other, feeling that unless we understand we shall never be united. Excuse these many words on a matter close to your heart, and not distant from ours who love peace and would ensue it.[72]

Fr George Tyrrell SJ wrote that he felt Halifax had expected too much.

[70] Michael de La Bedoyère (ed.), London 1964.
[71] William Barry, *Newman*, London 1904.
[72] Letter of 10th March 1897, HP A4.269.

> The majority . . . with us, as with every other body of mortals, is made up of those who take narrow and shortsighted views of every question, and whose zeal and good-will is greater than their discretion. Were not God's foolishness wiser than the wisdom of men we might despair of any good ever being accomplished: but if we have eyes of faith we can see him at work everywhere moulding good out of evil. I am afraid the same acrimonious bitterness has characterised every quarrel recorded in the pages of Church history; and one cannot pretend that the orthodox side has ever shown a too brilliant example of charity to the unorthodox. This I think is inevitable—taking human nature as it is in the many—wherever any difference of opinion creates *sides*, for thousands who care little about the truth love controversy and contest for its own sake, and eagerly join the fray, not to heal the breach but to enlarge it; not to reconcile differences but to accentuate them. Were it not for this class, Church papers could not subsist.[73]

Reference has already been made in several places to the fact that Vaughan's friend Wilfrid Ward was considerably more sympathetic to Halifax's ideas than the cardinal, although he understood Vaughan's criticisms and misgivings, and tried to interpret them to Halifax. Another dissenter from the line adopted by the cardinal was Fr Scannell, who owed his place on the commission to his dissenting views, and whom Lacey reported after the close of the commission's meetings to be apparently 'much disgusted with the *Tablet*',[74] which was the personal organ of Cardinal Vaughan. But the most important dissenting voice was that of Bishop W. R. Brownlow of Clifton, who had been a priest in the Church of England before he was received into the Roman Catholic Church by Newman. Wilfrid Ward reports Brownlow as saying:

> We all agree that reunion is a dream. It is not in the domain of practical politics. The real question is: is it a good dream to be encouraged or a bad one to be roughly dispelled?[75]

[73] Letter of 24th July 1897, HP A4.270, Part II.
[74] Lacey, *Roman Diary* 70, entry for 23rd May 1896.
[75] Cited from the *Morning Post*, 16th August 1910, 4 col. 6. Baron von Hügel wrote to his friend Loisy that Bishop Brownlow was in favour of permitting the *Revue Anglo-Romaine* (in which Loisy had collaborated) to continue publication after the condemnation of Anglican Orders, and that Brownlow 'did not approve of the Cardinal's [i.e. Vaughan's] intransigence' (cf. Loisy, *Memoires* i, 415).

Bishop Brownlow felt that the movement for corporate re-union was a good dream which should be encouraged.[76]

After the condemnation of the Orders Baron Friedrich von Hügel wrote to Cardinal Vaughan in his usual tortuous, half-German style:

> Bishop Brownlow represents, I think, in these matters, very much the tone and attitude that not only help me, but that have enabled me to be of some real help, I gratefully think, to a now not inconsiderable number of souls. I am very sure, from such direct experience (which, after all, but repeats, on a humbler scale, what can be seen writ large on the special influence of Cardinal Wiseman and Cardinal Newman) that there *are* souls, I suspect in increasing numbers, whom only such a tone would ever bring into the Church.[77]

Von Hügel went on to refer to Vaughan's very different attitude in terms which one would be compelled to regard as deliberately ironic, were it not that the baron's intense piety and lack of humour forbid such an interpretation.

> No doubt Your Eminence has evidence, at least as cogent, and no doubt much more multifarious, of the existence, possibly in much larger numbers, of souls that have been helped on by exactly the opposite tack.[78]

Von Hügel confided in the cardinal that the condemnation of the Orders filled him with apprehension.

> My extrinsic difficulty is purely general. It is a fear lest this decision may encourage in our rank and file a tone which, for now over a quarter of a century, has tried me much, all Catholic, and please God, devoted Catholic as I am—a tone which, I know full well, would have constituted an all but insuperable barrier to my becoming a Catholic, had I had the misfortune of being born outside the Church.[79]

That von Hügel's fear was not fanciful is abundantly demonstrated by the mass of polemic which has been produced in the seventy years since *Apostolicae curae*, all rubbing Anglican noses in the mud, and taunting Anglicans with belonging to a bogus church that dispenses purely illusory and worthless sacraments.

[76] Cf. Brownlow's remark after Vaughan's militant speech at Bristol in September 1895, pp. 95–6 above.

[77] *The Tablet* 137 (1937), 188 col. 2. The letter was written towards the end of 1896.

[78] Ibid. [79] Ibid.

The defence offered for Cardinal Vaughan by his biographer, as well as by Canon Moyes and others who had acted with him, was not that he had faithfully represented the opinion of all loyal Roman Catholics in England. This was simply assumed. For once all dissenting voices had been suppressed it was easy to assume that they did not exist. Even the most violent partisans could not but realise, however, that Vaughan's views and actions were unpopular with the public at large, and required some defence. This consisted of the claim, made many times in subsequent years in *The Tablet* articles, as well as by Gasquet in his *Leaves from My Diary* and by Vaughan's biographer, that the cardinal had from the start deprecated the raising of the Orders question at all. The record shows that while there may have been some truth to this claim at the very beginning of the affair, Cardinal Vaughan changed his attitude almost at once, and devoted all his energies to obtaining a public and solemn condemnation of Anglican Orders.

In a letter to the pope on 8th August 1895, in which he displayed considerable bitterness towards the French clergy who were co-operating with Halifax, Vaughan said that he had always advocated a thorough examination of the question of Anglican Orders. There is nothing in the letter to suggest that he regretted the matter having been raised.[80] It is entirely a plea that nothing should be done without the full participation of English Roman Catholics. This was an entirely reasonable request, and one which was granted to the full, as we have seen. It was to this letter that Vaughan was referring in his speech at Bristol in September 1895, which has been referred to in Chapter 5 above, and in which the cardinal said that he had 'earnestly pleaded' that the question of Anglican Orders 'be re-examined in Rome'.[81]

In season and out Vaughan insisted that the Church of England was thoroughly protestant, and that Halifax spoke

[80] Cf. the text of this letter in RMP ii, 527. This is the communication referred to by Vaughan in his letter to Gasquet reproduced on pp. 299f below.
[81] Cf. p. 95 above.

for only a tiny minority of Anglicans. The truth was considerably more complex. By the end of the nineteenth century the successors of the Tractarians had succeeded in persuading a very large number of the Anglican clergy of the fundamental principles of the Oxford Movement. In 1899 the Revd H. L. Jackson, Vicar of St Mary's, Huntingdon, who described himself as a 'Liberal Broad Churchman' and confessed his dislike of many features of the High Church position, admitted nevertheless that Anglo-Catholics had come to occupy a position of great strength.

> The High Churchman has, I think, deserved to win. Very patiently, very courageously has he worked. Most of the opposition he has met with has been fatuous in the last degree. The High Church position is largely warranted by our Church's formularies. It is, so it seems to me, only malice and ignorance that can determine otherwise.[82]

The laity are consistently the most conservative element in the church, and opposition to the Anglo-Catholic view of Anglicanism was still strong amongst the English laity at the end of the century, far stronger than amongst the clergy. This is especially true if one includes a very large number of laypeople whose adherence to the Church of England was entirely nominal, but who were always ready to respond to protestant agitation and cries of 'No Popery'. If judged by the attitude of the English laity, Cardinal Vaughan's statements contained a considerable element of truth. But there was a serious inconsistency in Vaughan's appeals to the religious sentiment of the Anglican laity, a large proportion of whom hardly practised their religion at all, as representative of the Anglican Church. For his view of his own church was, in accordance with the theology which he had been taught, almost exclusively clerical.

Cardinal Vaughan once confided in the Anglican convert priest and former Cowley Father Basil Maturin his puzzlement at the fact that despite all the vaunted conversions the

[82] Cited from Roger Lloyd, *The Church of England in the 20th Century* i, London 1946, 121.

movement towards Rome in England remained so small. He asked Fr Maturin what he thought was the chief obstacle which kept people back. 'If you want me to be perfectly frank with your Eminence,' Maturin replied, 'I should say it was yourself.' Vaughan was a genuinely humble man, to whom one could say that kind of thing. It was characteristic of him that he was not offended by this blunt expression of an opinion highly unfavourable to himself, and asked Fr Maturin to give his reasons for his view.

> In reply Father Maturin pointed out [his biographer writes] that the Cardinal seemed in his public utterance to cast doubt on the good faith of so many Christians outside the Catholic and Roman Church. To one who had lived among them as he himself had done their good faith did not admit of the faintest doubt, and a general line of *intransigence* only served to hurt their feelings unnecessarily and prevent them from drawing nearer to the Church. Of the High Church position in particular the view of the two men was diametrically opposed, the Cardinal regarding it [as] a dangerous and specious substitute keeping men back from the Church, Father Maturin looking on it as a teaching of Catholic truth educating them gradually to receive the fullness of truth in the Church.[83]

It is pleasant, however, to record what Fr Maturin wrote on Vaughan's death in 1903:

> The Cardinal is a great loss. I shall miss him very much. . . . He was really a saint. I think one of the humblest and certainly most unworldly men I ever met, perfectly simple and as straight as a die.[84]

Cardinal Vaughan honestly believed that the faith and the vital interests of the church entrusted to his pastoral care were threatened by what Lord Halifax and his French friends were proposing. He did what any conscientious bishop would do in such a situation: he defended to the uttermost the sheep for whose eternal welfare he knew himself to be answerable to God. It is, however, impossible to be happy about the methods used in that defence, especially when one compares them with those used on the other side. Fifteen

[83] Maisie Ward, *Father Maturin* 52; emphasis in original.
[84] Ibid. 52f.

years later, when tempers had cooled, Portal could still write to Halifax:

> Cardinal Vaughan and his lieutenants were wrong not to conduct themselves like christians. . . . Our adversaries conducted their campaign like a game of football or like any political campaign. They did not, I think, display any genuine intelligence. More intelligence would have caused them to adopt a different attitude. But above all they were not christian.[85]

And in another letter written about the same time the abbé told his friend:

> It is impossible for me to relive all that whole time without a feeling of deep sadness. But I find a great sweetness in it nevertheless. We acted as we believed we were bound to act. We employed only honest and Christian means, and that is something at any rate.[86]

These judgements are severe. Despite the fact that the preceding pages contain much evidence in their support, opinions are bound to differ on the question of whether Portal's judgements were too harsh, or whether they were simply what the facts here recounted demanded.[87] Vaughan could certainly have claimed, as did Portal, to have acted only as he felt bound to act. But this does not prove that he acted rightly.

An independent view of Vaughan's conduct, valuable

[85] Letter of 16th April 1911, HP A4.213.

[86] Letter of 3rd December 1910, HP A4.213.

[87] In the foregoing account much important detail has necessarily been omitted. A case in point is Cardinal Vaughan's treatment of the encyclical, *Satis cognitum*, issued by Leo XIII at the end of June 1896. This document emphasised the position of the pope as the inheritor of Christ's commission to St Peter, while asserting that the bishops inherited the commission given by Christ to the other apostles. Cardinal Vaughan sent a summary of this document to *The Times*, which published it on 30th June. The summary concentrated entirely upon the petrine and papal passages of the letter to the exclusion of its teaching about the episcopate. Vaughan also sent a covering letter in the same sense, in which he wrote that Halifax and his supporters 'had been under the strange delusion that it was in the power of the Holy Father to modify or dispense with the ancient terms of communion' with the Holy See—a statement for which there was no justification in anything Halifax had said or done. The net effect of this letter, together with the one-sided summary of the encyclical, was to create a wholly false impression. When Portal tried to set matters straight at the meeting in London on 14th July referred to on p. 189 n. 16 above, and explain how much more reasonable the encyclical was than the distorted impression of it which had been circulated in England, his remarks were gravely misrepresented and he was made the target of repeated bitter attacks (cf. loc. cit. above).

because it comes from a distinguished author and literary critic with no direct interest in the controversy himself, was that of Sir Edmund Gosse. He read the proofs of Halifax's book, *Leo XIII and Anglican Orders*, before publication, and helped Halifax by suggesting a number of stylistic changes and improvements.[88]

> It is all very interesting [Gosse wrote], very human and generous and ardent. Only wooden old Vaughan comes out as the villain of the piece. And I think he was a villain, a holy villain of course, one of those strange people who employ for sacred ends methods which applied to civic ends would be seen to be infamous.[89]

A judgement of Vaughan personally with which there can be no quarrel, and which is the more remarkable as coming from Lord Halifax only a few weeks after the condemnation of the Orders, while Vaughan was publicly triumphing over the fallen foe, is contained in a letter written by Halifax to his fellow Anglican layman and close friend Athelstan Riley.

> He is a person quite apart [Halifax wrote of Vaughan]. No one can the least understand him who does not know him. He is quite the oddest mixture of things that ever was. He is absolutely impervious to new ideas and combines with a great deal of magnanimity and stupidity a capacity for blundering which is marvellous. I like him and cannot help doing so despite all his enormities.[90]

The methods used by Vaughan and those who served him so efficiently behind the scenes to crush the reunion movement and obtain a solemn condemnation of Anglican Orders illustrate once again a fact frequently noted by keen observers of ecclesiastical affairs: that the sons of the counter-reformation are sometimes not very good at the natural virtues. Or, as Halifax himself said in a letter to the Bishop of Peterborough before the condemnation of the Orders:

'It is not the bad men who do the most mischief in the world.'[91]

[88] Cf. *Leo XIII* 3.

[89] Letter of Gosse to Halifax, 8th August 1911, HP A4.269. Gosse was at the time librarian of the House of Lords.

[90] Letter of 6th October 1896, HP A4.215. The quotation of this letter in Halifax's biography omits the next to last sentence: Lockhart *Halifax* ii, 87.

[91] Halifax to Mandell Creighton, 17th July 1896, HP A4.254.

PART TWO

THE HISTORICAL ARGUMENTS OF THE BULL

Infallibility has, happily, this time
ventured on reasons.

Archbishop Benson[1]

[1] A. C. Benson, *E. W. Benson* ii, 623. Benson wrote this the day before his sudden death during Matins in Hawarden Parish Church on Sunday 11th October 1896.

12
THE MARIAN RESTORATION

The question here is not about what was done, but what ought to have been done; and it does not appear that the facts and motives upon which they determined ought to determine us too.

—P. F. le Courayer [1]

Apostolicae curae begins its argument against Anglican Orders by an appeal to precedent. It is asserted that the Holy See has always treated the Orders as null and void whenever the question has arisen in practice, and that this policy of non-recognition can be traced back to the period of the Marian restoration from 1553–58. The Bull argues that in view of the unbroken practice of the Holy See,

> It must be clear to everyone that the controversy lately revived had been already definitely settled by the Apostolic See.[2]

This statement is surprising, for it naturally suggests the question, why any investigation was necessary or even possible if the matter was 'already definitely settled'. This difficulty was got round by the suggestion that the historical precedents appealed to in the Bull were not as well known as they might be.

> It is to the insufficient knowledge of these documents that we must perhaps attribute the fact that any Catholic writer should have considered it still an open question.[3]

We have already seen that the pope and his Secretary of State were amongst those who were ignorant of the documents here referred to, and who as recently as two years previously had fallen into the error of regarding the validity of Anglican Orders as an open question.[4]

[1] Pierre François le Courayer, *A Dissertation on the Validity of the Ordinations of the English* (translated by Daniel Williams), Oxford 1844, 229.
[2] AO(E) 9. [3] Ibid. [4] Cf. p. 59 above.

The precedents cited in the Bull are, first, those of the Marian restoration, and second, two decisions of the Holy Office, which in 1684 and 1704 treated orders conferred with the Anglican Ordinal, or supposed to have been so conferred, as null. Before discussing the Marian restoration in this chapter, and the two later cases in the chapter following, we must draw attention to the necessary limitation of the appeal to precedent in a matter of this kind. Even if it could be conclusively demonstrated that orders imparted with the rite of the Edwardine Ordinal had been treated from the very start and with complete consistency as null and void, this would not in itself prove that such orders were in fact invalid. For who can guarantee that the previous practice was sound? The existing practice of treating Anglican Orders as invalid was well known in 1896; the commission was charged with investigating this practice and the reasons for it. If the argument from precedent were decisive the investigation would have been superfluous. This was pointed out by Fr Wilfrid Knox, the Anglican brother of Mgr Ronald Knox, who said in 1919:

> The Bull itself is an admission of the fact that the mere historical precedent—the fact that it has always been the practice to reordain Anglicans—would not by itself be a bar to the adoption of the view that our Ordinal is valid. It would have been meaningless to reopen the question if there had been no possibility of a change of attitude.[5]

Precedents have the binding force of the reasons upon which they are based. *Apostolicae curae* claims, not very convincingly in view of the lengthy controversy and investigation which preceded it, that the question *is* decided on the basis of precedent. But the Bull betrays a consciousness that this argument alone will not carry ultimate conviction. For it goes on to argue at length that the precedents appealed to were in fact based upon solid and sound reasons. It is these reasons therefore which must be investigated, for there is no

[5] Wilfrid L. Knox, *Friend, I do thee no Wrong*, London (Soc. of SS Peter and Paul) 1919, 4.

guarantee that the Roman authorities in the sixteenth century or at any subsequent period were fully and accurately informed on the question; or, even presuming that they were so informed, that their decision was in fact the correct one.

Although the previous practice of the Holy See cannot be decisive, this does not mean that it can be ignored. It is appealed to by *Apostolicae curae*, and for that reason alone we must consider it. The Bull claims that ordinations carried out with the Edwardine Ordinal were consistently treated as null and void during the Marian restoration. Anglican apologists were accustomed to assert before 1896 that no distinction was made under Mary between clergy ordained with the Ordinal and those ordained with the Sarum Pontifical. They have continued to make this claim since the Bull, pointing out that the version of history presented by *Apostolicae curae* is not supported by the available evidence and that it raises as many fresh difficulties and contradictions as it solves.[6] Roman Catholics, on the other hand, have been accustomed to assert since the Bull that the rejection of Edwardine Orders under Mary is a clearly established fact. Messenger says flatly:

> This condemnation was complete, universal and authoritative.[7]

And Fr Clark has written:

> There is indeed abundant evidence from many independent sources showing plainly that in Mary's reign the Catholic authorities, both in England and Rome, deliberately and definitely rejected as invalid the ordinations which had been performed in the previous reign by use of the new English rite. Some controversialists, by clutching at a few ambiguities or anomalies in the records while ignoring the whole mass of proved historical facts which combine to put the matter beyond doubt, still try to maintain the contrary; but in this they are clinging to a lost cause.[8]

[6] Cf. for example Frere, *The Marian Reaction* 158ff n. 1 and the passage from the Anglican archbishops' Reply to the Bull cited on p. 270 below.

[7] RMP ii, 167.

[8] Francis Clark, *The Catholic Church and Anglican Orders* (t), London (CTS) 1962, 14; cf. also Fr Clark's 'Les ordinations anglicanes, problème oecuménique', Gr 45 (1964), 60–93, 71.

A careful examination of the historical evidence shows that such statements belong in the category of the remark pencilled in the margin of his sermon manuscript by a popular preacher: 'Argument weak: shout.' There is no question that Edwardine Orders were rejected on a number of occasions. But the 'few ambiguities and anomalies in the records' include the language of two papal documents issued by Paul IV in 1555, and cannot be so lightly dismissed. For they point to inconsistencies and ambiguities in practice quite sufficient to shake our confidence in the alleged unanimous and consistent rejection of Edwardine Orders during Mary's reign.

The difficulties of the enquiry

The available historical evidence is incomplete and tangled. After a lengthy study of all the available documents from all relevant sources both in Rome and England, as well as a careful consideration of the conflicting claims of partisans on both sides as to the meaning of these documents, one overriding conclusion emerges: the record is so full of ambiguities and uncertainties that no clear verdict for either side is possible on the basis of present knowledge. Anglican claims that the Orders were allowed, and catholic claims that they were consistently rejected, are both based upon special pleading. No really adequate study of the evidence has ever been published. Such a study would far transcend the bounds of this book. It would require the combined talents of an expert historian, able to find, read, and interpret the evidence contained in more than two dozen diocesan registers of the Marian period up and down England; and the analytical powers of a trained canonist, with the customs and subtleties of Roman curial practice at his fingertips, and the ability to deal with lengthy Latin legal documents, couched in the style of the fine print in an insurance contract, with a single sentence extending over two and more printed pages. A certain amount of research has been done into the deprivations of clergy under Mary. Frere is the only scholar who has studied the registers with a view to determining how Edwardine Orders were treated, and his investigation, published in 1896, was admittedly hasty and incomplete.[9] It has now been rendered partially obsolete by the appearance of further studies, none of them, however, motivated by an interest in the question of orders.[10] The only discussion of the question informed by a knowledge of Roman canon law is that of Messenger.[11] His is by far the lengthiest and most detailed treament of the subject to date, and it will therefore be necessary to refer to Messenger's statements at a number of points in the subsequent discussion. It is unfortunate that a work of over 1,300 pages, representing as it does such a vast amount of labour, should be disfigured throughout by such glaring faults. Messenger's identification of his sources is seldom complete; bibliographical references generally lack either the date or place of publication, and sometimes both; the same work is often referred to in different places under different titles; authors are apt to be identified by their surnames only. Messenger's pages, and especially his footnotes, abound in slips and errors. When the second volume of his work appeared it was found to contain fourteen pages of small print correcting mistakes and omissions in the first volume which had been spotted by reviewers—who are generally busy men with a deadline to meet and little time to verify references or details in a lengthy and closely packed work of this kind. Neither volume contains a bibliography. Even worse than these formal defects is the confusion which Dr Messenger introduces into almost every question he treats. Instead of elucidating, he frequently leaves the reader more perplexed than ever. Even as strong a partisan as Fr Clark refers to his predecessor's 'useful but somewhat ill-

[9] W. H. Frere, *The Marian Reaction*, London 1896.
[10] Cf. H. E. P. Grieve, 'The Deprived Married Clergy of Essex', *Transactions of the Royal Historical Society* 4th Series, xxii, 141–69; James E. Oxley, *The Reformation in Essex to the Death of Mary*, Manchester 1965, 180f.; A. G. Dickens, *The Marian Reaction in the Diocese of York: Part I, the Clergy*, London and York 1957.
[11] RMP ii 91–167 *passim*.

digested volumes',[12] a judgement which, on balance, must be termed generous.

Messenger undertook no independent research into the evidence of clerical deprivations and re-ordinations in the Marian registers, but relied entirely upon Frere's incomplete and hasty investigation in 1896. Nowhere is Messenger's habitual confusion of thought and treatment so evident as in his discussion of the tangled events and frequently obscure documents of the Marian period. At crucial points in his argument Messenger is forced to fall back on conjecture and upon assertions which are not susceptible of proof.[13]

The treatment of Edwardine Orders by Queen Mary and her bishops

We have already seen that the new Ordinal was not originally part of the First Prayer Book of Edward VI issued in 1549. An act of parliament in January 1550 authorised the compilation of new rites for ordination. A draft must have been prepared in advance, for the commission appointed to do the work appears to have completed its task within a week. Hooper, soon to be the new Bishop of Gloucester, saw the new rite in print on 5th March.[14] When the Second Prayer Book was issued in 1552, minor changes were made in the Ordinal. The delivery of the pastoral staff to the newly consecrated bishop was dropped, a bible being given to him instead. In the 1550 Ordinal the bible had been laid upon the neck of the kneeling bishop before delivery of the staff. The original rite for the ordination of priests contained the following rubric immediately after the essential form of ordination:

> The Bishop shall deliver to every one of them, the Bible in the one hand, and the Chalice or cup with the bread in the other hand . . . [15]

[12] ESR 192 n. 41.

[13] As the remainder of this chapter is concerned with technical points of no little complexity which cannot in any case be decisive, the general reader may, if he wishes, pass at once to Chapter 13 without substantial loss.

[14] Cf. Philip Hughes, *The Reformation in England* ii, London 1953, 113f.

[15] Gibson 312.

The 1552 version ordered the delivery of the bible only. Five bishops were consecrated with the first version of this rite, and one with the second version, the consecrators being in each case bishops themselves consecrated with the Sarum Pontifical.[16] Some 110 other clergy were ordained with the Ordinal, and it appears that seventy-one of these received the diaconate only.[17]

The young and sickly King Edward VI died on 6th July 1553. After an abortive attempt to place Lady Jane Grey on the throne, Edward's half-sister, Mary, was proclaimed queen on 19th July. Mary immediately set about to restore in England the catholic religion of her childhood. Within a fortnight the news of her accession reached Rome, where it was greeted with transports of joy. On 5th August Pope Julius III appointed Mary's cousin, Reginald Cardinal Pole,[18] as his legate to England to carry through the reconciliation of the kingdom to the Holy See. It was to be more than a year, however, before Pole could gain admission to his native country. He was detained on the Continent by a series of political complications which need not detain us here. In his absence Mary proceeded in good Tudor fashion to carry through the restoration of catholicism by virtue of her royal authority as Supreme Head of the Church which she had inherited from her father and half-brother. The fact that a catholic restoration should have been set in motion and so largely carried through in virtue of so un-catholic a principle

[16] Frere, *Marian Reaction* 90.

[17] Ibid, 105f. This tabulation is the only one we have and is based upon a hasty search of the registers undertaken by Frere in 1896, of which he himself wrote: 'It is too much to hope that the enquiry has been at all exhaustive or really final' (*Marian Reaction* 8). It is entirely possible, therefore, that future research may extend the list of Edwardine ordinations. Professor Dickens (op. cit. in n. 10 above) reports that Frere overlooked a great many deprivations recorded in the York registers. This lends colour to the suspicion that Frere's list of ordinations may also be incomplete.

[18] Pole and Henry VIII had a common great-grandfather, Richard Duke of York (1411–60), and a common great-grandmother, Margaret Beauchamp. Her first husband, Sir Oliver St John (d. 1437), was a great-grandfather of Pole; her second husband, John Duke of Somerset (1403–44), was a great-grandfather of Henry. Pole was thus a second cousin to Henry VIII and second cousin once removed to Mary (cf. the genealogical tables in W. Schenk, *Reginald Pole, Cardinal of England* London 1950, 172).

is a considerable embarrassment to Messenger. He goes to great pains to stress that Mary remained in close touch with Pole, who soon set up headquarters in Flanders, so that communication by messengers travelling back and forth between him and the Queen was comparatively easy.

The first indication of what was done with regard to Edwardine clergy in this early part of the new reign comes from a contemporary catholic apologist, Nicholas Sanders. Writing in the course of Elizabeth's reign, Sanders complained bitterly that under Mary the clergy who had been ordained with the Edwardine Ordinal at first continued to exercise their ministry on the same basis as clergy ordained with the Pontifical rite.

> But when they first began to restore the church the clergy everywhere fell into a grievous error. For the Queen (as has been reported) made it possible to practice the catholic faith, and soon many who had been in schism in the time of Henry and Edward flocked to the sacred altars and sacrifices quite casually and irreverently (to say nothing worse of men who sinned rather by neglecting canonical discipline than by despising it). They were oblivious of the church's canons and law, and did not consider what their status was nor examine the qualifications and status of the bishops who had ordained them, nor the manner in which they were ordained, nor whether they were hindered or impeded by any censures or irregularities.[19]

Sanders concludes the passage by saying that he has included these facts in his narrative as a warning for the future, so that sacrilege of this kind may be avoided in case the same situation should arise again elsewhere. Sanders' work, which was published posthumously and reprinted many times on the

[19] 'Sed in his primis restituendae Ecclesiis initiis, gravius a clero passim in eo peccatum est, quod Regina ita (uti dictum est) facultatem exercendae catholicae religionis concedente, mox multi ex superiore Henrici et Edouardi temporibus schismate, canonum et regulae Ecclesiasticae obliti, sine conditionis cuiusque suae consideratione, non examinantes, a quibus et qualibus Episcopis quove modo fuerant ordinati; utrum aliquo censurarum, vel irregularitatum vinculo aut impedimento innodati ac irreti, temere plane ac irreverenter (ne quid gravius de hominibus, ex canonica disciplina neglecta potius, quam contempta peccantibus dicam) ad sancta altaria et sacrificia convolabant: . . .' Nicholas Sanders, *De origine ac progressu schismatis Anglicani*, Ingolstadt 1586, 248. I am indebted to Studienrat Norbert Panhuysen for assistance in translating the abominable Latin of this passage.

Continent, forming for a considerable time the standard catholic account of the English reformation, is violently partisan. It is most unlikely therefore that he would have reported anything so discreditable to the catholic queen and her government unless there were solid evidence for the report. Sanders' biographer in the *Dictionary of National Biography* writes that:

> Recent historians have . . . shown that, notwithstanding his animus and the violence of his language, his narrative of facts is remarkably truthful. In almost every disputed point he has been proved right . . . [20]

It could be argued that what was done by Queen Mary prior to the arrival of the papal legate in no way compromised the Holy See. But we have already remarked that Mary was in touch with Pole throughout and consulted him constantly. It is most improbable that the Queen permitted anything to be done with regard to ecclesiastical affairs without Pole's advice and consent. Especially would this be true with regard to something as important as the admission of clergy with doubtful orders to the exercise of their sacredotal functions. Sanders' evidence indicates that at least at the beginning of the reign there was no settled policy with regard to Edwardine Orders.[21]

Frere has discovered in the episcopal registers of the Marian period evidence for a certain number of re-ordinations of clergy who had previously received the same orders with the Edwardine Ordinal. Owing to the uncertainty of identification in a few cases, estimates of the number of men re-ordained during the restoration vary between thirteen and fifteen.[22] It might be supposed that the fact of these

[20] DNB xvii, Oxford 1921, 750 col. 1; cf. also Thomas McN. Veech, *Dr Nicholas Sanders and the English Reformation 1530–1581*, Louvain 1935.

[21] It is interesting to note that Messenger nowhere refers to this passage from Sanders.

[22] Messenger gives the larger figure (RMP ii, 129) and Gregory Dix the smaller one (*The Question of Anglican Orders*, London [2]1956, 72). Dix's statement that Pole himself re-ordained Edwardine clergy 'in thirteen cases out of the hundreds involved' is a serious lapse. Almost all the re-ordinations took place in the early months of Mary's reign, long before Pole reached England. And Dix is wholly unjustified in speaking of 'hundreds' of Edwardine clergy. At the time he wrote less

re-ordinations establishes conclusively that Edwardine Orders were treated as null and void during the restoration. But this is only one of the many points at which further study shows that things are by no means as simple as they appear at first sight. In order to form a sound judgement about the significance of these few re-ordinations it would be necessary to know what motivated them. But it is precisely at this point that we lose the trail. Did the re-ordinations take place on the initiative of the ordinands themselves? And if so, is it not possible that they may have been motivated either by conscientious scruples (which might or might not have been well founded) or by a desire to impress the authorities by demonstrating their adherence to the new regime in this way? Either or both of these motives could also have been operative in the case of any re-ordinations which took place on the initiative of the ordaining bishops.

The first evidence we have of any initiative in the question from the side of the authorities comes nine months after Mary's accession—and here again, as at almost every point in this tangled history, it is uncertain how the evidence ought to be interpreted. On 4th March 1554 the Queen issued injunctions to the bishops for the restoration of good order in the church. Cardinal Pole's messenger, Goldwell, visited Mary just before these injunctions were issued; and both catholic and Anglican controversialists agree that the injunctions were issued with the legate's knowledge.[23] The bishops were ordered by the Queen to put down heresy and vice, to drive out married clergy, and to restore catholic usages everywhere. The fifteenth of these injunctions reads:

> Touching such persons as were heretofore promoted to any Orders, after the new sort and fashion of order, considering that they were not ordered in very deed, the bishop of the diocese finding otherwise sufficiency and

than a hundred and twenty had been counted. Even if further research into the Marian registers lengthens the list compiled by Frere, it is most unlikely that we shall ever be able to speak of 'hundreds' of ordinations in the three years in which the Ordinal was in use.

[23] Cf. RMP ii, 53, and Denny and Lacey, *De Hierarchia Anglicana* 148.

ability in these men, may supply that thing which wanted in them before and then, according to his discretion, admit them to minister.[24]

This might seem to imply that the Edwardine ordinations were regarded as null and void, and Messenger interprets the provision in this sense. On the other hand, the phrase 'supply that thing which wanted in them before' hardly accords with this interpretation. Messenger argues that it is governed by what has gone before, and that what was to be supplied was ordination.[25] But in that case we are left with the question why language was used which more naturally suggests some supplementary ceremony, like supplying the rites of solemn baptism (without actually baptising) to someone who has been baptised without these rites in an emergency. It is impossible to say with certainty what was intended. Nor does the fact that a certain number of re-ordinations had already taken place decide the matter. For there is no evidence that these ordinations were part of a deliberate policy to be followed in all cases. And Sanders' complaint already cited indicates that in this early period there was no consistent policy at all.

Bishop Bonner's treatment of Edwardine Orders

The next piece of evidence comes from the newly restored Bishop of London, Edmund Bonner, whom Gasquet and Bishop call 'a practical man but evidently no theologian'.[26] Bonner was the most zealous of the Marian bishops, relentless towards heretics, and made so much trouble for the government after his deprivation by Elizabeth five years later that he was the only one of the deprived Marian bishops who had to be kept in close confinement as long as he lived.[27]

[24] Burnet–Pocock v, 385. [25] Cf. RMP ii, 52.
[26] F. A. Gasquet and E. Bishop, *Edward VI and the Book of Common Prayer*, London 1890, 96.
[27] The others were kept under house arrest but allowed to live out their lives in peace and quiet. At least two lived as guests of the new Archbishop of Canterbury, Matthew Parker, who became quite fond of his enforced guests and treated them with a courtesy and christian charity all too rare in an age of religious intolerance and persecution (cf. R. F. Shirley, *Thomas Thirlby*, and V. J. K. Brook, *A Life of*

Bonner carried out a visitation of his diocese in accordance with the Queen's injunctions, which we have just discussed. The procedure in such a visitation was to send round to all parishes a list of questions to be answered. One of the questions from these visitation articles, dated September 1554, refers to Edwardine Orders.

> Art. 29. Whether any such as were ordered schismatical, and contrary to the old order and custom of the Catholic Church, or being unlawfully and schismatically married, after the late innovation and manner, being not yet reconciled nor admitted by the ordinary, have celebrated or said, either Mass or other divine service, within any cure or place of this city or diocese?[28]

It is claimed that this is a condemnation of Edwardine Orders. In fact it proves only that Edwardine clergy could not minister if they were 'not yet reconciled nor admitted by the ordinary'. From the canonical point of view all clergy ordained since the breach with Rome under King Henry VIII, even those ordained with the Pontifical rite, were 'ordered schismatical' and would need to be reconciled before they could properly exercise their orders. It is not clear from this question whether such reconciliation involved a re-ordination in the case of those ordained with the Ordinal. Messenger quotes a contemporary reformer, John Bale, in an attempt to show that these articles clearly rejected Edwardine Orders. But while Messenger's citations show that such orders were certainly held to be irregular, they do not prove that they were considered invalid.[29]

Clear evidence of Bonner's rejection of Edwardine Orders *is* supplied, however, by *A Profitable and necessary doctrine for every Christian Man*, which was issued by Bonner's authority in 1555 and commanded by him to be publicly read in all parishes in his diocese.

Archbishop Parker). Nicholas Heath, Mary's Archbishop of York, was soon set at liberty after his deprivation in 1559, and lived out his days in retirement on his own estate at Cobham in Surrey. He received several visits from Queen Elizabeth, whom he welcomed loyally. The DNB says that 'he was allowed to dispose of his property at will, and died of old age, respected by all, at the end of 1578'.

[28] Burnet-Pocock v, 388f.

[29] Cf. RMP ii, 54.

The late made ministers in the time of the schism, in their new devised ordination, having no authority at all given them to offer in the Mass the Body and Blood of our Saviour Christ, but both they so ordered (or rather disordered), and their schismatical orderers also, utterly despising and impugning not only the oblation or sacrifice of the Mass, but also the Real Presence of the Body and Blood of our Saviour Christ in the Sacrament of the Altar, therefore I say that all such damnably and presumptuously did offend against Almighty God, and also most pitifully beguiled the people of this realm, who by this means were defrauded of the most blessed Body and Blood of our Saviour Christ, and the most comfortable fruit thereof, and also of the Sacrifice of the Mass, and of the inestimable fruit which cometh thereby.[30]

This is the voice of Cardinal Vaughan and the Roman Catholic authorities in England for the last 400 years, who have felt that it was necessary to maintain not merely that the Anglican Church was schismatical and heretical but that it was no church at all. The most significant thing about this rejection of Edwardine Orders by a man whom two modern catholic apologists have called 'evidently no theologian'[31] is the reason given: 'having no authority at all given them to offer in the Mass the Body and Blood of our Saviour Christ'. This indicates that Bonner believed the essential form of ordination to be the words accompanying the tradition of chalice and paten to the ordinand in the Pontifical rite: 'Receive power to offer sacrifice in the Church for the living and the dead.' This would be in line with the common teaching of the theologians at that time that the tradition of the instruments with the accompanying words constituted the essential matter and form of the sacrament of orders.[32] Bonner's rejection of Edwardine Orders is clear. But the reason he gives for this rejection, being based upon the

[30] Op. cit., no pagination in the original. The passage is frequently quoted, e.g. by Messenger, RMP ii, 108.

[31] Cf. n. 26 above.

[32] Cf. pp. 134 and 139 above. The English reformer Ridley is reflecting this common sixteenth-century teaching when he writes that he does not know whether it will be granted that St Luke was a priest, 'and was able to receive the orders of priesthood which (they say) is given by virtue of these words said by the bishop, "Take authority to sacrifice for the quick and the dead" . . .' (Nicholas Ridley, *Works*, ed. by Henry Christmas (PS), Cambridge 1841, 19).

erroneous ideas of liturgical development current in his day, is unsound.

Papal treatment of Edwardine Orders in the Marian Period

The evidence we have examined thus far is inconclusive. The discussion has therefore tended to centre upon the instructions and actions of Cardinal Pole. At this point we encounter a veritable mare's nest of uncertainties, ambiguities, claims, and counter-claims. When Pole was appointed legate on 5th August 1553 by Pope Julius III he was given two sets of faculties. They are of great length and were designed to give the legate blanket authority to deal with a tremendous variety of matters.[33] It must be remembered that England had been in a state of schism for fifteen years or more, and that from the canonical point of view just about everything was at sixes and sevens: marriage dispensations had not been properly issued; the children of such marriages might be illegitimate; all institutions of bishops to their sees in this period, and of other clergy to their benefices, were irregular. Reconciliation therefore involved dealing with a large number of different matters, and for this purpose Pole was given the broadest possible authority. The really difficult problem was not the question of Edwardine Orders but that of the vast amount of church property which had been confiscated under Henry VIII, and which was now illegally in lay hands. It was made very clear to the legate that no reconciliation which involved the compulsory return of this property to the church stood any chance of success. The pope and the curia were prepared to accept the loss of church property if it could effect something as desirable as the return of England to unity with the Holy See.[34] But Pole was a devout and

[33] Text in M. A. Tierney, *Dodd's Church History of England* ii, London 1839, cviii–cxvii.

[34] Cf. A. M. Quirini (ed.), *Epistolarum Reginaldi Poli S. R. E. Cardinalis et aliorum ad ipsum* iv, Brescia 1752, 170ff.

pious man whose conscience would not permit him to enter into anything which savoured of a 'deal'. The reconciliation was delayed while the legate wrestled with his conscience and the lawyers prepared various formulas in an attempt to satisfy him.

Owing to the long delay before Pole reached England some question arose as to whether he might use his dispensing and reconciling powers while he was still on the Continent. During his enforced stay in Flanders English bishops sent over to Pole requesting reconciliation for themselves, and this was granted in a number of cases. To remove any doubt as to the legality of such actions Pope Julius III issued another lengthy document on 8th March 1554, enumerating once again all the powers which Pole possessed as legate and specifically authorising him to use these faculties prior to his arrival in England.[35] It was from this confirmation of the legate's faculties that Merry del Val cited in *Apostolicae curae*, claiming that the language of the document constituted a clear condemnation of orders conferred with the Ordinal.[36] This claim has always been vigorously disputed by Anglican controversialists,[37] and even Messenger admits that 'the Julius III documents, taken by themselves, do not explicitly decide the matter'.[38] And in 1895 Gasparri, who was already one of the leading canonists of the day, wrote that 'neither the validity nor the nullity of Anglican ordinations is clearly affirmed by Julius III in his Bull of March 8th 1554'.[39]

The legate finally reached England in November 1554. With his arrival the final reconciliation of the kingdom was carried out in due canonical form, Pole delegating his own faculties to the bishops for this purpose, so that they could use them in their own dioceses. Early in the following year

[35] Text in Burnet–Pocock vi, 322–7. [36] AO(E) 4f.
[37] Cf. the Reply of the Anglican Archbishops in 1897, AO(E) 27.
[38] RMP ii, 474; cf. 88.
[39] P. Gasparri, 'De la valeur des ordinations anglicanes', RAR i, 481–93, 529–57, 486.

an embassy was sent out to Rome under the leadership of Bishop Thirlby, Edward VI's Bishop of Norwich, newly promoted by Mary to the see of Ely, to explain everything that had been done in the reconciliation of the kingdom, and to obtain papal confirmation of the whole procedure.[40] This confirmation was granted on 20th June 1555 by the new pope, Paul IV, in the Bull *Praeclara carissimi*. It was this document and the later brief explaining it, *Regimini universalis*, issued a few months later and discussed below, which Bishop and Gasquet found in the Vatican Archives on 20th February 1895.[41]

Apostolicae curae quotes the following passage from *Praeclara carissimi*:

> Those who have been promoted to ecclesiastical Orders . . . by anyone but a bishop validly and lawfully ordained are bound to receive those Orders again.

And the Bull interprets this provision as follows:

> But who those bishops not 'validly and lawfully ordained' were had been made sufficiently clear by the foregoing documents and the faculties used in the said matter by the Legate: those, namely, who have been promoted to the Episcopate, as others to other Orders, 'not according to the accustomed form of the Church', or, as the Legate himself wrote to the Bishop of Norwich, 'the form and intention of the Church' not having been observed.[42] These were certainly those promoted according to the new form or rite, to the examination of which the Cardinals specially deputed had given their careful attention.[43]

[40] Thirlby is an interesting figure. He had originally been appointed by Henry VIII to the newly created suffragan see of Westminster in 1540, and was consecrated with the Pontifical. Although he had been promoted to Norwich, under Edward VI in 1550, he was found sufficiently catholic in the new reign to obtain preferment once more, and to be sent on this important mission to Rome as Pole's ambassador in 1555. There is an excellent modern biography of Thirlby by T. F. Shirley, *Thomas Thirlby, Tudor Bishop*, London 1964.

[41] Cf. Gasquet, *Leaves from My Diary* 18f. The text of the two documents was printed first in *The Tablet* 54 (1895), 499–503, and may also be found in A. Boudinhon, *De la Validité des Ordinations Anglicanes*, Paris 1895, 82ff, and in the Church Historical Society's (anonymous) *Treatise on the Bull* Apostolicae curae, London 1896, 55–61. These two documents of Paul IV had dropped from view completely for three centuries; the earlier Julius III documents already discussed above had always been known, and had been printed a number of times.

[42] Cf. pp. 271–5 below.

[43] AO(E) 5f.

In fact the identity of the bishops not 'validly and lawfully ordained' (the Latin phrase was *rite et recte ordinatus*) was *not* made sufficiently clear by the previous Julius III documents, as *Apostolicae curae* claims. This is shown by the fact that this provision of *Praeclara carissimi* caused confusion and doubts amongst ecclesiastics in England, who may be presumed to have been in a better position to understand what was meant than the thirty-one-year old author of *Apostolicae curae* 350 years later. These doubts are not difficult to understand. From the canonical point of view no bishop consecrated in England since the beginning of the schism under Henry VIII had been consecrated *rite et recte*. Could the pope be meaning to say, men asked in England, that *all* those who had received their orders from bishops consecrated since the schism must receive them over again? In order to allay doubts on this score the pope issued the brief *Regimini universalis* on 30th October 1555.

> We, wishing to remove the doubt and to provide opportunely for the peace of conscience of those who during the schism were promoted to Orders, by expressing more clearly the mind and intention We had in the aforesaid letters, declare that only those Bishops and Archbishops who were not ordained and consecrated in the form of the Church cannot be said to have been validly and lawfully ordained. Hence those persons promoted by them to those Orders have not received Orders, but ought and are bound to receive the said Orders anew.[44]

For the further quieting of troubled consciences in England the logical corollary of this provision was explicitly stated and affirmed.

> But those on whom Orders of this kind were conferred by Bishops and Archbishops who were themselves ordained and consecrated in the form of the Church—even though these Bishops and Archbishops were schismatics and received the churches over which they preside in former times from the hand of Henry VIII and Edward VI, pretended kings of England—*have received the character of those Orders which were bestowed on them* . . .[45]

[44] Translated from the text in Boudinhon and the Church Historical Society *Treatise* (cf. n. 41 above).
[45] Ibid., emphasis supplied.

The significant feature of these provisions is that they made the criterion of valid orders not the rite used in conferring them but the credentials of the ordaining bishop. If *he* was consecrated in 'the form of the Church', then *all* those whom he has ordained 'have received the character of those Orders which were bestowed on them'. The Brief makes no distinction between those ordained by such a bishop with the Pontifical rite and those he ordained with the Ordinal. Nor can it be pleaded that the Roman authorities failed to make such a distinction because they did not realise that under Edward VI Pontifical bishops in England had conferred orders with the Ordinal rite. For Thirlby had been at Rome while the ambiguous Bull, *Praeclara carissimi*, which caused all the trouble and misunderstanding, was being drafted; it was issued in response to the requests he submitted on Pole's behalf; and in 1896 Cardinal Vaughan's three representatives on the investigating commission pointed out that the Bull reflected the detailed information which Thirlby had given the curia about the English situation.[46] He could have told the Roman authorities, and it requires no little credulity to believe that he did not, that he and a number of other Pontifical bishops had continued to hold their sees throughout Edward's reign, and that a number of these men had conferred orders with the Ordinal during the three years it was in use. Such ordinations are known to have been carried out by Bishops Robert King of Oxford,[47] Lewis Thomas of Shrewsbury,[48] Pursglove of Hull,[49] and by the two Archbishops Cranmer[50] and Heath of York.[51]

[46] Cf. Moyes, Gasquet, and Fleming, *Responsio ad votum Rev.mi P. de Augustinis S.J.*, Roma 3rd April 1896 (privately printed): *Scholion de sensu et scopo Bullae et Brevis Pauli IV 1555*, 16ff.

[47] Cf. Frere, *The Marian Reaction*, 210.

[48] Ibid., 210–14.

[49] Ibid., 217. Cf. Hugh Aveling, *Northern Catholics*, London 1966, 38. Despite his conformity to the protestant changes in Edward's reign, illustrated especially by his willingness to confer orders with the new Ordinal, Pursglove 'was reconciled to the Catholic Church in Mary's reign and continued a pillar of the York ecclesiastical administration' (Aveling, loc. cit.). He refused to conform again under Elizabeth, but the degree of his adherence to the papist cause until his death in 1579 is disputed (cf. Aveling, op. cit. 38ff).

[50] Frere, op. cit. 218f.

[51] Cf. Philip Hughes, *Rome and the Counter-Reformation in England*, London 1942, 89.

That the Bull and Brief of Paul IV stop short of a condemnation of Edwardine Orders is the conclusion of several Roman Catholic scholars. The Abbé Marchal writes in the *Dictionnaire de Théologie Catholique*:

> Neither the Brief nor the Bull speak of those who were ordained priests or deacons by a properly ordained bishop but with the Edwardine Ordinal. The silence of these documents allows us to suppose that the priesthood and the diaconate were valid when conferred in this way. . . . It is possible that . . . Paul IV recognised in practice the value of the Orders so conferred.[52]

Even more significant is the judgement of two expert canonists, based in each case upon a careful analysis of the papal documents. A. Boudinhon, Professor of Canon Law at the Institut Catholique in Paris, wrote shortly before Anglican Orders were condemned:

> All the official documents emanating from Julius III, from Paul IV, and from Cardinal Pole are far more favourable than damaging to the validity of Anglican Orders. None of these documents explicitly denies the validity; several of them clearly presume it.[53]

And Gasparri wrote that under the provisions of the Bull and Brief of Paul IV

> deacons and priests ordained according to the rites of the Ordinal . . . by an heretical or schismatical bishop who was himself consecrated according to the Catholic rites . . . would be validly ordained.[54]

Accordingly Gasparri concludes that Paul IV recognised the sufficiency of the Ordinal rite for the two lower Orders, and rejected it only for the episcopate. He admits, however, that this conclusion involves an inconsistency. For

> if you admit the sufficiency of the Ordinal rite for the diaconate and priesthood, despite the modifications introduced, it will be quite impossible for you to give serious theological reasons for the insufficiency of the rite for the episcopate.[55]

[52] Op. cit. xi, col. 1170 (art. 'Ordinations anglicanes'); Messenger (RMP ii, 149) ascribes this article to 'Père Michel', a typical mistake.

[53] A. Boudinhon, 'Nouvelles observations sur la question des ordres anglicans' RAR ii, 625–32, 673–82, 779–91, cited from p. 791.

[54] Art. cit. in n. 39 above, 488.

[55] Ibid. n. 2.

Gasparri concludes therefore that the ruling of Paul IV was not intended to be a definitive decision of the question, but merely 'a practical rule for the time being,' the reasons for which we do not know.[56]

In the face of the plain language of *Regimini universalis* that *all* those ordained by a bishop consecrated in 'the form of the Church' *had* received the character of those Orders which were bestowed upon them', Messenger asserts:

> The brief was confined to the question of episcopal consecration, because that was the only point upon which doubt had arisen.[57]

In fact doubt had arisen with regard to the Orders of *all* clergy ordained since the beginning of the Henrician schism. And the pope ruled that their orders were valid so long as the credentials of the bishop who ordained them were in order. Messenger follows the three English commissioners in 1896[58] in arguing that the invalidity of the Ordinal rite for all the orders had already been established prior to Paul IV's Bull and Brief; and that therefore the only orders which could possibly be valid were those conferred with the Pontifical. To make assurance doubly sure, Messenger writes, the 'vigilant Cardinals in Curia' with 'their proverbial care and caution' inserted the additional provision that even ordinations according to the Pontifical rite would be invalid if carried out by a bishop consecrated according to the Ordinal.

> [The Cardinals'] proverbial care and caution [Messenger writes], and incidentally their knowledge that there had been, not only Edwardine priests, but also Edwardine bishops—knowledge which they could have obtained from Thirlby then in Rome, as from the Edwardine forms of ordination, which . . . had for some years been in the possession of the Curia—prompted them to add this important proviso. . . . Thus, the Bull plainly does not for one moment suggest or imply that the *only* source of invalidity of Edwardine Orders is their being conferred by an invalidly consecrated bishop, but it inserts this as an additional possible source of invalidity. . . .[59]

[56] Loc. cit. in n. 38 above.
[57] RMP ii, 148.
[58] Cf. loc. cit. in n. 46 above.
[59] RMP ii, 142f.

This purely conjectural argument fails to take account of the fact that Thirlby could have informed the 'vigilant Cardinals in Curia' not merely that there had been Edwardine bishops but that their total number was exactly six, and that not a single one of them had ever carried out any ordinations with the Pontifical rite or could ever conceivably do so. Two of these six bishops were already dead by the time Thirlby reached Rome: Taylor of Lincoln had died in December 1554, and Hooper of Gloucester had been burnt alive by Queen Mary's government on 9th February 1555 as part of the campaign to restore true religion in England. Three of the four remaining Ordinal bishops had fled to the Continent,[60] where there was as much likelihood of their ordaining men with the Pontifical as there was of the pope's ordaining men with the Ordinal. The sixth, John Harley of Hereford, had been deprived of his see in March 1554, not for lack of valid consecration, as we might expect, but because of his marriage and heresy.[61] His subsequent fate until his death in 1558 is unclear. But the thought of this deprived, married arch-protestant ordaining men with the Pontifical is, to anyone acquainted, as Thirlby was, with the realities of the religious situation in England in Mary's reign, simply ludicrous.

Messenger's interpretation of the disputed Paul IV documents amounts to this: that on the basis of Thirlby's information about the religious situation in England *another* ground of invalidity was added in the Bull and Brief of Paul IV (additional to the use of the invalid Ordinal rite) in order to cover an eventuality which, as Thirlby could have told the cardinals in Rome, had never occurred in the past and could not conceivably occur in the future. It is surely not unreasonable to entertain a doubt as to whether such an interpretation, which is admittedly pure conjecture, is in fact the correct one.

[60] They were: Scory of Chichester, Coverdale of Exeter, and Ponet (or Poynet) of Winchester, who died on 11th August 1556 in Strasbourg. Scory and Coverdale survived to consecrate Parker on 17th December 1559.

[61] Cf. Frere, *The Marian Reaction* 164.

Another interpretation of the provision that ordinations (by any rite at all) were invalid if carried out by a bishop not himself consecrated 'in the form of the Church' was offered in 1896 by Cardinal Vaughan's three representatives on the commission to investigate the Orders. They argued that this provision was inserted into the Bull, *Praeclara carissimi*, on the basis of information which Thirlby had given to the canonists at Rome, to cover the case of Ferrar. It will be recalled that Ferrar was consecrated on 9th September 1548, some eighteen months before the Ordinal was first issued. The Pontifical rite was used, with certain modifications in the direction of the coming changes.[62] We have already seen that the three authors of *Ordines Anglicani* claimed in this work that Ferrar was consecrated with the Ordinal, and that this statement was challenged in the commission by Duchesne.[63] In their *Reply to Fr de Augustinis*, which was issued after the commission had begun its deliberations, Cardinal Vaughan's three representatives retreated from their previous statement about Ferrar's consecration and claimed merely that he

> was made a bishop by some new rite (*secundum quemdam novum ritum*) and not with the ancient Catholic Pontifical.[64]

The only evidence that the three English commissioners were able to marshall in support of this statement was the fact that at his trial for heresy under Mary, Ferrar was degraded from the priesthood but not from the episcopate.

> But it is abundantly clear that the Catholics did not recognise Ferrar's episcopal character, since he was afterwards degraded from the presbyterate, but not from the episcopal Order.[65]

This assumes the very thing which has to be proved, namely that there was in fact a consistent policy with regard to Edwardine Orders under Mary. Anglican apologists claim that Ferrar was consecrated with the Pontifical rite,

[62] This was the account which Moyes gave of Ferrar's consecration in *The Tablet* 54 (1895), 459 col. 2.
[63] Cf. pp. 143 and 154 above. [64] Op. cit. 18. [65] Ibid.

and that the changes made were non-essential. They maintain further that the ignoring of Ferrar's episcopal character at his trial is an instance of the lack of any consistent policy with regard to Edwardine Orders in the Marian period.

Although Cardinal Vaughan's three representatives on the commission in 1896 found it impossible to maintain their original claim that Ferrar had been consecrated with the Ordinal, it was essential to their case to assert at least that he had not been consecrated in 'the form of the Church', but with 'some new rite' and hence invalidly. For they argued that the disputed provision in *Praeclara carissimi* was inserted to cover the possibility that Ferrar had ordained men with the Pontifical in the eighteen months between his (allegedly invalid) consecration in September 1548 and the introduction of the Ordinal in March 1550.[66] This interpretation raises two difficulties. First, the likelihood that Ferrar actually performed any ordinations with the Pontifical in this brief period is extremely remote, especially if the Pontifical rite was not used at his own consecration, despite the fact that it was then the only rite legally available (and the abandonment of the Pontifical rite at Ferrar's consecration is the crucial hypothesis upon which this whole argument is founded). The likelihood that Ferrar performed any ordinations with the Pontifical is diminished still further by the fact that he was thoroughly identified with the reforming party, and was placed on trial for heresy a few years later. And second, if the disputed provision in *Praeclara carissimi* had been inserted (as Moyes, Gasquet, and Fleming claimed) in response to Thirlby's information and in order to make it clear that Ferrar's Pontifical ordinations were invalid, then presumably Thirlby would have understood the meaning of the disputed provision, and could have explained it upon his return to England with the Bull. Had Thirlby furnished any such explanation there would have been no confusion, and no need for the explanatory Brief four months later. That

[66] Cf. *Responsio ad P. de Augustinis* 16ff.

this obviously did not happen is the surest indication that Thirlby himself shared the general uncertainty about the meaning of *Praeclara carissimi*. And if that be so, then the argument that its disputed clause was inserted in response to Thirlby's information, and solely to cover the case of Ferrar's (hypothetical and highly unlikely) ordinations according to the Pontifical, falls to the ground.

If there *was* a consistent and deliberate policy of rejecting all Edwardine Orders during Mary's reign, it is remarkable that none of the canonical documents contains an explicit and unequivocal condemnation of the Orders. It would have been very easy to have said categorically and explicitly that all orders conferred with the Ordinal were null and void. A single sentence in any one of the papal documents would have sufficed. No such sentence can be found. It is this fact, combined with the inconsistent and vague nature of the evidence as a whole, which leads us to conclude that on the basis of present knowledge we are not justified in asserting that Edwardine Orders were consistently rejected by the Holy See during the Marian restoration.

Should further evidence or investigation enable us to conclude with moral certainty in favour of such rejection, it would still be necessary to enquire into the reasons upon which it was based. And in view of the common sixteenth-century idea, to which we have already drawn attention twice above, that the essential form of ordination was to be found in the words accompanying the tradition of the instruments,[67] it is most probable that to the extent that Edwardine Orders were rejected in the Marian period such rejection was motivated by an understanding both of the rite of ordination and of the nature of the church's ministry which is now abandoned by catholic theologians.

[67] Cf. pp. 132f and 137f above.

The Holy See the best interpreter of its own acts?

It might be pleaded that precisely because the documents of the Marian period are so difficult to understand and interpret, we should simply accept the judgement of *Apostolicae curae* about these documents, on the principle that the Holy See is the best interpreter of its own acts. This argument is an attractive one, for if granted it offers a simple escape from difficulties of such complexity as to make an agreed solution well-nigh impossible. The argument rests, however, upon the legal fiction that the authority which issued the documents of Julius III and Paul IV in the middle of the sixteenth century is identical with the authority which said almost three and a half centuries later what they meant. So long as this authority is called in each case 'the Holy See', there appears to be a moral unity between the utterances so widely separated in time. But as soon as the facts are more closely examined, the argument collapses.

The interpretation of the documents of Julius III and Paul IV offered in *Apostolicae curae* is, as we have seen, the work of a thirty-one-year-old ecclesiastic, Raphael Merry del Val. He was a gifted linguist and a man of high intelligence. He was not specially qualified to pass an authoritative judgement upon ancient legal documents of no little complexity, the interpretation of which was disputed by acknowledged experts. He did not go to the sources, but relied entirely upon the texts, interpretations, and arguments set before him by Dom Francis Aidan Gasquet. In the first part of this book we have seen that Gasquet was a highly interested party whose concern with the documents under consideration was not to study them impartially in order to discover their true meaning but to find in them arguments to support his own preconceived view of the matter. Gasquet's customary inaccuracy in the transcription of texts appears to have been responsible for the fact that one of the texts he furnished to Merry del Val, and which is quoted in the Bull, differed in a vital detail from the version of the same document published by Gasquet only a year previously.[68] Merry del Val simply adopted Gasquet's interpretation of the documents in dispute. The resulting draft was submitted to several cardinals of the Holy Office, who made a few minor changes in it, and then placed it before an eighty-six-year old pope for his signature.

Weighing carefully the circumstances under which *Apostolicae curae* was actually written, it is clear that the Reply of the Anglican archbishops to Leo XIII can still stand, more than seventy years after it was first written.

> As regards the practice of the Roman Court and Legate in the XVIth century, although the Pope writes at some length, we believe that he is really as uncertain as ourselves. We see that he has nothing to add to the documents which are already well known, and that he quotes and argues from an imperfect copy of the letter of Paul IVth *Praeclara carissimi.*[69]

> Who in fact knows thoroughly either what was done in this matter or on what grounds it was done? We know part; of part we are ignorant. It can be proved however on our side that the work of that reconciliation under Queen Mary . . . was in very great measure finished, under royal and episcopal authority, before the arrival of Pole. In the conduct of which business there is evidence of much inconsistency and unevenness. . . . The principle of [Pole's] work appears to have been to recognise the state of things which he found in existence on his arrival, and to direct all his powers towards the restoration of Papal supremacy as easily as possible.[70]

[68] Cf. *The Tablet* 54 (1895), 499–503.

[69] The reference is to the fact that the text of this Bull which Gasquet had published in 1895 contained the word *concernentia* (loc. cit. in n. 68 above, p. 500 col. 1), which was omitted in the citation of the same Bull in *Apostolicae curae.* The point at issue is whether it was a question of dealing with clergy who had received dispensations and *orders* invalidly but *de facto* during the schism; or of clergy who had invalidly but in fact received *dispensations concerning* orders (as the original text of *Praeclara carissimi* published by Gasquet in 1895 said). In the latter case it was merely the dispensations to receive orders (necessary in case of an impediment, such as illegitimacy, for instance) which would have been received invalidly; the implication was that the Orders themselves were valid. Lacey argued that *Apostolicae curae*, by omitting the word 'concerning', not merely introduced an inaccuracy but 'an argument is drawn from it which depends on the inaccuracy' (*Roman Diary* 172 n. 1). Messenger argues that various subsidiary documents on which *Praeclara carissimi* was based show that the omission of this crucial word in *Apostolicae curae* does not make any difference anyway, as the sense of the quotation is the same in either case. The reader who feels competent to award the palm of victory to one or other of the contending parties will have gone more than half-way in mastering the intricate complexities of this tedious and confused controversy.

[70] AO(E) 26ff.

The 'form of the church' and the 'accustomed form'

There is no portion of the controversy about Anglican Orders which is as complicated and tedious as this one. The investigation is made subjectively more difficult by the knowledge that the question at issue is of purely academic interest, and cannot lead to any decisive result, for the reason stated at the beginning of this chapter: *whatever* was done by Julius III and Paul IV and Pole, there is no guarantee that their policy was correct. Even if we could be certain about what they did, it would still be necessary to ask whether it was right—in other words to consider the question of the Orders on its merits. The discussion above is based upon a lengthy study of the sources and of a large number of comments upon them, involving the careful weighing and comparison of a confusing mass of claims and counter-claims. But because the appeal to precedent can never be decisive in this matter, and in order to avoid wearying and perplexing the reader more than necessary, the discussion has been confined, so far as possible, to the absolute essentials.

For the sake of completeness, however, it is necessary to point out a further weakness in the argument of *Apostolicae curae*, arising out of the ambiguity of the words 'the form of the church'. The documents of the Marian period, and *Apostolicae curae* in quoting them, speak of two things which are not necessarily identical: 'the form of the Church' (*forma Ecclesiae*), and 'the accustomed form of the Church' (*forma Ecclesiae consueta*). Merry del Val ignored this distinction in drafting *Apostolicae curae*, and mentioned both things in a single sentence in such a way as to suggest that they were synonymous, which they are not.

The 'accustomed form' was, from the point of view of Pole and the popes in the Marian period, the old form in use in England before 1550 and found in the Sarum Pontifical. But there was a far greater variety of rites then, even in the west, than we have in the Latin church today. Large numbers of clergy had been validly ordained in the sixteenth century not according to the 'accustomed form' of the English church prior to 1550 but according to the forms of the various Pontificals in use elsewhere. Moreover the ordinations carried out by the very different forms of the various eastern churches were also valid, though how widely this was appreciated by Latin catholics in the 1550s may remain a moot point. The *forma Ecclesiae*, on the other hand, was simply the irreducible minimum common to all of these various rites. What this was is very difficult to say. The Council of Trent avoided this thorny problem, and the minimum necessary for the conferral of Holy Orders remains undefined even today.[71] A likely conjecture as to the irreducible minimum form necessary for the valid conferral of Holy Orders is that it consists simply of prayer for the imparting of the Holy Spirit and grace appropriate to the Order being conferred. Without the *forma Ecclesiae* in *this* sense, that is without prayer for the grace of Holy Orders, no order can be conferred. It is this which is insisted upon by the papal documents of the Marian period, and *not* the use of the 'accustomed form' of the Sarum Pontifical, which no one would have said was a *sine qua non* for the valid conferral of orders. The question of whether the Ordinal contained the irreducible minimum necessary for valid ordination, and could thus be called the *forma Ecclesiae*, was left in the papal documents to be decided by Pole and the English bishops in accordance with the prevailing (erroneous) theological principles of the day.

Fr T. B. Scannell drew attention to this distinction between the form and the accustomed form in a series of letters to *The Tablet* in the autumn of 1895, in which he also pointed out that Paul IV had insisted merely on the necessity of the church's form (in the sense of the irreducible minimum

[71] The Apostolic Constitution, *Sacramentum ordinis*, issued by Pope Pius XII in 1947 merely defines the essential form, of the present Latin rite. Cf. DS 3857–61 (2301).

necessary in any ordination), and that he left it to Pole to decide whether the Ordinal fulfilled this requirement. To the argument that it was nonsense to call a rite drawn up by heretics 'the Church's form' Scannell replied that this was precisely the position defended successfully by St Augustine in the controversy over Donatist baptisms.

> What is the principle which St Augustine maintains in his dispute with the Donatists? Precisely this: That baptism conferred by heretics is *the Church's own baptism*, that every valid rite used by heretics is *the Church's own rite*. . . . The Church considers as her own—as belonging to her and therefore as *forma Ecclesiae*—any and every form which in her judgement contains the essentials of a valid rite. And I do not hesitate to hold that the Baptismal rite in the Book of Common Prayer is 'the Church's own rite'. [72]

It was to these letters, and the clear and keen theological thinking which they displayed, that Scannell owed his place on the papal investigating commission of 1896.[73]

Apostolicae curae argues that the papal documents of the Marian period did not deal merely in general principles, leaving the application of these principles to Cardinal Pole, but that they legislated specifically for the existing state of things in England.

> And here, to interpret rightly the force of these documents, it is necessary to lay it down as a fundamental principle that they were certainly not intended to deal with an abstract state of things, but with a specific and concrete issue. For since the faculties given by these Pontiffs to the Apostolic Legate had reference to England only, and to the state of religion therein, and since the rules of action were laid down by them at

[72] *The Tablet* 54 (1895), 633 col. 2; cf. also pp. 305, 473, 552, and 594.

[73] Immediately after the publication of *Apostolicae curae* Scannell hastened to make the ritual 'submission' required by the ecclesiastical mores of the day. In the *Tablet* for 26th September 1896, the following letter appeared over Scannell's signature:

'It is hardly necessary for a priest to say that he submits to a Papal decision; but it may prevent some misunderstanding if you will allow me frankly to state that I heartily accept the recent Bull declaring Anglican Orders to be utterly null and void, and that I was wrong in my interpretation of Paul IV's decrees' (*The Tablet* 56 (1896), 497 col. 1).

Looking once again at Scannell's position with the perspective afforded by the passage of seventy years it appears highly doubtful whether Scannell was in fact wrong in his interpretation of Paul IV's decrees.

> the request of the said Legate, they could not have been mere directions for determining the necessary conditions for the validity of Ordinations in general. They must pertain directly to providing for Holy Orders in the said kingdom, as the recognised condition of the circumstances and times demanded. This besides being clear from the nature and form of the said documents, is also obvious from the fact that it would have been altogether irrelevant to thus instruct the Legate—one whose learning had been conspicuous in the Council of Trent—as to the conditions necessary for the bestowal of the Sacrament of Orders.[74]

It may be remarked in passing that Pole had never studied theology, and that if his ideas about the sacrament of orders were no better than what he wrote to Cranmer about the Eucharist,[75] he could have used a little instruction in the conditions necessary for the bestowal of the sacrament of orders. But leaving this subsidiary consideration on one side, we may remark that the main argument of this section of the Bull was taken over by Merry del Val directly from the English commissioners' *Reply to Fr de Augustinis*, a fact which Gasquet noted with satisfaction in the memorandum he drew up on board Mr Cave's yacht at Rouen as soon as he received the draft of the Bull on 24th August 1896.[76] De Augustinis had argued, like Scannell, that the phrase *forma Ecclesiae* referred not to the Pontifical rite (which he said was the *forma consueta Ecclesiae*) but simply to the *forma essentialis* (the irreducible minimum common to all rites), 'which

[74] AO(E) 4.
[75] Cf. A. M. Quirini, *Epistolarum Reginaldi Pole* . . . v, Brescia 1757, 238–74.
[76] Gasquet's memorandum says in part:

'4. States the documents—Card. Pole—must have had faculties to deal with quest. of H. Orders—we know his views—Pope didn't merely wish to give a general tract on *Orders*, but instruct[s] [i.e. instructions] practical to circumstances.

'5. Takes *our* views as to meaning of *rite ac legitime* in Julius III.—States the two *classes* of men existing in England with whom Pole had to deal—*Promoveri* means that the ordination they had rec[d] was *irrita*—Pole (Lett. to Bp. Norwich 29 Jan. 1555) shows he understood this "minus rite et non servata forma Ecclie consueta"—This can only mean those who had been ord. by Edw. Ordinal.

'6. Phil. & M. at Poles [*sic*] instig[ation] send oratores—(all about them)—*Thirlby* explains state—Paul IV issues his Bull & Brief—Take *our* view throughout—actually defines *Nulliter* as *invalide*. The *Brief* of Paul IV quoted & said to be absurd if it did not refer to the state of things in England—. Pole so understood & acted upon instructions' (GP).

For the circumstances in which this memorandum was written cf. p. 196 above.

might be found in the Anglican ritual or not'.[77] The English commissioners argued that this was impossible, and that the term *forma Ecclesiae* in the Paul IV documents must mean the Pontifical rite as distinct from the Ordinal. They claimed that de Augustinis' interpretation meant that the pope had said: 'He who is validly ordained is validly ordained'—which would be absurd. Moreover this would mean that the pope had left the decision about this vital matter to the legate's discretion. But this was incredible, the three English commissioners argued, since Pole had submitted a description of the Ordinal so that the Holy See might give a judgement about it. The very fact that the essential form of Holy Orders was a matter of dispute amongst the theologians of the time shows that the Holy See must have given a decision on the matter when it was necessary to do so.[78]

This final argument was especially weak, since papal decisions are generally reserved for cases where an agreed consensus has already been achieved amongst catholic theologians. Matters still in dispute in the schools are normally left open to further debate. This policy of prudent reserve affords the best reason for believing that Paul IV did in fact leave Cardinal Pole to decide whether the Ordinal contained the irreducible minimum necessary for the bestowal of Holy Orders. This made it unnecessary to decide what in fact this irreducible minimum (the *forma Ecclesiae*) was and is. This question remains undefined up to the present day.

[77] Cf. *Responsio ad P. de Augustinis* 14.

[78] Ibid. 15f.

13
A CLERICAL BRIDEGROOM AND AN EPISCOPAL SPY

The enquiry into Anglican Orders has ever been to me of the class which I must call dreary; for it is dreary surely to have to grope into the minute intricate passages and obscure corners of past occurrences in order to ascertain whether this man was ever consecrated, or that man used a valid form, or a certain sacramental intention came up to the mark, or the report, or register of an ecclesiastical act can be cleared of suspicion. On giving myself to consider the question, I never have been able to arrive at anything higher than a probable conclusion, which is most unsatisfactory except to antiquarians, who delight in researches into the past for their own sake.

—John Henry Newman[1]

After asserting that Edwardine Orders were consistently rejected during the Marian restoration, *Apostolicae curae* goes on to say that this rejection was the origin of the three-hundred-year old practice of re-ordaining convert Anglican clergy absolutely, adding that

> Since in the Church it has ever been a constant and established rule that it is sacrilegious to repeat the Sacrament of Order, it never could have come to pass that the Apostolic See should have silently acquiesced in and tolerated such a custom.[2]

Unfortunately this sacrilege is not the impossibility which it is here asserted to be, but an established and oft-repeated fact of history. The realisation that certain sacraments, when validly administered, impart to their recipient an indelible 'character', so that the sacrament cannot be repeated, is a relatively late development in the history of dogma. St Augustine was the great exponent of this truth in regard to the sacrament of baptism. Against strong opposition he asserted that the baptisms of the Donatists were valid and could not be repeated by Catholics. Acceptance of the same truth with regard to the sacrament of order came only many

[1] *Month*, September 1868, 269f.

[2] AO(E) 7.

centuries later. Up until the thirteenth century the re-ordination of clergy ordained by schismatical or simoniacal bishops was frequent. Reference to any standard theological encyclopedia or lexicon under the heading 'Re-ordination' will give further information and introduce the reader to the literature on the subject.

Nor may these re-ordinations be excused on the ground that they belong to the times of ignorance that God winked at, and that since then things have been better. A particularly flagrant example is furnished by Latin proselytising efforts in Abyssinia in the 1620s. Portuguese Jesuits managed to gain a brief ascendancy in the land at that time. They may be presumed to have been familiar with the teaching of the Council of Trent some six decades previously on the subject of the indelible character imparted by the sacraments of baptism, confirmation, and order.[3] This did not prevent these zealous missionaries, however, from simply disregarding the sacraments of the ancient Coptic Church in Abyssinia. They enforced re-baptism, re-ordination of the Abyssinian clergy, and the re-consecration of their churches.[4] The Abyssinian church was terribly decadent at this period, and ordinations were carried out very carelessly, so that there may well have been reason for considering the orders doubtful because it was not certain in every case that hands had actually been laid on all the candidates at an ordination. But practical abuses of this kind, while justifying conditional re-ordination, do nothing to make the policy followed by these Jesuit proselytisers legitimate. It was in fact a piece of ecclesiastical imperialism of the most flagrant kind. The case is an excellent example of the fact that the validity of

[3] Cf. DS 1609 (852), 1767 (960), 1774 (964).

[4] Cf. David Mathew, *Ethiopia, the Study of a Polity*, London 1947, 52; cf. also A. H. M. Jones and Elisabeth Monroe, *A History of Ethiopia*, Oxford 1962, 96f; and Sylvia Parkhurst, *Ethiopia, A Cultural History*, Woodford Green, Essex 1955, 354f, who adds that images, which were considered idolatrous by the Ethiopians, were set up in churches by these Jesuit missionaries, who also introduced the ancient catholic custom of spitting in church. I am indebted to Bro George Every, SSM, for drawing my attention to this neglected chapter on one of the little known byways of church history.

orders cannot be decided merely by an appeal to precedent. For there are bad precedents as well as good.

'A certain French Calvinist'

Two specific cases are cited as precedents by *Apostolicae curae*, involving decisions of the Holy Office in 1684 and 1704. For our knowledge of what was done on these occasions we are dependent upon the incomplete publication of the documents by an Italian Jesuit, Fr S. M. Brandi, who undertook the defence of *Apostolicae curae* against Anglican criticisms shortly after the Bull's appearance only to find, like others who have addressed themselves to this controversy before him and since, that he had embarked upon a Sisyphean task which was to occupy him for many years to come. The documents concerning the cases of 1684 and 1704 which Fr Brandi began to publish in 1896[5] from the archives of the Holy Office (still secret after a lapse of more than three centuries) did not remain unchallenged by Anglican controversialists, and Brandi felt compelled to keep on bringing out new and expanded versions of his work, which finally went through four editions in twelve years, each new version revealing additional ancient documents from the top-secret files of the Holy Office in an effort to meet his opponents' objections.[6] Even Brandi's final disclosures are incomplete, and most readers will probably feel that this method of controversy, despite its venerable history, is not particularly convincing. This was clearly the view of that veteran controversialist Canon Moyes, who wrote to Gasquet in an undated letter, probably from 1897:

> You are exceedingly right. I had looked into Brandi only cursorily, and have since examined the articles more closely, and quite agree with you that the whole proceeding is intolerable. Besides I do not believe that *his* is the answer we want in England. There are things which would leave

[5] Cf. *Civiltà Cattolica* Series xvi, Vol. 8 (21st November 1896), 433f.

[6] Cf. *La Condanna delle Ordinazioni Anglicane: Studio Storico-Teologico*, Rome ⁴1908.

us open to attack, and omissions which would weaken our position. Fr Sydney [Smith, SJ] called this morning. He takes a sensible view of the matter and will write to Brandi. If he should persist, which I do not anticipate, I will join you in publicly protesting.[7]

The 1684 case concerned 'a certain French Calvinist', as the Bull calls him. This otherwise unknown personage had been ordained to the priesthood in the Church of England. He subsequently returned to France, became a Roman Catholic, and wished to marry. The question was thus whether he had contracted a canonical impediment to marriage by valid reception of the priesthood. An investigation of the whole question of Anglican Orders was undertaken, opinions being obtained from theologians in Holland and Belgium. The Belgian consultor, a professor of history at Antwerp[8] named Snellaerts, gave it as his 'practically certain' opinion that the Ordinal rite for the priesthood would be sufficient if used in the catholic church or in the Greek Church.[9] Another consultor, Arnauld, was doubtful about the matter, but did not feel able to condemn the Orders out of hand.[10] A Dutch bishop, Mgr Neercassel, recommended that the Orders be

[7] GP. The reason for this proposed protest is explained by a letter which Merry del Val wrote to Gasquet on 6th February 1897 in which he said:

'I don't know what passed between Brandi and the Holy Father, but the latter certainly expressed a wish that the articles should be published in England. The Holy Father was pleased with them and thought they might do good' (GP).

In his letter to Gasquet, Moyes added that he was finding the continuing controversy over the Orders (which *Apostolicae curae* was supposed to have ended) wearying:

'In the meantime, I will hurry on with the book. The Cardinal wishes me to do the articles, but I hope to do them and the book together, so as to have the latter practically finished when the articles are ended. I wish I could work harder, but I get tired so soon latterly. However there must be in the nature of events a time when the question will be over, and one can turn to better work' (GP).

Moyes' book was not to appear for another decade, and then it turned out to be no more than a collection of his polemical articles over the years, not all of them on Anglican Orders (James Moyes, *Aspects of Anglicanism; or, Some comments on certain events in the 'nineties*, London 1906). The question which he and Gasquet thought they had settled for ever in 1896 was to outlive both of them by far.

[8] This is the description of Snellaerts given by Messenger (RMP ii, 469); Snellaerts' letter, as printed by Messenger, is dated 'Louvain, 2 March 1665' (loc. cit.).

[9] Snellaerts' opinion is quoted by P. F. Le Courayer, *Défense de la Dissertation* tôme ii, part ii, Brussels 1726, vii–xvi; excerpts in English translation in RMP ii, 471f.

[10] Cf. Le Courayer, op. cit. vif.

condemned, and this was done by the Holy Office, which refrained from publishing its decision, however, for reasons of expediency.[11] One's confidence in the value of this decision is seriously shaken upon discovering that in his two statements in favour of condemnation Cardinal Casanata, who was in charge of the case at Rome, banished residual doubts about the possible validity of the Orders by appealing to the existing practice of re-ordaining convert Anglican clergy absolutely.[12] A precedent which is itself arrived at in part by an appeal to the precedent of the Church's existing practice is clearly not worth very much.

The Gordon case

The second and final precedent cited by *Apostolicae curae* is that of John Clement Gordon, a ne'er-do-well cleric who became a Roman Catholic in France in 1703, and whose case has been the subject of a long and confused controversy. Seldom can so much ink have been spilled in a more worthless cause. The Anglican scholar T. F. Taylor, who has attempted to sort out the events of Gordon's chequered career, writes of him:

> He was not big enough to leave any considerable deposit of papers and so he is to be met with only where his lifeline intersects with others. He is known mostly as he bumps against his fellows.[13]

The facts of Gordon's life as far as Taylor has been able to piece them together seem to have been these. He was born in 1643 or 1644; his baptism is recorded as having taken place in the parish church of Ellon eighteen miles north of Aberdeen, on 19th July 1645. He was educated in Scotland

[11] The Holy Office decree is dated 13th August 1685. A Roman Catholic, James II, was on the throne of England, and it was hoped that if a judicious policy was followed England might be won back to the church. In the event the policies followed by James were so injudicious, however, that he fled during the 'Glorious Revolution' of 1688 and was replaced by Mary, his Anglican daughter by his first wife, who ruled jointly with her protestant husband, William of Orange.

[12] Cf. Brandi, op. cit. in n. 6 above, 189–93; RMP ii, 476–9.

[13] T. F. Taylor, *A Profest Papist, Bishop John Gordon*, London 1958, 5.

and his ordination may have taken place in 1668. The rite used is uncertain, but it is most unlikely to have been that of the Anglican Ordinal. The account Gordon gave of Anglican ordination in his petition to the Holy Office in 1704 is a travesty of the Ordinal rite. He is recorded as having been in New York as a royal chaplain in 1674, and there is reason to believe that he may previously have sought his bread upon the waters as a naval chaplain—'the last refuge of destitute or criminous clerks'.[14] At some subsequent date Gordon came into contact with the Duke of York, Charles II's Roman Catholic brother, who succeeded to the English throne as James II in 1685, and who employed Gordon in his service as a spy. After his accession to the throne the King rewarded Gordon for his services by naming him Bishop of Galloway. He was consecrated for that see on 18th September 1688, by what rite it is impossible to say. His episcopate was exceedingly brief, for episcopacy was abolished in Scotland in July of the following year, by which time Gordon had already fled to France in the wake of the revolution which sent his royal master, James, into exile. During the years 1689-90 Gordon was in Ireland, where James was trying to obtain a following in order to regain his throne. Gordon was considered a papist by the Irish during this period, and appears to have done well out of some shady legal dealings. He returned to France with James in 1690. Gordon remained in the circle around the exiled king at St Germains during the nineties, and is variously reported to have been an Anglican and a Roman Catholic. Taylor quotes a letter written by Gordon to the secretary of the British Embassy in Paris in June 1699 in which Gordon sought reinstatement in the Church of England. But three years later he appears to have abandoned this attempt at rehabilitation as an Anglican, for in 1702 he was sent as a Jacobite spy to Scotland. In 1703, after a few conferences with Bossuet, he was received into the Roman Catholic Church. He proceeded to Rome, where

[14] Taylor, op. cit. 13.

the pope, Clement XI, wished to appoint him to the sinecure benefice of the Abbey of St Clement, for which Gordon had to be at least in minor orders. This was the occasion of the enquiry into the validity of his previous orders. Gordon presented an account of his ordination designed to put it in the worst possible light from the catholic point of view. His petition recounted the Nag's Head Fable to show that there was no true succession of bishops in England. Although Gordon requested that his episcopal orders be declared null, it was his supposed priestly ordination that he described. And he closed with the now standard appeal to precedent: the existing practice of the church in treating the Orders of convert Anglican clergy as null and void.[15] This appeal to precedent was repeated at considerable length in the *votum* of one of the consultors of the Holy Office.[16] The documentation in this case is hardly more satisfactory than in that of the French Calvinist twenty years previously. Differing accounts of the rite used at Gordon's consecration and of the decree of the Holy Office are given by Le Quien[17] and by Estcourt,[18] the documents being certified in each case as authentic by an official of the Holy Office. A third version of the Holy Office decree was published by Brandi in November 1896 with the assertion that it was the authentic text, being published for the first time.[19] Here we read that Gordon requested a declaration that his episcopal consecration was null 'both on account of the want of legitimate succession of the bishops in England and Scotland, who had consecrated him, and on account of other reasons'[20]—a conveniently vague phrase. Gordon's request was granted, no reasons being given in accordance

[15] Gordon's petition is printed in Latin in M. Le Quien, *Nullité des Ordinations Anglicanes* ii, Paris 1725, lxix–lxxvi, and in English by A. S. Barnes, *The Popes and the Ordinal*, London ²1898, 134–7.

[16] Cf. the Latin text in Brandi, op. cit. in n. 6 above, 196f; English in RMP ii, 484f.

[17] Loc. cit. in n. 15 above.

[18] Cf. his *Question of Anglican Ordinations*, cxvf.

[19] Cf. art. cit. in n. 5 above.

[20] 'tum propter deficientiam legitimae successionis Episcoporum in Anglia et Scotia, qui illum consecraverunt, tum propter alia motiva', loc. cit. in n. 5 above.

with the usual practice of the Holy Office. This decision was taken in a 'Feria v' meeting on 17th April 1704 in the presence of Pope Clement XI, when it was ordered that Gordon was to be ordained absolutely to all orders, and that if not already confirmed he was to receive that sacrament first. In the event he never proceeded beyond the minor orders necessary to hold the benefice which was given him. Gordon lived for over twenty years after this decision, finally passing to the jurisdiction of a higher tribunal in 1726 at the age of about eighty-two. Because of the unusual solemnity surrounding the meeting at which the decision in the Gordon case was taken, this decision was frequently appealed to thereafter as a binding precedent, and is so mentioned in *Apostolicae curae*.

It is impossible to say with certainty why the decisions in these two cases were taken. Quite apart from the lack of complete documentation mentioned above, there can be no certainty that the decisions were based upon the reasons mentioned in such documents as have been published. We have seen that the *vota* in the earlier case were not completely negative. The available documents from both cases mention a defect of form and intention in the conferring of Anglican Orders. Since these are the two substantial reasons (in addition to the appeal to precedent) for which the Orders were condemned in 1896, any modern reappraisal of the validity of Anglican Orders will have to include a careful reconsideration of these alleged defects of form and intention.

14
A REAPPRAISAL OF ANGLICAN ORDERS?

The Reformers in England certainly desired one thing: viz. to insist only in doctrine and practice upon what could certainly claim primitive sanction, and to allow a great latitude outside this. Granting this desire, and admitting that there was much at the time to create and to justify such a desire, is it not wiser in the interest of Christendom at large, whatever mistakes may have been made in fact, to go all possible lengths in the way of putting a favourable construction on what was then done, rather than to adopt precisely the opposite course?

—Lord Halifax[1]

We have been concerned in this book primarily with history, and especially with the history of the papal condemnation of Anglican Orders in 1896. Theological considerations have been deliberately kept in the background, and referred to only where the narrative made such reference necessary. But the historical evidence alone does not permit a firm verdict either in favour of Anglican Orders or against them. Even if it were to be agreed that the 1896 investigation was bungled (and on so controversial a question unanimity can hardly be expected), this would not in itself prove that the verdict of *Apostolicae curae* was wrong. It is possible to reach a correct decision for bad reasons, and it is perfectly conceivable that this was what happened in 1896. Any reappraisal of the validity of Anglican Orders will have ultimately to face the theological issues in themselves, prescinding from the question of how they were treated seventy and more years ago. Such a task calls for a full-length study in its own right. We must be content here merely to indicate some of the questions which will have to receive fresh treatment in any future reappraisal of Anglican Orders[1a].

Despite the mountain of controversial literature on the

[1] *Leo XIII* 381f.

[1a] The theological issues are treated by the present writer in a sequel to this work, to be published shortly under the title *Stewards of the Lord*.

subject, to which the bibliography at the end of this volume, though still incomplete, bears eloquent testimony, a large amount of historical and especially of theological research remains to be done. We have already drawn attention in Chapter 12 above to the lack of any adequate modern study of the treatment of Anglican Orders during the Marian restoration. Nor do we possess any competent account of the arguments advanced by opponents and defenders of the Orders in the more than four centuries since the Anglican hierarchy was initiated, and with it the controversy over its spiritual credentials. There is no adequate investigation of the new situation created in recent decades by the participation in Anglican episcopal consecrations of bishops whose orders are recognised by the Holy See as certainly valid: most of the Anglican bishops in the world can now trace their orders to such sources. But above all we need a serious reappraisal of the theological grounds upon which the invalidity of Anglican Orders is asserted in *Apostolicae curae:* alleged defects of intention and form in the sixteenth century.

By far the most eloquent exponent and defender of the Bull is the English Jesuit Fr Francis Clark, whose impressive work of research has put all those who study the question of Anglican Orders in his debt, and who has given to the traditional arguments against the Orders the most detailed and scholarly statement they have yet received. In his first published study of the subject, *Anglican Orders and Defect of Intention,*[2] Fr Clark argued that the defects of form and intention alleged in *Apostolicae curae* were separate and distinct, and that much unnecessary confusion had been introduced into the controversy by the failure of partisans on both sides to distinguish clearly between these two defects. Clark has discovered in the writing of his fellow catholic apologists no less than seven different interpretations of whose or what intention is condemned in the Bull. Carefully analysing each

[2] London 1956, out of print.

of these seven intentions, he discards six, and offers a wealth of evidence to show that the intention condemned in 1896 was 'the internal intention of the minister in the strict theological sense; in particular of the consecrator(s) of Archbishop Parker' in 1559.[3] Clark concedes that these consecrators had a general intention to act as Christ's ministers to confer the ministry instituted by him, and that this is in itself sufficient. But he argues that Parker's consecrators had a second intention: to exclude 'the power of the consecrating and sacrificing priesthood'.[4] This intention was incompatible with the general intention of conferring the ministry instituted by Christ, Clark argues. It therefore cancelled out that intention by what he calls 'the principle of positive exclusion'. This is the principle that when the minister of a sacrament has simultaneously two conflicting intentions, and he does not consciously subordinate one to the other (because of the erroneous idea that the two are perfectly compatible), they invariably cancel each other out and invalidate the sacrament without any investigation of the question, which intention was in fact predominant, or which the minister would have chosen had he known that his two intentions could not co-exist. It is this principle, according to Clark, which lies behind the condemnation of intention in *Apostolicae curae*.

If this interpretation of the Bull be correct (and the evidence Clark offers in its favour is impressive), then we must ask whether the 'principle of positive exclusion' is itself sound. Significantly, a number of authors cited by Clark in favour of the principle actually deny it, if read in context. Moreover it is not clear that Parker's consecrators really had the second limiting intention upon the existence of which the argument of *Apostolicae curae*, on Clark's hypothesis, is based. Clark has himself gone to considerable pains in his second book, *Eucharistic Sacrifice and the Reformation*,[5]

[3] AODI 11. [4] AODI 161.
[5] London and Westminster, Md., 1960; second edition 1967.

to prove that the English reformers did not believe that the power of offering sacrifice in the mass existed anywhere or could be given by anyone. The question thus arises how they could, by a deliberate act of the will, have excluded in their intention a power which in their view was unreal and non-existent.[6] Although the final balance with regard to the alleged defect of intention in Anglican Orders has yet to be drawn, the evidence presently available suggests that this section of the Bull raises more difficulties than it solves. We may yet be compelled to grant the claim of Anglican apologists that appeal to the necessarily private intention of the minister of Holy Orders launches us upon such a sea of doubts as to call into question the validity not merely of Anglican Orders but ultimately of all orders everywhere.

The more important and fundamental reason for the Bull's condemnation was the alleged defect of form, and it is upon this point that discussion has tended in recent years to concentrate. *Apostolicae curae* says that the forms of ordination in use in the Anglican Church from 1550 to 1662 were incapable of conveying Holy Orders in the catholic sense because these forms were deliberately fashioned by the English reformers to express their denial of eucharistic sacrifice.[7] Hence the forms of the Edwardine Ordinal could never convey the 'sacrificing priesthood', which is asserted to be the priesthood of the catholic church and the only genuine christian priesthood there is. Anglican apologists have been accustomed to reply to this argument by saying that to the extent that the reformers denied the sacrifice of the mass[8] this denial must be understood against the

[6] For a brief discussion of the vitiating flaws in Clark's arguments about the defect of intention in Anglican Orders cf. the articles cited on p. 47 n.3 above. A fuller treatment will be given in the present writer's *Stewards of the Lord* (see n.1a above).

[7] *Apostolicae curae* avoids a direct judgement about the adequacy of the expanded forms in use since 1662.

[8] Anglican scholars disagree about the extent of this denial. One school, identified especially with the name of the late Dom Gregory Dix, maintains that the English reformers were as thoroughgoing protestants as their colleagues on the Continent, and that their denial of eucharistic sacrifice was unequivocal and complete. Others maintain that the English reformers carefully steered a middle course between the

background of 'late medieval errors' about eucharistic sacrifice which were allegedly widespread on the eve of the reformation. In his second book Fr Clark argues that these alleged 'late medieval errors' about the sacrifice of the mass rest either upon misunderstandings or upon foundations even less substantial. In an impressively documented work of almost 600 pages he maintains that the late medieval theology of eucharistic sacrifice followed staidly and unimaginatively in the path of earlier teaching, and that this theology was wholly orthodox. The writings of the English reformers are cited to show that they were well acquainted with this orthodox tradition, and that it was this which the reformers rejected, and not merely popular abuses. These have in any case been greatly exaggerated, Clark writes, and they can be paralleled in any age, since there will always be distortions and misunderstandings of the church's teaching, especially amongst the uneducated, the simple, and the credulous.

The wealth of original source material which the book contains makes it a valuable work of scholarship, and has earned for its author the unanimous praise of a host of critics. Clark's interpretation of the mass of evidence he has assembled has not met with the same degree of acceptance, however. One of the first to register dissent was the author's fellow English Jesuit Fr Anthony A. Stephenson, who in 1961 stated his conviction that 'the interesting material' contained in the book, 'so far from leading to the conclusion which the author draws from it, points in the diametrically opposite direction'.[9] This conviction has been echoed in the criticisms of several Anglican theologians, notably Dr E. L.

heretical extremes of continental protestantism and late medieval catholicism. Although associated principally with the nineteenth-century Tractarians and Anglo-Catholics, this view has found an able modern exponent in C. W. Dugmore, *The Mass and the English Reformers*, London 1958.

[9] A. A. Stephenson, 'Two Views of the Mass: Medieval Linguistic Ambiguities', ThSt 22 (1961), 588–609, 604. In December 1966 Fr Stephenson entered the Anglican Church with expressions of deep gratitude and affection towards the Roman Catholic Church, 'which gave me baptism and ordination' (Hamilton, Ont., *Spectator*, 6th January 1967, 7f). Since the Anglican Church recognises Roman Catholic Orders as identical with its own, Fr Stephenson was received as a priest.

Mascall[10] and Bro George Every.[11] The most outspoken dissent from Clark's interpretation of the reformation controversy over the mass, however, was that of the Austrian Jesuit Fr Hans Bernard Meyer, who in a lengthy review of the book praised his English colleague's achievement within his narrow self-imposed apologetic limits, but pointed out that at the point where Clark's investigations ended the real question began: what actually caused the reformation protest against eucharistic sacrifice, if the late medieval theology of sacrifice was really as sound as Clark had claimed? Meyer pointed out that it was not enough simply to examine the school theology of the later middle ages in isolation: one must also investigate the popular religious life of the age, and especially the practical mass system with which the reformers were confronted, as well as the theological ideas which were developed to explain and justify the vast multiplication of masses which was so prominent a feature of the world in which the reformers lived. Such an investigation, Meyer suggested, would show that there was much in early sixteenth-century catholic teaching and practice to justify the reformers' protest. This view has found support from no less an authority than Fr J. A. Jungmann, whose encyclopedic knowledge of liturgical history is unsurpassed amongst contemporary scholars, and whose judgements are invariably characterised by caution and reserve:

> The ferocity of the sixteenth century controversy, in which the Mass was least of the issues at stake . . . is explained by the fact that both sides in the controversy argued on the basis of a late medieval understanding of the Mass and a practical Mass system which obscured important elements of the Mass to the point at which it was well-nigh impossible to understand them at all. . . . It is not surprising to find that on more than one occasion [Luther's] protests were justified.[12]

Since Fr Clark himself argues that the English reformers owed their fundamental theological ideas to the continental

[10] Cf. E. L. Mascall, *Corpus Christi*, London² 1965, 111–15.
[11] Cf. *Sobornost* series 5, No. 6 (1962), 337–9.
[12] Foreword to H. B. Meyer, *Luther u. die Messe*, Paderborn 1965, 7.

reformers, we must reckon with the likelihood that Jungmann's judgement will prove to be equally applicable to English protests against the sacrifice of the mass.

Although the teaching of the English reformers about eucharistic sacrifice may seem to have little direct bearing on the validity of Anglican Orders, there is growing recognition that the relationship between the two questions is crucial. As long ago as 1957 Dr A. R. Vidler, one of the keenest minds amongst contemporary Anglican theologians, wrote:

> If there be scope for much further discussion of the Papal attitude to Anglican Orders one may hazard the guess that it will be centred on the question whether notions about the eucharistic sacrifice and a sacrificing priesthood that were prevalent in the late medieval church did or did not warrant a somewhat drastic pruning of current rites and ceremonies.[13]

Fr Clark has put historical and theological scholarship in his debt by checking irresponsible and loose talk about 'late medieval errors' concerning eucharistic sacrifice. The criticisms of his work cited above suggest, however, that Clark may have overlooked much important evidence; and we have already seen that his interpretation of such evidence as he does cite has failed to win general acceptance. Any reappraisal of the validity of Anglican Orders will have therefore to attempt to draw the balance between Clark and his critics. Was there really nothing in the practical mass system of the early sixteenth century and in the theology of the day to justify, or at the very least to explain, the violence of the reformers' attack on the mass? Can the depth and massiveness of the protest really be satisfactorily explained as due to nothing more than a basically dishonest polemic? It has been shown that on the Continent the catholic defence of eucharistic sacrifice in the reformation period was vacillating, weak, and inconsistent, so that the reformers never received the answers which their objections to the sacrifice of the mass deserved.[14] Significantly, the few catholic apologists

[13] JEH 8 (1957), 122, review of AODI.

[14] Cf. Erwin Iserloh, *Der Kampf um die Messe*, Münster 1952. Professor Hubert Jedin, the foremost catholic authority on the Council of Trent today, writes that as

who did manage to give the coherent account of catholic mass doctrine which the times so desperately demanded failed to gain a hearing. Inevitably the reformers saw the justice of their criticisms confirmed by the feebleness of the catholic response. If an investigation of the English apologetic for eucharistic sacrifice should reveal that it was no more convincing than what was offered on the Continent, then we shall have additional reason for believing that in rejecting the sacrifice of the mass (and with it all contemporary notions of 'sacrificing priesthood') the English reformers were denying not so much the truth as a caricature of it.

The Dutch catholic theologian and former Anglican, Professor W. D. van de Pol, has urged:

> The debate about the validity of Anglican ordinations . . . should be conducted on as wide an ecclesiological plan as possible. It is useless and senseless to renew the discussion . . . as long as there exists no agreement concerning the nature, structure, function and authority of the church and regarding the nature and practice of the sacraments, in particular of the Holy Eucharist.[15]

These remarks are particularly timely in view of the fact that hitherto all attacks on the Orders, and many defences from the Anglican side, have reflected a narrow theology of 'sacrificing priesthood' which received significant corrections at the Second Vatican Council,[16] and which is increasingly being called into question by catholic theologians.[17] There can be little doubt, after Clark's work, that the English reformers

late as 1562 the catholic controversialists 'had not been able to provide a satisfactory answer to the theological questions which Luther had raised' concerning the sacrifice of the mass (H. Jedin, *Crisis and Closure of the Council of Trent* London 1967, 68).

[15] W. H. van de Pol, *Anglicanism in Ecumenical Perspective*, Pittsburgh 1965, 58.

[16] Cf. *Const. on the Church* 20f and 25–9; *Decr. on the Ministry and Life of Presbyters*, *passim*.

[17] Cf. Nicholas Lash, *His Presence in the World*, London 1968, Chapter 6; Y. Congar, *Sacerdoce et laicat*, Paris 1962, esp. 92–5 and 112–15; *idem*, 'Ministère et laicat dans la théologie catholique romaine', *Verbum Caro* 71–2 (1964), 145–8; J. Colson, *Ministre de Jésus-Christ ou le sacerdoce de l'évangile*, Paris 1966; Seamus Ryan, 'Episcopal Consecration: the Legacy of the Schoolmen', IThQ 33 (1966), 3–38, 35–8; Cornelius Ernst, 'Priesthood and Ministry', *New Blackfriars* 49 (1967), 121–32.

rejected contemporary notions of 'sacrificing priesthood'. The question which remains to be investigated is whether late medieval notions of 'sacrificing priesthood' were or were not fairly representative of the church's full tradition with regard to her ministry. There is a steadily growing list of studies of the doctrine of the ministry, especially in the early centuries of christian history. Some of these works may prove to have much to contribute to a reappraisal of Anglican Orders.

Finally, we are witnessing the first halting attempts to reassess the traditional notion of apostolic succession and a valid ministry. The Swiss catholic theologian Hans Küng has suggested that the concept of a valid baptism 'of desire' might be extended to the sacrament of orders in the reformation churches.[18] And the Dutch Jesuit Fr F. J. van Beeck has argued in a lengthy article of no little complexity that a positive verdict on the validity of Anglican and protestant post-baptismal sacraments, including Holy Orders, might be reached by extending to these sacraments the principles of valid administration by an extraordinary minister in unusual circumstances.[19] The unproved hypotheses advanced by these two theologians have yet to win general acceptance, and require further study. Only time will tell whether a radically new approach to the problem of orders along lines such as these will lead to a way out of the present impasse and so render arguments of the kind which have been discussed above both obsolete and irrelevant.

Hitherto most catholic writing about Anglican Orders has been characterised by a desire to see how much could be said against the Orders, not how much could be said for them. The result of all such studies is a foregone conclusion. If the reformers of the sixteenth century were simply evil men, 'fallen priests' bent on the destruction of the church which

[18] Cf. H. Küng, *Structures of the Church*, London 1965, 184f. For a contrary view cf E. Schillebeeckx, *Christ the Sacrament*, London and New York 1963, 143.

[19] Cf. F. J. van Beeck, 'Towards an ecumenical understanding of the sacraments', *Doctrinal Development and Christian Unity*, ed. N. Lash, London 1967, Part 2; (pub. in US as *Progress towards Christian Unity*, Dayton, Ohio 1968).

had ordained them and of the faith she had taught them—and this is the underlying assumption of most existing catholic works on Anglican Orders[20]—then it is clear that we shall come closest to the truth by judging the reformers' deeds as strictly as possible, and by putting on their writings as anti-catholic an interpretation as the language permits. If, on the other hand, we believe that despite their exaggerations and the undoubted havoc which they wrought, the reformers were frequently moved by christian (and therefore catholic) concerns and motives; if we allow that they may have had a sense of genuine pastoral concern for the fate of countless souls whom they saw being led to spiritual ruin by a religious system which they believed was tolerating, if it did not actively teach, a false idea of man's relationship with God; if, moreover, we take to heart the statement of the second Vatican Council that the reformation divisions came about 'not without the fault of men on both sides';[21] and if we are open to the possibility that on the catholic side this fault may not have been confined entirely to the realm of morals and discipline, but that it perhaps included the teaching of a theology which, at least in certain of its implications, was sub-christian; then it is clear that in judging the reformers' work we shall come closer to the truth if we 'go to all possible lengths in the way of putting a favourable construction on what was then done, rather than to adopt precisely the opposite course'.[22]

It cannot be said that existing studies of Anglican Orders by Roman Catholic authors reflect such an approach. If this book has done something to show the desirability of a reappraisal of this question informed by such principles, then it will not have been written in vain.

[20] This assumption is explicitly made by Clark; cf. ESR 112–15.
[21] *Decr. on Ecumenism* 3.
[22] Cf. n. 1 above.

APPENDIX

APPENDIX

A Correspondence between Merry del Val and Vaughan and Gasquet, July–August 1895 (see pp. 97–100)

Merry del Val to Cardinal Vaughan[1]

✠

J.M.J.

Sunday night 21.vii.95 *Private*

My dear Lord Cardinal,

The enclosed (n.b. Worledge's art. in Philadelphia Cath. Times) was sent to the H[oly] Fr and he told me to write a translation of it for him in Italian which I did in the course of today and read to him in the evening. I pointed out to him the truth of what is stated in the interview about Lord H[alifax] and the Ritualist position, the position of the different sections of the Establishment. I took advantage of the opportunity to tell the H.Fr of Ld. H's Memorandum, the way in which he endeavoured to make people believe that you and he do not take the same view of the Ang. Church etc. etc. I told him of the harm this was doing, the confusion it brought about and how it kept back conversions, as I am assured from all sides. The H. Fr was much impressed, I will almost say displeased and said that something must be done to stop this. He suggested there and then one or two measures but he decided upon none and told me to think over it and that he would see. He spoke of writing a letter to you, then of Card. Rampolla writing one to Halifax stating what the Pope means when he speaks of reunion. He suggested that I might take the letter to you, when I go to England, for you to see and remark upon. I understand that this letter would not be for publication but a private one to Halifax. Then he spoke of sending for 'Portal' and giving him a letter and a warning to convey to H., setting things right. However he came to no decision, and in the meantime I write to ask you what you would think best under the circumstances. The *Hierarchia Anglicana* has done and does harm on account of its false statements and dressing up of facts, but I do not think it has *convinced* anybody here, and what Worledge says on that head is rather beyond the mark. I also warned the H. Fr of the policy of praising him up to the skies and this throwing dust in people's eyes and ignoring the real points at issue.

[1] Copy in Gasquet's hand: GP

I think it is still the H.F's intention to start a 'Commission of Cardinals' to examine into Ang. Orders etc. next winter and indeed it is to be hoped he will and that a definite decree will be issued, now that it has been so much talked about.

I shall be glad to have your opinion upon the proposal of the H.F. as soon as possible.

Yours affectionately in Christ,
Raphael M.d.V.

Merry del Val to Cardinal Vaughan[2]

✠

J.M.J.

24.vii.95 *Private*

My dear Lord Cardinal,

I have no good news for you tonight and I am rather out of spirits. The H.F. sent for me this morning to talk over the effect of Halifax's action upon would-be converts etc., and this led to a long talk on the prospects of reunion, Ang. O[rders] etc.

The H.F. said he could not possibly allow a misunderstanding to subsist as to the real basis of reunion or a misrepresentation which would delay or prevent conversions, that he considered it his duty to provide in some way. He contemplates a kind letter to Lord H. instead of to you because this latter might be interpreted as provoked by yourself and thus lose its authority. He would very gently but clearly state the basis of true union and put things in their true light. He would publish this letter if H. did not.

We were talking over all this, the position of the Ritualists, etc. etc. when Card. Rampolla was announced and the H.F. had him introduced at once wishing me to be present, and there began an anxious and rather painful time for me. The Cardinal is an earnest upholder of H. He has to my mind been completely hoodwinked by him and he evidently has no grasp of the situation in England. He knew nothing of H's speeches since his return from Rome or of their relation to your address at Preston. Though it was most unpleasant I felt bound in conscience to speak out and tried to show the fallacy of H's position, his belief in the English Church, his idea of union, the value of Catholic expressions on his lips, the capital he was making of kindness shown, of Duchesne's medal,[3] his objection to individual secession, his speech at the Leeds Church institute, the theory of a national Church, his statement that

[2] Copy in Gasquet's hand: GP

[3] The pope had sent Duchesne a medal and Halifax had mentioned this in a speech to the English Church Union at the end of June 1895. (Cf. *The Tablet* 54 [1895], 40 col. 1.)

what had been said at Preston did[n't] represent the mind of Leo XIII etc.[4] All this and a great deal more I said but the Cardinal was full of Halifax. Nothing that he had said here was in conformity with what I stated of him, on the contrary. Not only is H. in earnest but according to the Card. he quite understands and intends reunion in the true Catholic sense as we understand it, that he believes in the infallibility of the Popes, in the Church, in everything in fact and that all there is, is a mere difference of opinion between him and you as to the way in which to proceed; that he maintained the advisability of corporate reunion and that you believed in individual secessions. We got no further. The H.F. saw my point and said something must be done and in the mean time instructed me to prepare translations of Halifax's speeches and of other documents. I will give him an extract of your address at Preston. But of course with Card. R. against me it is hard work. I am alone entirely and I am nobody, he is the Card. Sec'y and has numberless Italian and French Portals to back up his impressions. We must pray God most earnestly to help or there will be some dreadful blunders made. I shall take the first opportunity of pointing out to the H.F. the difficult position you are gradually being placed in, as no longer authorised to declare what is the Catholic position.

As to Ang. Orders: I am not at all sure that the first plan is going to be carried out. Several documents are being drawn up and printed (not published) and they will form the basis of a first discussion; in what exact form I am unable to say as yet. But as you may suppose nearly all those papers will be in favour. It would be of incalculable utility that Canon Moyes should print (not publish) a few copies in *Latin*, Italian or French of his work[5] and place it in the H.F.'s hands. I don't think *De Hier. Anglicana* has *convinced* anybody, but a great deal of it will be accepted by several and Duchesne will do the rest. I say all this in the strictest confidence. I feel you ought to know of course you may tell Fr Gasquet in confidence too. I am not at all sure that things will turn out as easily as we hoped. I see a growing conviction on the part of the H.F. and of course of Card. R. that any concession that could be made on the point of A.O. would be a step towards reunion and help on conversions!! I may be taking a doleful view, but the discussion this morning has produced a sad impression upon me and seemed to show that we have gone back.

I must stop for it is very late. I will write again soon. Excuse haste.

Yours etc. in Corde Jesu,
Raphael M.d.V.

[4] Cf. p. 62 above.

[5] The reference is apparently to a series of articles currently appearing in *The Tablet* (February–December 1895) dealing with various aspects of the Anglican Orders controversy.

Merry del Val to Cardinal Vaughan[6]

✠

J.M.J.

29.vii.95 *Private*

My dear Lord Cardinal,

I have your letter of the 16th in answer to my first and I am so glad I forestalled your judgement with regard to the advisability of a letter to Halifax. The H.F. seemed quite bent on it but he has agreed now that it would not be wise to follow out that idea. I was with him on Friday night after writing my second letter to you and took him the translation of your address at Preston, of Lord H's at Bristol and to the E[nglish] C[hurch] U[nion] on his return from Rome and last of all the Abp of Canterbury's address to the diocesan conference.[7] I did my very best to explain the whole position to him, the strange conception of the Church in the minds of many, the theory of continuity, the impression produced by every little incident, e.g. Duchesne's medal etc. etc. He was much interested in all and I really think I have conveyed something of the truth to his mind, if I may judge by what he said to me and to somebody else the next day. I will tell you more about this when I see you. The H.Fr was at a loss to realize how people could call themselves Catholic, apostolic without meaning exactly what we mean. He remarked that this was not the case some years ago to his knowledge, and that when a person said Catholic they meant Roman Catholic. Card. Rampolla has read the translations above mentioned and as far as I can see they have had some effect. But however he has hit upon your expression of 'rebels' and takes exception at it as irritating and unbecoming though of course he readily admits that all you say is true and that the doctrinal basis you put forward is beyond criticism. But the above mentioned expression has rather confirmed him in the idea that there is a harshness between you and Halifax, due to a different appreciation of the situation (!!), that he bids for corporate reunion and you for individual conversions. It seems to me that in the expression quoted you are only asserting a fact in the history of the Church, which Anglicans would admit when brought to the point, though they might seek to justify or to excuse the rebellion on the ground of an authority asserting itself beyond measure.

We must pray hard, very hard, that our Lord may turn the question of A[nglican] O[rder]s into the right channels. I am not without anxiety,

[6] Copy in Gasquet's hand: GP.

[7] Benson had spoken appreciatively of the pope's appeal in *Ad Anglos*, but said Leo XIII had written as if Englishmen had no church of their own; reunion, Benson added, must include the Orthodox and Protestants as well as Roman Catholics; the pattern of this reunion, for which all should work and pray, was not yet visible. (Cf. *The Tablet* 54 [1895], 71f.)

from different things I have heard. I am more than ever convinced that a treatise in Latin or Italian putting things in their true light and distributed here might prevent endless mischief.

Can you tell me anything of the reported group of Anglicans who are ready to submit unconditionally and spoken of in the Tablet?

Yours affectly and devotedly in Xt
Raphael M d V

Merry del Val to Dom Gasquet[8]

✠
J.M.J.

29.vii.95

My dear Father Gasquet,

Very many thanks for your letter which confirmed what I had already heard from another quarter. Of course the incident of the medal is of no importance in itself, in fact as far as I can make out it was given rather as a general recognition of merit than as reward for anything Duchesne had done in this particular question. But no doubt it was very imprudent.

I do hope and pray that the plan of action you heard of here may be carried out in all its parts, but I go through moments of terrible anxiety at times, when I see the ups and downs of impressions received, and the misleading action of those who are quite strangers to the whole question and to the situation in England.

We must pray hard.

Could you procure me a copy of the 'Hier. Anglicana' and let me know what it costs. I hope I am not troubling you too much with this request. It is terribly warm in Rome just now.

I hope I may see you, if I get to England in September.

Yours very sincerely in Xt
Raph. Merry del Val

Cardinal Vaughan to Dom Gasquet[8]

Llandrindod Aug. 7 [1895]

My dear Frank

I am writing a strong letter direct to the H. Father confining myself to the point that mischief beyond words will be done if any decision, as to A[nglican] O[rders] changing the practice of the Church for 300 years, be come to without the fullest investigation or without the cooperation of the representatives of the C[atholic] C[hurch] in England. I ask for a full Investigation and a Decision, but protest against this being attempted behind our back etc. etc.

A letter from the Bishops may come later, if needed.

[8] Original in GP.

Meanwhile I propose to call a meeting after the Assumption of say, yourself, Moyes, Sydney Smith and Breen? Is there anyone else worth having, to discuss and study the theological side of the question, and be prepared for Rome in the winter?

In my letter I remind the H.F. of his promise to me in this matter and say we are preparing to be ready for the winter.

Yours affly
H[erbert] C[ardinal] V[aughan]

Merry del Val to Dom Gasquet[9]

✠

J.M.J.

20.viii.95

My dear Fr Gasquet,

I start tonight for England. I should be very grateful to you if you would let me know your whereabouts during the next few weeks. My address will be 'Writtle Park, Chelmsford', but as I shall have to come up to town I hope to call on you. Things have taken a more favourable turn, and though there is some danger still I think we are pretty sure now by hook or by crook of getting the question properly sifted, when it does come on. My last interview with the H. Fr. has been satisfactory. I think he quite reckons with *you* now at all events and I am most thankful you came to Rome for this has been the corner of the wedge. Thank God for it all.

Hoping to see you shortly, I am, my dear Fr Gasquet,

Yrs very sincerely in Xt
Raph. Merry del Val

B Complete text of the letter from Cardinal Merry del Val to Canon Moyes cited on pp. 162 and 191[10]

Note: Moyes' questions, which occasioned this letter, can no longer be found.

My dear Mgr Moyes,

I have received your welcome letter of December 6th and I have seen Lacey's book which Abbot Gasquet kindly sent me, though I have not got it before me as I write, as I have lent it to Father David [Fleming].

[9] Original in GP

[10] Original in Moyes Papers, Westminster Archives; reproduced by kind permission of Cardinal Heenan, Archbishop of Westminster.

I return your 'quarenda' [*sic*] in regard to which let me make a few remarks and suggestions.

1 The method of discussion at the sittings of the Commission was first 'De documentis' Bulls, Brief etc Cardinal Pole's enactments, decisions of the H Office and their interpretation and purport in the light of historical facts, or fundamental theology and of the practice of Holy Church in regard to Ordinations generally and in connection with Anglican Ordinations in particular. Then, if I remember right we passed on to the subject of 'De Ministro'. From a note in my posession [*sic*] I can affirm that Barlow was not discussed until the 7th meeting and his case was certainly not discussed for more than three hours at the very most and then dropped, it being generally agreed that interesting as his case was, it did not constitute the 'crux' of the question and could be set aside.—It is possible that Lacey and Co, having settled in their own minds that Barlow's case would be one of the first and chief questions discussed, when, through their informant, who had no scruples about the 'secreto pontificio', they realised that Barlow was being discussed at such an advanced stage of the work, they concluded that the Commission had spent all its time over Barlow and that the other matters were hurriedly dismissed and that the Commission then broke up.—After the 7th meeting the Commission as a matter of fact discussed 'De Ritu' in all its parts and thus covered the whole ground in twelve sittings. I therefore answer 'affirmative' to your first question. Father David can look up my minutes of the sittings, which are at the Holy Office and complete this information which I am giving from memory and from some stray notes in my possession. I can answer for the accuracy of my minutes. They were practically stenographed and, as you know, they were read and approved by the Commission.

I answer 'affirmative' without hesitation to your No 2.

As to No 3. The statement made is mischievous and a monstrous untruth. The Commission had of course to consider the importance and purport of the Gordon Case but it was left entirely free to 'go behind it', and for that purpose all available documents were procured from the Holy Office concerning Ordinations and were placed at the disposal of the Commission. I got them myself by order of the Cardinal President and cases were referred to which had been considered centuries before Gordon. Those documents brought out the fact that an absolute reordination, without the 'sub-conditione' only existed in the case of Anglican Orders. The benefit of the doubt was always admitted when a legitimate rite had been used and each case was considered separately and was only discussed in connection with the manner in which the Ordination had taken place and the use of the Rite. In that respect the English Ordinal stands alone. You may certainly state that the Commission was free to adduce any argument available from theology, or from the latest results of liturgical or historical research from the earliest periods of the Church.

No 4. You may certainly explain the prohibition in the way you mention. And now I come to No 5. I have asked Father David to look up my minutes and it will be easy to settle the point of the votes. My impression is that they were as follows: Gasquet, Moyes, David and Llevaneras voted for the invalidity, Duchesne and De Augustinis for the validity. Gasparri and Scannell for a doubtful validity and therefore a 'sub-conditione'. If, as Father David thinks, Scannel [*sic*] voted for the validity with Duchesne and De Augustinis, in a sense, the validity was lost by one vote. I do not think it would be allowable, at present at all events for you to say publicly that—so many were for absolute Invalidity, and so many were for the validity, and so many for reordination sub conditione. First because this would require special leave and might not be advisable for many reasons. Secondly and chiefly because it would be misleading as to the purport and character of the Commission. And this could only help Lacey. The Commission had no authority or mission to decide the matter. The Validity could not be lost or won at the Commission, even if the Commission had been unanimous in one or other sense. The Commission was a body of technical Consultors. The Cardinals of the Holy Office worked on the report of the Commission. They did so very carefully, and in view of the importance of the matter before them, after they had studied it at home, they discussed the question finally and gave their vota 'coram Pontifice' in a 'Feria v'. As you are aware the Cardinals were unanimous for the absolute Invalidity. But even this was not a decision, though carrying great weight.

The Validity was not even then either lost or won. The Holy Father did not there and then sanction the vote of the Cardinals, giving it the form of a Decree of the Holy Office approved by his Holiness. He wished to give greater solemnity and authority to the decision and to reserve to himself the *manner* and *time* of publishing his final verdict. Finally He [*sic*] drew up and published the Bull. Then indeed the Validity was lost: lost in a sense at the Commission of Consultors where some tried to make out a case for Anglican Orders: lost at the solemn meeting of the Holy Office, no doubt, but really lost and finally lost when The Holy Father spoke with all the solemnity and authority of a Pontifical Bull. I think it would be a mistake to let people think with Lacey that the decision practically rested with the Commission. Consultors very often report to the Holy Office or to a Congregation in one sense and the Holy Office or that other Congregation, ie the Cardinals reverse the conclusion. Sometimes the Holy Office or another Congregation comes to a decision, unanimously or otherwise, and the Holy Father does not accept the verdict, though of course this does not happen as often as the former case which is not rare.

I should like to add one or two remarks: 1 I consider it essential that we should again and again disclose and refute the long standing equivocation which lies at the bottom of the whole controversy and which Lacey goes on using as if nothing had been said. He sees clearly that is the crucial question. I mean the equivocation regarding the 'sacerdotium' and what is meant by 'Validity'. We mean of course a sacrificing priesthood and the validity of Orders for a sacrificing priesthood. Lacey, like so many others, goes on playing with the word 'priest' and 'priesthood' which can be used for different kinds of ministry, and for the simple ministry of preaching the Word with a Sacrament more or less. He knows that the great body of Anglicans and those who are entitled to speak for and govern the Anglican Church do not uphold a valid priesthood in the sense of a valid sacerdotium for a real sacrifice and a sacrificing priesthood, but still he goes on. It is of course true that the Church has not defined what exactly constitutes the matter and form of the Sacrament of Orders, but whatever the essential form is, and whatever the Rite, it must include explicitly or implicitly the 'sacerdotium' in the Catholic sense, or it is invalid, and as we have shown times without number, the Anglican Form (Edwardine) was expressly manufactured to exclude the 'sacerdotium' and the sacrificing priesthood. It is this equivocation that misleads so many and hurts their feelings when we say that their Orders are invalid: whereas they do not pretend that they are valid in our sense. Secondly, I think it most necessary to refute Lacey's assertions as to the procedure of the Holy Office and of the Congregations generally. According to him the Cardinals simply sit round a table and mysteriously utter the words 'affirmative' or 'negative' or 'dilata', without discussion or argument. We all know that that is nonsense. I can testify with regard to Anglican Orders, that the Cardinals were given all the documents with full time to consider and study them at home, after the Commission had done its work. I can testify that the Feria v lasted at least two hours and a half. I was in attendance on the Holy Father and I spent all that long time in the Holy Father's private chapel, saying my office and praying for the blessing of God on the meeting. I remember coming out from time to time wondering at the length of the proceedings and rejoicing that the matter should be so fully discussed. It did not take five or six Cardinals two hours and a half to say 'affirmative' or 'negative' or 'dilata'. Each one must have spoken at length and you know that their verdict was unanimous

Please forgive this rambling and perhaps useless letter. I have written it amidst all manner of interruptions, just as if I had been talking to you in my room, and perhaps I have talked too much.

I enclose some rough notes of yours which I had by me and which you handed to me after our meetings to help me to be accurate in reporting what you had said. They may perhaps be useful to refresh your memory.

With every best wish for Xmas and begging a remembrance in your prayers, I am, my dear Canon Moyes,

13.xii [1910. Date in Merry del Val's clearly identifiable handwriting; signature and year cut out of original.]

C Letter from Merry del Val to Gasquet, August 1896 (see p. 192)[11]

✠

J.M.J.

I.viii.96 *Private*

My dear Fr. Gasquet,

For the purpose of making an exact quotation which can stand the scrutiny of the severest critics, I am in need of some 'data' regarding the Bulls and Briefs attributed to Julius III in your 'Documents ad Leg: Card: Poli spectantia'. As these documents will be referred to in the coming pronouncement it is necessary to distinguish them carefully and quote them accurately with their right name, place and value. I trust I am not troubling you too much but I should be grateful if you could help me to clear up the following questions:

(1) What is your exact authority for stating that *two* Bulls were issued on the *same* day, 5th Aug. 1553, one for ordinary faculties, the other extraordinary? Is this only a supposition or can you quote the Bulls accurately? Was not all contained in the Bull which constituted Pole Legate for the reconciliation of England, after the Consistory of Aug. 5th and Legate for France to negotiate a peace with the Emperor? Does this Bull exist and how can it be quoted?

(2) Why do you speak of three documents (Haec tria documenta in una quasi complexa coadunantur) and then apparently only find two clearly distinguishable in the context? How is it that the date 5th Aug. 1553 is nowhere to be found in the context?

(3) What authority have you for supposing that any of the documents given in the text, or any portion of that text are *Bulls*, when the form of a Bull is absent (Servus servorum etc.) and the 'Dilecte Fili' points decidedly and almost exclusively to a *Brief* and not to a Bull? (sub plumbo)

(4) On page 7, before what appears to be an extension of Pole's faculties there is the sentence 'ac diversas alias facultates per *diversas* alias nostras *tam sub plumbo*, quam in forma *brevis* confectas litteras'. This points to at least *two* other Bulls and *two* other Briefs: '*diversas* alias

[11] Original in GP.

nostras *sub plumbo*' must signify at least two Bulls—and '*diversas* alias nostras . . . in forma brevis confectas litteras' must signify at least two Briefs. Can they be safely quoted and how?

(5) If the document before us is a later compilation of several documents, why is the form of Brief only 'Dilecte fili'? Is this conclusion based only on intrinsic evidence, is it more than an opinion, and in any case how are the several documents to be accurately quoted with their dates and calling them by their proper names, Bull or Brief, so as to bar the way to all adverse criticism of the accuracy of the Papal document?

I don't know whether I have expressed myself clearly. You will tell me if you fail to see any point.

I will not trouble you further today and I feel remorseful at tormenting you so much, but you will readily understand how necessary it is to be on the safe side in a case like this even in the smallest details.

Prayers are still needful to carry this matter through.

Yours affectly in Xt
Raph. Merry del Val

D Complete text of the letter from Cardinal Vaughan to Lord Halifax quoted on p. 203[12]

Oct. 5, 96

The Oaks
Woodford Green
Essex

My dear Lord

I have yet to thank you very sincerely for your affectionate letter and for sending me a copy of what you wrote to the Abbé Portal.

I believe the time will come when you will judge things differently. I hope that you will come to see that the actual Pope, as Head of the Church, has the same right and duty that his predecessors had in the 16 [*sic*] century and in the centuries preceding that. If after a new investigation, he has felt bound to repeat the judgment on Anglican Orders passed by his predecessors, it must be really a gain that he should have done so—unless the supposition be made (which we Catholics cannot admit) that the Supreme Judge has been wrong from the beginning.

I should have thought that, from the point of view of piety and devotion to Our Lord, you and I ought to rejoice to think that men have not had the power to profane and dishonour Our Lord in the B. Eucharist during the last three centuries which they would have had were their Orders valid. Think of how the bread and wine have been treated, not

[12] Original in HP (A4.240).

only by clergymen but by sacristans and the people generally, who disbelieved in any real presence. Think of how shocking it would be if men were actually producing Our Lord—not to be honoured and adored, but in truth to be disowned and dishonoured by themselves and the people.

This is a consideration which cannot fail to suggest itself to a devout mind like your own.

But is it not good and useful that, instead of groping in the mist of uncertainty, we should be brought face to face with test questions? Such a question is, the Supremacy of the Pope and the necessity of submission to the Church—the Church of which the Pope is the legitimate Head. No doubt such submission requires humility, for human nature is filled with that spirit of pride and independence which has been the ruin of an angelic as well as of a human race. But it is to this test that Our Lord seems to call those who would hear His Church. But I must not go on, or I should weary you with a volume.

I hope you know that the Abbé Duchesne has fully accepted the decision of the Holy See on Anglican Orders. He writes thus: 'Vous savez que je n'avais jamais admis la suffisance du rituel pour le Diaconat; pour la prêtrise, plus j'étudiais la formule, et moins elle m'inspirait de confiance. Quant à l'Episcopat, j'espérais qu'on pourrait admettre le doute, bien qu'il y ait, là aussi, une objection assez grave. Dans ces conditions vous voyez que je n'avais pas à faire un grand sacrifice d'opinion pour accepter la solution du S. Père. Du reste, il ne pouvait me venir à l'idée d'hésiter dans la soumission. Dans ces choses religeuses le Pape, même en dehors de toute considération surnaturelle, a des lumières que n'ont pas les simples mortels.—Je ne puis comme historien refuser d'admettre ce fait très grave, découvert par les Anglicans eux-mêmes au cours du débat, que les réordinations nombreuses ont eu lieu sous la reine Marie.'

But, however interesting this may be, the real question between us is, where is the Divine Teacher to be found? In a small but respectable section of the Church of England or in the Church of which the Pope is the Head. This is the question to which I hope all your attention will be given, with constant earnest and humble prayer for guidance. I ought to have answered your letter before this—but I have been away, and much overworked. I send this to Shrewsbury, as I hear you are to be there. Believe me

Your faithful and devoted [illegible]
Herbert Card Vaughan

The Lord Halifax

Note on this letter

The passage cited in French above is from a letter written by the Abbé Duchesne to Baron von Hügel and sent on (or cited?) by him to Vaughan (cf. Messenger, RMP ii, 549 and 583f). The next to last sentence of this citation is startling. Aside from the difficulty of finding any dogmatic basis in the teaching of the Roman Catholic Church for the claim that in religious matters the pope 'even apart from all supernatural considerations, is possessed of lights not available to simple mortals', such a statement seems utterly foreign to the ever-caustic and irreverent Duchesne. Was he writing tongue in cheek to the good baron and exercising once again that celebrated gift for irony which, as Portal reported in another connection, was 'terribly irritating to everyone'? (Cf. p. 167 above.)

BIBLIOGRAPHY

BIBLIOGRAPHY

I Unpublished sources
II Works dealing with Anglican Orders or their condemnation
III General works

An attempt has been made to compile in Part II of the following bibliography as complete a list as possible of all works dealing with Anglican Orders from the English reformation to the present day, to serve as the basis for a complete history of the controversy, which has yet to be written. To assist the student, passages dealing with Anglican Orders in longer or more general works have been identified, where possible, by page numbers in parentheses following the place and date of publication. Although this list is certainly incomplete, it is by far the lengthiest yet compiled, as comparison with the bibliography in Fr Clark's *Anglican Orders and Defect of Intention* (the best and most complete bibliography of the subject up to that time) will show. Clark's list has been of great assistance in compiling Part II of the following bibliography, which includes all titles listed by Fr Clark.

Part I—Unpublished Sources

Edmund Bishop Papers Gasquet Papers	Downside Abbey, Stratton on the Fosse near Bath
Hickleton Papers of the second Viscount Halifax	In possession of the Earl of Halifax, Garrowby, Stamford Bridge, York
Portal Papers	Villa Béthanie, 95 Montsoult, France
Archbishop Benson's Diary	Trinity College, Cambridge. (Extensive excerpts published in Benson's Life by his son, A. C. Benson.)
Westminster Archives	Archbishop's House, Westminster, London SW1

Part II—Works dealing with Anglican Orders or their condemnation

ABERCROMBIE, Nigel	*The Life and Work of Edmund Bishop*, London 1959
ABRAHAM, C. T.	*The Church of England Catholic and Continuous in her history* (t), London 1903
AINSLIE, J. L.	*The Doctrines of Ministerial Order in the Reformed Churches of the Sixteenth and Seventeenth Centuries*, Edinburgh 1940
ALETHES, Clerophilus	see CONSTABLE, John
ALLEN, William	*An Apologie and true Declaration of the Institution and Endevours of the two English Colleges, the one in Rome, the other now resident in Rhemes, against certain sinister informations given up against the same*, Mounts in Henault, Mons., 1581 (fol. 88–9)
ALLIES, T. W.	*The Royal Supremacy Viewed in Reference to the two Spiritual Powers of Order and Jurisdiction* (t), London 1850
ANDROUTSOS, Chrestos	*The Validity of English Ordinations from an Orthodox Catholic point of View*, London 1909. (Translation of Greek original published in Constantinople in 1903.)
anon.	'L'anglicanisme et la Papauté', *Questions Actuelles* 40 (Paris 1897), 66–83
ARCHBISHOPS OF CANTERBURY AND YORK (Frederick Temple and W. D. MacLagan)	*Responsio Archiepiscoporum Angliae ad Litteras Apostolicas Leonis Papae XIII de Ordinationibus Anglicanis*, London 1897. Translations in English, French, and Greek published simultaneously. Reprinted in Latin and English for the Church Historical Society by SPCK, London at various dates between 1943 and 1957
ARCHAEOPHILUS, Constantius	*Memoirs of the Reformation in England ... collected chiefly from Acts of Parliament and Protestant Historians*, London 1826 (217–45)
B., W.	see L., H.P.
BAILEY, Thomas John	*English Orders and Papal Supremacy* (t), London and Oxford 1868
—	*A Defence of Holy Orders in the Church of England*, London 1870 (separate Latin version published simultaneously)
—	*Are Ministers of the 'Reformed Episcopal Church' validly ordained?* (t), London 1879

BAKER, E. A. — *Have Anglicans Valid Orders?*, Art & Book Co., before 1896

BAMPTON, Joseph M. — *The Papal Bull on Anglican Orders* (t), London 1897

BARBER, S. C. — see MORTIMER, C. G.

BARNES, Arthur S. — *The Popes and the Ordinal*, London 1896

— *No Sacrifice, No Priest; or Why Anglican Orders were Condemned* (t), London 1897

— *Bishop Barlow and Anglican Orders*, London 1922 (refuted by JENKINS, Claude, q.v.)

BARTER, William B. — *A Word in Defence of our Altars and Catholic Church* (t), London 1843; contained in

— *Tracts in Defence of the Christian Sabbath, the Church, her Priesthood and her Sacraments*, London 1851 (139–71); and in

— *The English Church not in Schism*, London 1845 (207–83)

BASSET, Joshua — *An Essay towards a Proposal for Catholick Communion . . . by a Minister of the Church of England*, London 1704, ^{2}1801

BAUM, Gregory — 'Reopen the Question of Anglican Orders?' JES 4 (1967), 716 f.

BEDOYÈRE, Michael de la — *The Life of Baron von Hügel*, London 1951 (80–92)

BEECK, F. J. van — 'Towards an Ecumenical Understanding of the Sacraments, JES 3 (1966), 57–112; reprinted in *Doctrinal Development and Christian Unity*, ed. N. Lash, London 1967 (in US, in *Progress Towards Christian Unity*, ed. N. Lash, Dayton, Ohio 1968)

BEEVOR, Humphrey — *The Anglican Armoury*, Canterbury 1934

BELL, G. K. A. — *Randall Davidson* i, London 1935 (228–37)

— *Christian Unity, the Anglican Position*, London 1948

BELLASIS, Edward — *Anglican Orders. By an Anglican since become a Catholic* (t), London 1872

— *Was Barlow a Bishop?* (t), London 1890

BELLESHEIM, Alfons — 'Zwei römische Tagebücher aus der Zeit der Bulle *Apostolicae curae*', *Archiv für Kirchenrecht* 91 (1911), 391–423

BENSON, Arthur C. — *The Life of Edward White Benson* 2 vols., London 1900

BENSON, Arthur H. T. — *The Pope's Bull on Anglican Orders* (t), Dublin 1896

BÉVENOT, Maurice — *Are they Priests? The Nature of Anglican Orders* (t), London 1946, ^{2}1953

Bill, E. G. W. (ed.) — *Anglican Initiatives in Christian Unity*, London 1967

Birbeck, Mrs — *Life and Letters of W. J. Birbeck*, London 1922

Birbeck, W. J. — *Cardinal Vaughan and the Russian Church* (t), London 1897

Birkenhead, Earl of — *The Life of Lord Halifax*, London 1964

Bliss, W. H. W. — *Continuity, A Dream* (t), London 1928

Bolton, Anselm — *A Catholic Memorial of Lord Halifax and Cardinal Mercier*, London 1935

Bonner, Edmund — *A Profitable and Necessary Doctrine*, London 1554

Boudinhon, A. — *Étude théologique sur les ordinations Anglicanes* (t), Paris 1895

— *De la Validité des Ordinations Anglicanes* (t), Paris 1895

— *Ordinations schismatiques Coptes et Ordinations Anglicanes* (t), Paris 1895 (=*Canoniste Contemporain* 18 [1895], 213–23, 263–81)

— 'Les aspects moraux de la question des Ordres Anglicans', *Can. Contemporain* 19 (1896), 193–210

— 'Nouvelles observations sur la question des Ordres Anglicans', RAR 2 (1896), 625–32, 673–82, 770–91

Brady, W. Maziere — *The Alleged Conversion of the Irish Bishops to the Reformed Religion at the Accession of Queen Elizabeth and the assumed descent of the present Established Hierarchy in Ireland from the Ancient Irish Church, disproved*, London 1866, ^{5}1867

— *The Episcopal Succession in England, Scotland and Ireland, A.D. 1400 to 1875* 3 vols., Rome 1876–77

Bramhall, John — 'A Replication to the Bishop of Chalcedon', London 1656; in Bramhall's 'Works' (LACT) ii, Oxford 1842

— 'The Consecration and Succession of Protestant Bishops Justified', The Hague 1658 and London 1659; in 'Works' (LACT) iii, Oxford 1844.

— 'Protestants' Ordination Defended; or an Answer to the Twentieth Chapter of the Guide of Faith', Dublin 1676; in 'Works' (LACT) v, Oxford 1845

Brandi, S. M. — 'The Pontifical Declaration of the Invalidity of Anglican Ordinations', AER 16 (1897), 22–54,

BRANDI, S. M. 138–47, 267–89, 363–81 (translations of articles in *Civiltà Cattolica*)

— *Roma e Canterbury*, Rome [3]1897; French trans., *Rome et Cantorbéry*, Paris 1898

— *La Condanna delle Ordinazioni Anglicane: Studio Storico-Teologico*, Rome [4]1908

see also SMITH, Sydney

BREEN, John Dunstan *Anglican Orders, Are they Valid?* (t), London 1877, [2]1885

see also MCCAVE, James

BRETT, Thomas *The Divine Right of Episcopacy and the Necessity of an Episcopal Commission for Preaching God's Word and for the Valid Ministration of the Christian Sacraments Proved from Holy Scriptures and the Doctrine and Practice of the Primitive Church . . . also the Valid Succession of our English Bishops Vindicated . . . and the Popish Fable of the Nags-Head Consecration of Archbishop Parker fully refuted*, London [2]1728

BRIDGETT, T. E. 'Early Catholic Witness on Anglican Orders', *Dublin Review* 118 (1896), 1–40

BRIGGS, Charles A. 'Orders in the Church of England', *Critical Review* 7 (London 1910)

— *Church Unity: Studies of its most important Problems*, London and New York 1910

BRIGHTMAN, F. E. *What objections have been made to Anglican Orders?* (t), London 1896

— *The English Rite*, 2 vols., London 1915

BRISTOW, Richard *A Brief Treatise of diuerse plaine and sure wayes to find out the truthe in this doubtful and dangerous time of Heresie: conteyning sundry worthy Motiues vnto the Catholike faith, or considerations to moue a man to beleue the Catholikes and not the Heretikes*, Antwerp 1574 (93ff)

— *Demaundes to be proponed of Catholikes to the Heretics*, n.d., n.p.

— 'An Offer made by a Catholike to a learned Protestant' in John de Albine, *Notable Discourse*, Douai 1575

— *Reply to Fulke in Defense of M. D. Allen's Scroll of Articles and Booke of Purgatorie*, Louvain 1580 (317–30)

— *Motives inducint to the Catholike Faith*, [Douai?] 1641

BROOK, V. J. K. *A Life of Archbishop Parker*, Oxford 1962

BROWN, John *The Historic Episcopate* (t), London 1891

— *Apostolical Succession in the Light of History and Fact*, London 1898

BROWNE SJ, Fr (ed.) *The City of Peace by Those who have Entered It*, London 1903 (67–88)

BROWNE, George Forrest *Anglican Orders. A speech delivered in ... the Church House ... Oct. 15, 1896*, London 1896

— *The Continuity of the Holy Catholic Church in England*, London 1896

— *What is the Catholic Church in England?*, London 1897

BROWNE, Thomas *Concio ad clerum habita coram Academia Cantabrigiensi Junii II^{0} a^{0} 1687 ... ubi vindicatur vera et valida cleri Anglicani, ineunte reformatione, ordinatio ... Annexum est instrumentum consecrationis Matt. Parker archiepiscopi Cantuarensis, etc.*, Cambridge 1688

— *The Story of the Ordination of our First Bishop in Queen Elizabeth's Reign at the Nag's-Head Tavern in Chapside, Thoroughly Examined; and proved to be a Late-invented, Inconsistent, Self-contradicting, and Absurd Fable ... etc.* London 1731

BROWNLOW, W. R. *The Reunion of England and Rome*, London 1896.

BULGAKOFF, A. *The Question of Anglican Orders in respect of a Vindication of the Papal Decision, which was drawn up by the English Roman Catholic Bishops at the end of 1897* (t), trans. by W. J. Birbeck, London

BURNET, Gilbert *A Vindication of Ordinations of the Church of England*, London ^{2}1688
(see also Part III: General Works)

BURN-MURDOCH, H. *Rome's Denials of Anglican Orders* (t), London 1956

BUTLER, Charles *Reply to Bishop Philpotts' Fourth Letter*, London 1826

BUTLER, Montagu R. *Rome's Tribute to Anglican Orders: A Defence of the Episcopal Succession and Priesthood of the Church of England, founded on the testimony of the best Roman Catholic authorities* (t), London 1893

— *A Brief Catechism on English Orders* (t), London 1895

C., R. *A Scholasticall Discourse ... wherein is answered all which is alleged by Erastus Senior against the*

C., R. — *order and jurisdiction of the Bishops of the Church of England*, London 1663

CALMEYN, J. — *Origines de l'Anglicanisme* (t), Brussels 1938

CAMM, Bede — 'La controverse sur les ordinations Anglicanes', RBén 11 (1894), 530–40; 12 (1895), 123–33

— *The English Martyrs and Anglican Orders* (t), London 1929

CARDINAL ARCHBISHOP AND BISHOPS OF THE PROVINCE OF WESTMINSTER, see VAUGHAN, Herbert

CARR, Thomas — *The Church of England and the Church Catholic* (t), Melbourne 1895

CARSON, W. R. — *Reunion Essays, with an Appendix on the Non-Infallible Dogmatic Force of the Bull 'Apostolicae curae'* . . ., London 1903

CARRIER, Benjamin — *Letter to King James*, London 1649

CARTER, T. T. — *The Recent Action of the Archbishop of Dublin and its Consequences* (t), London 1892

'CATHOLICUS' — 'The Pope and the Anglicans; (ii) The Policy of the Bull', *Contemporary Review* (London 1896), 804–9

CENCI, Pio — *Il Cardinale Raffaele Merry del Val*, Rome and Turin 1933

CHAMPNEY, Anthony — *A treatise on the Vocation of Bishops . . . proving . . . in particular the pretended Bishops in England to be no true Bishops*, Douai 1616; Latin edition Paris 1618

CHAPMAN, John — *Bishop Gore and the Catholic Claims*, London 1905

CHARLES I, King — 'Papers concerning Church Government: 1664' in *The Workes of King Charles the Martyr*, London 1662, 153–89

CHRISTIE, Joseph — *Anglicans Anonymous; a comment on 'Infallible Fallicies'* (t), London 1953

CHRYSOSTOM, K. — *Hai Anglikanikai Cheirotoniai*, Constantinople 1921 (in Greek)

CHURCH HISTORICAL SOCIETY — *The Doctrine of Intention, with special Reference to the Validity of Ordinations in the English Church* (t), London 1895

— *Has the English Church preserved the Episcopal Succession?* (t), London 1896

— *Treatise on the Bull 'Apostolicae curae'*, London 1896

— *Priesthood in the English Church: a Study of the Vindication of the Bull 'Apostolicae curae'* (t), London 1898

CHURTON, W. R.	*Defence of the English Ordinal*, London 1872
CIRLOT, Felix	*Apostolic Succession and Anglicanism*, Lexington, Ky., 1946
CLARA, Sancta	see DAVENPORT, Christopher
CLARK, Francis	*Anglican Orders and Defect of Intention*, London 1956
—	*The Defect of Form in Anglican Ordinations*, Rome 1958 (printed extract from doctoral dissertation at the Gregorian University)
—	*Eucharistic Sacrifice and the Reformation*, London and Westminster, Md., 1960, ^{2}1967
—	'A Roman Document of 1853 concerning Anglican Orders', *Heythrop Journal* 2 (1961), 355f.
—	'A Reopening of the Question of Anglican Orders', ClRev 47 (1962), 555–60
—	*The Catholic Church and Anglican Orders* (t), London 1962
—	'Les ordinations anglicanes, problème oecuménique', Gr 45 (1964), 60–93
CLARK, James	*De Successione Apostolica necnon Missione et Jurisdictione Hierarchiae Anglicanae et Catholicae*, Georgetown, Brit. Guiana, 1890
CLARK, R. E. D.	*The Problem of Ordination in the Church of England* (t), Cambridge 1930
CLARK, William	*The Anglican Reformation*, Edinburgh 1897 (147–54, 265–76)
COHU, J. R.	*'No Bishop, no Church'; or Anglo-Catholic Claims examined* (t), London 1917
[COLERIDGE, H. J.]	'Cardinal Pole and the Anglican Ordinal', *Month* 4 (1866), 60–7
[—]	'Anglican Sacerdotalism', *Month* 9 (1868), 249–71; 10 (1869), 41–57
COLLINS, H.	*The Probable Validity of Anglican Orders etc.; to which is added Suggestions on Re-union*, London 1860
COLLINS, William E.	*The Internal Evidence of the Letter, 'Apostolicae curae', as to its own Origin and Value* (t), London 1897
CONSTABLE, John	*Remarks upon F. Le Courayer's Book in Defence of the English Ordinations*, London c. 1730 (by 'Clerophilus Alethes').
COSIN, John	'Works' (LACT) iv, Oxford 1851
COUTURIER, J.	*Le 'Book of Common Prayer' et l'Église Anglicane*, Paris 1928; Eng. trans. London 1930

COVENTRY, Francis — see DAVENPORT, Christopher

CRANE, A. B. — 'The Anglican Claim to Continuity', *Quarterly Review*, July 1909

CREIGHTON, Louise — *Life and Letters of Mandell Creighton* 2 vols., London 1904–5

CRESSY, Hugh Paulin de — *Exomologesis: or, a faithful narrative of the occasion and motives of the Conversion unto Catholique Unity of Hugh Palin de Cressy*, Paris 1647, [2]1653

— *Epistle Apologeticall to a Person of Honour*, London 1674

CROWE, Jeremiah — 'Anglican Orders and the Doctrine of Intention', IER 16 (1895)

— 'The Papal Bull on Anglican Orders', IER 17 (1896)

CUDSEMIUS, Peter — *De desperato Calvini Causa, Tractatus brevis*, Mainz 1609 (408)

'DALBUS' — see PORTAL, Fernand

DALPIAZ, Vigilio — *Cardinal Merry del Val*, London 1937

DARK, Sidney — *Lord Halifax, a Tribute*, London 1934

DART, J. L. C. — *Anglican Orders and the Papal Decree of 1948 on the Matter and Form of Holy Orders* (t), London, n.d.

DAVENPORT, Christopher — *Deus, Natura, Gratia*, Lyon and Paris 1634

— *Enchiridion of Faith*, Douai [2]1655

— *Summa Veteris Theologiae Discipulis meis Missionariis propinata*, Douai 1667

— *The Articles of the Anglican Church Paraphrastically Considered and Explained* (ed. F. G. Lee), London 1865

DAVIES, E. T. — *Episcopacy and the Royal Supremacy in the Church of England in the XVI Century*, Oxford 1950

DELASGE, Gustave — *Validité des Ordinations Anglicanes* (t), Paris and Poitiers 1895

anon. — *A Demonstration by English Protestant pretended Bishops and Ministers against their owne pretended Bishops and Mynestery*, Douai 1616

DENNY, Edward — *Anglican Orders and Jurisdiction*, London 1893

— *The English Church and the Ministry of the Reformed Churches* (t), London 1900.

DENNY, Edward and LACEY, T. A. — *De Hierarchia Anglicana*, London 1895

DIDIOT, Jules — *Lettre d'un Prêtre Catholique Romain aux Métropolitains Anglicans de Cantorbéry et d'York sur leur Réponse au Pape Léon XIII* (t), Arras 1897

DIMOCK, N. — *The Christian Doctrine of the Sacerdotium*, London ²1897

— *Some Notes on the Vindication of the Bull 'Apostolicae curae' by the 'Cardinal and Bishops of the Province of Westminster'* (t), London 1898

DIX, Gregory — *The Question of Anglican Orders*, London 1944, ²1956

DIX, Morgan — *The Authority of the Church*, London 1891 (63–85)

DIXON, R. W. — *History of the Church of England* v, Oxford 1902 (209–48)

DOCKERY, John B. — *Christopher Davenport, Friar and Diplomat*, London 1960 (Chapter v., Appendices D and E)

DODD, Charles — *The Church History of England*, Brussels 1737; ed. M. A. Tierney (*Dodd's Church History*), ii, London 1839 (cclxxii–cccxi)

DODWELL, Henry — *Two Letters of Advice*, Dublin 1672

DÖLLINGER, J. J. I. von — *Lectures on the Reunion of the Churches*, London 1872 (103–35)

DOUGLAS, Gerald W. — *Ordination and Apostolical Succession* (t), London 1907

DOUGLAS, J. A. — *The Relations of the Anglican Churches with the Eastern-Orthodox especially in regard to Anglican Orders*, London 1921

DUCHESNE, L. — Review of DALBUS, 'Les Ordinations Anglicanes', *Bulletin Critique* 5 (1894), 262ff; reprinted in HEADLAM, A. C., *The Doctrine of the Church and Reunion* (q.v.)

ECK, H. V. S. — *The Continuity of the Church of England* (t), London 1928

ELRINGTON, Thomas — *The Clergy of the Church of England Truly Ordained and not Obliged to subscribe to Damnable Contradictions*, Dublin 1808

— *The Validity of the English Ordinations Established*, Dublin 1818

ELYS, Edmund — *Letter to Dr L. Mumoulin, on the Validity of English Ordinations, with an Appendix concerning the Sacrilegious and Schismatical Action of the Church of Rome in Ordaining Anew*, London 1680

ELYS, Edmund	*Sacri Ordinis Episcopalis Vindiciae contra Salmasium*, n.p. 1705
anon.	*England's Conversion and Reformation Compared, or, the Young Gentleman Directed in the Choice of his Religion* ('printed for R.C. and C.F.'), Antwerp 1725 (257f, 261f, 321–6)
ESTCOURT, E. E.	*The Question of Anglican Ordinations Discussed*, London 1873
EVEREST, W. F.	*The Gift of the Keys and other Essays*, London 1895
anon.	*An examination of the Arguments in the Papal Letter on Anglican Orders; and the Pope's Criteria applied to the Roman Ordinal* (t), Philadelphia 1897
FABER, Frederick W.	*Grounds for Remaining in the Anglican Communion; A Letter to a High-Church Friend* (t), London 1846
FAIRWEATHER, E. R., and HETTLINGER, R. F.	*Episcopacy and Reunion*, London 1953
FENNELL, E.	*Dissertation sur la Validité des Ordinations des Anglais* 2 vols., Paris 1726
FERN, Henry	*Examination of Anthony Champney's Exceptions against the lawful Calling and Ordination of the Protestant Bishops*, London 1653
FERREY, Abbé	'Les Ordinations Anglicanes', *Revue du Monde Catholique* 11 (1896), 441–56; and 13 (1897), 5–25
FFOULKES, Edmund S.	*Christendom's Divisions*, London 1865 (198–207)
—	*The Church's Creed or the Crown's Creed, A Letter to the Most Rev'd Archbishop Manning, etc.*, London 1868
FIRKINS, Harold H.	*As in Times Past* (t), London 1931
FIRMINGER, W. K.	*The Attitude of the Church of England to Non-Episcopal 'Ordinations'* (t), London 1894
—	*The Purity of the Apostolic Succession in the Church of England* (t), Zanzibar, Oxford, and London 1895
—	*The Alterations in the Ordinal of 1662: Why were they made?* (t), London 1898
—	*Some Comments on 'The Vindication of the Bull "Apostolicae curae"* (t), Calcutta 1898

FIRMINGER, W. K. — 'Some Ancient Ordination Ceremonies', *Indian Church Review* (Calcutta), October 1901, 429–50

FISHER, Francis — *The Validity of English Orders; Archbishop Parker's Consecrators proved to have been Acknowledged by the Church of Rome as Lawful Bishops*, London 1857

FITZHERBERT, Thomas — *A Supplement to the Discussion of M. B. Barlow's Answer to the Judgment of a Catholike Englishman etc.* (by 'F.T.'), St. Omer 1613

— — *A Confutation of certaine Absurdities, Falsities, and Follies, uttered by M. D. Andrews in his Answer to Cardinall Belarmine's Apology* (by 'F.T.'), St. Omer 1613

FITZSIMON, Henry — *Britannomachia Ministrorum in plerisque fidei fundamentis et articulis dissidentium*, Douai 1614

FLETCHER, John — *A Comparative View of the Grounds of the Catholic, and Protestant, Churches*, London 1826 (208–41)

FLEURY, Claude — *Histoire Ecclésiastique* tôme 31, Paris 1733 (335–8); the actual author of this volume is J. C. Fabre

FORREST, Michael D. — *Nightmare of Infallible Fallacies* (t), London 1954

FORRESTER, H. — *Christian Unity and the Historic Episcopate*, New York 1889

FRASER, J. A. L. — *Apostolical Succession* (t), London 1905

FRERE, Walter Howard — *What is the Position of the Roman Catholic Body in England?* (t), London 1896

— — *The Marian Reaction*, London 1896

— (ed.) — *Registrum Matthaei Parker, Diocesis Cantuarensis, 1559–1575* (Canterbury and York Society, Vol. 35), Oxford 1928

— and KENNEDY, W. M. — *Visitation Articles and Injunctions of the Period of the Reformation* vols. 1 and 2 (Alcuin Club Collections xv), London 1910

FULKE, William — 'T. Stapleton and Martiall (two Popish Heretikes) confuted, and of their particular heresies detected', London 1580: in Fulke's *Works* (PS) ii, Cambridge 1848 (117f)

— — *Answere of the Christian Protestant to the proud Challenge of a Popish Catholic*, London 1577

— — *A Retentive to stay good Christians, in true faith and religion, against the motives of R. Bristow . . .*, London 1580 (69)

FULKE, William — *Briefe Confutation of a Popish Discourse by John Howlet or some other Birde of the Night*, London 1581 (fol. 37–8)

FULLER, Morris — *Our Established Church: with a Dissertation on the Anglican Form of Ordination*, London 1878

— *The Anglican Ordinal* (t), London 1897

FULLER, Reginald — see HANSON, Richard

FULLER, Samuel — *Canonica Successio ministerii Ecclesiae Anglicanae reformatae tam contra Pontificios quam schismaticos vindicata*, Cambridge 1690

GALWEY, Peter — *Twelve Lectures on Ritualism* ii, London 1879

— *Thoughts on Apostolic Succession to Help Catholics in Discussion with their Anglican Friends* (t), London 1889

— *Apostolic Succession; a Hand-Book*, London ^{2}1889

GASPARRI, Pietro — *De la Valeur des Ordinations Anglicanes*, Paris 1895; reprinted with corrections and additions in RAR i, 481–93 and 529–57

GASQUET, Francis Aidan — *Leaves from My Diary, 1894–96*, London 1911

— *England under the Old Religion*, London 1912 (144–93)

— *Breaking with the Past, or Catholic Principles Abandoned at the Reformation*, New York 1914

— *England's Breach with Rome* (t), London 1920

— and MOYES, James — *Risposta all' Opuscolo intitolato 'De Re Anglicana'*, Rome 1896 (printed privately)

GERVAISE, Armand-François — *Lettres d'un théologien à un ecclésiastique de ses amis sur une dissertation touchant la validité des ordinations anglicanes*, Paris 1724

GIBSON, Edmund — *A Preservative Against Popery* ii, London 1848 (109–225)

GIBSON, E. C. S. (ed.) — *The First and Second Prayer Books of Edward VI*, London and New York 1910 (Everyman Edition), numerous reprintings.

[GILLE, Albert] — *A Catholic Plea for Reunion* (by 'Fr Jerome'), London 1934

GODWIN, F. — *De Praesulibus Anglicae Commentarius: omnium Episcoporum necnon et Cardinalium ejusdem gents Nomina, Tempora, Seriem atque actiones maxime memorabiles* (ed. G. Richardson), Cambridge 1743

GONDON, Jules	*Conversion de soixante ministres anglicans ou membres des Universités Anglaises et de cinquante personnes de distinction . . .*, Paris 1846, ²1847
—	*Motifs de conversion de dix ministres anglicans, exposés* par eux-mêmes, *et rétraction du Révérend J. H. Newman; . . .*, Paris 1847
—	*Les récentes conversions en Angleterre*, Paris 1851
GORDON George, R. E.	'The Church in France in its Relation to Christian Unity', *Theology* 13 (1926), 21–30
GORE, Charles	*Roman Catholic Claims*, London ⁹1905
—	*Orders and Unity*, London 1908
GOUDGE, H. L.	*Priest and Prophet* (t), London 1930
GRAFTON, Charles C.	*Works* i, New York 1914 (188–216); vi, New York 1914 (288–354)
GRATIEUX, A.	*L'amitié au service de réunion*, Paris 1952
— and GUITTON, Jean	*Trois Serviteurs de l'Unité chrétienne: le Père Portal, Lord Halifax, le Cardinal Mercier*, Paris 1937
GREGG, J. A. F.	*Anglican Orders and the Prospect of Reunion* (t), London 1929
GREGORY, J. Robinson	*Anglican Orders and Apostolical Succession* (t), London 1893
GRIEVE, H. E. P.	'The Deprived Married Clergy of Essex', *Transactions of the Royal Historical Society*, 4th series, xxii, 141–69
GUITTON, Jean	*Dialogue avec les Précurseurs*, Paris 1962
HACKELBERG-LANDAU, Reichsfreiherr von	*Die anglikanischen Weihen u. ihre neueste Apologie* (t), Graz 1897
HADDAN, A. W.	*Apostolical Succession in the Church of England*, London 1869
HALIFAX, Earl of	*Fullness of Days*, London 1957
HALIFAX, Viscount	*Leo XIII and Anglican Orders*, London 1912
—	*Further Considerations on Behalf of Reunion*, London 1923
HALL, A. C. A.	*The Apostolic Ministry* (t), London 1910
HALL, Herbert E.	*Anglican Orders and the Papal Bull* (t), London 1896
—	*The Shadow of Peter*, London 1914
HALSEY, Joseph	*The Question of Apostolical Succession as raised by Mr Gladstone's letter to the Pope . . .* (t), Anerley 1896
HAMMOND, Joseph	*Apostolical Succession* (t), London 1884

HANSON, Richard, and FULLER, Reginald — *The Church of Rome: A Dissuasive*, London 1948

HARDOUIN, P. — *La Dissertation du R. P. Le Courayer sur la Validité des Ordinations des Anglais refutée*, Paris 1724

— *La Défense de la Dissertation . . . refutée*, Paris 1727

HARDY, Edward R. — *Orthodox Statements on Anglican Orders*, New York and London 1946

HARDY, Thomas J. — *Catholic or Roman Catholic?*, London 1916 (Chapter vi)

HARENT, S. — 'La forme sacramentelle dans les Ordinations Anglicanes', *Études* 68 (1896), 177–204

HARPER, C. H. R. — *Our Clergy, whence and what* (t), London 1900

HARRINGTON, E. C. — *Succession of Bishops in the Church of England Unbroken* (t), London 1852

— *Pope Pius IV and the Book of Common Prayer*, London 1856

HARRISON, D. E. W. — *The Book of Common Prayer*, London 1946

HASTINGS, Adrian — *One and Apostolic*, London 1963

HEAD, F. W. — *Our Catholic Heritage in the Church of England* (t), London 1940

HEADLAM. A. C. — *The Doctrine of the Church and Christian Reunion*, London ²1920

HEMMER, Hippolyte — *M. Portal: Apôtre de l'Union des Églises* (t), Paris 1926 (reprinted from *Le Correspondant*, 19th July 1926).

— *et al.* — *Monsieur Portal, Prêtre de la Mission (1885–1926)*, Paris 1947. (*Note:* '1885' is a misprint for '1855'.)

HENSON, H. Hensley — *Anglicanism*, London 1921

— *Continuity* (t), London 1924

HETTLINGEN, Viktor von — *Raphael Kardinal Merry del Val*, Einsiedeln and Köln 1937

HETTLINGER, R. F. — see FAIRWEATHER, E. R.

HEYLIN, Peter — 'Ecclesia Vindicata, or the Church of England Justified' in *The Historical and Miscellaneous Tracts of the Rev'd and Learned Peter Heylin D.D.*, London 1681 (20 unnumbered pages and 1–43)

HICKEY, E. H. — 'George Leicester, Priest', AER 36 (1907), 381–99

HOARE, Charles — *Continuity*, London 1938

— *Anglican Ordinations in the Reign of Queen Mary* (t), St Leonards-on-Sea 1957

HOARE, Charles	*The Edwardine Ordinal*, Bristol 1957
—	*Chart of Apostolic Succession, with explanatory key* (t), St Leonards-on-Sea 1959
HODGES, G. F.	*The Roman Catholic Doctrine of Intention and Anglican Orders* (t), London 1896
HOLDEN, G. F.	*The Special Bases of the Anglican Claim*, London 1916
HOLGATE, Clifford W.	*The Form and Manner of Making Deacons and of Ordering of Priests according to the order of the Church of England* (t), Salisbury 1894
HOLYWOOD, Christopher ('à Sacrobosco')	*De Investiganda vera ac visibili Christi Ecclesia libellus*, Antwerp 1604
HOOKER, Richard	'Of the Laws of Ecclesiastical Polity', Book v, lxxvi–lxxviii: in Hooker's *Works*, ed. by John Keble (7th rev. ed. R. W. Church and F. Paget), Oxford 1888 (444–83)
HORNYHOLD, Vincent	*Catholic Orders and Anglican Orders* (t), London 1917
HOW, F. D.	*Archbishop Maclagan*, London 1911 (339–53)
HOWARD, J. G. Morton	*Epistola ad Romanos* (t), London 1933
—	*Holy Orders in the Church of England* (t), London 1943
HOWELLS, T. B.	*Roman and Anglican Claims. A Free Church View*, London 1933
HRAUDA, C. F.	'Anglican Ordinations: A Posthumous Thesis', *Reunion* 5–6 (London 1945–46)
HUBY, Joseph	'Lord Halifax', *Études* 230 (1937), 596–610, 756–73
HUGHES, John Jay	'Ministerial Intention in the Administration of the Sacraments', ClRev 51 (1966), 763–6
—	'Two English Cardinals on Anglican Orders', JES 4 (1967), 1–26
—	'The Papal Condemnation of Anglican Orders: 1896', JES 4 (1967), 235–67 (341)
—	'Recent Studies of the Validity of Anglican Orders', *Concilium* (London) 4 (1968), 68–73
—	'The Unresolved Problem of Anglican Orders', *Ampleforth Journal* 73 (1968), 16–24
HUNKIN, J. W.	*Episcopal Ordination and Confirmation in relation to Inter-communion and Reunion*, Cambridge 1929
HUSENBETH, F. C.	*A Reply to the Rev. G. S. Faber's Supplement to his Difficulties on Romanism*, London and Norwich 1829 (328–44)

HUTCHINSON, D. R. — *Orders and Reunion* (t), London 1943

HUTTON, A. W. — *The Anglican Ministry*, London 1879

HUTTON, William H. — *Letters of William Stubbs, Bishop of Oxford*, London 1904 (346–9)

INCE, William — *The Scriptural and Anglican View of the functions of the Christian Ministry* (t), Oxford 1895

INGRAM, A. K. — *The Anglo-Catholic Case* (t), London 1923

JAMES, L. J. — *The Historic Continuity of the Church*, Bangor 1907

JEAFFRESON, Herbert H. — *A letter on the Papal Bull 'Apostolicae curae'* (t), London 1897

JENKINS, Claude — *Bishop Barlow's Consecration and Archbishop Parker's Register: with some new documents*. London 1935 (reprinted from JThS, October 1922)

'JEROME, Fr' — see GILLE, Albert

JEWEL, John — 'Defence of the Apology', London 1567; in Jewel's *Works* (ed. J. Ayre, PS) iii, Cambridge 1848 (320–36)

JOHNSON, Humphrey J. T. — *Anglicanism in Transition*, London 1938

JOHNSON, Vernon C. — *The Church of England always Catholic* (t), London 1925

— *One Lord, One Faith*, London 1929

KELLISON, Matthew — *Survey of the New Religion. Detecting manie grosse absurdities which it implieth*, Douai 1603, [2]1605

— *Kellison's Reply to Sotcliffe's Answer . . ., in which most partes of the Catholike doctrine is explicated, and al is averred and confirmed; and almost al points of the New Faith of England disproved*, Rheims 1608

— *Examen Reformationis novae praesertim Calvinianae, in quo Synagoga et Doctrina Calvini, sicut et reliquorum hujus temporis novatorum tota fere ex suis principiis refutatur*, Douai 1616 (100–83)

KENNEDY, W. M. — see FRERE, W. H.

KIDD, B. J. — *Validity, Name and Thing* (t), London 1937 (reprinted from *Theology*, January 1937)

KING, William	*An Answer to the Considerations which obliged Peter Manby . . . to Embrace, what he calls, the Catholick Religion*, London 1687
KIÖRNINGIO, Olao	*Commentatio Historico-Theologica qua Nobilissima Controversia de Consecrationibvs Episcoporvm Anglorvm recensetvr et diivdicatvr*, Helmstedt 1739
KNOWLES, David	*The Historian and Character and other Essays*, Cambridge 1963
KNOX, Wilfred L.	*Friend, I do Thee no Wrong* (t), London 1919
—	*The Catholic Movement in the Church of England*, London 1923
	see also MILNER-WHITE, Eric
L., H.P., and B., W.	*Are Clergymen of the English Church rightly Ordained?*, London 1872 (by 'H.P.L. and W. B.')
LACEY, T. A.	*L'imposition des mains dans la consecration des Évêques* (t), Paris and London 1896
—	*Dissertationis Apologeticae de Hierarchia Anglicana Supplementum*, Rome 1896 (printed privately)
—	*De Re Anglicana* (t), Rome 1896 (printed privately)
—	*A Roman Diary and other Documents relating to the Papal Inquiry into English Ordinations 1896*, London 1910 (includes several articles reprinted from periodicals)
—	Article 'Intention' in Hastings' *Encyclopaedia of Religion and Ethics* vii
—	*The Continuity of the Church of England*, London 1928
—	see also articles in RAR and DENNY, Edward
LANGFORD-JAMES, R. I.	*The Doctrine of Intention*, London 1924
LAWLOR, H. J.	*The Reformation and the Irish Episcopate* (t), London 1906
LAURAIN, P.	'Le Renouvellement des Ordinations', *Le Canoniste Contemporain* (Paris 1895) 193–212
'LAYMAN, A.'	*Leo XIII versus Paulus IV* (t), London 1898
LEA, J. W.	*The Succession of Spiritual Jurisdiction in every See of the Catholic Church in England at the Epochs of the Reformation and Revolution exhibited in a series of Tables*, London n.d.
LEBOURLIER, Jean	'A propos des ordinations anglicanes', *Mélanges de science religieuse* (Lille) 12 (1955), 201–8

LE COURAYER, Pierre François — *Dissertation sur la Validité des Ordinations des Anglois et sur la succession des évêques de l'église anglicane, avec les preuves justificatives des faits avancés*, Brussels 1723; Eng. trans. D. Williams 1728 and 1844

— *Défense de la Dissertation*, Brussels 1726

— *Supplément aux deux Ouvrages faits pour la Défense de la Validité des Ordinations Anglicanes*, Amsterdam 1732

LEE, Alfred T. — *The Irish Episcopal Succession*, London 1867

LEE, Frederick George — *The Question of Anglican Orders Discussed* (t), [London 1873] (printed privately)

— *The Validity of the Holy Orders of the Church of England*, London 1869

LEE, William — *Some Strictures on Dr Brady's Pamphlet in which he denied the descent of the hierarchy of the present Church of Ireland from the ancient Irish Church* (t), Dublin 1866

LEHMKUHL, Aug. — 'Intentio u. Forma bei den Sakramenten', *Theologisch-praktische Monats-Schrift*, Passau 1895, 599–604

— 'Die anglikanische Hierarchie in anglikanischem und in katholischem Licht', *Stimmen aus Maria Laach* 49 (1895)

LE NEVE, J. — *Fasti Ecclesiae Anglicanae*, London 1715; Oxford ^{2}1854 (3 vols.); being reissued by the Athlone Press, 2 Gower St, London W.C. 1, in a series of volumes beginning 1962

LEO XIII, Pope — 'Apostolicae curae', ASS 29 (1896–97)

LE QUIEN, Michel — *La Nullité des Ordinations Anglicanes*, 2 vols., Paris 1725

— *La Nullité des Ordinations Anglicanes demontrée de nouveau contre la Défense du R. P. Courayer*, Paris 1730

LESLIE, Shane — *Cardinal Gasquet, A Memoir*, London 1953

anon. — *Lettre Latine anonyme sur les Ordinations Angloises*, Paris 1668

LEWGAR, John — *Erastus Junior: a solid Demonstration by Principles, Forms of Ordination, Common Laws, Acts of Parliament, that no Bishop, Minister, nor Presbyter, hath any Authority to preach etc., from Christ, but from the Parliament*, London 1659–60

— *Erastus Senior, scholastically demonstrating this*

	Conclusion, That (admitting their Lambeth Records for true) those called Bishops here in England are no Bishops either in order or jurisdiction, or so much as legal, [London?] 1662, London ²1844 and ³1850; Sydney 1848, New York 1850 with erroneous attribution to Peter TALBOT (q.v.)
LEWIN, G. H. R.	*Continuity of the English Church*, London 1886
LEWIS, George F.	*The Papacy and Anglican Orders*, London 1957
—	*Towards Anglican-Roman Catholic Unity* (t), Toronto 1962
LINGARD, John	*The History of England* 8 vols., London 1818–30 (cf. esp. v [1823], 155f and 630f)
—	'Three Letters on Protestant Ordinations', *The Catholic Magazine and Review* 5 (Birmingham 1834), 499–503, 704–15, 774–82
LINDSAY, John	*A Vindication of the Church of England and of the Lawful Ministry thereof . . . of the Succession, Election, Confirmation, and Consecration of Bishops, etc.*, London 1728, ²1734, ³1778; (translation of F. MASON, *Vindicatio Ecclesiae Anglicanae* [q.v.] with introduction by Lindsay and two sermons by Mason)
LITTLE, W. J. Knox	*Sacerdotalism if Rightly Understood, the Teaching of the Church of England*, London 1894
LITTLEDALE, R. F.	*Anglican Orders: a Summary of Historical Evidence*, London 1871
—	*Words for truth: replies to Roman cavils*, London 1888
LIVIUS, T.	'Anglican Orders', IER 16 (1895), 137–45
LOCKE, J. A.	'Anglican Answers to the Pope's Bull', *Catholic World*, February 1897
LOCKHART, J. G.	*Charles Lindley, Viscount Halifax*, 2 vols., London 1935–36
LOISY, Alfred	*Mémoires pour servir à l'histoire religeuse de notre temps* i, Paris 1930
LOWNDES, Arthur	*Vindication of Anglican Orders* 2 vols., New York 1897
MCCAVE, James, and BREEN, J. D.	*'Continuity' or Collapse?*, London ²1891 (Lecture iv)
MCCLELLAN, William H.	'A Convert's Letter to an Anglican Friend', AER 39 (1908), 148–69

MacColl, Malcolm — *The Reformation Settlement*, London 1899 (460–519)

MacDevitt, J. — *Are Anglican Orders Valid?* (t), Dublin 1896

Macdonald, T. M. — *Are the clergy absolving priests?* (t), Manchester 1889

McCormack, Arthur — *Cardinal Vaughan*, London 1966

Machyn, Henry — *The Diary of Henry Machyn, Citizen and Merchant-Taylor of London, from A.D. 1550 to A.D. 1563* (ed. J. G. Nichols, Camden Society), London 1848

Mackenzie, Kenneth D. — *The Case for Episcopacy*, London 1929

Macmillan, Arthur T. — *Fernand Portal (1855–1926), Apostle of Unity*, London 1961

Manby, Peter — *The Considerations which obliged Peter Manby, Dean of Derry, to embrace the Catholique Religion* (t), Dublin and London 1687

Marchal, L. — Article 'Ordinations Anglicanes' in DTC xi, Paris 1931

Marot, Hillaire — 'Les ordinations anglicanes', *Lumière et Vie* 12, No. 64 (August–October 1963), 87–116

Marshall, A. F. — 'The Moral Aspects of the Question of Anglican Orders', *American Catholic Quarterly Review*, January 1896

Mascall, Eric L. — *Priesthood and South India* (t), London 1943

— *The Convocations and South India* (t), London 1955

— *Corpus Christi*, London ²1965

Mason, A. J. — *The Church of England and Episcopacy*, Cambridge 1914

Mason, Francis — *Of the Consecration of Bishops in the Church of England*, London 1613; revised edition:

— *Vindiciae Ecclesiae Anglicanae*, London 1625; Eng. trans. Lindsay, John (q.v.)

Mathew, A. H. — *Are Anglican Orders Valid?*, London 1910

Maturin, Basil W. — *The Price of Unity*, London 1917 (47–54)

Messenger, E. C. — *Epistle from the Romans* (t), London 1933

— *The Lutheran Origin of the Anglican Ordinal*, London 1934

— *Bishop Bonner and Anglican Orders* (t), London 1936

— *The Reformation, the Mass and the Priesthood* 2 vols, London 1936–37

— 'The Condemnation of Anglican Orders; New Light from Unpublished Documents', *The Tablet* 137 (1937), 117f, 151–4, 186–9

MESSENGER, E. C.	*Rome and Reunion; a Collection of Papal Pronouncements*, London 1934
MIDDLETON, Edmund S.	*Unity and Rome*, New York 1922
MILBOURNE, Luke	*A Short Defence of the Orders of the Church of England, against some scattered objections of Mr Webster of Linne. By a Presbyter of the Diocese of Norwich*, London 1688
—	*A Legacy to the Church of England, vindicating her Orders from the Objections of Papists and Dissenters* 2 vols., London 1722
MILNER, John	*The End of Religious Controversy* ii, London 1818 (169–85)
—	*Letters to a Prebendary*, Derby 1843
MILNER-WHITE, Eric and KNOX, W. L.	*One God and Father of All; a Reply to Father Vernon*, London 1929
MOBERLY, R. C.	*Ministerial Priesthood*, London 1897, ²1905
MOORE, Aubrey L.	*Lectures and Papers on the History of the Reformation in England and on the Continent*, London 1890 (191–200, 222ff, 245–52)
MORAN, Patrick F.	*The Episcopal Succession in Ireland during the Reign of Elizabeth* (t), Dublin 1866 (reprinted from IER)
MORETON, H.-A.	*La Réforme Anglicane au XVIe Siècle*, Paris 1930
MORSE, Herbert G.	*Apostolical Succession. A Plain Treatise on Holy Orders and Jurisdiction in the Church of England*, London 1887
MORTIMER, C. G.	*Anglican Orders* (t), London 1913
— and BARBER, S. C.	*The English Bishops and the Reformation 1530–1560: with a Table of Descent*, London 1936
MOSS, C. B.	*The Old Catholic Movement, its Origins and History*, London 1948
MOYES, James	Thirty-one articles in *The Tablet*, February–December 1895; nineteen articles in *The Tablet* February–July 1897
—	*Aspects of Anglicanism; or, Some comments on certain events in the 'nineties*, London 1906 see also GASQUET, F. A.
MOYES, James, GASQUET, F. A., and FLEMING, David	*Ordines Anglicani: Expositio Historica et Theologica, Cura et Studio Commissionis ab Em.o et Rev.o D. D. Herberto Cardinali Vaughan ad hoc institutae*, London 1896 (printed privately)
—	*Brevis Conspectus Ritualium Ordinationum in Oriente et Occidente adhibitarum quoad Formam*

consecratoriam cum manuum impositione conjunctam, Rome 5th May 1896 (privately printed by Befani).

MOYES, James, GASQUET, F. A., and FLEMING, David — *Novae quaedam Animadversiones in Ordinationes Anglicanorum*, Rome 1896 (privately printed by Henricus Filiziani)

— *Responsio ad votum Rev.mi P. de Augustinis S.J.*, Rome 3rd April 1896 (printed privately)

— *Documenta ad legationem Cardinalis Poli spectantia*, Rome 5th May 1896 (privately printed)

NEWMAN, John Henry — *Letters and Diaries* (ed. C. S. Dessain) xi, London 1961, 148 and 151; xii, London 1962, 15

— Letter in the *Month*, September 1868, 269ff

— *Tracts for the Times* No. 1, 'Thoughts on the Ministerial Commission . . .', London 1833 (see also anon., *Tracts for the Times*)

NORRIS, Sylvester — *The Guide of Faith: or, A Third Part of the Antidote against the Pestiferous writings of all English Sectaries . . ., wherein the Truth, and perpetual Visible Succession, of the Catholique Roman Church, is clearly Demonstrated by S.N., Doctour of Divinity*, n.p. 1621

OLDKNOW, J. — *The Validity of the Holy Orders in the Church of England briefly discussed and proved*, London 1857

OLDROYD, A. E. — *Continuity of the English Church* (t), London 1892

O'ROURKE, William J. — *The Doctrine of Apostolic Succession according to Anglican Theologians*, Paris 1966 (unpublished doctoral thesis: Institut Catholique)

OVERTON, J. H. — *Anglican Orders. A Sermon preached in Lincoln Cathedral* (t), Lincoln, 1879

OXENHAM, F. Nutcombe — *An Eirenicon of the Eighteenth Century; Proposal for Catholic Communion by a Minister of the Church of England*, London 1879 (Chapter xvii). (This is a later edition of the work by Joshua BASSET cited above, q.v.)

— *Some Considerations suggested by the Letter of Leo XIII on Anglican Orders* (t), London 1896

[—?] Two letters in the *Union Review* 6 (London 1868), 549–60

PALMER, William — *Apostolical Jurisdiction and Succession of the English Episcopacy vindicated against the Objections of Dr Wiseman in the Dublin Review*, London 1840

— *A Treatise on the Church of Christ* 2 vols., London ³1842 (cf. esp. ii, 338–59)

PARKER, Matthew — *De Antiquitate Britannicae Ecclesiae et Priuilegiis Ecclesiae Cantuariensis, cum Archiepiscopis eiusdem 70*, privately printed at Lambeth by John Day, 1572

— *Correspondence of Matthew Parker, Archbishop of Canterbury* (ed. T. T. Perowne, PS), Cambridge 1853

see also FRERE, W. H.

PALMIERE, F. A. — 'The Validity of Anglican Ordinations in modern Russian Theology', *Catholic Quarterly Review* (USA), April 1916

PAPADOPOULOS, Chrysostom — *The Validity of Anglican Orders* (trans. by J. A. Douglas), London 1930

PARSONS, Daniel — *Are Clergymen of the Church of England rightly ordained?*, London 1881

PARSONS, Robert — *A brief discovrs contayning certayne reasons why Catholiques refuse to goe to Church*, Douai, John Lyon, [London] 1580 (fol. 41)

— *A Discussion of the Answer of M. William Barlow, Doctor of Diuinity, to the book intituled, The Judgment of a Catholic Englishman*, St Omers 1612

PECK, A. L. — *Anglicanism and Episcopacy, a Re-Examination of Evidence . . . together with an Essay on Validity*, London and New York 1958

PELLETIER, Claude de — *Denonciation aux Evêques de France, d'un livre intulé: 'Défense de la Dissertation sur la validité des Ordinations des Anglois' . . .*, Paris 1727

PERCEVAL, A. P. — *An Apology for the Doctrine of Apostolical Succession with an Appendix on the English Orders*, London 1839, ²1841

PLUMMER, A. — *Continuity of the English Church* (t), Kendal 1887

anon. — *Pastoral Epistle of His Holiness the Pope to some Members of the University of Oxford* (t), London ²1836

PILKINGTON, James — *The burnynge of Paules church in London, etc.*, London 1563: in Pilkington's *Works* (ed. J. Scholefield, PS), Cambridge 1842 (487–616)

PIXELL, C. H. V. — *Anglican Orders and Jurisdiction* (t), London 1891

POL, W. H. van de — *Anglicanism in Ecumenical Perspective*, Pittsburgh 1965

POLLARD, G. F. — *Ecclesia Anglicana*, London 1930 (329–42)

POPE, George — *The Old Paths ...; or, the Continuity of the Church of England* (t), London 1885

PORTAL, Fernand — *Les Ordinations Anglicanes* ('by F. Dalbus'), Arras 1894; Paris and Lyon ²1894

— *Notice sur Lord Halifax* (t), Paris 1895

PORTER, G. — 'Canon Estcourt on Anglican Ordinations', *Month* 18 (1873), 456–70

POWERS, C. J. — 'Are Anglican Orders Valid?', *Catholic World*, September 1896

PRECLIN, E. — *L'union des Églises gallicane et anglicane: une Tentative au Temps de Luois XV*, Paris 1928

PRIDEAUX, Humphrey — *The Validity of the Orders of the Church of England*, London 1688

PULLER, F. W. — *Les Ordinations Anglicanes et le Sacrifice de la Messe*, London and Paris 1896 (originally published in RAR No. 9, 1895)

— *The Bull 'Apostolicae curae' and the Edwardine Ordinal* (t), London 1896

— *Essays and Letters on Orders and Jurisdiction*, London 1925

PUSEY, E. B. — *An Earnest Remonstrance to the Author of the 'Pope's Pastoral Letter to Certain Members of the University of Oxford'*, London 1836

RADFORD, Daniel — *The Providential Character of the recent Papal Bull* (t), London 1897

RAGEY, Père — *La Crise Religieuse en Angleterre*, Paris 1896

— *L'Anglo-Catholicisme*, Paris 1897; with a Preface by Cardinal Vaughan

— 'Le Concile Anglican de Lambeth', *Le Correspondant* (Paris 1897), 208–21, 520–39

RAINY, R. — 'The Pope and the Archbishops', *Contemporary Review*, May 1897

RAMSEY, Arthur Michael — *The Gospel and the Catholic Church*, London ²1956 (Chapters vi, xii, xiv)

RAWLINSON, A. E. J. — *Problems of Reunion*, London 1950 (96–8)

RAYNAL, Paul W. — *Letter on the Validity of Anglican Orders* (t), London 1870

— *The Ordinal of Edward VI*, London 1871

anon. *Recent Secessions and Corporate Reunion, A Letter to an Anglican Friend* (t), London 1868

REINKENS, J. H. and FRIEDRICH, Johann 'Von der Gültigkeit der anglikanischen Weihen', *Revue Internationale de Théologie* (Berne), January–March 1895

RÉNÉ, Theodoric de S. *Justification de l'Église romaine . . . ou Réponse à la Dissertation*, 2 vols., Paris 1728

Report of the Archbishops' Commission on Doctrine in the Church of England, London 1938

Report of the Joint Doctrinal Commission appointed by the Oecumenical Patriarch and the Archbishop of Canterbury for Consultation on the Points of Agreement and the Differences between the Anglican and Eastern Orthodox Churches, London 1932

RENWART, L. 'Ordinations anglicanes et intention du ministre', NRTh 89 (1957), 1027–53

RICHARDSON, Austin *What are the Catholic Claims?*, London 1889 (119–32)

RICHEY, T. *Leo XIII and Anglican Orders: the Proper Gift of a Christian Ministry*, New York 1897

RICKABY, Joseph *What Cranmer meant to do and did* (t), London 1922, [2]1945

RIVINGTON, Luke *Dependence, or the insecurity of the Anglican position*, London 1889

— *Tekel: or the Anglican Archbishops arraigned at the Bar of Logic and Convicted of 75 Flaws* (t), London 1897

— 'Since the condemnation of Anglican Orders', *Catholic World*, December 1897

— 'A Vindication of the Bull, *Apostolicae curae*', *Month* 91 (1898), 113–20

ROBERTS, Victor *In Terra Aliena* (t), n.p. 1949, printed privately

ROBINSON, J. Armitage *The Apostolic Succession* (t), London 1920
Congé d'Élire (t), London 1921

ROE, Henry *The Continuity of the Church of England and the Papal Encyclical 'Apostolicae curae'* (t), Quebec 1897

anon. *The Roman Catholic and Anglican Churches proved to be nearer to each other than most men imagine*, n.p. 1842

ROPE, H. E. G. *Matthew Parker's Witness against Continuity* (t), London 1931

ROSS, K. M. *Why I am not a Roman Catholic*, London 1953

RULE, Martin *Apostolical Succession Not a Doctrine of the Church of England; an Historical Essay*, London 1870

RUSSELL, J. F. — *Anglican Orders Valid*, London 1846

RUST, Paul R. — *Anglican Orders Invalid? Why?* (t), St Paul, Minn., 1961

RYDER, H. D. — *Critique of Mr Ffoulkes' Letter* (t), London 1869

ST JOHN, Henry — 'The Anglo-Catholic Problem', *Blackfriars* 10 (1929), 1176–83

SAMPSON, Gerard — *Catholic Truth and Unity; the Confessions of a Non-Convert*, London 1914

SANCTA CLARA — see DAVENPORT, Christopher

SANDAY, W. — *The Conception of Priesthood in the Early Church and in the Church of England*, London ²1899

— (ed.) — *Different Conceptions of Priesthood and Sacrifice*, London 1900

SANDERS, Nicholas — *De origine ac progressu schismatis Anglicani*, Ingolstadt 1586 (numerous editions in various places); Eng. trans. David Lewis, London 1877

SANDFORD, C. W. — *Papal Claims and Anglican Orders* (t), London 1897

SANDFORD, E. G. (ed.) — *Memoirs of Archbishop Temple by Seven Friends* ii, London 1906 (206ff, 388–97)

SCHAIK, G. C. van — *De la validité des Ordinations anglicanes. Lettre à l'épiscopat vieux-catholique de Hollande*, Rotterdam 1893

SCHANZ, D. — 'Form und Intention bei den Sakramenten', *Theologische Quartalschrift*, 1899

SCOTT, S. H. — *General Councils and Anglican Claims in the light of the Council of Ephesus* (t), London 1927

SEABURY, W. J. — *Lectures on Haddan's Apostolical Succession*, New York 1893

[SEGNA, Cardinal] — 'Les ordinations anglicanes à propos d'une brochure', RAR, February 1896 (anonymous)

— — *Breves Animadversiones in Responsionem Archiepiscoporum Anglicanorum ad Litteras Apostolicas Leonis PP.XIII Apostolicae curae*, Rome 1897

SERJEANT, John — *Transactions Relating to the English Secular Clergy*, London 1706

SERLE, S. E. B. — *The Validity of Anglican Ordinations* (t), London 1907

SEVIÈRE, J. de la — 'La controverse sur la valeur des ordinations anglicanes, d'après des publications récentes', *Études* 132 (1912), 658–66

SHELFORD, Robert — *A Vindication of Five Pious and Learned Discourses, by Robert Shelford of Ringsfield in*

Suffolk, Priest, with an appendix concerning Master Doctor Goffe, Cambridge 1662

SHIRLEY, F. J. — *Elizabeth's First Archbishop*, London 1948

SIMMONS, A. H. — *To all that be in Rome* (t), Aldershot, Hants., 1965

SIMPSON, W. J. S. — *The Ministry and the Eucharist*, London 1942

SINCLAIR, W. M. — *Points at issue between the Church of England and the Church of Rome*, London 1896

SMITH, G. D. — *Anglican Orders—Still No Case* (t), London 1946

— 'The Church and her Sacraments', ClRev 35 (1950), 217–31

SMITH, H. — *The Ordination of the Ministers of the Established Church examined upon Protestant principles and Protestant testimonies, and found to be merely a Commission from the Crown without any right or title to Apostolical succession* (t), London 1841

SMITH, Sydney F. — *The Alleged Antiquity of Anglicanism*, London 1888

— 'M. Dalbus on Anglican Orders', *Month* 82 (1894), 184–204, 380–401, 543–70. Later reprinted as:

— *Reasons for Rejecting Anglican Orders* (t), London 1895

— *The Doctrine of Intention* (t), London 1895 (= *Month* 82 [1894], 411–17)

— 'The Condemnation of Anglican Orders', *Month* 88 (1896), 153–6, 305–29

— *Le Mouvement de Réunion en Angleterre* (t), Paris 1896 (= *Études* 69 [1896], 5–33)

— 'The Anglican Bishops and the "Vindication" ', *Month* 91 (1898), 337–41

— 'Anglican Criticisms of the "Vindication" ', *Month* 91 (1898), 227–37

— *A Last Word on Anglican Ordinations*, New York 1897 (annotated translation of articles by S. M. BRANDI [q.v.]).

— Article 'Anglican Orders' in *Catholic Encyclopaedia* i, 1907

— Article 'Ordinations Anglicanes' in DAFC iii

— 'Leo XIII and Anglican Orders', *Month* 119 (1912), 337–54

— (ed.) *Historical Papers* iii, London 1898 ('Rome's Witness against Anglican Orders', 49–92)

SMITH, Sydney F. (ed.) *Some Aspects of the Anglican Position*, London 1914

SMITH, John Bainbridge *English Orders: Whence Obtained* (t), London 1893

— *Ordinals Past and Present, and their witness to the validity of English Orders*, London 1898

SLESSER, Henry H. *The Anglican Dilemma*, London 1952

SNEAD-COX, J. G. *Life of Cardinal Vaughan* 2 vols., London 1910

SOKOLOFF, V. *Ierarkhija Anglicanskoi Episkopaljnoi Tzverki*, Moscow 1897 (in Russian)

— *An Enquiry into the Hierarchy of the Anglican Episcopal Church* (trans. of one chapter by W. J. Birbeck), London 1897

SPARROW-SIMPSON, W. J. *The Ministry and the Eucharist*, London and New York 1942

SPOTTISWOODE, George A. *The Holy Orders of the Church of England* (t), London 1898

STALEY, Vernon *Are our Clergy rightly ordained?* (t), Oxford 1897

STAPLETON, Thomas *Returne of vntruthes vpon M. Iewels Replie*, Antwerp 1566

— *A Fortresse of the Faith first planted amonge vs Englishmen, and continued hitherto in the vniuersall Church of Christ. The faith of which time Protestants call, Papistry*, Antwerp 1565

— *A Counterblast to M. Hornes vayne blaste against M. Fekenham*, Louvain 1567

— *Triplicatio inchoata adversus Whitakeri duplicationem*, Antwerp 1596 (240f)

— *Principiorum Fidei doctrinalium Relectio* . . . Antwerp 1596 (250ff)

STEPHENSON, Anthony A. *Anglican Orders*, London 1955 (reprinted from the *Month*, July–September 1955). Withdrawn by the author in June 1960: cf. *The Old Palace* (Oxford), No. 22 (1961), 31

STOKES, G. T. *The Pope on Anglican Orders; two introductory Lectures on the religious relations between Rome and England* (t), Dublin 1896

STONE, Darwell *Episcopacy and Valid Orders in the Primitive Church* (t), London 1910 (Pusey House Occasional Paper No. 6)

— *Episcopacy and Valid Orders in the Primitive Church* (t), London 1910, ^{2}1926

Stone, Darwell *To Kyros tōn anglikanikōn Cheirotoniōn*, Athens 1939 (in Greek)

Stopford, Edward A. *The Unity of the Anglican Church, and the Succession of Irish Bishops*, Dublin 1867

Story, Robert Herbert *The Pope and Anglican Orders* (t), Edinburgh 1896

Stubbs, William *The Apostolical Succession in the Church of England; a Letter to a Russian Friend* (t), London 1866

— *A Charge . . . at his second Visitation*, Oxford 1893

— *A Charge . . . at his third Visitation*, Oxford 1896.

— *Registrum Sacrum Anglicanum*, Oxford 1858, ^{2}1897

Sutcliff, Matthew *The Examination and confutation of a certaine scurrilous treatise entituled, The Survey of the new Religion, published by M. Kellison, in disgrace of true religion professed in the Church of England*, London 1606

Swete, Henry B. *A Letter on the Bull 'Apostolicae curae'* (t), Cambridge 1896

Sykes, Norman *William Wake* i, Cambridge 1957 (315–66)

— *Old Priest and New Presbyter*, Cambridge 1957

T., H. *A manuel of Controversies clearly demonstrating the truth of Catholique Religion* (by 'H.T.'), Douai 1671 (30–6)

Talbot, M. d'Arcy *Third Letter to Rev. Wm. Palmer on auricular confession . . . also the nullity of the Church of England's ordinations* (t), London 1841

Talbot, Peter *A Treatise on the nature of Catholick Faith and Heresie* (by 'N.N.'), Rouen 1657 (7–28)

— *The Nullity of the Protestant Church of England and its Clergy*, Brussels 1658

— *The Nullity of the Prelatic Clergy, etc.* (by 'N.N'), Antwerp 1659

— *Protestant Bishops proved to be no real Bishops . . . in a little work entitled 'Erastus Senior' first printed in 1662 . . .*, London 1850

Taylor, T. F. *A Profest Papist, Bishop John Gordon*, London 1958

Thompson, Beatrice M. Hamilton *The Consecration of Archbishop Parker*, London 1934

Thureau-Dangin, Paul *Le Cardinal Vaughan*, Paris 1911

TIERNEY, M. A. — see DODD, Charles

TILLARD, Jean-Marie — 'Sacramental Questions: The Intentions of Minister and Recipient', *Concilium* 4 (1968), 61–7

TORRY, John — *The Papal Hierarchy and the Scottish Bishops* (t), Edinburgh 1878

TOURNEBIZE, F. — 'L'Église d'Angleterre a-t-elle réellement le Sacerdoce?', *Études* 64 (1895), 400–23, 574–605

— 'Le Mouvement Religieux en Angleterre', *Études* 65 (1895), 513–28

— 'Le Mouvement vers l'Union en Angleterre', *Études* 67 (1896), 159–70

— *Ordres Anglicans et Ministères des Églises Réformées* (t), Paris 1896 (= *Études* 69 (1896), 651–76)

— 'La réponse des Archevêques Anglicans à la lettre du Léon XIII sur les ordinations anglicanes', *Études* 72 (1897), 304–18, 487–510

TOWNSEND, G. F. — *The Christian Ministry. A Christian Priesthood: Its Office, Authority, and Duties* (t), London 1838

'*Tracts for the Times*' — No. 15: 'On the Apostolical Succession in the Church of England', London 1833

No. 74: 'Catena Patrum: Testimony of Writers in the Later English Church to the Doctrine of Apostolical Succession', London 1836

No. 81: 'Catena Patrum No IV: Testimony of Writers of the Later English Church to the Doctrine of Eucharistic Sacrifice with an historical account of the changes made in the Liturgy as to the expression of that doctrine', London 1837

(see also NEWMAN, J. H.)

VANE, Thomas — *A Lost Sheep returned home; or the Motives of the Conversion to the Catholike Faith of Thomas Vane*, Paris ²1648, ⁴1649 (245f, 252)

VAUGHAN, Herbert — *The Reunion of Christendom*, London 1894, ²1896

— *Leo XIII and the Reunion of Christendom* (t), London 1896

— *The Anglican Archbishops and the Pope* (t), London 1897

— *Vindication of the Bull 'Apostolicae curae'*, London 1898

see also RAGEY, Père

VAUGHAN, Roger B. — *Vindication of the Bull 'Apostolicae curae'; A Letter on Anglican Orders*, London 1898

VERDIN, G. — 'Les ordinations anglicanes au tribunal de l'ancienne Église catholique', *Internationale kirchliche Zeitschrift* (Bern) 1929, 209–21

'VERITAS' — *The Mass and the Church of England* (t), Exeter 1925

'VERNON, Fr' — see JOHNSON, Vernon C.

VIVANT, François — *La vraie manière de contribuer à la Réunion de l'Église Anglicane à l'Église Catholique*, Paris 1728

W., D. — *The Case of Mr. Doctor Stephen Goffe, Priest and Chaplaine to His Late Majesty, as set fforth and Determined at the Sorbonne, etc.*, London 1652

WADSWORTH, James — *Copies of Certain Letters which have Passed between Spain and England in the Matter of Religion, etc., between Master James Wadesworth, a late Pensioner of the Holy Inquisition at Sivill, and W. Bedell, a Minister of the Gospel in Suffolke*, London 1624

WALCOTT, M. E. C. — *The English Ordinal, its History, Validity, and Catholicity*, London 1851

WALKER, E. T. M. — *The Popes and Ordination* (t), London 1906

WALSH, Peter — *The History and Vindication of the Loyal Formulary, or Irish Remonstrance, so graciously received by his Majesty, anno 1661, etc.*, London 1674 (Preface 'To the Reader')

— *Controversial Letters Concerning the Pope's Authority over the Whole Earth*, London 1674 ('Preface to Four Letters')

WARD, Maisie — *The Wilfrid Wards and the Transition*, London 1934 (277–99)

— *Fr. Maturin: A Memoir*, London 1920 (154ff, 172–80)

WARD, Thomas — *Some Queries to the Protestants concerning the English Reformation* (by 'T. W., Gent.'), London 1687

— *The Controversye of ordination truely stated*, London 1719

WARD, Wilfrid — *The Life and Times of Cardinal Wiseman*, 2 vols., London 1897 (i, 300; ii, 481)

— 'Cardinal Vaughan, a Personal Appreciation', *Morning Post* (London), 16th August 1910

[WARD, William George]	*Strictures on Mr Ffoulkes' Letter to Archbishop Manning by the Editor of the 'Dublin Review'* (t), London 1869
WARE, James	*De Praesulibus Hiberniae*, Dublin 1665; ed. by Walter Harris, *The Whole Works of Sir James Ware*, 3 vols., Dublin 1739–64
WATSON, E. W.	*Life of Bishop John Wordsworth*, London 1915
WENGER, A.	'L'Église Orthodoxe et les Ordinations Anglicanes', NRTh 76 (1954), 44–55
WHARTON, H.	*Anglia Sacra*, London 1691
WHITEBROOK, J. C.	*The Consecration of Matthew Parker*, London 1945
WHITFELD, William	*A Defence of the Ordinations and Ministry of the Church of England*, London 1688
WHITHAM, A. R.	*Holy Orders*, London 1903 (160–3)
WHITNEY, J. P.	*The Episcopate and the Reformation: our Outlook*, London and Milwaukee 1917
WHITTON, T.	*The Necessity for Catholic Reunion*, London 1933
WILLIAMS, Daniel	*The Succession of Protestant Bishops Asserted*, London 1721
WILLIAMS, John	*Letters on Anglican Orders and other Matters*, London 1859, [2]1864
WILLIAMSON, Hugh Ross	'A Convert Explains', *Month*, November 1955
WILLIS, F. W.	*Anglican Orders* (t), Liverpool 1896
[WILSHERE, C. W.]	*Leo XIII an Paulus IV: auctore laico* (by 'Fidelis') (t), London and Paris 1900
WISEMAN, Nicholas	*The Anglican Claim of Apostolical Succession* (t), London 1894 (reprinted from the *Dublin Review*, August 1839)
WOODLOCK, Frank	*Constantinople, Canterbury and Rome*, London 1923 (Lecture iv)
WOODHOUSE, H. F.	*The Doctrine of the Church in Anglican Theology 1547–1603*, London 1954 (73–123)
WORDSWORTH, Christopher	*Theophilus Anglicanus; or Manual of Instruction on the Church and the Anglican Branch of It*, London 1843, [2]1895
WORDSWORTH, John	*De Successione Episcoporum in Ecclesia Anglicana* (t), London 1890 (Eng. trans. 1892)
—	*De Validitate Ordinum Anglicanorum: Responsio ad Batavos* (t), London 1894
—	*Trois lettres sur la position de l'Église Anglicane* (t), Salisbury and London 1894
—	*The Ministry of Grace*, London 1901

WORDSWORTH, John	*Ordination Problems*, London 1909
—	*Bishop Serapion's Prayer Book*, London [2]1923 (51ff, 72ff)
WYBORNE, Percivall	*Check of M. Howlet's untimely Skreeching*, London 1581 (fol. 160–3)
Y., D.	*Legenda Lignea: with An Answer to Mr Birchley's Moderator (pleading for a toleration of Popery): And a Character of some Hopeful Saints Revolted to the Church of Rome*, London 1653; (the 'Epistle to the Reader' is signed 'D.Y.')

Part III—General or miscellaneous works

BURNET, Gilbert	*The History of the Reformation of the Church of England* (ed. Nicholas Pocock) 7 vols., Oxford 1865
DICKENS, A. C.	*The Marian Reaction in the Diocese of York: Part I, The Clergy*, London and York 1957
—	*The English Reformation*, London 1964
HUGHES, Philip	*The Reformation in England* 3 vols., London 1950–54
—	*Rome and the Counter-Reformation in England*, London 1942
POLE, Reginald	*Reformatio Angliae ex Decretis Reginaldi Poli Cardinalis*, Rome 1562; Eng. trans. by RAIKES, Henry (q.v.)
QUIRINI, A. M. (ed.)	*Epistolarum Reginaldi Poli S.R.E. Cardinalis et aliorum ad ipsum* 5 vols., Brescia 1744–57
RAIKES, Henry	*The Reform of England by the Decrees of Cardinal Pole*, Chester 1839

INDEX OF NAMES

ABBOT, George, Archbishop of Canterbury, 19–20
Abercrombie, Nigel, 68
Act of Supremacy (1559), 10
Act of Uniformity (1559), 10, 13, 14
Ad Anglos, papal letter, 81–3, 85–6, 90–1, 146, 179
Angeli, Mgr Rinaldo, 101, 103, 105, 225
Apostolicae Curae, papal Bull (1896), 1–4, 25–6, 28, 35, 59, 89–90, 104, 127, 166, 167, **192–9**, 214, 215, 235, 237, 245–7, 259–62, 269–71, 276, 278, 280, 283–7
Aquinas, St Thomas, 1, 127
Arnauld, consultor in papal investigation of AO, 1684, 279
Arundel of Wardour, Lord, 228
St Augustine
and the Donatists, 273, 276

BALE, John, Bishop of Ossory, 14, 256
Barlow, William, Bishop of Chichester, 14–17
controversy over his consecration, 21–4, 26, 35, 46, 134, 145, 156, 159, 161, 194–5, 301
Barnes, Arthur S., 23, 25–6
Barry, Revd William Francis, 235
Bath and Wells, Bishop of, (1559), 13
Beauchamp, Margaret, 251
Bell, G. K. A., Bishop of Chichester, 3, 200
Bellarmine, St Robert, 219
Benedict XV, pope, 110, 224
Benson, Edward White, Archbishop of Canterbury, 43, 46, 52–7, 61–3, 65, 79–80, 91, 176, 179, 180, 184, 190, 200–3, 243, 298
Benson, Robert Hugh, 231
Bird, John, Bishop of Chester, 143
Bishop, Edmund, 72–3, 81–2, 85–7, 90, 94, 107–10, 114, 146, 148, 149, 155–6, 186, 193, 204, 217–20, 222, 255, 260, *see also* Gasquet, Dom Francis Aidan
'Black Rubric' of 1552 Prayer Book, 11, 130, 141
Bolt, Dr W. J., 3
Bonner, Edmund, Bishop of London, 16, 19, 24, 131, 143–4, **255–8**
Borromeo, St Charles, 50
Bossuet, Jacques-Benigne, 281
Botton, Dom Anselm, 228
Boudinhon, Professor A., 263
Bourne, Francis, cardinal, Archbishop of Westminster, 210, 234
Bramhall, John, 96
Brandi, Fr S. M., 278–9, 282
Brechin, Bishop of, (1896), 78
Breen, J. D., 300
Brown, Mgr H. Barton, 76
Brownlow, William Robert, Bishop of Clifton, 96, 236–7
Bucer, Martin, 130
Butler, Dom Cuthbert, 146

CAMM, Dom Bede, 109
Capovilla, Mgr Loris, 209
Casanata, Cardinal, 280
Catholic Truth Society, the, 62, 95
Cave, Mr, friend of Gasquet, 195

Cecil, William, Lord Burghley, 14
Champney, Anthony, 21
Charles II, King of England, 281
Clark, Francis, 121, 138, 142, 144, 215, 247, 249–50, 285–91, 308
Clement XI, pope, 165, 282–3
Council of Trent, 272, 274, 277
Coverdale, Miles, Bishop of Exeter, (1551–53), 14–17, 265
Cranmer, Thomas, Archbishop of Canterbury, 122–5, 129–30, 134, 137, 140, 142, 262, 274
Creighton, Dr Mandell, Bishop of Peterborough, 49, 50, 58, 111, 176, 184
Creighton, Mrs Mandell, 53
Curwen, Hugh, Bishop of Oxford, 24

'DALBUS, F.' (pseudonym of Abbé Portal), 46–8, 59
Davenport, Christopher, 144
Davidson, Randall, Bishop of Rochester, 21, 34
Day, George, Bishop of Chichester, 130
De Augustinis, Fr Aemilius M., 105, 106, 111–12, 116, 131, 151, 152–3, 158, 274–5, 302
Decree for the Armenians, 132–3
De Dominis, Marco Antonio, Archbishop of Spalato, 25, 133
della Chiesa, Giacomo, 224; *see also* Benedict XV, pope
de Llaveneras, Fr Calasanzio, 113–14, 146, 153, 158, 162, 164, 185, 187, 302
de Lugo, 144–5
Denny, Edward, 23, 24, 63, 87
De Re Anglicana, 169–76, 215
Dickens, A. G., Professor, 251
di Pietro, cardinal, 197
Dix, Gregory, 253, 287
Dublin Review, the, 106
Duchesne, Abbé Louis, 32, 43, 48–9, 52, 63, 79, 82, 84, 93, 101, 102, 105, 106, 110–11, 116, 119–20, 143, 150–2, 154, 155, 158, 160–2, 165–8, 190, 266, 296, 298–9, 302, 306–7
Duggan, Revd James, 234
Dupanloup, Bishop, 32

EDWARD VI, King of England, 131 140, 171–3, 251–2, 260–2
Edward VII, King of England, 28
Eeles, Francis Carolus, 73
Elizabeth I, Queen of England, 9, 10, 12–14, 24, 130, 131, 133, 173, 216, 255
English Church Union, the, 28, 36, 53, 76, 92, 200
Estcourt, Canon E. E., 1, 63, 282
Eugene IV, pope, 132
Everest, Canon, W. F., 96
Every, Bro. George, 289

FERRAR, Robert, Bishop of St David's, 143, 154, 266–8
Fleming, Fr David, 76, 106–7, 112, 121, 148, 152, 155, 157, 162, 186, 199, 220–1, 267, 300–2
Fleury, Claude, 20
Francis a Sancta Clara, *see* Davenport, Christopher
Franzelin, Cardinal, 149
Frere, Walter Howard, 250–1 253

GAIRDNER, James, 222
Gardiner, Bishop, 131
Gasparri, Mgr Pietro, 20, 63–4, 82, 102, 106, 110–11, 114, 116, 119, 150–4, 156, 158, 160,

162–4, 166–7, 188, 190, 192, 259, 263–4
Gasquet, Dom Francis Aidan, 81–90, 94, 100, 102–4, 106, 112–14, 116, 121, 134, 140, 146, 147, 151–6, 158, 160, 162–3, 186–200, 215, 225, 238, 255, 260, 267, 269–70, 278–9, 299–300, 302, 304, *see also* Bishop Edmund
biographical, 72–73, 217–23
historical methods, 107–10
and the *Risposta*, 169–75, 177–80, 184
George, R. E. Gordon, 227
on Abbé Portal, 212–14
Gille, Fr Albert, 233–4
Gladstone, W. E., 168, 178–9, 181
Goldwell, Thomas, 254
Gordon case, the, 165–7, 191, 280–3, 301
Gosse, Sir Edmund, 242
Grey, Lady Jane, 251
Guitton, Jean, 209–10

HARDING, Thomas, controversy with Jewel, 17–18
Harley, John, Bishop of Hereford, 265
Halifax, Charles Lindley Wood, second Viscount, 2, 6, 21, 28–39, 45, 46, 48–58, 60–81, 83, 86–9, 92–9, 101–2, 104, 111, 114, 121, 123, 147–8, 150, 152, 176–9, 184, 187–91, 211–12, 214, 222, 225–30, 232–3, 235, 238, 241–2, 284, 295–8, 305–6
biographical, 28–32, 199–210
Heath, Nicholas, Archbishop of York, 256, 262
Heenan, John Carmel, cardinal, Archbishop of Westminster, 3
Henry VIII, King of England, 10, 125, 128, 172, 251–2, 256, 258, 260–2
Hodgkin, John, suffragan bishop of Bedford, 14–17, 133
Holywood, Christopher, 19
Hooper, John, Bishop of Gloucester, 250, 265
von Hügel, Baron Friedrich, 114, 190, 237, 306
Hughes, Mgr Philip, 128
Huddlestone, Trevor, Bishop of Masai, 2

JACKSON, Revd H. L., 239
Jacob, Edgar, 179
James I, King of England, 19
James II, King of England, 280–1
Jedin, Professor Hubert, 290
Jenkins, Dr Claude, 23
Jewel, John, Bishop of Salisbury, 17–18
John XXIII, pope, 33, 57, 204–6, 208–9
Johnson, Dr Humphrey, 38, 44, 182
Julius III, pope, 192, 251, 259, 261, 263, 269, 271, 274, 304
Jungmann, Fr J. A., 289–90

KENRICK, Peter, Archbishop of St Louis, 20
King, Robert, Bishop of Oxford, 262
Kitchin, Anthony, Bishop of Llandaff, 12–14, 19
Klein, Abbé, 32, 200
Knowles, Professor David,
on Gasquet, 107–10, 218, 222–3
Knox, Fr Wilfrid, 246
Küng, Hans, 292

LACEY, Revd Thomas Alexander, 23, 24, 63, 72, 79, 82–3, 87, 96,

111, 115, 117–20, 146, 149, 150–5, 161–2, 166, 168–77, 179, 181, 184, 187–8, 191, 194, 211, 215–16, 236, 300–3, *see also* Puller, Fr F. W.
Lake, William Charles, Dean of Durham, 49
Lambeth Synod (1555–6), 132
Laud, William, Archbishop of Canterbury, 24, 125
Legg, Wickham, 73
Leo XIII, pope, 30, 34, 35, 55–7, 59–62, 66–71, 73, 75–6, 79–88, 90, 94, 97–100, 114, 117, 140, 141, 165, 183, 186–9, 200, 208, 211, 214, 218, 224–5, 230, 245, 270, 295–300
Le Quien, Michel, 282
Leslie, Sir Shane, 152
Lightfoot, John, Bishop of Durham, 125
Lincoln, Bishop of, (1896), 80
Lingard, John, 20
Loisy, Alfred, 32, 102, 190, 220
Lombard, Peter, 127
Luther, Martin, 289

MACHYN, Henry, 16
Maclagen, Dr W. D., Archbishop of York, 50, 56–7, 60–1, 63, 80, 96, 211
Manning, Henry Edward, cardinal, Archbishop of Westminster, 40, 76, 128, 213, 233
Marshall, Abbot of Colchester, 109
Mertel, Teodolfo, Cardinal, 188
Mary I, Queen of England, 9, 24, 154, 172, 192, 247–54, 260, 266, 268, 270
Mascall, Dr E. L., 289
Maturin, Fr B. W., 177, 228–9, 239–40
Maxwell, Constable, 228
Mazella, Cardinal, 113, 153–5, 157–62, 166–7, 190–1, 197, 235
Mercier, Cardinal, 31, 214, 234
Merry del Val, Mgr Raphael, 86, 90, 97–101, 103, 105, 106, 113, 152, 156–8, 161–5, 181, 184, 188–9, 191–9, 215, 220–1, 259, 269–71, 274, 279, 295–307
biographical, 223–7
Messenger, Dr E. C., 121, 152, 186, 249–50, 252–3, 255–7, 259, 263–5, 270, 279
Meyer, Fr Hans Bernard, 289
Moberly, R. C., 203
Monteigne, George, Bishop of London, 25
Month, the, 69
Morris, Dr Edwin, Archbishop of Wales, 4
Moyes, Canon James, 99, 103, 104, 106, 111, 112, 121, 134, 140, 143–4, 146–8, 152–64, 166, 169–78, 181–7, 190–1, 195, 199, 220–1, 225, 238, 267, 278–9, 297, 300–4
biographical, 214–17

'NAG'S HEAD FABLE', the, 19–21, 132, 282
Neercassel, Bishop, 279
'Neo-Anglicanism', 125–6, 137
Newman, J. H., cardinal, 44, 145, 204, 233, 235–7, 276

OATH OF SUPREMACY, 10, 12
Ordinal, the (compiled 1550, revised 1552), 13–15, 17, 46–7, 124, 127, 130–6, 138–45, 157, 164–5, 246–7, 250–6, 259, 262, 264, 267–8, 272–5, 281, 287, 301

Ordines Anglicani, 121–45, 148, 163, 266
Oxenham, Francis Nutcombe, 145
Oxford Movement, the, 28, 37, 55, 59, 126, 169, 176, 239

PARFEW, Robert, Bishop of Hereford, 172
Parker, Matthew, Archbishop of Canterbury, 9, 12–15, 17–24, 32–3, 35, 46, 133, 137, 145, 156, 255, 286
'Parliament bishops', 18
Parocchi, Cardinal, 235
Paul IV, pope, 153, 196, 248, 260, 263–6, 269, 271–5
Paul VI, pope, 207
Peterborough, Bishop of, (1559), 13
Phillimore, Sir Walter, 190
Pierotti, Fr, cardinal, 185, 187
Pius II, pope, 110
Pius IX, pope, 178, 179
Pius X, pope, 224, 226
Pius XII, pope, 135
Pole, Reginald, cardinal, Archbishop of Canterbury, 9, 131–3, 144, 154, 172–3, 192, 251, 253–5, 270–5, 301
  biographical, 258–63
Ponet, John, Bishop of Winchester, 265
Portal, Etienne Fernand, 2, 6, 28, 31–9, 43, 45, 46–72, 74, 79, 87, 89, 92–3, 98, 101–4, 112, 113, 121, 147–8, 151, 152, 161, 166–8, 176, 178, 187–9, 191, 199, 203–4, 208, 225–6, 229, 233, 241, 295, 297, 305, 307
  biographical, 32–4, 210–14
Praeclara carissimi, papal Bull (1555), 132, 260–8, 270
Prayer Book (1549), 127–30, 140
Prayer Book (1552), 10, 11, 13, 127, 130–1, 140, 173, 250
Puller, Fr F. W., 46, 117–20, 146, 150, 153, 155, 168, 171, 178, 187, 211, *see also* Lacey, Revd Thomas Alexander
Puritans, the, 12, 136, 174
Pursglove, Robert, Bishop of Hull, 262
Pusey, E. B., 37

RAHNER, Karl, 232
Rampolla, Cardinal Secretary of State, 54, 56, 58–62, 64, 65, 80–2, 85, 88–9, 97–9, 114, 150, 168, 176, 187–90, 197, 202–3, 211, 226, 232, 245, 295–8
Ramsey, A. M., Archbishop of Canterbury, 207
Regimini universalis, papal Brief (1555), 132, 260–8
Revue Anglo-Romaine, 101–4, 111, 117, 153, 189, 199
Riley, Athelstan, 38, 67, 69, 76, 202, 242
Riposta all' Opuscolo De Re Anglicana, 169–82, 184, 187, 215–16, 229
Robinson, John, Bishop of Woolwich, 2

ST JOHN, Fr Henry, 232
St John, Sir Oliver, 251
Saliège, Cardinal, Archbishop of Toulouse, 209–10
Salisbury, John, suffragan bishop of Thetford, 14
Sanders, Nicholas, 252, 255
Satis cognitum, encyclical (1896), 241
Scannell, Revd T. B., 113–15, 153, 156, 158, 162, 236, 272–3, 302

Scory, John, Bishop of Hereford, 14–17, 19, 143–4, 265
Segna, Cardinal, 164
Smith, Fr Sidney, 68–9, 279, 300
Snellaerts, consultor in papal investigation of AO, 1684, 279
Somerset, John, Duke of, 251
Stephenson, Fr Anthony A., 288
Swinburne, Algernon Charles, 204

Tablet, The, 40, 42, 68, 76, 83, 99, 101, 103, 106, 114, 119, 134, 143–4, 146, 151, 163, 166, 177, 189, 194, 215, 236, 238, 272, 299
Tarozzi, Mgr Vincenzo, 192, 196–7
Taylor, John, Bishop of Lincoln, 131, 265
Taylor, T. F., 280
Temple, William, Archbishop of Canterbury, 44
Thirlby, Thomas, Bishop of Ely, 132, 172, 196, 260, 262, 264–8
Thomas, Lewis, Bishop of Shrewsbury, 262
Thorndike, Herbert, 96
Times, The, 90, 179–80
Thureau-Daugin, Paul, 35, 50, 230
Tunstall, Cuthbert, Bishop of Durham, 13
Tyrrell, George, 235–6

VAN BEECK, F. J., 292
Van de Pol, W. D., 291
Vannutelli, Serafino, cardinal, 187, 197
Vatican Council I, 128, 178, 190
Vatican Council II, 233, 291, 293
Vaughan, Herbert, cardinal, Archbishop of Westminster, 51–2 57, 62, 64, 65–76, 79, 80–7, 89, 92–3, 95–107, 111, 115, 118, 121–2, 151, 160, 164, 176–86, 189, 190, 198, 201–4, 210, 214, 220–6, 257, 295–300, 305–7
biographical, 37–45, 227–42
Vidler, Dr A. R., 290

WARD, Wilfrid, 41, 44, 65, 66, 69, 70, 74, 79, 102, 123, 178, 182, 203, 211, 236
Warre, Dr Edmund, 61
Willebrands, Bishop Jan G. M., 207
William and Mary, King and Queen of England, 280
Wiseman, Cardinal, 70, 177, 213–14
Wood, Revd E. G., 168
Woodlock, Fr Francis, 164
Wordsworth, John, Bishop of Salisbury, 46
Worledge, writer in *Philadelphia Catholic Times*, 295

YORK, Richard, Duke of, 251